AQA

AS
Economics

Ray Powell

Philip Allan Updates, an imprint of Hodder Education, an Hachette UK company, Market Place, Deddington, Oxfordshire OX15 0SE

Orders

Bookpoint Ltd, 130 Milton Park, Abingdon, Oxfordshire OX14 4SB
tel: 01235 827827
fax: 01235 400401
e-mail: education@bookpoint.co.uk

Lines are open 9.00 a.m.–5.00 p.m., Monday to Saturday, with a 24-hour message answering service. You can also order through the Philip Allan Updates website: www.philipallan.co.uk

© Philip Allan Updates 2008

ISBN 978-0-340-94750-0

Impression number   8
Year 2013   2012

This textbook has been written specifically to support students studying AQA AS economics. The content has been neither approved nor endorsed by AQA and remains the sole responsibility of the author.

All website addresses included in this book are correct at the time of going to press but may subsequently change.

The front cover is reproduced by permission of Comstock Images/Alamy.

Printed in Dubai.

Hachette UK's policy is to use papers that are natural, renewable and recyclable products and made from wood grown in sustainable forests. The logging and manufacturing processes are expected to conform to the environmental regulations of the country of origin.

P01932

AQA
AS
Economics

177788

Contents

Foreword

This book has three main objectives. The first and most important is to help you achieve the highest possible grades in the AQA AS economics examinations.

The second objective is to help you to become a good economist. For those of you who are not intending to study economics at university, I hope that reading the book will enable you to contribute thoughtfully and informatively when discussing economic issues with family or friends, or with prospective employers you need to impress. And for those of you who decide to study economics or an economics-related subject at university, I hope the book sets you on the right path and provides you with an enjoyable introduction to economics that prepares you for studying the subject at a higher level.

The third objective, which relates to those already stated, is to encourage you to study economics at A2, and for you to achieve a high A-level pass at the end of your 2-year course. With this in mind, I recommend that you re-read, toward the end of your AS course, the part of Chapter 1 which introduces you to 'what economists do'.

The content of the AQA AS economics specification is thoroughly covered in this book. Most chapters also include extension material which provides a link between AS and A2 economics. On occasion, the extension material goes further, explaining what it takes to become a good economist.

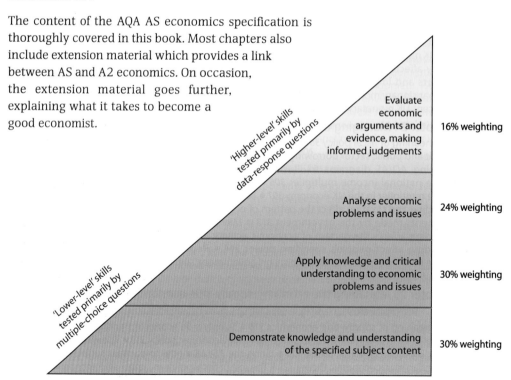

The 'incline of difficulty', showing the skills required to do well at AS

To meet my first objective of helping you to achieve a good grade, each chapter explains the topic in the depth required for an A-grade at AS. However, doing well in the examination requires demonstration of appropriate and required examination skills too. The required skills are summarised in the diagram opposite, which also indicates the importance of each of the four skills in the AS examinations.

Economists sometimes distinguish between the necessary and sufficient conditions required for a particular outcome to be achieved. For example, a necessary condition for doing well at AS is to turn up and answer the questions in all or most of the examinations. (For medical reasons, it may not always be necessary for a student to sit every Unit examination.) However, merely attending an examination cannot guarantee success — it is a necessary but insufficient condition for doing well. The quality and relevance of what you write in the exam room is more important.

Likewise, possession of knowledge about the economy and economic theory is a necessary but insufficient condition for doing well. Knowledge is necessary, but on its own contributes in a limited way to examination success. To achieve a high grade, you must show understanding of knowledge, together with the ability to apply, analyse, and evaluate. Throughout this textbook, I introduce you to these skills, which I also explain in more depth in the final chapter. To acquire and practise these skills, you should also use the online material. This contains a number of exam-style questions covering the main AS topics.

Using this book

The book is organised into three sections. In the introductory section Chapter 1 provides a general introduction to economics and to 'what economists do', while Chapter 2 introduces and explains the central economic problem of scarcity and the resulting need for choice. It is important that you familiarise yourselves with Chapter 2 because the central economic problem is what economics is all about. Consequently, it is relevant to every chapter in the textbook.

The main body of the textbook covers the content of the AS Units 1 and 2. The chapters closely follow the specification.

Key terms boxes provide definitions of important economic terms or concepts relevant to the topics in the chapter. **Examiner's voice** inserts explain how the chapter content is relevant for the AS examinations. In some instances, the insert highlights the presence of useful background information in the text, designed to increase the reader's depth of knowledge and understanding. Full marks for a question can be earned without this background information but it supports your knowledge.

In an exam answer do not try to display 'all you know', regardless of the relevance of the information to the actual question. And do not make the mistake of rewriting questions to fit a pre-prepared answer, rather than adapting what you know to the needs of the questions.

The AQA economics specification requires that, for the Unit 2 exam:

> Candidates should have a good knowledge of developments in the UK economy and government policies over the past 10 years (before the date of the exam), but should be able to illustrate the economic cycle from the UK experience, taking as a starting point the boom of the late 1980s, followed by the recession of the early 1990s, and then the subsequent recovery.

Apart from when they relate to the economic cycle (the ups and downs of the economy), examination questions do not require knowledge of events earlier than 10 years before the Unit 2 examination. (Candidates are, however, sometimes asked to describe or to compare data series extending back more than 10 years.) However, a basic knowledge of economic history and of different schools of economic thought, such as Keynesianism and monetarism, is useful to your understanding. Where I think it helps, I have adopted a historical approach, particularly in the explanation of macroeconomic topics such as theories of inflation and unemployment, and in the way monetary policy, fiscal policy and supply-side economics have developed over the years.

At the end of each chapter, there are a number of self-testing **questions**. These can be used to test your knowledge. Answers are given in the *AQA AS Economics Teacher Guide*, available from Philip Allan Updates.

The online material includes a selection of examination-style questions. Objective test and data-response questions and commentary on students' answers are available, along with summary specification coverage, in the *Student Unit Guides* for Units 1 and 2 AQA economics published by Philip Allan Updates.

Starting AS economics

If you are starting an AS course in economics, you should begin by reading Chapters 1 and 2, which introduce you to the subject. How you then use the book will depend on whether you are studying the course unit-by-unit (in which case you are probably studying Unit 1 before Unit 2, and are probably being taught by just one teacher), or whether you are studying Unit 1 and Unit 2 'side-by-side' (in which case, you are probably being taught by at least two teachers).

As you read each chapter or section of a chapter, answer the self-testing questions at the end of the chapter. Then check your answers against the chapter content. Refer also to the exam-style questions in the online material.

I hope that you find this book a useful adjunct to the course that your teacher(s) deliver. I wish you every success in the AS examinations and hope that you go on to study for the full A-level qualification in economics. And while 'luck' is by no means the only ingredient in eventual examination success, may I wish you the best of luck in the course, in the examinations and in your future life!

Ray Powell

Introduction

Chapter 1

What is economics and what do economists do?

For most of my readers, welcome to a new subject. Unless you have studied economics at GCSE, it is only in the last week or so that you have given thought to the nature of the economy in which you live, and to what you must learn about the economy in the next nine months. This chapter aims to ease you into the subject so that you quickly build up a broad idea of what you are going to study at AS in economics.

Learning outcomes

This chapter will introduce you to:
- economics as a social science and a current affairs subject
- the difference between microeconomics and macroeconomics
- economic problems and economic policies
- what economists do

Starting from a position of ignorance?

At the beginning of an economics course you are not expected to know anything about economics. For the last 2 years all your mental energy has been directed at the GCSE subjects you have been studying, and economics has not been one of them.

It usually takes at least a term to settle into a new subject. This is certainly the case with economics, which is different in many important respects from any subject you have previously studied. I hope that by February or March next year you will have settled, but if not, don't in the first instance blame yourself, blame the subject.

Economics is a current affairs related subject, so it will help if you can become interested in what is going on in the country you live in, and also in the wider world outside the UK. (However, I don't expect you to possess this knowledge at the beginning of the course. Any relevant current affairs knowledge you already possess is a bonus, not a requirement.)

Nevertheless, if you are not prepared to read about current affairs in newspapers or on web pages such as BBC News (**http://news.bbc.co.uk**), you are unlikely to enjoy economics or to do very well in the course. So start reading newspapers (getting advice from your teachers as you go on what to read), and don't switch off the television whenever the news or the BBC2 *Newsnight* programme starts.

What is economics?

When answering this question, a good point to start is the fact that **economics** is a social science. Social science is the branch of science that studies society and the relationships of individuals within a society. Besides economics, psychology, sociology and political science are also social sciences, as are important elements of history and geography.

> **key term**
>
> **Economics** is the study of choice and decision making in a world with limited resources.

Psychology studies the behaviour and mental processes of an *individual*. Sociology studies the *social* relationships between people in the context of *society*. By contrast, economics, as the name suggests, studies the *economic behaviour* of both individuals and groups of people and the *economic relationships* between individuals and groups.

Let me give you two examples of what I mean.

I have taken my first example, about *individual behaviour*, from an important part of economics known as demand theory. This is covered early in the book, in Chapter 3. The theory addresses consumer behaviour, or how we behave when we go shopping. Why, for example, do people generally buy more strawberries as the price of strawberries falls?

My second example introduces an important *economic relationship*. Having explained demand, we must go a stage further and look at how consumers interact with firms or producers. Firms supply and sell the goods that consumers buy, and economists call the 'place' in which goods are bought and sold a market. Market interactions between consumers and producers are also explained early in the book (see Chapter 5). Indeed, before you started this economics course, you may very well have heard the words '**supply**' and '**demand**' and thought that is what economics is about. Well, in large measure that is true, particularly in the early chapters of this book.

> **key terms**
>
> **Demand** is the quantity of a good households are willing to buy in a market.
>
> **Supply** is the quantity of a good firms are prepared to sell in a market.

Economics involves, however, a lot more than theories of individual behaviour and economic relationships between groups of individuals.

A second possible starting point for answering the question 'What is economics?' is in the word itself: 'economics'. Related to *economics* is the verb '*to economise*'. In large part, economics is the study of *economising* — the study of how people make choices on what to produce, how to produce and for whom to produce, in a world

in which most resources are limited or scarce. How best can people make decisions on how scarce resources should be allocated among competing uses, so as to improve and maximise human happiness and welfare? This is the economic problem, which we explain in greater detail in Chapter 2.

Introducing microeconomics and macroeconomics

The subject of economics is usually divided into two parts, called **microeconomics** and **macroeconomics**. The AQA AS economics course is organised in this way:

- Unit 1 Markets and Market Failure is microeconomic
- Unit 2 The National Economy is macroeconomic

*k***ey terms**
Macroeconomics examines the economy as a whole.

Microeconomics examines individual consumers, firms and markets in the economy.

Microeconomics is the part of economics concerned with economic behaviour in the individual markets that make up the economy. Questions such as 'What determines the price of bread?' and 'How many workers might an employer wish to hire?' are microeconomic questions. Essentially, microeconomics investigates the 'little bits' of the economy, namely individual consumers, firms, markets and industries.

By contrast, macroeconomics is the part of economics that attempts to explain how the whole economy works. Macroeconomics addresses questions such as 'What determines the average price level?' and 'How do we explain the overall levels of employment and unemployment in the economy?' Macroeconomics examines the aggregates rather than the little bits of the economy: the aggregate levels of output, income, prices, employment and unemployment, and the trade flows that make up the balance of payments.

Economic problems and economic policies

One of the most interesting areas of economics lies in studying the economic problems facing governments and the economic policies governments use to try to get rid of or reduce the problems. Economic problems can be microeconomic or macroeconomic, though some have both micro and macro elements.

At the micro level, covered by AQA Unit 1, the main problems lie in the field of market failure. As we shall see in Chapters 9 to 12, market failure occurs whenever markets do not perform very well — and in extreme cases fail to perform at all. Perhaps the best-known recent and current market failure stems from environmental pollution and the subsequent global warming. We shall be examining a number of different government policies aimed at correcting market failures. These include taxation, subsidy and the use of regulations. In Chapters 13 and 14 I also explain how government failure results when government policies are ineffective or even downright damaging.

At the macro level, which is covered by AQA Unit 2, the main economic problems are unemployment, a failure to achieve and sustain a satisfactory rate of economic growth, inflation and an unsatisfactory trading and balance of payments position. Chapter 17, together with Chapters 20 to 22, investigates these macro-economic problems. The final chapters of the book then examine the main macro-economic policies that are used to try to solve these problems. The main policies are fiscal policy, monetary policy and supply-side policy.

Positive and normative statements in economics

A lot of economics is concerned with what people *ought* to do. This is particularly true of the government. *Ought* the government try to reduce unemployment, control inflation and achieve a 'fair' distribution of income and wealth? Most people probably think that all these objectives are desirable. However, they all fall within the remit of **normative** economics. Normative economics is about value judgements and opinions, but because people have different opinions about what is right and wrong, normative statements cannot be scientifically tested. They are just opinions.

By contrast, a **positive statement** can be scientifically tested to see if it is incorrect. If a positive statement does not pass the test, it is *falsified.* Some positive statements are obviously correct, for example the statement that an apple is a type of fruit. But a positive statement does not have to be true. For example the statement that the Earth is flat is a positive statement. Although once believed to be true, the statement was falsified with the growth of scientific evidence. The key point is that positive statements can in principle be tested and possibly falsified, while normative statements cannot. Words such as *ought, should, better, worse* and *good* and *bad* (used as adjectives) often provide clues that a statement is normative.

> **k**ey terms
>
> **Normative** means an opinion that cannot be scientifically tested.
>
> **Positive statement** A statement that can be scientifically tested and possibly falsified.

How much maths do I need to know?

At the beginning of an economics course, students often seek advice about the amount of mathematics they need to know or must learn to help them with their studies. For AS and A2 economics, the answer is not very much.

The two skills you do need to develop are:
- drawing and interpreting graphs
- interpreting statistics presented in a variety of forms: tables, line graphs, bar graphs and pie charts

You will be introduced to economics graphs and to the different ways of presenting statistics as you proceed through this book.

Nevertheless, I must issue two warnings. First, economics contains a large number of abstract ideas and concepts, similar to those employed in maths, summed up in the saying 'to an economist, real life is a special case'. A logical mind, capable of handling abstractions, will be of great help if you are to become a good economist. My second warning is that, unlike AS and A-level economics, university economics is definitely mathematical. Thinking ahead, however good your eventual A-level economics grade, you should only study economics at university if you are good

at and enjoy mathematics. If you are weak at mathematics or if you have dropped the subject, it would be far better to consider a joint honours degree, for example economics and history, economics and French, or economics and politics.

What do economists do?

It has been said that 'economics is useful as a form of employment for economists'. This essentially means that economists give advice to other people who pay them for the service they provide. Some economists act as private consultants, but others are employed by central and local government, and by the Bank of England.

Box 1.1 How about working in the City of London?

The UK financial services industry creates employment for 3 million people, with nearly half a million in banks alone. Although they make up only a small fraction of this number, economists enjoy some of the most prestigious jobs in the City of London. The financial services industry makes a £50bn contribution to the UK economy, representing 8.5% of the UK's gross domestic product (GDP), equivalent to around £850 for every man, woman and child in the country.

The financial firms that employ economists include banks, research companies and accountancy firms such as Deloitte. High street banks such as Barclays own investment banking subsidiaries. Until about 30 years ago, investment banks were known by the old-fashioned name of 'merchant banks'. This name is sometimes still used today, but 'investment bank' has become a rather sexier label.

In the old days, merchant banks were relatively small companies, often family-owned and affected by nepotism in the sense that top jobs would be handed down from father to son. (Women were only employed as secretaries or cleaners.) This has now largely changed and City employees are rewarded according to their talents. Nevertheless, 'glass ceilings' sometimes prevent women from getting the top City jobs that their skills deserve. The demise of Baring Brothers provides a case study of how family-owned City firms have given way to a new breed of company in which talent is the requirement for success. These days, most investment banks are owned by international multinational financial and banking corporations such as Deutsche Bank.

The City of London is a prestigious place to work

Lombard Street Research is an important City-based consultancy, specialising in the field of monetary economics, and which employs a number of leading economists. The firm was founded in 1989 by the economist Professor Tim Congdon. Lombard Street Research quickly established a reputation as a leading provider of independent macroeconomic research. The firm's aim is to provide accurate economic forecasts in order to improve the investment thinking and strategic decisions of financial institutions, banks and corporations worldwide.

To find out more about what the economists employed by Lombard do, access **www.lombardstreetresearch.com/about_us.html**.

Follow-up questions

1 Find the website: **www.economistjobs.co.uk** and research the current UK job opportunities being advertised for economists.

2 Now go to **www.efinancecareers.co.uk** to research a wider field of job opportunities in financial service industries.

City firms such as investment banks, leading companies such as Marks and Spencer and trade unions are big employers of economists. Indeed, virtually every large UK organisation (except perhaps religious institutions) either employs its own economists or seeks the advice of economic consultancy firms. And, of course, there are also thousands of economics teachers hired by universities, schools and colleges.

The Government Economic Service (GES) is the UK's largest employer of professional economists, with over 1,000 economists based in 30 government departments and agencies such as the Treasury and the Department for Business, Enterprise and Regulatory Reform, which until 2007 was within the Department of Trade and Industry (DTI).

Box 1.2 Working for the government

Central government is the biggest employer of economists in the UK. Here is how a major government ministry, the **Department for Environment, Food and Rural Affairs (DEFRA)** advertises for economists on the government website: **www.ges.gov.uk/whatdo.htm**.

DEFRA Economists

Some of the biggest challenges currently facing the UK are dealt with by DEFRA. As an Assistant Economist in DEFRA you might, for example, find yourself:

■ considering the most efficient way to tackle climate change
■ advising on waste and recycling policy in the UK
■ investigating social exclusion in rural areas
■ ensuring biodiversity and natural resource issues are considered in policy design and delivery
■ investigating air and water quality issues
■ considering economic aspects of ethical trading and the environmental impacts of food transport

Our work

Working as an economist in DEFRA is exciting, challenging and rewarding as you will be working on high profile, dynamic areas of economics with plenty of opportunity to shape policy.

A large proportion of DEFRA's work is at the cutting edge of economic analysis. As a department we deal with instances of externalities and the resulting market failures in many different areas and Defra's economists work in fields as diverse as the EU Emissions Trading Scheme, Common Agricultural Policy reform, rural productivity, avian influenza and assessing the regulatory burden imposed by the department.

Follow-up question

Go to the government website: **www.ges.gov.uk** and research the jobs currently being advertised, for example, under Fast Stream Assistant Economist Appointments.

As well as providing advice to employers or clients, economists undertake research and are involved in forecasting activity. It has been said that 'An economist is a trained professional paid to guess wrong about the economy'. The question has also been asked 'What makes a good economist?' For the non-economist, the answer is 'An unshakeable grasp of the obvious!'

But, joking apart, economics pundits to look out for include Evan Davis and Stephanie Flanders, who work for the BBC, and City economists such as Roger Bootle and Stephen King (who write respectively in the *Daily Telegraph* and the *Independent* newspapers). The public face of the economics profession centres on television appearances of economic experts or analysts giving advice on such issues as rising or falling share prices, exchange rates or interest rates. Whether the advice of such professional economists is useful, I shall leave you to judge as you continue your studies over the next few months. Whether or not you have faith in economists, I hope you enjoy the course.

Summary

- You don't need to know anything about economics or about the economy before you start the AS course.
- Economics is a social science and a current affairs subject.
- Economics divides into microeconomics and macroeconomics.
- Microeconomics looks at the 'little bits' of the economy.
- Macroeconomics examines the economy in aggregate.
- Government economic policies aim to reduce or eliminate economic problems.
- Microeconomic policies aim to prevent or correct market failures.
- Fiscal policy, monetary policy and supply-side policy are examples of macroeconomic policies.
- Unemployment, too low a rate of economic growth, inflation, and the balance of payments pose the main macroeconomic problems.

■ Positive statements in economics are statements that can be scientifically tested and possibly falsified, whereas normative statements are statement of opinion, involving value judgements.

■ Professional economists undertake research, engage in economic forecasting and provide economic advice to clients.

Questions

1 Compare economics to other social sciences such as psychology and sociology.
2 What is the difference between microeconomics and macroeconomics?
3 What is a market?
4 What is meant by market failure?
5 Name three significant macroeconomic problems.
6 Find out how many economists are employed by different government departments in the UK.

Chapter 2

The economic problem

In Chapter 1, I defined economics as the study of choice and decision making in a world with limited resources. I also mentioned that economics is the study of economising — how people make choices on what to produce, how to produce and for whom to produce, in a world in which most resources are limited or scarce. This chapter explains and explores the central economic problem in greater depth.

Learning outcomes

This chapter will:
- relate the economic problem to scarcity and choice
- use production possibility curve diagrams to illustrate scarcity
- introduce the concept of opportunity cost
- explain the meaning of production
- explain the role of factors of production in the economy
- explain how different economic systems attempt to deal with the economic problem
- explain how recent UK governments have changed the UK economic system in recent decades

Economics and the economic problem

A definition of economics, similar to the one I have already given you was put forward by Professor Lionel Robbins in *An Essay on the Nature and Significance of Economic Science* in 1932. Robbins defined economics as:

> The science which studies human behaviour as a relationship between ends and scarce means which have alternative uses.

Professor Robbins' long-established definition provides perhaps the most well-known starting point for introducing and understanding what economics is about. How best can people make decisions on the allocation of scarce resources among competing uses, so as to improve and maximise human happiness and welfare? This is the **economic problem**.

The economic problem, scarcity and choice

key term

The **economic problem** is that only a limited amount of resources are available to produce the unlimited quantity of goods and services people desire.

To repeat, economics is literally the study of economising — the study of how human beings make choices on what to produce, how to produce and for whom to produce, in a world in which most resources are limited. The economic problem exists because both goods and the resources needed to produce goods are scarce. Scarcity also means that people (even the very rich) have limited incomes.

Now, if goods are scarce and incomes are limited, choices have to be made. Consider, for example, a family with a weekly income of £1,000. The family currently spends £300 on housing, £250 on food, £250 on other goods and services, including heating and lighting, and £120 on entertainment. The family's total weekly spending on goods and services is thus £920, meaning the family manages to save £80. Suddenly, the cost of housing rises to £400. To avoid getting into debt, and assuming that family income can't increase, one or more probably unpleasant choices will have to be made. An obvious possibility is to cut down on entertainment, such as visits to the cinema. Other possibilities could be spending less on home heating, buying cheaper food, cutting down on alcoholic drink and stopping saving. Something will have to be given up. Unless the family gets into debt or its income increases, it will have to economise.

The economic problem illustrated on a production possibility diagram

So far, I have explained how scarcity and choice may affect an ordinary family. In much the same way, but on an obviously much grander scale, the economy of the nation as a whole faces a similar need for choice. To explain how the economic problem affects the whole economy, I shall make use of a diagram which you will come across again and again in your economics course, a **production possibility diagram**.

key term

A **production possibility diagram** shows different possible combinations of goods that can be produced using available resources.

The key feature of a production possibility diagram is a production possibility frontier (or production possibility curve). I shall call this the *PPF* curve. A *PPF* curve illustrates the different combinations of two goods, or two sets of goods, that can be produced with a fixed quantity of resource, providing we assume that all available resources are being utilised to the full. The *PPF* curve drawn in Figure 2.1 illustrates the different combinations of **consumer goods** and **capital goods** that the whole economy can produce when all the economy's resources are employed, with no spare capacity. To put it another way, the *PPF* curve shows what the economy can produce, assuming that all the labour, capital and

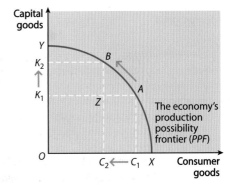

Figure 2.1 Using a production possibility frontier diagram to illustrate the economic problem

land at the country's disposal are employed to the full, and assuming a given state of **technical progress**.

Given that resources and capacity are limited, a choice has to be made on the type of good to produce. Look closely at points X and Y on the diagram. Point X shows the maximum possible output of consumer goods, assuming that the economy only produces consumer goods (i.e. no capital goods are produced). Likewise, point Y shows the maximum possible output of capital goods, assuming that the economy only produces capital goods. In fact, points X and Y show the two extreme production possibilities, since all goods are either consumer goods or capital goods. Finally, the line drawn between points X and Y in Figure 2.1 shows all the different possible combinations of consumer goods and capital goods the economy can produce, given the available resources and given the state of technical knowledge. This line is the economy's production possibility frontier (*PPF*).

Capital goods are goods such as raw materials and machines that are used to produce other goods. They are also known as producer goods and intermediate goods. Capital goods are very important for economic growth. By contrast, consumer goods (which are also known as final goods) are goods bought by individuals and households to satisfy their wants and needs. Goods such as iPods and television sets are **consumer durable goods** whereas food and washing powder are **non-durable consumer goods**.

The purchase of capital goods (by firms) is known as **investment**. Likewise, the purchase of consumer goods (by individuals or households) is called **consumption**. As a general rule, if an economy decides to produce capital goods rather than consumer goods, economic growth will take place at a faster rate than if the people had chosen to enjoy a higher level of consumption.

An iPod is a consumer durable good

Now consider point A on the *PPF* curve (Figure 2.1), which shows the economy producing K_1 capital goods and C_1 consumer goods. If people want faster economic growth, more scarce resources must be devoted to the production of capital goods and fewer to producing consumer goods. In other words, there has to be a movement from point A to a position such as point B on the *PPF*. Given this movement, capital good production rises to K_2, but at the expense of a fall in consumer good production to C_2. Society's choice has been to produce more capital goods at the expense of fewer consumer goods.

Opportunity cost

The movement from point A to point B on the *PPF* curve in Figure 2.1 illustrates a very important aspect of the economic problem, namely the principle of **opportunity cost**. The opportunity cost of any choice, decision or course of action is measured in terms of the alternatives that have to be given up. Hence the opportunity cost of increasing the production of capital goods from K_1 to K_2 is the fall in consumer goods from C_1 to C_2.

> **key term**
>
> **Opportunity cost** The cost of the next best alternative sacrificed.

Indeed, the concept of opportunity cost can be developed a stage further. Economists generally assume that economic agents (for example, individuals, households or firms) behave rationally. Rational behaviour means people try to make decisions in their self-interest or to maximise the agent's private benefit. When a choice has to be made, the best alternative is always chosen, which means that the second best or next best alternative is rejected. Providing people are rational, the opportunity cost of any decision or choice is the next best alternative sacrificed or foregone.

Extension material

Suppose the economy is initially producing at point Z in Figure 2.1. Because it is producing inside its *PPF*, there must be idle resources, including unemployed labour, in the economy. In this situation, the opportunity cost of increasing capital good production from C_1 to C_2 is not a fall in the production of capital goods. Instead, it is the sacrificed opportunity for resources to remain idle.

The type of unemployment that occurs when the economy produces inside its *PPF* is called *demand-deficient unemployment*. I shall explain this in some detail in Chapter 20. In Chapter 17 I explain how an outward movement of the economy's *PPF* curve illustrates *economic growth*.

The nature of production

As I explained in Chapter 1, the ultimate purpose of economic activity is to improve people's economic welfare and standard of living. For this to happen, material goods and services must be consumed, although quality of life factors, such as the pleasure derived from family and friends, also form an important part of welfare and human contentment.

But with the exception of goods that are freely available at absolutely no cost, which are known as **free goods**, almost all the goods we consume must first be produced. This requires the use of economic resources. **Finite economic resources** are used up when they are employed to produce goods and services, and hence are not then available for further use. By contrast, as the name indicates, **renewable economic resources** can be

> **key terms**
>
> **Finite resource** A resource, such as oil, which is scarce and runs out as it is used.
>
> **Free good** A good, such as air, for which there are no costs of production and no scarcity.
>
> **Renewable resource** A resource, such as timber, that with careful management can be renewed as it is used.

used again and again, with careful management, and do not run out as **production** takes place.

The basic nature of production is shown in Figure 2.2. Production is a process, or set of processes, that converts inputs into outputs. The eventual outputs are the consumer goods and services that go to make up our standard of living, though inputs are of course also used to produce the capital goods that are necessary for the eventual production of consumer goods.

key term

Production
A process, or set of processes, that converts inputs into outputs.

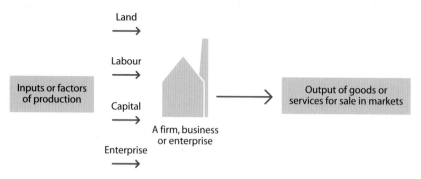

Figure 2.2 The nature of production

Factors of production

Economists call the inputs of the production process **factors of production**. Four factors of production are usually identified. These are **land**, **labour**, **capital** and **enterprise**, the last often being called the **entrepreneurial input**. The **entrepreneur** is different from the other factors of production. He or she is the person who addresses the issues I introduced in Chapter 1, deciding what to produce, how to produce it and for whom to produce it. The entrepreneur decides how much of the other factors of production, including labour, to employ. The cost of employing land, labour and capital, together with the cost of the entrepreneur's own services, become the firm's costs of production. In essence, the entrepreneur is a financial risk taker and decision maker. **Profit**, which is the entrepreneur's financial reward, results from successful decision making. Entrepreneurial profit is the profit left over after the cost of employing the other factors of production is deducted from the sales revenue gained from the sale of the goods and services the entrepreneur decides to produce.

key term

Factors of production Inputs into the production process, such as land, labour, capital and enterprise.

The economic problem and economic systems

An economic system is a set of institutional arrangements whose function is to employ most efficiently scarce resources to meet the ends of society.

The United Nations Dictionary of Social Science

Although the problem of scarcity is fundamental and common to all forms of human society — from humble tribal groupings of hunter-gatherers in the Amazonian forest to rich nations such as the USA — different societies have produced different institutional frameworks and methods for allocating scarce resources among competing uses. The set of institutions within which a community decides what, how and for whom to produce is called an **economic system**.

Classification of economic systems by allocative mechanism

Perhaps the most widely used method of defining and classifying economic systems is according to the type of allocative mechanism by which scarce resources reach the people who eventually consume or use them.

There are a variety of ways in which wealth and purchasing power can be allocated among individuals, including inheritance and other types of gift, theft and chance (such as winning a fortune on the National Lottery). However, the two allocative mechanisms by which economic systems are defined are the **market mechanism** (or **price mechanism**) and the **command mechanism** (or **planning mechanism**). An economic system in which goods and services are purchased through the price mechanism in a system of markets is called a **market economy**, whereas one in which government officials or planners allocate economic resources to firms and other productive enterprises is called a **command economy** (or **planned economy**).

> **key terms**
>
> **Command economy**
> The planning mechanism allocates resources between competing uses.
>
> **Market economy** Markets and prices allocate resources between competing uses.

Market economies

In a pure market economy, the market mechanism (the price mechanism and market forces) performs the central economic task of allocating scarce resources among competing uses. A market economy comprises a large number of markets varying in the degree to which they are separated from and interrelated with each other.

A **market** is a meeting of buyers and sellers in which goods or services are exchanged for other goods or services. Occasionally, the exchange is direct and is known as barter. More usually, however, the exchange is indirect with buyers and sellers using money. One good or service, such as labour, is exchanged for money, which is then traded a second time for other goods or services, sometimes immediately but often some time later. The exchange must be voluntary; if one party forces a transaction upon the other, it is not a market transaction.

Transport costs and lack of information may create barriers that separate or break up markets. In past centuries, such barriers often prevented markets from operating outside the relatively small geographical areas of a single country or even a small region within a country. However, while some markets exist in a particular geographical location — for example, a street market and until quite recently the London Stock Exchange — many markets do not. In recent years,

modern developments have allowed goods to be transported more easily and at lower cost, and have helped in the transmission of market information via telephone, fax and increasingly the internet. This has enabled many markets, especially commodity and raw material markets and markets in financial services, to become truly global or international markets functioning on a worldwide basis.

Command economies

A complete command economy is an economy in which all decisions about what, how, how much, when, where and for whom to produce are taken by a central planning authority, issuing commands or directives to all the households and producers in the society. Such a system could only exist within a very rigid and probably totalitarian political framework because of the restrictions on individual decision making that are obviously implied.

In fact, in much the same way that a pure market economy, in which the price mechanism alone allocates resources, is a theoretical abstraction, so no economy in the real world can properly be described as a complete or pure command economy. Before the collapse of the communist political system around 1990, the countries of eastern Europe were command economies. However, they were not pure command economies. Production but not consumption was planned. Consumers often had to queue to get consumer goods, whose prices were fixed by the planners. Shortages resulted, which, together with the generally inferior quality of consumer goods, contributed to the breakdown of the command economies. Some communist countries still exist, namely the People's Republic of China, North Korea, Vietnam and Cuba. However, all these countries, with the exception until recently of North Korea, have encouraged the growth of markets to a greater or lesser extent. They have communist political systems, but they have moved away from being pure command economies.

Classification by ownership

So far I have defined economic systems in terms of the allocative mechanism (the market mechanism or the planning mechanism) used to solve the economic problem. Economic systems can also be defined in terms of who owns the means of production: **private individuals** or the **state**.

Capitalist economies

Capitalism is a system in which the means of production are privately owned by individuals (or capitalists), who employ labour to operate the capital they own, so as to produce output for sale at a profit.

Socialist economies

In contrast to capitalism, in a **socialist** economic system the means of production are owned by the state on behalf of the people.

k*ey terms*

Capitalism The means of production are privately owned.

Socialism The means of production are socially owned.

Classification by allocative mechanism and ownership

Mixed economies

Many economies, particularly those of the developed countries of western Europe such as the UK, are called **mixed economies**. A mixed economy, as the name suggests, is a mixture of different types of economic system. Figure 2.3 shows how a mixed economy can be defined both in terms of the mechanism for allocating resources and in terms of ownership. The upper panel of the diagram shows that a mixed economy is intermediate between a market economy and a command economy. Defined in this way, a mixed economy contains a large **market sector** and a large **non-market sector**. The lower panel of the diagram shows that a mixed economy contains a large **public sector** and a large **private sector**.

*k*ey term

A **mixed economy** contains both market and non-market sectors and a substantial public sector as well as a private sector.

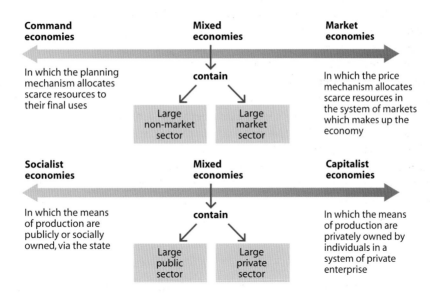

Figure 2.3 Different types of economic system

The UK as a mixed economy

The development of the mixed economy

A mixed economy developed quickly in the UK in the 1940s, when a number of important industries such as coal, rail and steel were nationalised and taken into public ownership. At the same time, the 1944 Education Act and the creation of the National Health Service extended state provision of education and healthcare.

For about 30 years after the end of the Second World War, from the 1940s to the 1970s, the majority of UK citizens (and the major political parties) agreed that the mixed economy was working well. Most people believed that certain types of

economic activity, particularly the production and distribution of consumer goods and services, were best suited to private enterprise and the market economy. But people also accepted that some industries, the utility industries, which at the time were natural monopolies, ought to be nationalised, and that important services such as education, healthcare and roads should be provided by government outside the market and financed through the tax system. In short, a consensus existed around the belief that the mixed economy was right for the UK.

Box 2.1 The mixed economy and models of capitalism

The UK mixed economy came into existence in the 1940s, in the aftermath of the Second World War. As the next section explains, the nature of the mix in the UK mixed economy has changed over the years since then. The economies of most of the continental countries of northwest Europe have also been mixed economies. More so than the UK, continental economies have also reflected the social market model of capitalism, with an emphasis on the paternalist role of the state. The UK economy, by contrast, to a much greater extent now reflects the Anglo-American model of capitalism in which the role of the state is more limited. I include below an extract from an article in the *Financial Times*, which comments on changes that occurred in the early 2000s in continental European mixed economies.

Slump intervenes in capitalist culture-clash

Paul Betts, European Business Correspondent

A revisionist spirit is sweeping continental Europe. Governments, businesses and investors are all reassessing what appeared barely a decade ago as the winning capitalistic model — the competitive market economy pioneered by the USA, adopted by the UK under Margaret Thatcher and increasingly embraced on the continent. It is a step back that has given fresh weight to the question: are the European and British ways of doing business part of an implacable clash of cultures or are they both changing in a way that represents a slow but certain convergence?

New rightwing liberal governments in Europe, rather than pursuing aggressive privatisation programmes, are reverting to interventionist instincts.

Historically, European countries had relied for their postwar reconstruction on a mixed economy system in which a paternal state or, in the case of Germany, the banking system, propped up and helped revive the corporate sector. This also involved a far greater attention to social welfare, absent in the American business model, in an attempt to combine a competitive market approach with a high degree of social awareness.

Until the 1980s, this mixed economy system delivered better rates of economic growth than the American system. But from the 1980s, the American economy, under the impulse of its 'Reagonomic' neoliberal revolution, outperformed Europe. Since the mid-1980s, all European countries, in different degrees, have sought to implement structural reforms to reduce the state's role, stimulate private initiative and adapt to a global market system.

Financial Times, 6 November 2002

Follow-up question

The UK economy provides an example of the Anglo-American model of capitalism. France, by contrast illustrates the social market model. Explain the difference between the two.

Privatisation of state-owned industry in the UK occurred in the 1980s

Recent changes in the UK mixed economy

From the 1960s onward, however, a growing minority (and perhaps eventually a majority) of economists and politicians blamed the mixed economy for the UK's deteriorating economic performance, relative to that of its main competitors in western Europe and Japan. Critics argued that the public and non-market sectors of the economy are very often inefficient and wealth consuming rather than wealth creating. The public and non-market sectors had become too big and needed cutting down to size. Critics of the mixed economy argued that a concerted effort should be made to change fundamentally the nature of the UK economy by increasing private ownership and market production.

During the 1980s and early and mid-1990s, Conservative governments implemented policies that succeeded in changing the nature of the mix in favour of private ownership and market forces, at the expense of public ownership and state planning. The UK economy is now much closer to being a pure market and private enterprise economy than it was 30 years ago. The three main policies used to change the nature of the UK economy have been:

- **privatisation** — selling off state-owned assets such as nationalised industries to private ownership
- **marketisation** or **commercialisation** — charging a market price for goods and services that the state previously provided 'free'
- **deregulation** — removing barriers to entry and government red tape and bureaucracy from the operation of markets

These policies of economic liberalisation were first introduced by Margaret Thatcher's Conservative governments in the 1980s. Thatcher believed that the mixed economy she inherited in 1979 was actually a mixed-up economy, performing inefficiently and uncompetitively. To a large extent, she established a new agenda that Tony Blair's New Labour governments also accepted, continuing the process of reform (or reaction?) that they inherited. It remains to be seen whether Gordon Brown's Labour administration (June 2007 onward), or any government which achieves office in the near future, will maintain the policies of economic liberalisation implemented in the UK economy in recent decades.

Box 2.2 The end of history?

Few of you reading this book were born at the time of the collapse of the old command economies in eastern Europe at the end of the 1980s and the beginning of the 1990s. At the time, as the article below indicates, political and economic analysts, particularly those living in the USA, claimed that this was a triumph for capitalism and the market economy.

But by 1995, when the article containing the extract was written, some analysts such as Francis Fukuyama were changing their views, arguing that capitalism and markets on their own are not enough for social cohesion in an economy. In fact, when you read the whole of the article, you may well conclude that in 1995 Fukuyama was stressing the virtues of a form of mixed economy, but with a central feature of the mix being the role of non-governmental organisations (NGOs) that lie between markets and the state.

The space in between — the Western system depends on neither free market nor state alone

Ian Davidson

After the fall of the Berlin Wall and the collapse of the Soviet Union, the US political analyst Francis Fukuyama declared that the triumph of the West was so complete that it had brought us to *The End of History*.

The western system, based on free markets, was not just the best, the most victorious system; it was now the only valid system. This was total victory.

Many people at the time claimed that his triumphalism was overstated. But not many predicted that so much of the euphoria would by now have disappeared.

The main reason is that the triumph of free markets, so far from providing a 'peace dividend' for the victors in the cold war, is

proving much more painful, divisive, unjust and destabilising within western societies than the economic gurus had ever led us to expect.

Five years after the fall of the Berlin Wall, Francis Fukuyama is still persuaded that there is no historical alternative to market structures and free markets. But Fukuyama now believes that what really counts, in the functioning western model, is not mainly the performance of the individual and the market, nor the performance of the state, but what occupies the space between.

The 'space between' means all the myriad forms of intermediate associations, which include companies and churches and charities. Francis Fukuyama argues that the vitality of this intermediate layer of civil society is critical to the functioning both of the market and of the state. And he claims that those countries that have had the most dynamic economies are those that have had the most vigorous networks of intermediate associations: the USA, Germany and Japan.

Today's problem, as he sees it, is that the associational network is beginning to disintegrate, in the USA at least, under the stresses of headlong economic change. The USA faces a crisis of associational life. The art of associating is an important economic virtue, because it is an inherently flexible manner of facing challenges. People who trust each other and feel responsible to each other are good at adapting to new conditions. When all that is left of the rich texture of society is a contract between individuals, then the USA will be in real trouble. Undeniably, that is where we seem headed.

Financial Times, 1 February 1995

Follow-up questions

1 The article was written nearly 15 years ago. Do you think that events since 1995 support or refute Fukuyama's views?

2 Do some research on the internet to see if Fukuyama has again changed his views since 1995.

Summary

■ The economic problem is limited resources in relation to people's desires and wants.

■ The economic problem results from scarcity.

■ Scarcity results in the need for choice.

■ Whenever a choice has to be made there is an opportunity cost.

■ The opportunity cost of any decision is the next best alternative foregone.

■ Economists generally assume that people are rational, choosing the best alternative available.

■ Scarcity, opportunity cost and choice can be illustrated on a production possibility diagram.

■ Production is a process, or set of processes, that converts input into outputs.

■ The inputs into the production process are called factors of production.

■ The entrepreneur is the factor of production that decides what to produce, how to produce and for whom to produce.

■ Different economic systems allocate resources between different uses in different ways.

■ In a market economy, the price mechanism performs the allocative task.

■ The UK economy is a mixed economy, containing a mix of market and non-market sectors, and private and public sectors.

■ The nature of the UK mixed economy has changed during the last 30 years.

Questions

1 What is the central economic problem?
2 Explain how a production possibility frontier illustrates the problem of scarcity.
3 What is meant by 'opportunity cost' and what might be the opportunity cost of answering this question?
4 What are factors of production?
5 What are the two main methods by which resources are allocated between competing uses?
6 Distinguish between a market economy, a command economy and a mixed economy.
7 Distinguish between capitalism and socialism.
8 How has the UK mixed economy changed in recent years?

Unit 1

Markets and market failure

Chapter 3

The demand for goods and services

Suppose you ask a person the question 'what is meant by economics?' As well as some less printable replies, the answer you may get is 'supply and demand'. Such a reply is actually very sensible, because a lot of economics is about how markets work, and about how ordinary individuals such as you and I demand or supply goods and services in markets. This chapter, which focuses on demand, is followed by two chapters, the first of which considers supply, while the second brings demand and supply together to allow us to see how a market taken as a whole functions.

Learning outcomes

This chapter will:

■ explain the difference between wants, desire and effective demand

■ distinguish between individual demand and market demand

■ explain the 'law of demand'

■ examine the slope of a market demand curve

■ explain shifts of demand and the conditions of demand

■ distinguish between complementary goods and substitute goods

■ explain how normal goods differ from inferior goods

■ distinguish between composite demand and derived demand

■ explain the difference between a shift of demand and a movement along a demand curve

■ consider circumstances in which consumers may respond to higher prices by increasing demand

Wants, desire and effective demand

For several years, an old 'bag lady' used to walk past my house. All her possessions were in the trolley she dragged behind her. From what I could gather, she had no income apart from the charity local people gave her. Her life lay outside the welfare benefit system operated by the state that is supposed to act as a safety net for poor and downtrodden people, the cast-offs of society. Then suddenly, the poor woman vanished. A few days later, my local newspaper reported starkly that the body of an old lady had been discovered in a churchyard near my house. The lady's death was apparently due to hypothermia linked to malnutrition.

From this sad story, you can gather that my local bag lady lacked the wherewithal to meet her basic wants, namely sufficient food to provide a reasonable diet, warm clothing and shelter — the very things that most of us take for granted.

Now let's compare this poor lady's situation (when she was alive) with mine. I enjoy a comfortable middle-class life in which all my basic wants are met. However, I have a schoolboy dream to own a bright red new Ferrari. Unfortunately the price is £182,940. By borrowing up to the hilt, I could possibly buy the car, but no way can I pay for it out of my income. I desire the car, but to my chagrin, I cannot exercise an effective demand for a brand-new Ferrari, or at least the model I have set my sights on.

I cannot exercise an effective demand for a new Ferrari

When economists refer to **demand**, they always mean **effective demand**. Effective demand is desire backed up by an ability to pay. Unlike the poor bag lady, most of us can exercise an effective demand for the goods that fulfil our basic wants, but unless we are extremely rich, with money no object, we are not in a position to buy *all* the goods we desire.

Individual demand and market demand

Normally when economists refer to demand, they mean **market demand**. This is the quantity of a good or service that all the consumers in the market wish to, and are able to, buy at different prices. By contrast, **individual demand** is the quantity that a particular individual, such as you or I, would like to buy. The relationship between market and individual demand is simple. Market demand is just the sum or addition

> **key terms**
>
> **Demand** The quantity of a good or service that consumers are willing and able to buy at given prices in a given period of time. For economists, demand is always **effective demand**.
>
> **Market demand** The quantity of a good or service that all the consumers in a market are willing and able to buy.

of the demand of all the consumers in the market. Thus, if in the UK, 40 million people are prepared to buy nectarines at prices ranging between 0 and £5 a kilo, market demand is the sum of the individual demand of 40 million people.

The 'law' of demand

The 'law' of demand states that as a good's price falls, more is demanded. There is thus an inverse relationship between price and quantity demanded. Note the word 'law' is in inverted commas. This is because a law in economics is not as strong or watertight as a law in a natural science subject such as physics or astronomy. Whereas a law in physics will always hold, a social science law always has ifs and buts attached. More of a good is usually demanded as its price falls, but there are exceptions. To find out more, read the Extension material later in the chapter.

The market demand curve

The market demand curve drawn in Figure 3.1 illustrates the 'law' of demand. If the price starts off high, for example at P_1, household demand is Q_1. But if the price falls to P_2, demand increases to Q_2.

Demand for a good varies according to the time period being considered. For example, weekly demand is different from daily, monthly and annual demand. For this reason, I have written 'Quantity demanded per period of time' on the horizontal axis in Figure 3.1. In later diagrams, I shall use the label 'Quantity'. Always remember that this is a shortcut, and stands for 'Quantity demanded per period of time'.

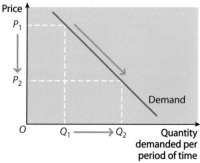

Figure 3.1 A market demand curve

examiner's voice

You don't need to write 'Quantity demanded per period of time' on the horizontal axis of a demand curve diagram. When answering AQA exam questions, the label 'Quantity' is adequate.

Shifts of demand

When we draw a market demand curve to show how much of the good or service households plan to demand at various possible prices, we assume that all the other variables that may also influence demand are held unchanged or constant. This is the **ceteris paribus** assumption. Ceteris paribus means 'other things being equal'. Among the variables whose values are held constant or unchanged when we draw a demand curve are disposable income and tastes or fashion. Collectively, the variables (other than the good's own price) whose values determine planned demand are often called the **conditions of demand**.

key term

Condition of demand
A determinant of demand, other than the good's own price, that fixes the position of the demand curve.

The conditions of demand

The main conditions of demand are:
- the prices of **substitute goods** (or **goods in competing demand**)
- the prices of **complementary goods** (or **goods in joint demand**)
- personal **income** (or more strictly **personal disposable income**, i.e. income after tax and receipt of benefits)
- tastes and preferences
- population size, which influences total market size

If any of the conditions of demand change, the position of the demand curve changes, shifting either rightward or leftward. Figure 3.2 illustrates a rightward shift of the demand curve, which is also called an **increase in demand**. Following a rightward shift of demand, more of the good is demanded at all prices. For example, at a price of P_1, the quantity demanded increases from Q_1 to Q_2. Conversely, a leftward shift of demand (known as a **decrease in demand**) causes the quantity demanded to fall at all prices.

key terms

Decrease in demand
A leftward shift of the demand curve.

Increase in demand
A rightward shift of the demand curve.

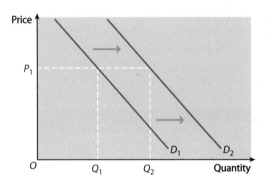

Figure 3.2 The effect of a rightward shift of demand

Among events that might cause a rightward shift of demand are:
- an increase in the price of a substitute good or good in competing demand
- a fall in the price of a complementary good or good in joint demand
- an increase in personal disposable income (but see the qualification below this list)
- a successful advertising campaign making people think more favourably about the good
- an increase in population

Complementary goods and substitute goods

An increase in the price of a complementary good (or a good in joint demand) has the opposite effect to an increase in the price of a substitute good (or a good in competing demand). For example, CD players and CDs are complementary goods in joint demand, but CD players and MP3 players may be in competing demand – if people regard them as substitutes

examiner's voice

Chapter 6 develops the analysis of complementary and substitute goods and normal and inferior goods.

for each other. Following a significant rise in the price of CD players, demand for CD players falls, which in turn reduces the demand for CDs. The demand curve for CDs shifts leftward. However, the demand curve for MP3 players shifts rightward, assuming that consumers consider an MP3 player to be a substitute good.

Box 3.1 Demand for healthy foods

As the news story below shows, demand for healthy foods has been growing rapidly in recent years. Meanwhile, demand for many foods which are perceived as unhealthy, such as hamburgers, have at times declined.

Britain gets fruity with smoothies

Vivianne Ihekweazu, senior market analyst at market analysis company Mintel, recently stated that 'Smoothies have been the true drinks success story of the twenty-first century and are clearly no longer a niche market.

'Healthy eating, and in particular the 5 a day fruit and vegetable campaign, has been the driving force behind continuing rates of exceptional growth. .

'With UK consumers becoming increasingly health conscious and in light of growing concerns about obesity in adults and children, the smoothie market is set to see significant future growth.'

Research published in January 2007 by Mintel found that over the five years from 2001 to 2006, the smoothies market has enjoyed a real burst of energy, with sales growing by no less than 523% to reach £134 million in 2006.

Mintel announced that Brits knocked back 34 million litres of smoothies in 2006 — enough to fill almost 14 Olympic size pools — and up from just 6.3 million litres in 2001.

Despite the huge growth in the market, less than a third of the adult population currently buy smoothies. The young 15–19 and 25–34 age groups are the most likely to reach for a smoothie, perhaps due to their busy on-the-go lifestyle or even as a hangover cure. Smoothies are most popular in London and the South as they may be more widely available in urban areas, but as availability widens, consumption should also increase in line with this.

Adapted from a Mintel press release

Follow-up questions

1 Explain, and illustrate on a supply and demand diagram, how the events in the passage have affected the demand curve for smoothies.
2 How have fast food companies such as McDonald's and Burger King reacted to changes in demand for their traditional products?

Normal and inferior goods

When disposable income increases, a demand curve shifts rightward, but only if the good is a normal good. A **normal good** is a good for which demand increases as income increases. However, some goods are **inferior goods**. In the case of an inferior good, demand decreases as income increases, and an increase in income shifts the demand curve leftward.

To take an example, private car transport and bus travel are not just substitutes for each other; one is a normal good and the other is an inferior good. As people's incomes rise, demand for cars generally increases, while, at the same time, demand for public transport usually falls. If people respond in this way to changes in income then private transport is a normal good, but public transport is an inferior good.

For an individual, whether a good is normal or inferior depends on personal income, tastes and, possibly, age. For young children, junk food such as sweets is usually a normal good. When parents increase small children's pocket money, they generally buy more sweets. But as children get older, tastes change, and sweets may very well become an inferior good.

key terms

Inferior good A good for which demand decreases as income rises.

Normal good A good for which demand increases as income rises.

Composite demand and derived demand

Students often confuse competing demand, which occurs in the case of substitutes, with composite demand and derived demand. **Composite demand** is demand for a good which has more than one use. This means that an increase in demand for one use of the good reduces the supply of the good for an alternative use, e.g. if more wheat is used for biofuel, less is available for food, unless wheat growing increases significantly. By contrast, **derived demand** for a good occurs when a good is necessary for the production of other goods. The demand for capital goods such as machinery and raw materials is derived from the demand for consumer goods or finished goods. If the demand for cars falls, so does the demand for engines, gear boxes and other car components.

Movement along a demand curve and shift of a demand curve

Another source of confusion lies in the difference between a movement along (or adjustment along) a demand curve and a shift of a demand curve. A **movement along a demand curve** takes place only when the good's price changes. As I have explained, provided the demand curve slopes downward, a *fall* in price results in *more* of the good being demanded. This is sometimes called an **extension of demand**. Likewise, a **contraction of demand** occurs when a *rise* in price leads to *less* being demanded.

> **e**xaminer's voice
> Unit 1 exam questions at AS often test understanding of the difference between a movement along a demand or supply curve and a shift of the curve.

By contrast, as I have also explained, a change in a condition of demand shifts the demand curve to a new position. As I have already explained a rightward shift of demand, for example caused by the effect of increased income on demand for a normal good, is often called an increase of demand. Conversely, a decrease of demand occurs when an event such as a rise in the price of a complementary good causes less of the good to be demanded, shifting the demand curve leftward.

Extension material

A demand function

A functional relationship exists between two variables whenever a change in one variable, known as the independent variable or explanatory variable, causes a change in a second variable, which is the dependent variable. The relationship between quantity demanded and price, illustrated in Figure 3.1, can be written as:

$$Q_d = f(P)$$

This tells us that the quantity demanded of a good (Q_d) is a function of the good's price (P). The symbol (f) indicates that a change in the value of the independent variable (shown inside the brackets) causes a change in the dependent variable (on the left-hand side of the equality sign). In a demand function, changes in the good's price are assumed to cause changes in the quantity demanded.

$Q_d = f(P)$ does not indicate the precise nature of the functional relationship, but as the demand curve slopes downward to the right, the relationship is negative or inverse: an increase in price causes a decrease in the quantity demanded.

$Q_d = f(P)$ is an example of a single explanatory variable demand function. But, as we have seen, there are many other variables besides the good's own price that influence demand. Other influences, such as the level of disposable income and tastes and preferences, I have called the conditions of demand. The functional relationship $Q_d = f(P)$, and the demand curve in Figure 3.1, result from the ceteris paribus assumption (or the assumption that the conditions of demand remain unchanged). Indeed, we can write:

$$Q_d = f(P), \text{ceteris paribus}$$

Dropping the ceteris paribus assumption, the demand function becomes:

$$Q_d = f(P, P_S, P_C, Y_d, \text{tastes, population size} \ldots)$$

This is a multi-explanatory variable demand function. All the symbols inside the brackets except the good's own price (P) are the conditions of demand. As we have seen, if any of them change then the demand curve shifts to a new position. P_S, P_C, Y_d are respectively the symbols for the prices of substitute goods, the prices of complementary goods and disposable income. The dots at the end of the symbols represent any other explanatory variables that influence demand, but which have not been indicated explicitly.

Upward-sloping demand curves

Demand curves don't have to slope downwards, though they usually do. In Chapter 6, I explain circumstances in which a demand curve may be horizontal or vertical. However, as Figure 3.3 illustrates, a demand curve may also slope upward, showing that more is demanded as the good's price increases.

There are a number of possible explanations for upward-sloping demand curves. Two of these,

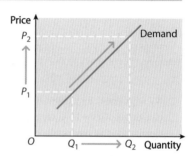

Figure 3.3 An upward-sloping demand curve

Veblen goods and goods for which consumers perceive a high price to be an indicator of high quality, are explained in the Extension material below.

There are two other situations in which consumers may respond to higher prices by demanding more of a good.

The first is **speculative demand**. If the price of a good such as housing, shares or a foreign currency starts to rise, people may speculate that in the near future the price will rise even further. In this situation, demand is likely to increase. In the case of rising house prices, young people who wish to become first-time buyers may scramble to buy houses, fearing that it they wait, they may never be able to afford to buy a house.

The final type of good with an upward-sloping demand curve is known as a **Giffen good**. However, there is very little evidence that Giffen goods actually exist. A Giffen good is a highly inferior good that forms a large part of the total spending of extremely poor people. Consider a situation in which a very poor family buys only two foods — potatoes and meat. Potatoes, the inferior good, are the family's main foodstuff. Meat is the luxury, which the family only eats on Sunday. In this situation, a rise in the price of potatoes means that the family's real income falls. The fall in real income increases the family's demand for potatoes, which as I have said, are inferior goods (at least for this family). In effect, higher potato prices mean that the family buys even more potatoes because they can no longer afford meat.

Many students make the mistake of believing that *all* inferior goods are Giffen goods, with upward-sloping demand curves. This is wrong. Most, and possibly all, inferior goods have conventional downward-sloping demand curves. A good has to be highly inferior for it to be a Giffen good, and in any case the Giffen phenomenon can only exist for extremely poor families. While it is true that all Giffen goods (if they exist) must be inferior goods, the reverse is not true. Few, if any inferior goods are Giffen goods.

*e*xaminer's voice

The AQA economics specification does not require knowledge of upward-sloping demand curves. Nevertheless, exam candidates often make the mistake of referring to inferior goods as Giffen goods.

Extension material

Are there any exceptions to the 'law' of demand?

According to the 'law' of demand, firms that lower their prices should sell more. Sometimes, however, you may come across a company that tries to persuade us to buy more of whatever the firm is selling precisely because its goods are more expensive than those of its competitors. The 'reassuringly expensive' advertising campaign for Stella Artois beer is a good example.

A few years ago, Interbrew, the Belgian company that owns the Stella brand, decided to sell its beer as a premium brand. Interbrew hoped that high prices would attract more customers. (Those readers enjoying a misspent youth who regularly buy beer may have noticed that in recent years, Stella has changed tack, selling its beers on the 'stack 'em high, sell 'em fast' principle, at discounted prices.)

Perhaps more could be done to justify Stella's ridiculous price.

Aaah the exquisite Stella taste.

Aargh the excruciating Stella price. Sadly, there's very little we can do about it.

Even offering small incentives like the one on the left is beyond our means.

Making Stella properly just costs far too much money.

We could, you might suppose, adulterate our premium barley with a few bags of a more questionable grain.

Substitute ordinary hops for the rare Czech Saaz variety.

Or hoist Stella out of the vat before the customary six weeks maturation.

While these expedients might produce a price that's not ridiculous, we're afraid the same could not be said of the beer.

Stella Artois. Reassuringly expensive.

ADVERTISING ARCHIVES

An economist might argue that the 'reassuringly expensive' campaign shows that Stella was marketing its beer as a Veblen good, named after the Norwegian economist Thornstein Veblen. A Veblen good is a good of exclusive or ostentatious consumption, or a 'snob' good. Veblen goods are sometimes called positional goods, though strictly a positional good is so scarce that only few people can ever acquire it. Some people wish to consume Veblen goods, such as the Ferrari car I mentioned earlier in the chapter, because possession of such goods indicates how well a person has done in society. Flaunting Veblen or positional goods sends signals to other (hopefully envious) people about how well off you are.

Don't confuse a Veblen good with another type of good which might attract more demand at higher prices, namely a good for which consumers use price as a short-cut for information about quality. Consumers may lack accurate information about the quality of some of the goods they are considering buying, particularly goods such as second-hand cars, computers and, in the example below, horses. In this situation, a potential buyer may fear that a low price means low quality, and that conversely a high price means high quality.

This reflects a problem which, according to economist George Akerlof (winner of the 2001 Nobel Prize for Economics), is as old as markets themselves. It concerns how horse traders respond to the question: 'If he wants to sell that horse, do I really want to buy it?' Akerlof believes that such questioning is fundamental to the market for horses and used cars, and it is also at least minimally present in every market transaction.

Summary

- Demand means effective demand, based on ability as well as willingness to pay.
- Market demand is sum of the individual demand of all the consumers in the market.
- The 'law' of demand states that as a good's price falls, more is demanded.
- Market demand (and individual demand) can be represented on a demand curve.
- For most goods, demand curves slope downward.
- If any of the conditions of demand change, the demand curve shifts to a new position.
- The conditions of demand include the prices of substitute goods and goods in joint demand, disposable income and tastes and preferences.
- Goods can be divided into normal goods and inferior goods.
- Composite demand is demand for a good which has more than one use.
- Derived demand for a good occurs when a good is necessary for the production of other goods.
- A movement along a demand curve must not be confused with a shift of a demand curve.
- A few goods may have upward-sloping demand curves. These are Veblen goods, goods for which price is an indicator of quality, goods in speculative demand and, possibly, Giffen goods.

Questions

1 What is effective demand?
2 What is meant by the ceteris paribus assumption and what are its implications?
3 Why may a demand curve shift?
4 With examples, distinguish between a complementary good and a substitute good.
5 What is the difference between composite demand and derived demand?
6 Under what circumstances may a demand curve slope upward?

Chapter 4

The supply of goods and services

Chapter 2 introduced you to the fact that a market is a voluntary meeting of buyers and sellers, with the buyers deciding how much of a good or service they wish to buy while firms or suppliers decide how much to sell. Chapter 3 then explained how individuals and households exercise demand in a market. This chapter looks at the other side of market transactions, investigating how firms or producers decide how much of a good they would like to supply and sell.

As you proceed through this chapter, you will note how it is similar to the previous chapter which explains the nature of demand. The similarity is no accident. For the most part, this chapter applies the same logic and line of reasoning used to explain demand in Chapter 3, to explain supply. Much of the explanation is similar, but do note the differences between the theory of supply and the theory of demand.

Learning outcomes

This chapter will:
- distinguish between the supply of a single firm in a market and market supply
- explain the 'law' of supply
- examine the slope of a market supply curve
- explain shifts of supply and the conditions of supply
- explain how expenditure taxes and subsidies shift supply curves
- distinguish between joint supply and competing supply

Supply by a single firm and market supply

Normally when economists refer to **supply**, they mean market supply. **Market supply** is the quantity of a good or service that all the firms or producers in the market *plan* to sell at different prices. By contrast, as the name indicates, supply by a single firm is the quantity that a particular firm *within* the market would like to sell. As with demand, the relationship between the two is simple. Market supply is just the sum of the supply of all the firms or producers in the market. Thus, if in the UK, 20,000 farmers are prepared to sell tomatoes at various prices ranging from very low to very high, market supply sums the supply decision of all the farmers in the market.

key terms

Market supply The quantity of a good or service that all the firms in a market are willing to sell.

Supply The quantity of a good or service that firms plan to sell at given prices in a given period of time.

The 'law' of supply

The 'law' of supply states that as a good's price rises, more is supplied. There is thus a positive or direct relationship between price and quantity supplied. (There are exceptions to the 'law' of supply. To find out more, read the Extension material that follows the next section on the market supply curve.)

The market supply curve

The market supply curve drawn in Figure 4.1 illustrates the 'law' of supply. If the price starts off low, for example at P_1, firms are willing to supply Q_1. But if the price rises to P_2, planned supply increases to Q_2.

The main reason for upward-sloping supply curves stems from the business objective which economists generally assume that firms have. This is the **profit-maximising objective**. It is assumed that firms always aim to make the biggest possible **profit**. From this it follows that a firm will only want to supply more of a good if it is profitable so to do.

For a firm, profit is the difference between the sales revenue the firm receives when selling the goods or services it produces and the costs of producing the goods. Now, the cost of producing extra units of a good generally increases as firms produce more of the good. As a result, it is unprofitable to produce and sell extra units of a good unless the price rises to compensate for the extra cost of production. The result is the upward-sloping market supply curve shown in Figure 4.1.

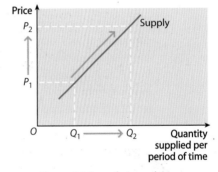

Figure 4.1 A market supply curve

key term

Profit is the difference between total sales revenue and total costs of production.

examiner's voice

Figure 4.1 shows a linear supply curve, i.e. a straight line. However, neither supply curves nor demand curves have to be linear. A non-linear supply or demand curve is depicted by a curved curve. Both linear and non-linear curves are possible. In an exam it does not matter which you draw — providing the curve is meant to be upward sloping. Supply curves usually slope upward, though, as the Extension material explains, other shapes of supply curve are possible.

As with demand, the supply of a good varies according to the time period being considered. Hence the words 'Quantity supplied per period of time' on the horizontal axis in Figure 4.1. In later diagrams, I shall shorten this to 'Quantity'. But again, as with demand, remember that this is a shortcut.

Extension material

Backward-bending supply curves

Occasionally, supply curves do not slope upwards. A backward-bending supply curve, illustrated here, has been observed in the market for oil. After the rapid rises in the price of oil caused by the first oil crisis in 1973, oil-exporting member countries of the Organization of Oil Exporting Countries (OPEC) *decreased* production of oil. To find out more, read page 157 in the 17th edition of a classic American textbook, *Economics*, written by Paul Samuelson and William Nordhaus, published by McGraw Hill.

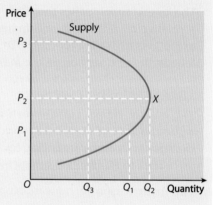

In Figure 4.2, the supply curve slopes upward in a conventional way until point X is reached. Thus, supply increases from Q_1 to Q_2 following a price rise from P_1 to P_2. However, any further price increase, for example from P_2 to P_3, causes producers to supply less of the good. Supply falls to Q_3 in this case.

Figure 4.2

Shifts of supply

In Chapter 3, I explained how a market demand curve shows how much all the consumers in the market plan to buy at different prices of the good, assuming all the other factors that influence demand remain constant. I called these 'other factors' the conditions of demand and explained how, if any of them change, the demand curve shifts to a new position.

In exactly the same way, a market supply curve shows the quantities of the good that all the firms in the market plan to supply at different possible prices, assuming the **conditions of supply** remain unchanged. Again, if the ceteris paribus assumption no longer holds, one or more of the conditions of supply change, and the supply curve shifts to a new position.

The conditions of supply

The main conditions of supply are:

- costs of production, including
  - wage costs
  - raw material costs

*k*ey term

Condition of supply A determinant of supply, other than the good's own price, that fixes the position of the supply curve.

– energy costs
– costs of borrowing
- technical progress
- taxes imposed on firms, such as VAT, excise duties, the business rate
- subsidies granted by the government to firms

key terms

Decrease in supply
A leftward shift of the supply curve.

Increase in supply
A rightward shift of the supply curve.

As I have noted, if any of the conditions of supply change, the supply curve shifts to a new position. A rightward shift of supply is also known as an **increase in supply**, whereas a leftward shift is known as a **decrease in supply**. An increase in wage costs, which for many firms are the most important cost of production, shifts the supply curve leftward (or upward). Firms reduce the quantity of the good they are prepared to supply because production costs have risen. For example, when the price is P_1 in Figure 4.3, a leftward shift of supply from S_1 to S_2 causes the quantity firms are prepared to supply to fall from Q_1 to Q_2.

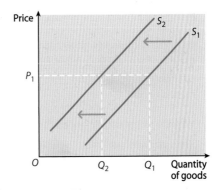

Figure 4.3 *A leftward shift of the supply curve*

examiner's voice
Chapter 5 explains how, following an increase and a decrease in supply, there is a resulting adjustment or movement along the demand curve. Likewise an increase or decrease of demand results in an adjustment or movement along the supply curve. Examination questions often test your understanding of the difference between a shift of a curve and an adjustment in response to a price change along the other curve which has not shifted.

Supply curves also shift when technical progress occurs, or when firms enter or leave the market. Technical progress generally reduces production costs and shifts supply curves rightward. The entry of new firms into the market has a similar effect. Conversely, the supply curve shifts leftward when firms leave the market.

Box 4.1 Fluctuations in commodity prices

The Unit 1 exam sometimes contains data about changing conditions of demand or supply for a product, and the reasons for, or consequences of, a shift of a demand curve or a supply curve in the market. Very often the market is a commodity market, for an industrial raw material such as copper or a source of energy such as oil. Here is a description of how commodity prices have changed over the decades, followed by an explanation of why the prices of commodities such as oil and natural gas fluctuate so much.

The history of commodity prices

Between 1906 and 1923, the world experienced a long commodity-price boom. Then between 1923 and 1933 commodity prices fell sharply. After that, a strong commodity-price boom started that lasted a full 20 years, until 1953. There followed a 15-year downturn in commodity prices that lasted until 1968. Afterwards came the great commodity price boom of the 1970s. We saw the long commodity downturn between the early 1980s and 1999, followed finally by the commodity-price boom that we're seeing right now.

Why do commodity prices fluctuate?

The answer is that, while commodity production and demand do in fact respond to price changes, there is a long time lag in most cases, particularly with regard to production. Because commodity prices fluctuate so much, many producers want to wait and see if we're really on an upward path before investing. But far more importantly, particularly in the cases of mining and drilling for oil and natural gas, it takes quite a while to find new sources; to determine whether or not mining or drilling is really economically viable; to overcome red tape and objections from government bureaucrats and environmentalists; and finally to go deep into the ground and actually extract it. Any of these things can take a decade or more.

Money Week, 23 November 2007

Follow-up question

Using the information in the data, explain why the long-run supply curve of a commodity such as oil is likely to differ from the short-run supply curve for the product.

How expenditure taxes and subsidies shift supply curves

A supply curve also shifts leftward (or upward) when the government imposes an **expenditure tax** such as customs and excise duties or value-added tax (VAT) on firms. From a firm's point of view, the tax is similar to a rise in production costs, so the supply curve shifts leftward. Firms try to pass the tax onto consumers by increasing the price of the good. For this reason, expenditure taxes provide examples of **indirect taxes**. The higher price charged means consumers indirectly pay the tax, even though the firms and not the consumers pay the tax to the government (see Figure 6.9 in Chapter 6 for an example).

How the supply curve shifts depends on whether the tax firms are forced to pay an *ad valorem* tax or a **specific tax**. In the case of an *ad valorem* tax such as value-added tax (VAT), which is levied at the same percentage rate (e.g. 17.5%) on whatever the price would be without the tax, the new supply curve is steeper than the old supply curve. This is shown in the

Key terms

Ad valorem tax A percentage expenditure tax such as VAT.

Expenditure tax A tax levied by the government on spending by consumers. The firms selling the good pay the tax to the government, but consumers indirectly pay via the resulting price rise.

Unit tax or **specific tax** A tax levied on a unit of a good, irrespective of the good's price.

left-hand panel of Figure 4.4. But in the case of a specific tax or unit tax, such as the excise duty levied on tobacco, alcohol or petrol, the tax levied on each unit of the good is not affected by the good's price before the tax was imposed. Because of this, the new and old supply curves are parallel to each other, as the right-hand panel of Figure 4.4 illustrates.

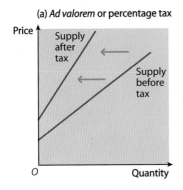

(a) *Ad valorem* or percentage tax

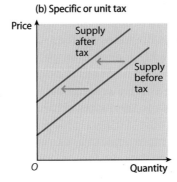

(b) **Specific or unit tax**

Figure 4.4
An expenditure tax shifting a supply curve

How subsidies shift supply curves

A **subsidy** given by the government to producers has the opposite effect to an expenditure tax. In the case of a specific subsidy, which is illustrated in Figure 4.5, the sum of money paid to firms for each unit of the good produced is the same whatever the price of the good. By contrast, the size of the subsidy would vary if the subsidy was dependent on the price of the good before the subsidy was paid.

key term
Subsidy Money given by the government to firms to reduce the price and offset some of the costs of production.

Joint supply and competing supply

In Chapter 3, I explained the difference between complementary goods (or goods in joint demand) and substitutes (or goods in competing demand). I then went on to explain how if the price of a complementary good increased, the demand curve for the other good in joint demand shifts leftward. In the case of substitute goods, the opposite relationship holds: a rise in the price of the substitute leads to the demand curve for the good in competing demand to shift rightward.

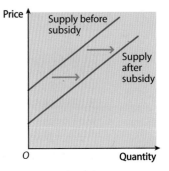

Figure 4.5 A specific or unit subsidy shifting a supply curve

With supply curves, there are rather similar relationships when goods are in **joint supply** and when they are in **competing supply**. These relationships are, however, a little bit different from the demand relationships I have just described. Joint supply occurs when production of one good leads also to the supply of a by-product. For example, the slaughter of a cow to provide meat leads to production of one extra cow hide, which increases the supply of leather. In this example, meat is the main product and leather is the by-product, though the relationship could be reversed.

Suppose now the price of beef increases and farmers believe the high price will continue in future years. More cattle will be bred for slaughter, and the supply of leather will also increase. Thus a rise in the price of the first good (beef) shifts the supply curve of the other good in joint supply.

Now consider what happens if two goods are in competing supply rather than in joint supply. The recent relationship between food and biofuel provides a highly topical example. As Box 4.2 explains, increased demand for biofuels such as ethanol has diverted crop production away from food supply to the supply of fuel for motor vehicles. Because farmers producing crops such as wheat, maize and sugar can earn a higher price by selling their produce to energy companies, the supply curve of such products for food is shifting leftward.

More cattle will be bred if the price of beef increases

examiner's voice

Think how you could use a production possibility curve diagram to illustrate how competing supply involves switching productive resources between different forms of production.

Box 4.2 Competing supply: biofuel and food

The agonies of agflation

The soaring prices of bushels of wheat and barrels of oil are not unconnected. The cost of agricultural commodities, just like oil and metals, has gone up sharply over the past couple of years. Aside from wheat, the prices of corn, rice and barley have all risen by over a third since 2005. Food prices around the world are rising so quickly that a new term has been coined to describe the ballooning price of breakfast staples and dinner-time favourites: agflation.

Demand for grain is accelerating, not to feed humans or livestock but to fill petrol tanks. Compared with 2000, three-times more corn is used to make ethanol in the USA; distilleries that produce biofuels hoover up a fifth of the country's corn supplies. Demand for cleaner energy in turn keeps demand for corn growing.

Farmers are having trouble keeping pace with the burgeoning biofuel industry. And to produce more corn farmers are switching production from wheat and soya, pushing up the prices of those crops too.

The Economist, 25 August 2007

Follow-up question

Relate the concept of competing supply to the concept of composite demand explained in Chapter 3.

Summary

- A market supply curve shows how much of a good all the firms in the market plan or intend to supply at different prices.
- A market supply curve is derived by adding together the individual supply curves of all the firms or producers in the market.
- If one or more of the conditions of supply change, the supply curve shifts to a new position.
- If costs of production, such as wage costs, increase, the supply curve shifts leftward or upward.
- Technical progress usually reduces production costs and shifts the supply curve rightward or downward.
- An expenditure tax shifts the supply curve leftward or upward.
- A subsidy granted to producers shifts the supply curve rightward or downward.

Questions

1 What is the relationship between a firm's supply and market supply?
2 Why does a market supply curve slope upward?
3 What are the conditions of supply?
4 Why may a supply curve shift?
5 Distinguish between joint supply and competing supply.
6 Compare the effect of the imposition of an *ad valorem* tax on supply with that of a unit tax.
7 How does a subsidy given by the government to farmers affect the supply of an agricultural good?

Chapter 5

Bringing demand and supply together in a competitive market

The comedian Sacha Baron Cohen, in his guise as Ali G, once interviewed the eminent, now sadly deceased, economist J. K. Galbraith, then in his late eighties. Ali G asked: 'What is supply and demand? Is it like with me Julie? I supply it and she demand it.'

Poor old JKG replied 'Supply and demand is an old economic expression...', but was unable to complete his sentence. I am sure that had he been able to do so, Professor Galbraith would have summarised some of the rest of this chapter, though of course what he might have said would be much more eloquently expressed. I am not going to repeat the rest of the 'interview', interesting as it was; the language hardly befits an economics textbook. If you are interested, you can of course find the whole interview on the internet.

Learning outcomes

This chapter will:

- distinguish between goods markets and factor markets in the economy
- explain the difference between a competitive market and an uncompetitive market
- bring demand and supply curves together in a supply and demand diagram
- distinguish between market equilibrium and disequilibrium
- explain how a shift of supply or demand disturbs market equilibrium
- distinguish between a shift of a supply or demand curve and an adjustment along a curve
- examine the adjustment process that restores equilibrium in a market
- survey the functions that prices perform in a market or mixed economy

Goods markets and factor markets

Market economies and mixed economies contain a large number of markets. Many of these markets can be grouped under the heading of either **goods markets** (or **product markets**) or **factor markets**. These markets are respectively markets for *outputs* or *final* goods and services (consumer goods and services) and markets for the factors of production or *inputs* necessary for final goods eventually to be produced. Households and firms operate simultaneously in both sets of markets. In goods markets, households exercise demand for consumer goods and services produced and supplied by firms. For household demand in the goods market to be an *effective* demand, i.e. demand backed up by an ability to pay, households must sell their labour, or possibly the services of any capital or land they own, in factor markets. In these factor markets it is the firms who exercise the demand for the factor services sold by the households as inputs into the production process.

Competitive markets and uncompetitive markets

The extent to which markets are **competitive** or **uncompetitive** is of great importance. At one extreme a market is highly competitive when the very large number of firms in the market produce uniform products, incur similar costs of production and have no ability to influence the ruling market price (or equilibrium price) set by supply and demand in the market as a whole. Highly competitive markets lack **entry barriers**, which means that new firms can enter the market. Likewise, firms already in the market can leave if they wish to. Because there is also a high degree of transparency in the market, firms can find out what their competitors are doing.

At the other extreme is a market in which there is no competition at all, simply because there is only one firm in the market, protected by entry barriers. Such a market is called a **monopoly**. As Chapter 12 explains, monopolies can often exploit consumers, for example by hiking up the price, restricting the output they make available and also restricting consumer choice.

Real-world markets usually lie somewhere between the extremes of a high degree of competition and monopoly. In many markets, such as the market for mobile phones, real-world firms use factors such as style and fashion to make one firm's product differ from the competitors' products. As a result, prices usually vary for the branded products sold by each of the firms in the market. However,

Tomato farmers produce a similar, uniform product

the ability to influence consumers in this way is not nearly so prevalent in the market for an agricultural good such as tomatoes, where large numbers of farmers produce a similar uniform product. The next sections of this chapter explain how such a market functions.

Box 5.1 To do with the price of fish

The extract below is taken from an article in *The Economist* and shows that for food markets to work efficiently it is essential for there to be good information on the supply and demand of a product.

For a market to be competitive, buyers and sellers need accurate information about what is going on in the market. In the market for newly caught fish in south-west India, lack of adequate information about conditions of supply and prices being charged led to small, separated and relatively uncompetitive fish markets, with almost identical fish being traded at different prices in each market. The case study below shows how, by improving the exchange of information between fishermen, mobile phone technology has contributed to the growth of a larger and much more competitive market.

Imagine you are a fisherman off the coast of northern Kerala, a region in the south of India. Visiting your usual fishing ground, you bring in an unusually good catch of sardines. That means other fishermen in the area will probably have done well too, so there will be plenty of supply at the local beach market: prices will be low, and you may not even be able to sell your catch. Should you head for the usual market anyway, or should you go down the coast in the hope that fishermen in that area will not have done so well and your fish will fetch a better price? If you make the wrong choice you cannot visit another market because fuel is costly. Since fish are perishable, any that

cannot be sold will have to be dumped into the sea.

This was the situation facing Kerala's fishermen until 1997. In practice, fishermen chose to stick with their home markets all the time. This was wasteful because when a particular market is oversupplied, fish are thrown away, even though there may be buyers for them a little farther along the coast. There were also wide variations in the price of sardines along the coast.

But starting in 1997 mobile phones were introduced in Kerala. As phone coverage spread between 1997 and 2000, fishermen started to buy phones and use them to call coastal markets while still at sea. Instead of selling their fish at beach auctions, the fishermen would call around to find the best price. The proportion of fishermen who ventured beyond their home markets to sell their catches jumped from 0% to around 35% as soon as coverage became available in each region. At that point, no fish were wasted and the variation in prices fell dramatically. Waste had been eliminated and the 'law of one price' — the idea that in an efficient market identical goods should cost the same — had come into effect, in the form of a single rate for sardines along the coast.

The Economist, 10 May 2007

Follow-up questions

1 Explain how the passage illustrates the way in which good information is needed for markets to be highly competitive.

2 Can you think of any markets in the UK that have been made more competitive by the use of mobile phones?

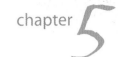
Bringing demand and supply curves together in a competitive market

I shall now bring together the market demand and market supply curves (explained in Chapters 3 and 4) to see how the equilibrium price is achieved within a single competitive goods market in the economy. The market we shall look at is the tomato market. The essential features of the market are shown in Figure 5.1.

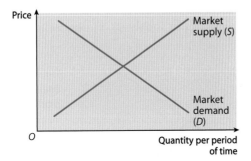

Figure 5.1 A supply and demand graph for the tomato market

Note that later diagrams in this chapter label the curves *D* and *S*, and the horizontal axis is labelled 'Quantity'. *D*, *S* and 'Quantity' are shorthand for 'market demand', 'market supply' and 'Quantity per period of time'.

The market demand curve drawn in Figure 5.1 shows how many tomatoes all the consumers in the market plan to purchase at different prices in a particular period of time. In a similar way, the market supply curve shows how many tomatoes all the farmers and firms in the market wish to supply at different prices in the same time period.

The equilibrium price

The concepts of **equilibrium** and its opposite, **disequilibrium**, are of great importance in economic theory and analysis. You should think of equilibrium as a *state of rest* or a *state of balance between opposing forces*. In a market, the opposing forces are supply and demand. **Market equilibrium**, which is shown in Figure 5.2, occurs where the demand curve and the supply curve cross each other. At price *P**, households

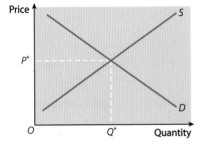

Figure 5.2 Market equilibrium in the tomato market

key terms

Equilibrium A state of rest or balance between opposing forces.

Market equilibrium When planned demand equals planned supply in the market.

examiner's voice

It is important to understand the concepts of equilibrium and disequilibrium in economics. You will come across many other examples besides market equilibrium and disequilibrium explained in this chapter. In your later studies, look out for macro-economic equilibrium and balance of payments equilibrium.

plan to demand exactly the same quantity of tomatoes that firms *plan* to supply. P^* therefore is the equilibrium price, with Q^* being the equilibrium quantity.

Disequilibrium in the market

It is impossible at *most* prices for both households and firms simultaneously to fulfil their market plans. In Figure 5.3, P_1 is a **disequilibrium** price for tomatoes because the tomato growers and sellers cannot fulfil their plans at this price. When price is P_1 in Figure 5.3, firms would like to supply Q_2, but households are only willing to purchase Q_1.

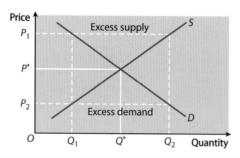

Figure 5.3 Disequilibrium and equilibrium in the tomato market

key terms

Excess supply When firms wish to sell more than consumers wish to buy, with the price above the equilibrium price.

Market disequilibrium When the market fails to clear. The market plans of consumers and firms are inconsistent with each other.

To explain this further, it is useful to divide the market into two 'sides' — the *short side* and the *long side*. When the price is P_1, households, or the people wishing to buy tomatoes, are on the short side of the market, while tomato producers are on the long side. The economic agents on the short side can always fulfil their market plans, but those on the long side cannot! Thus, when the price is P_1, households can purchase exactly the quantity of tomatoes they wish to, namely Q_1. Farmers and other tomato producers, however, are in a different situation. They would like to sell Q_2, but can only sell Q_1, as long as the price remains at P_1. The difference between Q_2 and Q_1 is **excess supply** or unsold stock.

examiner's voice

Many students never really get to grips with microeconomic analysis because they fail to understand the difference between market plans and market action. Your market plans are what you *want* to do when you go shopping; your market action is what you *end up* doing.

At P_1, as at any other price, *actual* or *realised* demand equals *actual* or *realised* supply. However, this is largely irrelevant; the key point is that at price P_1, *planned* supply exceeds *planned* demand.

The market is also in disequilibrium at price P_2, because households are unable to buy as much as they wish to at this price. Households would like to buy Q_2 of tomatoes, but they can't, because at this price tomato producers are only willing to supply Q_1. The situation is now reversed compared to P_1. Tomato buyers are on the long side of the market and farmers and tomato sellers are now on the short side. In this case, the difference between Q_2 and Q_1 is **excess demand** or unfulfilled demand. Households end up buying Q_1 of tomatoes because this is the maximum quantity tomato producers are prepared to sell at this price. Once again, *actual* demand equals *actual* supply (namely Q_1), but *planned* supply is now less than *planned* demand.

key term

Excess demand When consumers wish to buy more than firms wish to sell, with the price below the equilibrium price.

I shall now introduce a most important assumption about economic behaviour which recurs throughout economic theory and analysis. I shall assume that whenever an economic agent, such as a household or firm, fails to fulfil its market plans, it has an incentive to change its market behaviour. When excess supply exists in the market (as at P_1 in the tomato market), the market mechanism or price mechanism swings into action to get rid of unsold stocks. By doing this, the price mechanism moves the market towards equilibrium. Economists assume that firms react to stocks of unsold goods by accepting a lower price. Eventually the price falls until the amount the households wish to buy equals exactly the quantity firms are prepared to supply. In the tomato market, equilibrium is reached at price P^*.

In the case of excess demand, it is useful to divide households into two groups of customers. In the tomato market, the first group, depicted by the distance from O to Q_1, are *lucky* customers who buy the good at price P_1 before the available quantity runs out. By contrast, *unlucky* households, shown by the distance from Q_1 to Q_2, cannot buy the good at P_1, possibly because they turned up too late. However, in order to be able to purchase the good, unlucky consumers bid up the price until, once again, equilibrium is reached at P^*.

The equilibrium price, P^*, is the *only* price which satisfies both households and firms. Consequently, once this price is reached, neither group has reason to change their market plans. At P^*, planned demand equals planned supply and the market clears.

Here is a summary of the main conclusions of this very important part of the chapter.
- A market is in disequilibrium when:
  (a) planned demand < planned supply, in which case the price falls, or when
  (b) planned demand > planned supply, in which case the price rises.
- A market is in equilibrium when:
  (c) planned demand = planned supply, in which case the price does not change.

How a shift of supply disturbs market equilibrium

Once supply equals demand in a market, for example at point X in Figure 5.4, the market remains in equilibrium until an external event hits the market and causes either the market supply curve or the market demand curve to shift to a new position. Figure 5.4 illustrates what happens in the tomato market when an event such as a bumper harvest causes the supply curve of tomatoes to shift rightward, from S_1 to S_2. Before the shift of the supply curve, P_1 was the equilibrium price of

tomatoes. However, once the supply curve shifts, P_1 becomes a disequilibrium price. Too many tomatoes are offered for sale at this price, which means there is excess supply in the market. The excess supply is shown by the distance Q_2 minus Q_1, or from X to V. To get rid of this unsold stock, tomato producers reduce the price they are prepared to accept. The market price falls from P_1 to P_2, which eliminates the excess supply. In the new equilibrium planned supply once again equals planned demand, but at the lower equilibrium price of P_2.

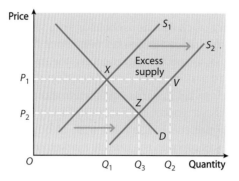

Figure 5.4 *The effect of a rightward shift of the market supply curve of tomatoes*

*e*xaminer's voice

Make sure you can distinguish between a *shift* of a supply or demand curve, and the adjustment to a new equilibrium along the curve that does not shift.

Shifts of supply or demand curves and adjustments along a curve

As noted in Chapter 3 students often confuse a *shift* of a supply or demand curve with an *adjustment* or *movement* along a curve. I shall use Figure 5.4 to explain the distinction again.

In Figure 5.4, the market supply curve of tomatoes *shifts* from S_1 to S_2, creating excess supply equal to the distance between X and V. The adjustment process then kicks in, reducing the price from P_1 to P_2. The adjustment involves a movement *along* the demand curve from X to Z (and also along the supply curve from V to Z). The shift of the supply curve is often called an increase in supply, whereas the resulting adjustment along the demand curve is known as an extension of demand.

The next diagram, Figure 5.5, shows an increase in demand, followed by an extension of supply. I shall leave it up to you to draw diagrams which illustrate (a) a decrease in supply and a contraction of demand and (b) a decrease in demand and a contraction of supply. You should also at this point go back to Chapters 3 and 4 to refresh your knowledge of the different conditions of demand and conditions of supply that determine the position of demand and supply curves.

*e*xaminer's voice

AQA does not require use of terms such as an increase or an extension of demand. By all means use these terms, but explain what you mean on the first occasion you introduce the terms.

A bumper harvest shifts the supply curve of tomatoes rightward, and a change in consumers' incomes, described in the next section, shifts the market demand curve.

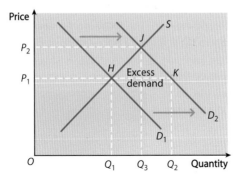

Figure 5.5 The effect of a rightward shift of the market demand curve for tomatoes

How a shift of demand disturbs market equilibrium

Figure 5.5 shows what happens in the market for tomatoes following an increase in consumers' incomes.

People who enjoy eating tomatoes usually consider tomatoes to be a normal good, i.e. a good for which demand increases as income increases. Before the increase in consumers' incomes, the equilibrium price of tomatoes was P_1, determined at the intersection of curves D_1 and S. At this price, planned demand equals planned supply. However, increased incomes shift the market demand curve rightward from D_1 to D_2. Immediately, disequilibrium replaces equilibrium in the market. The rightward shift of demand creates excess demand in the market, as long as the price remains at P_1. Excess demand is shown by Q_2 minus Q_1, or the distance between H and K.

The market adjustment mechanism now swings into action to get rid of the excess demand. The price increases to P_2 to eliminate the excess demand, and the quantity of tomatoes bought and sold rises to Q_3. In response to the increase in demand from H to K, there is an adjustment along the supply curve between H and J (an extension of supply) to establish the new equilibrium.

Extension material

Auctions and establishing an equilibrium price

These days almost all students are aware of eBay, the internet-based auction on which all new and second-hand goods that you can think of are traded. Economists believe that auctions provide a quick, and indeed an almost instantaneous, way of eliminating excess demand and establishing market equilibrium. Consider, for example, the situation shown in Figure 5.5 immediately following the increase in demand. If tomatoes were to be auctioned the price would rise to that offered by the highest bidder at P_2. The market would clear instantly. But would it? It is highly unlikely that a single consumer would wish to buy all the tomatoes sold in the market. The auction would have to be more complicated, perhaps enabling different consumers to buy at different prices between P_1 and P_2. Auctions are in fact quite rare. To relate auctions to other ways of setting prices read Box 5.2.

Box 5.2 The heyday of the auction

In theory, an auction provides a quick and efficient method of establishing equilibrium in a market. But auctions are quite rare in real-world markets. The following extract, taken from an article in *The Economist* compares auctions to two other forms of price-setting: haggling and fixed price lists (menu pricing).

Online auctions may be one of the most valuable innovations brought by the internet. Economists have long recognised the virtues of auctions. In 1880, Léon Walras, a French economist, described the entire price mechanism as an auctioneer, attaching a body to Adam Smith's 'invisible hand'. The 'Walrasian auctioneer' would call out a price, see how many buyers and sellers there were and, if these did not balance, adjust the price until demand equalled supply.

But in practice, for most of human history, auctions have not played a starring role in the price-setting process. Mostly they have been limited to agricultural and other commodity markets, fine art and antiques, and — of increasing importance in recent decades — some types of financial securities.

Two other forms of price-setting have been dominant: one-to-one negotiation (haggling) and the non-negotiable menu of prices offered by seller to buyer. These two approaches are not bad: the price mechanism based on them obviously does a much better job of allocating scarce resources than do centrally planned systems that eschew prices altogether.

But each method has important flaws. Menu prices can be 'sticky' — slow to adjust to changes in the balance of supply and demand. One-to-one haggling carries a big risk: that the seller or buyer may not be negotiating with the best person (i.e. the one willing to pay the most or sell for least).

Auctions can overcome these shortcomings by soliciting a wide range of bids from many people. And the internet, thanks to its cheap interconnection of millions of people, makes well-functioning auctions far easier. They are now possible for many goods and services that used to rely on haggling or menus. And even in markets where auctions have long been used to set prices, the internet can make them much more sophisticated than ever before.

Steve Kaplan, an economist at the University of Chicago, points out that online auctions have a big economic advantage over traditional online menu-priced sites, such as that pioneered by Amazon. Such sites cut out the cost of going to the shops, and make it cheaper to compare prices with other retailers. But Amazon's customers are no better off if it attracts more users. Whereas the more buyers and sellers turn up on eBay, the better their chances of getting a good deal, as the auction becomes deeper and more liquid.

The Economist, 23 July 1999

Follow-up questions

1 eBay is the best known and the largest internet-based auction. Give your views on the advantages and disadvantages of trading goods on eBay.

2 Explain how the use of the internet has affected the costs consumers incur when searching for goods they want to buy.

The functions prices perform in the economy

Chapters 2, 3 and 4, and indeed this chapter, have provided you with lots of information about the role of prices in a market economy or a mixed economy. So far, however, I have not explained the *precise* functions that prices perform in an economy. I shall conclude this chapter by explaining these functions. They are:

- the **signalling function**
- the **incentive function**
- the **rationing or allocative function**

The signalling function

Prices provide information that allows all the traders in the market to plan and co-ordinate their economic activities. Let me provide one example. Most Friday afternoons, I visit my local street market to buy fruit and vegetables, including tomatoes and lettuce. The prices, which are shown on white plastic tabs stuck into each tray of produce, help me to decide what to buy. Of course, information about prices alone is not enough. I also need information about the quality of the goods on sale, which I try to get by looking carefully at the size of the produce and for blemishes such as bruising on apples or pears.

> **k**ey terms
>
> **Incentive function** Prices create incentives for consumers and firms to behave in certain ways.
>
> **Rationing or allocative function** Prices allocate scarce resources between competing uses.
>
> **Signalling function** Prices provide information to buyers and sellers.

The incentive function

The information signalled by relative prices, such as the price of tomatoes relative to the price of lettuce, creates incentives for people to alter their economic behaviour. Suppose, for example, I go to my local market intending to buy, along with other vegetables, a kilo of tomatoes and one lettuce. As it is Friday afternoon, by the time I arrive at the market, the street traders have cut the price of tomatoes by 50% to try to prevent unsold stock accumulating, whose quality might deteriorate overnight. A fall in the price of tomatoes, relative to the price of other goods that I could buy, creates an incentive for me to buy more tomatoes, provided of course I believe the quality hasn't deteriorated.

The rationing or allocative function

Suppose I respond to a fall in the relative price of tomatoes by buying more, say two kilos rather than the single kilo I had intended to buy as I made my way to market. Because my income is limited, spending more on one good usually means I spend less on other goods. Prices, together with income, ration the way people spend their money. Suppose tomato prices fall, not only in my local street market on a Friday afternoon, but throughout the economy for a sustained period of time. Tomatoes are now cheaper relative to other goods in the economy. On the one hand, the lower relative price causes

households to increase their demand for tomatoes, substituting tomatoes in place of other vegetables. But, on the other hand, a lower relative price may indicate that growing tomatoes is not a very profitable activity. In response, farmers grow fewer tomatoes. If these events happen, the information signalled by changing relative prices creates incentives for economic agents to alter their market behaviour, and changes the way scarce resources are rationed and allocated between competing uses.

examiner's voice

It is important to recognise that when markets perform well, prices convey accurate information and create suitable incentives for economic agents to respond to. But when one or more of the three functions of prices performs unsatisfactorily, or in extreme cases breaks down completely, market failure occurs.

Summary

- A competitive market contains a large number of firms producing similar goods or services.
- New firms can easily enter a competitive market, and incumbent firms can easily leave.
- The price mechanism allocates scarce resources between competing uses in a competitive market.
- In a competitive market, a good's price is determined by supply and demand.
- When planned demand equals planned supply, a market is in equilibrium.
- Market disequilibrium means that excess demand or excess supply exists in the market.
- Firms respond to excess supply by reducing the quantity of the good they are prepared to supply.
- Consumers respond to excess demand by bidding up the price of the good.
- A shift of a supply or demand curve disturbs equilibrium and leads to excess supply or demand.
- A rightward shift of demand, known as an increase in demand, leads to an extension of supply.
- A rightward shift of supply, known as an increase in supply, leads to an extension of demand.
- Prices perform three functions in a market or mixed economy: signalling, creating incentives, and rationing and allocating resources between competing uses.

Questions

1. Distinguish between goods markets and factor markets in an economy.
2. Explain why the market for tomatoes is competitive whereas the market for tap water is uncompetitive.
3. What is meant by the word 'equilibrium' in economics?
4. Explain why, when 'planned demand = planned supply', a market is in equilibrium.
5. Why does realised demand always equal realised supply, even when a market is in disequilibrium?
6. Distinguish between excess demand and excess supply.
7. What happens when there is excess demand in a market?
8. Draw a diagram to illustrate a decrease in supply and a contraction of demand. Explain the diagram.
9. List and explain the three functions prices perform in a market.

Chapter 6

Elasticity

Whenever a change in one variable (such as a good's price) causes a change to occur in a second variable (such as the quantity of the good that firms are prepared to supply), an elasticity can be calculated. The elasticity measures the proportionate responsiveness of the second variable to the change in the first variable. For example, if a 5% increase in price were to cause firms to increase supply more than proportionately (say by 10%), supply would be elastic. In this example, a change in price induces a more than proportionate response by the producers. But if the response were less than proportionate (for example an increase in supply of only 3%), supply would be inelastic. And if the change in price were to induce an exactly proportionate change in supply, supply would be neither elastic nor inelastic — this is called unit elasticity of supply. Elasticity is a useful descriptive statistic of the relationship between two variables because it is independent of the units, such as price and quantity units, in which the variables are measured.

Learning outcomes

This chapter will:
- explain the elasticities you need to know
- investigate price elasticity of demand
- distinguish between the slope of a curve and its elasticity
- outline the factors determining price elasticity of demand and price elasticity of supply
- relate price elasticities to the shapes of demand and supply curves
- explain how price elasticity of supply and the shape of supply curves is different in the short run and the long run
- relate income elasticity of demand to normal goods and inferior goods
- relate cross-elasticity of demand to goods in joint demand and to substitute goods
- analyse how price elasticity of demand affects who bears the burden of an expenditure tax

The elasticities you need to know

Although, in principle, economists could calculate a great many **elasticities**, indeed one for each of the economic relationships in which they are interested, the four main elasticities you must know are:

- price elasticity of demand
- price elasticity of supply
- income elasticity of demand
- cross-elasticity of demand

The following formulas are used for calculating these elasticities:

$$\text{price elasticity of demand} = \frac{\text{proportionate change in quantity demanded}}{\text{proportionate change in price}}$$

$$\text{price elasticity of supply} = \frac{\text{proportionate change in quantity supplied}}{\text{proportionate change in price}}$$

$$\text{income elasticity of demand} = \frac{\text{proportionate change in quantity demanded}}{\text{proportionate change in income}}$$

$$\begin{array}{l}\text{cross-elasticity of}\\\text{demand for good } A\\\text{with respect to the}\\\text{price of } B\end{array} = \frac{\text{proportionate change in quantity of } A \text{ demanded}}{\text{proportionate change in price of } B}$$

Price elasticity of demand

Price elasticity of demand measures consumers' responsiveness to a change in a good's price. (Price elasticity of demand is sometimes called an 'own price' elasticity of demand to distinguish it from cross-elasticity of demand. Cross-elasticity of demand measures the responsiveness of demand for a particular good to a change in the price of a completely different good.)

A simple rule for detecting whether demand is price elastic or inelastic
As an alternative to using the formula stated above to calculate price elasticity of demand between two points on a demand curve, a simple rule can be used to determine the general nature of the elasticity between any two points on the demand curve:

- if total consumer expenditure increases in response to a price fall, demand is elastic

- if total consumer expenditure decreases in response to a price fall, demand is inelastic
- if total consumer expenditure remains constant in response to a price fall, demand is neither elastic nor inelastic: i.e. elasticity = unity (1)

Price elasticity of demand and slope

It is important not to confuse the absolute response indicated by the slope of a curve with the proportionate response measured by elasticity. Take a careful look at the two demand curves in Figure 6.1. In Figure 6.1 (a), a straight line (or linear) demand curve has been drawn. Obviously, a straight line has a constant slope. But although the slope is the same at all points on the curve, the elasticity is not. Moving down a negatively sloping linear demand curve, the price elasticity of demand falls from point to point along the curve. Demand is elastic (or greater than unity) at all points along the top half of the curve. Elasticity equals unity exactly half way along the curve, falling below unity and towards zero along the bottom half of the curve.

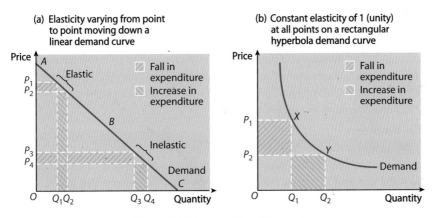

Figure 6.1 Price elasticity of demand

If elasticity falls from point to point moving down a linear demand curve, it follows that a non-linear curve (i.e. a curved line) is needed to show the same elasticity at all points on the curve. Figure 6.1 (b) shows a demand curve with a constant elasticity of 1 at all points on the curve, i.e. elasticity equals unity at all points on the curve. Mathematicians call this a rectangular hyperbola. Whenever the price falls, the proportionate change in quantity demanded exactly equals the proportionate change in price. In this case, consumer expenditure remains unchanged following a rise or fall in price.

examiner's voice

It is easy to confuse elasticity with the slope of a curve. Remember to include the word proportionate (or a % sign) above and below the dividing line when calculating elasticities.

Infinite price elasticity of demand and zero price elasticity of demand

Horizontal and vertical demand curves have constant elasticities at all points on the curve. A horizontal demand curve, such as the demand curve in Figure 6.2 (a), is infinitely elastic or perfectly elastic. At the other extreme, the vertical demand

curve in Figure 6.2 (b) is completely inelastic, displaying a zero price elasticity of demand at all points on the curve. When the price falls, for example from P_1 to P_2, the quantity demanded is unchanged.

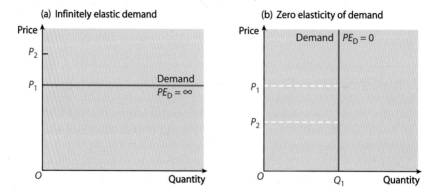

Figure 6.2 Horizontal and vertical demand curves

Extension material

Mathematicians draw demand and supply diagrams with quantity on the vertical axis and price on the horizontal axis. When demand and supply diagrams are drawn in this way, vertical curves are infinitely elastic, while horizontal curves have a zero elasticity. This is the opposite to the way economists draw demand and supply diagrams.

Negative elasticities
Usually demand curves are neither horizontal nor vertical, but have a negative slope, showing that as the good's price falls, the quantity demanded rises. In this situation, elasticity as well as slope is also negative. However, economists often ignore the minus sign of the elasticity. Ignoring the minus sign, all elasticities larger than 1 are elastic and all less than 1 are inelastic.

Summary: different demand curves and their price elasticities

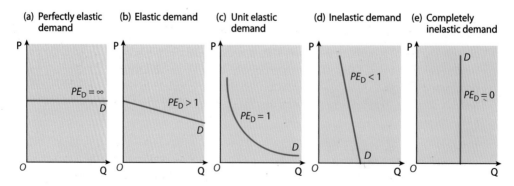

Figure 6.3 The five demand curves you need to know

Box 6.1 Elasticity and tobacco taxation

Examination questions often ask candidates to calculate an elasticity statistic from information supplied in the question. Questions can also ask for a discussion of why knowledge of elasticity is important for businesses and for governments. The following data are about tobacco consumption in South Korea, a country where cigarette smoking is still common. The Korean government wants to reduce it significantly.

South Korean smokers face the pain of withdrawal

South Korea has the highest proportion of male smokers (62%) in the world's developed countries. The government has recently embarked on an all-out campaign to encourage Koreans to quit through advertising, as well as by imposing large tax increases.

At the end of 2003, the price of a packet of cigarettes was 78 pence, in UK money. Having increased the price of a packet of cigarettes by 26 pence in 2004, the Korean government intended to increase the tax by the same amount in 2005. The health ministry estimates the 2004 increase led to an 8.3% fall in smoking among Korean males.

But there remains a sizeable group of smokers not deterred by price rises. 'I'm going to buy cigarettes even if they cost £5.00', says Lee Young-Hoon, a computer engineer. 'This campaign is silly. I may decrease smoking but I will never quit.' Cigarette manufacturers are, on the whole, resisting any change. Korea Tobacco and Ginseng, the former state-owned monopoly which commands more than 75% of the market, claims price rises have no long-term effect. 'Past data shows the rate of smoking reduction doesn't last long. Demand usually goes back to the ordinary level a few months after the increase', said a spokesman for Korea Tobacco and Ginseng.

Anna Fifield, *Financial Times*, 3 May 2005

Follow-up questions

1 Calculate the price elasticity of demand for a packet of cigarettes from the information in the passage.

2 What effects may the increased taxation have on the Korean government, cigarette manufacturers and smokers?

The factors determining price elasticity of demand

Substitutability

Substitutability is the most important determinant of price elasticity of demand. When a substitute exists for a product, consumers respond to a price rise by switching expenditure away from the good, buying instead a substitute whose price has not risen. When very close substitutes are available, demand for the product is highly elastic. Conversely, demand is likely to be inelastic when no substitutes are available.

Percentage of income

The demand curves for goods or services upon which households spend a large proportion of their income tend to be more elastic than those of small items which account for only a small fraction of income.

Necessities or luxuries

It is sometimes said that the demand for necessities is price inelastic, whereas demand for luxuries is elastic. However, this statement should be treated with caution. When no obvious substitute exists, demand for a luxury good may be inelastic, while at the other extreme, demand for particular types of basic food stuffs is likely to be elastic if other staple foods are available as substitutes. The existence of substitutes really determines price elasticity of demand, not the issue of whether the good is a luxury or necessity.

The 'width' of the market definition

The wider the definition of the market under consideration, the lower the price elasticity of demand. Thus the demand for the bread produced by a particular bakery is likely to be more elastic than the demand for bread produced by all bakeries. Quite obviously, the bread baked in other bakeries provides a number of close substitutes for the bread produced in just one bakery. And widening the possible market we are considering still further, the elasticity of demand for bread produced by all the bakeries will be greater than that for food as a whole.

Motorists may 'overreact' to petrol price rises in the short term

Time

The time period in question will also affect the price elasticity of demand. For many goods and services, demand is more elastic in the long run than in the short run because it takes time to respond to a price change. For example, if the price of petrol rises relative to the price of diesel fuel, it will take time for motorists to respond because they will be 'locked-in' to their existing investment in petrol-engine automobiles. However, in certain circumstances, the response might be greater in the short run than in the long run. A sudden rise in the price of petrol might cause motorists to economise in its use for a few weeks before getting used to the price and drifting back to their old motoring habits.

Price elasticity of supply

Whereas demand curves are generally downward sloping, supply curves usually slope upwards. A rise in price causes firms to respond by supplying more of the good. The mathematical properties of upward-sloping (or positive) supply curves are different from those of downward-sloping (or negative) demand curves. As with demand curves, the 'flatness' or 'steepness' of a supply curve is a misleading indicator of elasticity. The key point is not the slope of the curve, but whether the supply curve intersects the price axis or the quantity axis.

> **k**ey term
> **Price elasticity of supply** The proportionate change in supply of a good following an initial proportionate change in the good's own price.

Upward-sloping straight-line (linear) supply curves display the following price elasticities:

- if the supply curve intersects the price axis, the curve is elastic at all points, though elasticity falls towards unity moving from point to point up the curve
- if the supply curve intersects the quantity axis, the curve is inelastic at all points, though elasticity rises towards unity moving from point to point up the curve
- if the supply curve passes through the origin, elasticity equals unity (+1) at all points on the curve

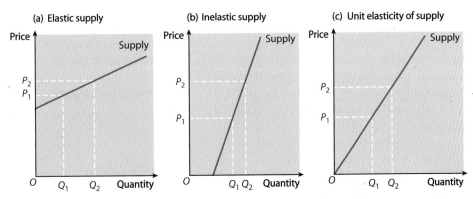

Figure 6.4 *Price elasticity of supply and linear supply curves*

---

examiner's voice

It is useful to understand why the elasticity of upward-sloping supply curves differs from the elasticity of downward-sloping demand curves.

However, exam questions test your knowledge of the economics of elasticity rather than the mathematics of elasticity.

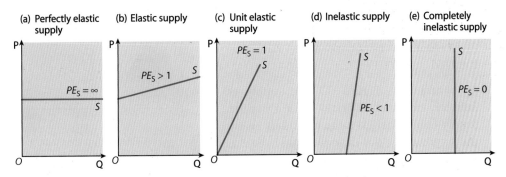

Figure 6.5 *The five linear supply curves you need to know*

Non-linear supply curves

Figure 6.6 shows how elasticity can be observed at any point on an upward-sloping non-linear supply curve. This is done by drawing a tangent to the point and noting the axis which the tangent intersects. Because the line drawn tangential to point *A* intersects the price axis, supply is elastic at point *A*. The tangent to

point *B* intersects at the origin, so supply at point *B* is unit elastic. Finally, the tangent to point *C* intersects the quantity axis, so supply is inelastic at point *C*. With this supply curve, elasticity falls moving from point to point up the curve. Supply is elastic in the lower section and inelastic in the upper section of the curve.

A closer look at perfectly elastic demand and supply

In the next diagram, I have drawn a perfectly elastic demand curve and a perfectly elastic supply curve. (These can also be labelled infinitely elastic demand and infinitely elastic supply.) Although the two parts of Figure 6.7 appear to be identical (apart from the labels), this is very misleading. The apparent similarity disguises a significant difference between perfectly elastic demand and perfectly elastic supply. In Figure 6.7 (a), demand is infinitely elastic at all prices on or *below* the demand curve, though if the price *rises* above the demand curve (for example from P_1 to P_2), the amount demanded immediately falls to zero. This is because perfect substitutes are available when demand is perfectly price elastic. Customers cease to buy the good as soon as the price *rises* above the demand curve, switching spending to the perfect substitutes whose prices have not changed.

By contrast, in Figure 6.7 (b), supply is infinitely elastic at *all* prices on or *above* the supply curve, though if the price *falls* below the supply curve (for example from P_1 to P_2), the amount supplied immediately drops to zero. P_1 is the minimum price acceptable to firms. If they are paid this price (or any higher price), firms stay in the market, but the incentive to stay in the market disappears at any lower price. Firms leave the market, unable to make sufficient profit.

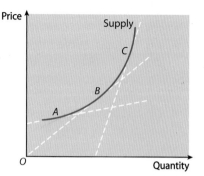

Figure 6.6 Price elasticity of supply and a non-linear supply curve

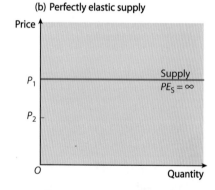

Figure 6.7 Perfectly price elastic demand and supply curves

examiner's voice

Exam candidates often confuse perfectly elastic demand with perfectly elastic supply.

AQA AS Economics

Box 6.2 Elasticity and housing markets

Examination questions on elasticity may cover more than one of the four elasticities you need to know. Here is an example adapted from a past AS data-response question on housing markets. The question required candidates (a) to define price elasticity of supply, (b) to compare the price elasticities of supply for new housing in selected European countries, and (c) to use a supply and demand diagram and the information about elasticities in the data, to explain how an increase in household income affects the price of housing in the UK.

Housing market elasticities in the UK

UK households have an income elasticity of demand for housing that exceeds +1. However, demand for housing is price inelastic. These demand elasticities, combined with a low price elasticity of supply for housing, push the UK's housing market towards long-term rising prices.

New housing would need to have a price elasticity of supply of +10 for supply to equal demand in the long term. But if the price elasticity of supply for new housing remains low, as the table shows, house prices will never be stable in the UK when the demand for housing is increasing.

The price elasticity of supply of new housing in selected countries

Country	Price elasticity of supply
Netherlands	+0.3
UK	+0.5
Denmark	+0.7
France	+1.1
USA	+1.4
Germany	+2.1

Follow-up questions

1 Compare the price elasticities of supply of housing in the various countries shown in the table.
2 Evaluate whether demand conditions have been more important than supply conditions in determining the prices of houses in the UK in recent years.

The factors determining price elasticity of supply

The length of the production period

If firms can convert raw materials into finished goods very quickly, e.g. in just a few hours or days, supply will tend be more elastic than when several months are involved, as with many agricultural goods.

The availability of spare capacity

When a firm possesses spare capacity, and if labour and raw materials are readily available, production can generally be increased quite quickly in the short run.

The ease of accumulating stocks

When stocks of unsold finished goods are stored at low cost, firms can respond quickly to a sudden increase in demand. Alternatively, firms can respond to a price fall by diverting current production away from sales and into stock accumulation. Likewise, the ease with which stocks of raw materials or components can be bought from outside suppliers and then stored has a similar effect.

The ease of switching between alternative methods of production

When firms can quickly alter the way they produce goods, for example by switching between the use of capital and labour, supply tends to be more elastic than when there is little or no choice. In a similar way, if firms produce a range of products and can switch raw materials, labour or machines from one type of production to another, the supply of any one product tends to be elastic.

The number of firms in the market and the ease of entering the market

Generally, the more firms there are in the market, and the greater the ease with which a firm can enter or leave, the greater the elasticity of supply.

Time

I have already noted that *demand* is more elastic in the long run than in the short run because it takes time to respond to a price change. The same is true for supply. Figure 6.8 shows three supply curves of increasing elasticity, S_1, S_2 and S_3, which illustrate respectively market period supply, short-run supply and long-run supply.

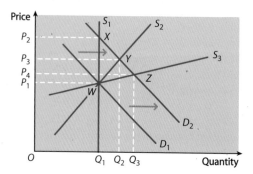

Figure 6.8 The effect of the time period upon price elasticity of supply

- **Market period supply** – the market period supply curve S_1 is shown by a vertical line. S_1 depicts the situation facing firms following a sudden and unexpected rightward shift of demand from D_1 to D_2. When surprised by a sudden increase in demand, firms can't immediately increase output. In the market period, supply is completely inelastic, and the price rises from P_1 to P_2 to eliminate the excess demand brought about by the rightward shift of the demand curve.
- **Short-run supply** – the higher price means that higher profits can be made, creating the incentive for firms to increase output. In the short run, firms increase output by hiring more variable factors of production such as labour. The short-run increase in output is shown by the movement up the short-run supply curve, S_2. The short-run supply curve is more elastic than the market period supply curve, S_1. In the short run, supply increases to Q_2, and the price falls from P_2 to P_3.
- **Long-run supply** – if firms believe the increase in demand will be long lasting, and not just a

> **examiner's voice**
> You should remember that, for most goods, both the demand curve and the supply curve are more price elastic in the long run than in the short run.

temporary phenomenon, they may increase the scale of production by employing more capital and other factors of production that are fixed in the short run, but variable in the long run. When this happens, firms move along the long-run supply curve S_3. Output rises to Q_3, and the price falls once again, in this case to P_4.

In a competitive industry with low or non-existent barriers to entry, elasticity of supply is greater in the long run than in the short run, because in the long run (but not the short run) firms can enter or leave the market. Short-run supply is less elastic because supply is restricted to the firms already in the industry.

Income elasticity of demand

The nature of **income elasticity of demand** — which measures how demand responds to a change in income — depends on whether the good is a normal good or an inferior good. Income elasticity of demand is always negative for an inferior good and positive for a normal good. This is because the quantity demanded of an inferior good falls as income rises, whereas the quantity demanded of a normal good rises with income. Normal goods can be further divided into superior goods or luxuries, for which the income elasticity of demand is greater than +1, and basic goods, with an income elasticity lying between 0 and +1. Although the quantity demanded of a normal good always rises with income, it rises more than proportionately for a superior good (such as a luxury car). Conversely, demand for a basic good such as shoe polish rises at a slower rate than income.

Cross-elasticity of demand

Cross-elasticity of demand measures how the demand for one good responds to changes in the price of another good. The cross-elasticity of demand between two goods or services indicates the nature of the demand relationship between the goods. There are three possibilities:

- joint demand (or complementary goods)
- competing demand (or substitutes)
- an absence of any discernible demand relationship

> **key terms**
>
> **Cross-elasticity of demand**
> The proportionate change in demand for a good following an initial proportionate change in price of another good.
>
> **Income elasticity of demand** The proportionate change in demand for a good following an initial proportionate change in consumers' income.

Joint demand or complementary goods

Complementary goods, such as computer games consoles and computer games, have negative cross-elasticities of demand. If the manufacturer increases the price of the games consoles (the hardware), demand for the consoles falls. This causes the demand for games (the software) to use in the consoles also to fall. A rise in the price of one good leads to a fall in demand for the other good.

Competing demand or substitutes

The cross-elasticity of demand between two goods which are substitutes for each other is positive. A rise in the price of one good causes demand to switch to the substitute good whose price has not risen. Demand for the substitute good increases.

No discernible demand relationship

If we select two goods at random, for example pencils and bicycles, the cross-elasticity of demand between the two goods will be zero. A rise in the price of one good will have no measurable effect upon the demand for the other good.

> **examiner's voice**
>
> The size and sign (positive or negative) of income and cross-elasticities of demand affects how a good's demand curve shifts following a change in income or a change in the price of a substitute or good in joint demand.

How the effect of an expenditure tax depends on elasticity of demand

If you refer back to Figure 4.3 in Chapter 4, you will see that an expenditure tax imposed by the government on firms shifts the good's supply curve leftward. From the point of view of the firms that produce and sell the good, the tax has the same effect as a rise in costs of production, for example a rise in wage costs or raw material costs. As is the case with cost increases, by raising the price of the good to cover the tax, firms try to increase the price charged to customers by the full amount of the tax. However, their ability to do this depends on price elasticity of demand (or on the elasticity of the curve that hasn't shifted). Figure 6.9 shows that when demand is relatively elastic, consumer resistance means that some, but not all, of a tax (in this case a specific tax) is passed onto consumers as a price rise. The tax per unit (labelled T in Figure 6.9) is measured by the vertical distance between S_1 (the supply curve before the tax was imposed) and S_2 (the supply curve after the tax was imposed). Immediately after the imposition of the tax, firms may try to raise the price to $P_1 + T$, passing all the tax on to consumers. However, there is excess supply at this price. Via the market mechanism, the price falls to P_2, thereby eliminating the excess supply. In the new equilibrium, part, but not all, of the tax has been passed onto consumers as a price rise. When demand is relatively elastic, as in Figure 6.9, this amounts to less than 50% of the tax.

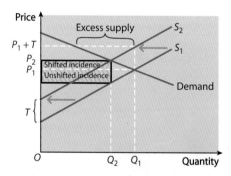

Figure 6.9 Shifting the incidence of a tax when demand is price elastic

The part of the tax passed on to consumers as a price rise is called the **shifted incidence** of the tax. The rest of the tax (the **unshifted incidence**) is borne by firms or producers. In Figure 6.9, the total tax revenue paid by firms to the government is shown by the rectangle bounded by heavy black lines. The part of the tax rectangle above what was the equilibrium price (P_1) before the tax was imposed, shows the shifted incidence of the tax. The part of the tax rectangle below P_1 shows the unshifted incidence.

You should now draw diagrams similar to Figure 6.9, but with perfectly elastic, unit elastic, relatively inelastic and completely inelastic demand curves. The diagrams will show that firms' ability to pass the incidence of a tax onto consumers as a price rise is greatest when demand is completely inelastic, and non-existent when demand is perfectly elastic.

Students often confuse the effect of an increase in an indirect tax imposed on firms with the effect of a direct tax such as income tax imposed on individuals. Whereas a tax imposed on firms shifts the supply curve of a good, by reducing consumers' incomes, income tax shifts the demand curve for a good. An increase in income tax shifts the demand curve for normal goods leftward, but if the good is an inferior good, the demand curve shifts rightward.

Finally, note that subsidies granted to firms have the opposite effect to taxes imposed on firms. Subsidies shift the supply curve rightward or downward, showing that firms are prepared to supply more of the good at all prices.

Shifts of demand and supply curves, and adjustments along demand and supply curves

examiner's voice

You should apply elasticity analysis when answering exam questions on the effects of a shift of a demand or supply curve. The extent to which the good's price or equilibrium level of output changes depends on the price elasticity of the curve that has not shifted. For example, when the supply curve shifts leftward, the price elasticity of the demand curve determines the extent to which the good's price and quantity changes.

The extent to which price or output change following a shift of demand or supply depends upon the slope and elasticity of the curve that has not shifted. Figure 6.10 shows a demand curve shifting rightward — along a gently sloping supply curve in Figure 6.10 (a) and along a much more steeply sloping supply curve in Figure 6.10 (b). Prior to the shift of demand, equilibrium occurs at point X in both

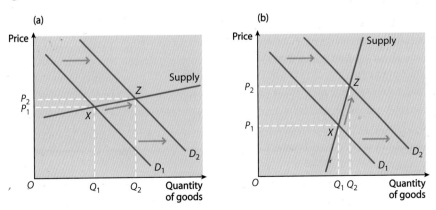

Figure 6.10 *The adjustment to a new equilibrium following a shift of demand*

panels of the diagram. In each case, the rightward shift of demand induces an adjustment along the supply curve to a new equilibrium depicted at point Z. With the elastic supply curve shown in Figure 6.10 (a), the quantity adjustment is greater than the price adjustment. The reverse is true in Figure 6.10 (b), where the supply curve is inelastic.

Summary

■ Elasticity measures the proportionate responsiveness of a second variable to an initial change in a first variable.

■ You need to know about price elasticities of demand and supply, and income and cross-elasticity of demand.

■ Make sure you know the formulas for all four elasticities.

■ Don't confuse elasticity with the slope of a curve.

■ It is important to understand the determinants of all the elasticities of demand and supply.

■ The availability of substitute products is the main determinant of price elasticity of demand.

■ Income elasticity of demand is positive for normal goods and negative for inferior goods.

■ Cross-elasticity of demand is positive for substitute goods and negative for complementary goods or goods in joint demand.

■ Knowledge of elasticities, particularly price and income elasticity of demand, provides useful information that aids decision making by businesses and the government.

Questions

1 State the formulas for demand and supply elasticities.
2 How does price elasticity of demand affect total consumer spending when a good's price falls?
3 Contrast perfectly elastic demand with perfectly elastic supply.
4 What is the most important determinant of price elasticity of demand?
5 List the determinants of price elasticity of supply.
6 What is the 'market period'?
7 Contrast the income elasticity of demand of normal and inferior goods.
8 What can be inferred about the demand relationship between two goods with a cross-elasticity of (+)0.3?
9 If demand is inelastic, what effect will a price fall have on a firm's total sales revenue?
10 If demand is inelastic, what effect might a unit sales tax have on: (a) the price of the good; and (b) the quantity bought and sold?

Chapter 7

Markets at work

In Chapters 3 to 6, I have explained the theory of how a market for a good or service operates. In this chapter, I apply supply and demand theory to a number of real world markets and sets of markets, concentrating on markets which could provide the scenario for a Unit 1 data-response question on how a market functions. The markets we shall look at are agricultural markets, markets for other primary products (such as oil and metals), housing markets and sports markets.

Learning outcomes

This chapter will:

- explain why markets for farm products and other primary products are prone to unstable prices
- explain how speculation affects markets for primary products such as the markets for metals
- describe how OPEC affects the market for crude oil
- investigate the factors determining demand and supply in UK housing markets
- examine some of the characteristics of sports markets

Why prices are often unstable in agricultural markets

Throughout recent history, agricultural markets for foodstuffs and **primary products** such as rubber have experienced two closely related problems. First, there has been a long-run trend for agricultural prices to fall relative to those of manufactured goods and, second, prices have fluctuated considerably from year to year. Agricultural markets are prone to disequilibrium and random shifts of the supply curve from year to year, caused by climatic factors. This leads to unacceptable fluctuations in agricultural prices that, as Chapter 14 explains, require government intervention to stabilise the price.

The long-run fall in agricultural prices

The long-run downward trend can be explained by shifts of the demand and supply curves for agricultural products over extended periods of time. This is shown in

Figure 7.1, where the equilibrium price for an agricultural product in an early historical period is P_1. Over time, both the demand and supply curves have shifted rightward, caused for example by rising incomes and population growth shifting the demand curve, while improved methods of farming have increased supply. But for many farm products, the shift of supply, brought about by improved crop yields and increased agricultural productivity, has greatly exceeded the shift of demand, resulting in the fall to the lower equilibrium price P_2.

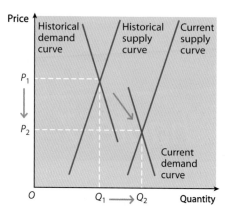

Figure 7.1 The long-run fall in the price of agricultural products

However, in 2007/2008 it seemed we might be seeing the beginning of a long-run trend for food prices to rise. Can you think of reasons why this might be happening?

Short-run fluctuations in agricultural prices

Figure 7.2 provides an explanation of fluctuating farm prices. In the diagram, price volatility is caused by random shifts of the short-run supply curve in response to fluctuations in the harvest. The diagram shows two short-run supply curves: a 'good harvest' supply curve, S_1, and a 'bad harvest' supply curve, S_2. Weather conditions and other factors outside farmers' control shift the position of the supply curve from year to year between the limits set by S_1 and S_2. As a result, market prices fluctuate from year to year within the range of P_1 to P_2.

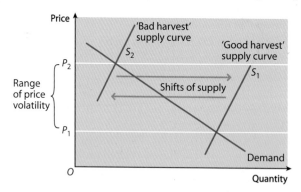

Figure 7.2 Fluctuating agricultural prices caused by shifts of supply

If you turn forward to Chapter 14, you will see that the government or a government agency, or indeed a co-operative of the farmers themselves, can try to stabilise the price of an agricultural good with a support-buying policy, which involves the accumulation of a **buffer stock**. Buffer stock intervention has sometimes also been used to stabilise the prices of other primary products, particularly metals.

*e***xaminer's voice**

Support buying and buffer stocks are explained in Chapter 14. Exam questions are often set on methods of government intervention in primary product markets.

Box 7.1 Rising commodity prices

Commodities can be divided into hard commodities, such as metals, and soft commodities, such as food.

In 2006, partly as a result of speculation and partly due to the growth of emerging economies such as China and India, metal and oil prices rose tremendously. The boom was soon over, but in 2007 and 2008, oil and food prices again rose. The long-term trend is rising prices as demand outstrips supply. There is nothing much that governments can do to stop this.

IMF warns on commodity price boom

The commodity price boom over the last three years is unsustainable and will result in sharp price declines by the end of the decade, the International Monetary Fund has warned.

High commodity prices have boosted the economies of resource-rich nations in the Middle East, South America, Africa, as well as Canada and Australia, but have added to the import bill in consuming countries in North America, Europe and Asia.

'The real annual price of aluminium and copper will decline from current levels by 35% and 57% respectively by 2010,' the IMF said in its World Economic Outlook, which was released on Wednesday.

The IMF said that metals' price declines would be a result of current high prices damping demand, and the expansion of mine and smelter production over the next five years.

Krishna Guha, *Financial Times*, 6 September 2006

Follow-up questions

1 Why do the prices of commodities such as wheat and copper fluctuate more from year to year than the prices of consumer goods such as cars?

2 Using a demand and supply graph, explain the effects of commodity speculation on the price of a commodity such as gold.

Extension material

The cobweb theory

Agricultural production often has a relatively long production period, compared for example with many types of manufacturing. Arable farmers make decisions to grow crops several months before the harvest, while, in a similar way, livestock farmers must breed animals for meat production many months before slaughter. As a result, farmers may form market plans on how much to supply on the basis of last year's price rather than on the prices current this year. The length of the production period means there is a supply lag between the decision to produce and the actual supply coming onto the market. A possible effect of a supply lag can be explained by the cobweb theory illustrated in Figure 7.3.

Figure 7.3 shows a stable cobweb in the pig market, in which the market price eventually converges to equilibrium

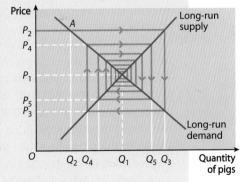

Figure 7.3

at price P_1, located where the long-run demand and supply curves intersect. Suppose an outbreak of swine disease reduces pig supply from Q_1 to Q_2 in Year 1 (but does not affect the position of the demand curve or the supply of healthy pigs in future years). In the current year (Year 1), the maximum number of pigs that can be sold on the market is shown by a vertical line drawn through Q_2. The vertical line is the short-run supply curve for Year 1. This means that the price rises to P_2, determined at point A on the vertical line. The now higher price of P_2 encourages farmers to breed Q_3 pigs for slaughter in Year 2.

The cobweb theory can explain the possible effect of a supply lag

When Year 2 arrives, the vertical line drawn through Q_3 depicts maximum possible supply. But the slaughter of Q_3 pigs causes the market price to fall to P_3, which means that farmers breed fewer pigs (Q_4) for slaughter in Year 3. In subsequent years, price and output continue to oscillate in a series of decreasing fluctuations until eventually — in the absence of any further shock hitting the market — the market converges again to a long-run equilibrium.

In the diagram, the cobweb eventually converges to a long-run equilibrium because the long-run demand curve has a gentler slope than the long-run supply curve. This is a stable cobweb. However, an unstable cobweb is also possible. Instability occurs if the long-run demand curve is steeper than the long-run supply curve. In this case, the market diverges in a series of yearly oscillations further and further away from the long-run equilibrium.

The effect of speculative activity in commodity markets

The importance of speculative demand

Farm products are not the only goods whose prices fluctuate wildly from year to year. The same is true for many primary products, especially metals such as copper and nickel. Part of the reason for this stems from the fact that it takes years to open new mines, with the result that sudden increases in demand cannot easily be met from supply.

Another reason is **speculation**. Many of the people and organisations that buy and sell commodities such as copper never intend to use the metal, or indeed ever to actually see or take delivery of the product. Instead, when they think that the price of copper is going to rise, probably in conditions of increasing global demand while supply is limited, speculators step into the market and buy copper, believing that the price will then rise still further in the future. If speculative demand is large enough, the speculators themselves force the price up. In these circumstances, higher future prices become self-fulfilling. In a similar way, when speculators start to sell in the belief that copper prices are going to fall, the act of speculative selling forces down the price of copper.

> **Key term**
>
> **Speculation** occurs when people buy or sell a good or service because they believe the price is going to rise or fall in the future. Successful speculation means people benefit from capital gains or avoid capital losses.

Box 7.2 Speculative demand and the price of nickel

The extract below, adapted from articles in the *Financial Times* from 2003, describes how, along with other influences on the world market for nickel in 2003, speculative demand was also a factor.

During 2003, the price of nickel rose from under $8,000 to over $14,000 a tonne. Two-thirds of the world output of nickel goes into the production of stainless steel, used for products such as cutlery and kitchen sinks. The factors that influenced the price of nickel included:

- A strike by workers at a large nickel mine in Canada. The mine normally produces 9% of the world output of nickel. 9,000 tonnes of nickel production was lost each month for several months.
- Early in 2003, Russian producers sold 36,000 tonnes of nickel from their stockpile, which was the largest in the world. In June 2003, the Russians sold a further 24,000 tonnes to offset supply concerns caused by the strike in Canada.

- Output of manufactured goods grew throughout the world in 2003. In China, surging output of stainless steel affected the nickel market.
- Speculative demand also affected the market. When speculators believe prices are going to rise, they buy the commodity in order to make a profit by selling at a higher price in the future. In the nickel market, changing demand conditions and running down of stocks led to speculative activity in 2003. Stocks had been the only buffer in the market stabilising the price of nickel.

Follow-up question

Draw a supply and demand diagram to illustrate the effect of speculative demands on the price of nickel.

The price of crude oil

Speculation has also affected the price of crude oil, but for this product, as Box 7.3 explains, rising world demand and the activities of the Organization of Petroleum Exporting Countries (OPEC, a producers' organisation) have been the main factors determining the price of oil.

The headline in the BBC news item in Box 7.3 describes OPEC as a cartel. Cartels are price rings which sometimes restrict output in order to raise the price of a good. Read the information in Box 7.3 carefully — the factors determining the price of crude oil have come up in data-response questions in a number of past Unit 1 examination questions.

examiner's voice

Exam questions have often been set on the market for crude oil, or on the markets for petrol and diesel fuel.

Cartels will not appear explicitly in AS questions, but questions have been set on the way OPEC has restricted supply.

Box 7.3 OPEC and the price of crude oil

Most people are familiar with the price of crude oil, often when moaning about the high price of petrol or diesel fuel. In the UK, however, the high prices of these fuels is largely a result of the high expenditure tax that the British government levies. But, as Figure 7.4 shows, the world price of crude oil has generally been

rising rapidly in recent years, though in real terms it is not (as yet) as high as it was around 1980. Part of the reason for high oil prices lies in the activities of OPEC, the Organization of Petroleum Exporting Countries.

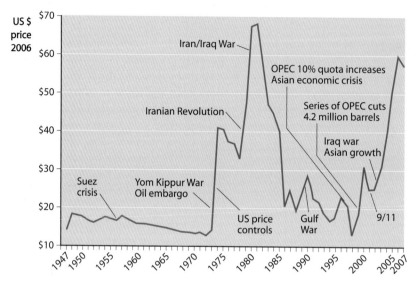

Figure 7.4
The changing world price of crude oil, 1947–2007

How OPEC affects the market for crude oil

The Organization of Petroleum Exporting Countries (OPEC) was created in 1960 to protect the interests of oil-producing countries. OPEC allows oil-producing countries to guarantee their income by co-ordinating policies and prices among them. The creation of OPEC was a response to the efforts of Western oil companies to drive oil prices down.

Two-thirds of world oil reserves are located in OPEC countries and OPEC members are responsible for half of the world's oil exports.

OPEC's aim has been to keep crude oil prices within a particular range. To do that, OPEC countries attempt to control the amount of crude oil they export and avoid flooding or squeezing the international marketplace. But the oil market is notoriously difficult to balance, as demonstrated by sharp price swings in the years since OPEC was set up. OPEC members do not necessarily have identical interests, and often find it difficult to agree on their price and output strategies.

In the early 2000s, the range was between about $25 and $30 a barrel, later upped to between about $55 and $65 a barrel. The fact that by late 2007, crude oil's price had risen to over $90, with occasional spikes to over $100, shows that OPEC has not been successful in controlling the price of oil.

OPEC attempts to control the price of crude oil, not through a buffer stock scheme, but by altering the rate at which its members release or supply oil onto the market. This is an example of a **retention scheme**, which operates through shifting the supply curve of a product rather than through purchasing a stockpile of the good.

Some OPEC economies, such as Saudi Arabia, are completely reliant on oil. Their long-term interest is to prevent oil prices rising too high, as this would speed up research in industrialised countries for alternatives to oil. Oil producers such as Dubai realise that they must diversify their economies before oil runs out. They are using oil revenues to finance the growth of other industries, particularly financial services and tourism. But other OPEC members, such as Nigeria, are swayed by the short-term interest to keep oil prices as high as possible to finance the champagne life-style of ruling elites and the consequent need to pay for luxury imports.

Follow-up questions

1 Using supply and demand diagrams, explain the difference between a retention scheme and a buffer stock scheme. (See Chapter 14 for information about buffer stock schemes.)

2 Why would it not be sensible for OPEC countries to try and stabilise the price of crude oil through buffer stock intervention in the world's oil market?

Housing markets in the UK

Housing markets can be separated according to the type of property (flats, semi-detached and detached houses etc.), but most importantly by the type of tenure enjoyed by the household living in the property. (A household is not the same as a family. For example, a family placing an elderly grandparent in sheltered accommodation creates a new one-person household. Likewise a teenager leaving the family home to live in a flat becomes a new household.)

> **examiner's voice**
>
> Exam questions may be set on aspects of the UK housing market.

There are two main types of tenure in the UK housing market. These are **owner-occupation**, which means that at least one member of the household living in the property owns the accommodation, and **privately rented housing**. In the latter case, a private landlord owns the property, which is rented to a tenant. There are also various forms of **socially owned housing** such as **council houses** and flats (owned by local authorities) and **housing associations**. The UK housing market can be divided into sub-markets containing different types of property.

Regional housing markets

Newspapers often refer to the North–South divide, which certainly exists in the UK housing market. House prices and private rents are much higher in London and the southeast region than they are in other UK regions, though there are pockets of high-priced housing outside the southeast in locations such as the Manchester and Leeds commuter belts and Edinburgh. By 2007, the average price of houses in Greater London had risen above £300,000 and the number of 'millionaire' properties was proliferating, while at the other extreme, run-down houses in declining and increasingly derelict northern manufacturing regions were selling for less than £5,000 — if a buyer could be found.

The factors explaining differences in regional house prices include the immobility of housing, the poor quality of housing in some locations (though much badly built housing in London now commands high prices), but primarily supply and demand factors.

Factors affecting the supply of housing in different regions include the availability of building land and the operation of planning controls. Demand factors, which relate strongly to the relative success of regional economies, include population density and growth (both of which are in turn affected by migration between regions), and marked regional differences in personal income and wealth, together with the lending policies of financial intermediaries such as banks and building societies.

The markets for new and second-hand housing

New houses are mostly bought from specialist house-building companies. A few, large, house-building companies account for most of the new houses built in the UK. Second-hand houses are generally bought from their existing occupiers who wish to sell. With these transactions, the act of selling a house simultaneously creates a demand, in the sense that the seller needs another house to live in.

The long-run rise in the price of housing

There has been a long-run trend for house prices to rise in the UK, ignoring short-run booms and busts. Both the demand for and the supply of housing have increased (or shifted rightwards) in the long run, but unlike in the case of agricultural goods which I described earlier, demand has increased faster.

The impact of the building cycle

Supply has increased because the quantity of new houses added to the housing stock each year exceeds the number demolished or converted to other uses. The supply of housing for owner-occupancy has generally increased even faster because landlords have withdrawn from the rental market and sold their properties. Sometimes, however, when housing market conditions are more favourable for private letting, the reverse happens. The main causes of the long-run rightward shift of demand have been: population growth; the growth in the number of households; real income growth (housing being a normal good with a positive income elasticity of demand); and people switching to owner-occupancy, which they treat as a superior good (income elasticity of demand > +1) and away from the perceived inferior substitute, rented accommodation.

The level of economic activity in the national economy also affects the construction industry. Since the 1970s, the house-building industry has become increasingly dominated by a small number of 'volume' builders. The building companies buy land and hold the land in a 'land bank'. Houses are then built in the expectation of being sold during or shortly after construction. The process tends to be speculative — very few houses are built to meet customers' specific requirements. The construction process itself is sometimes contracted out to smaller builders, who depend on hired plant and equipment and who mainly employ casual labour. In recessions or economic slow-downs, there is often a high level of bankruptcy among smaller building firms and subcontractors, and unemployment among building workers soars.

Short-run fluctuations in the price of housing

Short-run price fluctuations are explained primarily by the short-run demand curve shifting rightward or leftward along the near-vertical short-run supply curve. Figure 7.5 shows the demand curve increasing, shifting rightward from D_1 to D_2, causing house prices to rise from P_1 to P_2, with a smaller resulting expansion of supply.

The short-run supply of housing

In the short run, as Figure 7.5 shows, the supply of housing is highly price inelastic or unresponsive to price changes. The factors that explain this include: the general shortage of land; the effect of planning controls, which make it difficult to convert land from other uses; and the length of time taken to build a new house.

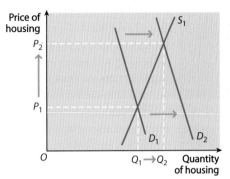

Figure 7.5 Short-term changes in the price of housing

examiner's voice
Practise drawing this diagram. It is the most important diagram on the housing market.

Box 7.4 A tale of two newspapers

In the UK, house prices are always in the newspaper headlines, especially in the mid-market tabloids the *Daily Mail* and the *Daily Express*. Indeed, the satirical magazine, *Private Eye*, often parodies the *Daily Mail*'s obsession with house prices, with headlines mimicking the newspaper's approach, such as 'Influx of asylum seekers causes house values to plummet'. Sometimes, as on 31 May 2007, the two newspapers can interpret the news about house prices in completely different ways!

House prices still soaring

House prices are continuing to soar in defiance of interest rate rises, official figures revealed yesterday.

The average home in England and Wales went up by more than £1,200 every month in the past year despite Bank of England attempts to dampen the market with hikes to the base rate.

And in welcome news for homeowners, experts claim the possibility of a housing crash is becoming more and more remote.

Daily Express, 31 May 2007

House price boom over?

For the first time in 7 years, the housing market is falling in over half the country. This could signal the end of the 11-year property boom. Alarm bells sounded after official figures from the Land Registry showed prices slipping in four of the ten regions into which it divides England and Wales.

The bubble appears to be bursting. Many estate agents outside London are gloomy: 'The market is cooling.'

Because the report covers April, it does not include the effects of the latest interest rate increase earlier this month. The situation now is likely to be even worse.

Daily Mail, 31 May 2007

Box 7.5 The problem of mortgage debt

Newspapers such as the *Independent* are less obsessed about house prices as such, preferring instead to focus on related issues such as the effect of mortgage debt upon house buyers. Here are the headlines from the front page of the *Independent* on 11 July 2007, just over a month after the *Daily Mail* and *Daily Express* headlines shown in Box 7.4. The story focuses on the worries caused because house owners with mortgages were becoming squeezed by rising interest rates and mortgage loans which were several multiples of household income and increasingly unaffordable. Consider what is meant by a loan default, and the implications of house repossessions.

Mortgage madness

Mortgage misery

Mortgage meltdown?

Independent, 11 July 2007

A financial crisis that began in the US…is coming to a home near you

Independent, 7 November 2007

Follow-up questions

1 Using a demand and supply diagram, explain the likely effect of a 'mortgage meltdown' on UK house prices.

2 Why do most people who buy houses in the UK need to mortgage the property they are buying in order to finance its purchase?

The demand for housing

As with all consumer goods, people demand housing for the utility or welfare derived from the consumer services that houses provide. All houses provide basic shelter, but each and every house also has a particular combination of other consumer attributes, such as location, a view, a garden, car parking and rooms suitable for work, leisure and hospitality. However, the demand for housing is also affected by a number of special factors. Housing is a consumer durable good, delivering a stream of consumer services over a very long period, often a century or more. Unlike most durable goods, such as cars and television sets, which **depreciate** and lose value during their lives, most houses – or certainly the land on which they are built – **appreciate** and gain value. This means that the demand for housing is determined not only by people's need for shelter, but by the fact that people treat housing as a form of investment. Housing is an attractive wealth asset – indeed, the main wealth asset owned by many UK residents.

As a result, far from reducing demand, a rise in house prices can trigger a speculative bubble in the house market in which rising prices drive up demand, causing a further rise in prices, with the process continuing until the bubble bursts. Rising house prices mean that owner-occupiers already on the 'housing ladder' have a vested interest in further price rises. Existing owner-occupiers become wealthier because the value of their property rises but the value of their **mortgages** generally stays the same. They benefit from **capital gains** – the difference between the price paid for the house and its current higher market value. In this situation, there is an

In a rising house market, first-time buyers may try to buy before houses become unaffordable

increase in the number of 'first-time buyers', as young people, desperate to get on the 'housing ladder', try to buy houses before they become unaffordable. Moreover, wishing to become even more wealthy, existing owner-occupiers put their houses on the market and 'trade up' to buy larger properties or houses in more desirable locations. Both these events shift the demand curve for housing rightwards and fuel a further rise in house prices. During house market booms, activity in the housing market soars with increases in both the number of people trying to sell and the number trying to buy property. However, demand rises faster than supply.

> **examiner's voice**
> House prices can be determined by speculative demand, and also by the fact that people treat housing as an investment good.

Sports markets

It is not possible in this chapter for me to examine all the special features of sports markets that make such markets interesting. I shall start by introducing a feature of markets not previously explained: the possibility of a **secondary market** or **black market** emerging. I shall then examine shifts of demand in sports markets for sports in competing demand (or substitutes) and also for sporting activities which are in joint demand (complementary goods). I shall complete the chapter by looking at pricing at different sporting events, while Box 7.6 explains a peculiar feature of competition in the market for competitive sports such as football or rugby.

Secondary markets in tickets for sports events

Secondary markets that occur when governments impose maximum price laws or price ceilings are of course illegal, though criminalised trading still takes place in such markets. However, some secondary markets are perfectly legal, for example

markets in tickets for popular sports events such as the FA Cup Final. In these cases, the secondary market emerges because the agency promoting the event under-prices tickets. This is illustrated in Figure 7.6 (a). The supply curve for tickets is vertical, reflecting the capacity of the stadium in which the event takes place. The number of seats in the stadium is around 90,000. Given the position of the demand curve, if tickets were priced at £150, the primary market would work efficiently. There would be no excess demand, and hence no need for a secondary market. But if the Football Association prices tickets at £50, 150,000 fans want to see the match. Excess demand is 60,000. In this situation, a secondary market enables 'unlucky' supporters, who are prepared to pay more than £50 to watch the match, to buy tickets sold by 'lucky' fans, who are prepared to sell at a price above £50.

*e**xaminer's voice***

Black markets or secondary markets occur when demand exceeds supply in sports markets. Such black markets are not necessarily illegal.

Figure 7.6 (b) shows a situation more common in lower league football and in other less popular sports. Because of the position of the demand curve, only 5,000 tickets are sold at the price set by the club hosting a lower league football match, even though stadium capacity is 20,000. There is an excess supply of 15,000 seats at the price set by the football club. Indeed, in this example, some seats would remain empty even if tickets were given away free. To fill the stadium, the club would have to pay people to watch the match.

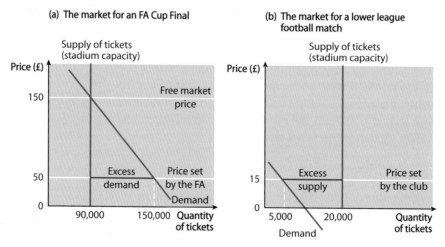

Figure 7.6 Excess demand and excess supply at football matches

Shifts of demand in leisure markets

When two leisure activities are substitutes or complementary goods, a change in the price of one leisure activity causes the demand curve for the other to shift. Suppose, for example, there is a fall in the price of tickets to see soccer matches (association football). This might lead to a leftward shift of the demand curve for tickets for rugby football matches. This is shown in Figure 7.7 (a). The size of the leftward shift will depend on the extent to which, from a spectator's point of view, the two types of football are substitutes for each other. However, a fall in the price of tickets for soccer matches will trigger a rightward shift in the demand curve for complementary goods, such as the replica shirts worn by many spectators. This is shown in Figure 7.7 (b).

examiner's voice

Sports markets provide plenty of examples of substitute and complementary good relationships.

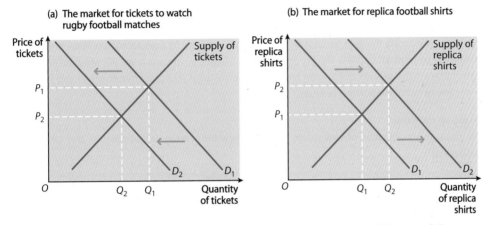

(a) The market for tickets to watch rugby football matches

(b) The market for replica football shirts

Figure 7.7 Shifts of demand for substitute and complementary goods, following a fall in admission prices to soccer matches

Charging different prices at a sports event

One way in which the providers of sport and leisure facilities can increase revenue is by charging different prices, both for different events available at the facility and for different customers. Football clubs charge higher prices for big games: for example, against a top club or a local rival. Likewise, some theatres charge different prices for different plays or shows. Also, sports fans are charged different prices for seats in different parts of the stadium. Some seats provide a better view than others, so the quality of the product varies according to where the seat is located. Customers are prepared to pay more for a high-quality view and comfort than for lower quality. Lower prices for children and old age pensioners are a common feature of pricing for sports and leisure events and facility use. A further variant is lower prices for frequent users: for example, in the form of season ticket pricing.

Box 7.6 The strange nature of competition in competitive sports

Some professional sports markets, such as the football market, provide an interesting mix of competition and monopoly. (Monopoly is one firm only in a market.) In football, clubs or teams compete in a league. The purpose of competition is to win the league and to be generally successful from year to year.

In most conventional markets, becoming a monopoly by driving rivals out of business represents ultimate success for a firm. But if a soccer club bankrupts all its rivals, there is no one to play against!

If Manchester United were to win the Premiership too many times with too much ease, the league would become boring and fans would lose interest. Scottish football, where Celtic and Rangers dominate, has already suffered this problem, though the two leading teams are still well supported.

The top teams in the UK, and in other European countries such as Spain and Italy, might seek to solve the problem by abandoning national leagues, and forming a new 'super league' where competition promises to be stiffer and the market more interesting for fans. Though there is a way that such a market could be less interesting if the clubs forming the super league decided they could never be relegated from the league.

In the 1990s, with the aim of allowing firms in all markets to compete on a level playing field undistorted by artificial barriers, the European Union created a single market. An ultimate logic of the single market is the growth of EU-wide leagues in professional sports such as football and rugby, and the decline of national sporting leagues.

Follow-up question

Why does the possibility of relegation make competition more interesting in the UK football premiership?

Summary

- Prices in markets for primary products, including agricultural goods, are often unstable.

- For many agricultural goods, there has been a long-run fall in prices caused by supply curves shifting rightward by more than the rightward shift of demand.

- Short-run fluctuations in agricultural prices are often caused by good and bad harvests, resulting from changing weather conditions.

- Speculation affects prices in commodity markets and also in the housing market.

- Prices of crude oil and of petrol and diesel fuel have been affected by OPEC — a producers' organisation and price ring.

- In the short run, the main determinant of house prices has been the demand curve for housing shifting up and down the inelastic supply curve for housing.

- Black markets or secondary markets are common in the markets for tickets for sports events.

- Substitute and complementary good relationships are common in sports markets.

Questions

1 Why are agricultural prices often unstable?
2 How has OPEC affected the world price of crude oil?
3 Distinguish between an owner-occupier, a landlord and a tenant.
4 Relate the terms 'stock' and 'flow' to the supply of housing.
5 Explain the main reasons for changes in average house prices in the UK.
6 How has owner-occupancy affected labour mobility in the UK?
7 Outline the factors affecting the supply of a particular sport or leisure activity.
8 Why would a soccer club charge different prices for tickets for different games?
9 What can happen in a competitive sport if one team becomes too dominant?

Chapter 8

Production, specialisation and exchange

I first explained the meaning of production in Chapter 2 — in the context of the role of production in trying to solve the fundamental economic problem of scarcity. This chapter begins by reminding you of the meaning of production, before introducing and explaining a number of production-related concepts, namely productivity, productive efficiency, the division of labour and specialisation. For specialisation and the division of labour to be worthwhile, the exchange of goods and services must be possible. Exchange can take place through barter, but in modern economies, money is almost always used as the medium which allows exchange to take place. I complete the chapter by explaining the main features of a firm's average cost curve and then use average cost curves to illustrate economies and diseconomies of scale.

Learning outcomes

This chapter will:
- remind you of the meaning of production
- distinguish between production and productivity
- explain the various forms of productivity, including labour productivity
- introduce the concepts of specialisation and the division of labour
- explain how successful specialisation and division of labour require exchange to take place
- introduce average cost curves
- explain the meaning of productive efficiency
- with the use of cost curves, explain economies and diseconomies of scale

Production

Earlier in the book, in Chapter 2, I explained the meaning of **production**, and also the roles of factors of production such as labour and capital in the production

> **K**ey term
> **Production** converts inputs or factor services into outputs of goods.

process. Before proceeding any further with this chapter, refer back to Chapter 2 and read again the section on production. The key point to remember is that production converts inputs, or the services of factors of production such as capital and labour, into final outputs of goods and services.

Also remember that production is a *means to an end*, and not the end itself. I cannot stress too often that the purpose of economic activity is to increase human happiness or economic welfare in a sustainable way, without destroying the ability of future generations to enjoy the resources the planet provides. Most, but not all, economic welfare is obtained from consumer goods and services, which have ultimately been produced by extracting and then using the earth's natural resources. Production is a necessary precondition for eventual consumption; without production human life as we know it would not be possible.

Productivity

Students often confuse productivity with production. While closely related, they do not have the same meaning. At AS, **productivity** usually means **labour productivity**, which is output per worker. However, **capital productivity** and **land productivity** can also be measured, as can **entrepreneurial productivity**. In reality of course, all the employed factors of production contribute to both a firm's current level of output and to any increase in the level of output. To reflect the fact that *all* the factors of production contribute to production, **total factor productivity (TFP)** can be measured. A change in total factor productivity measures the change in a firm's total output when more than one factor of production is changed.

examiner's voice
Productivity is a key concept in both AS Unit 1 and Unit 2. Questions usually centre on labour productivity, although candidates should be aware of other meanings of the term. Questions could also mention the UK's productivity gap, which is the difference in productivity levels between the UK and competitor countries.

key term
Productivity
Output per unit of input, e.g. labour productivity is output per worker.

Labour productivity or output per worker is extremely significant in manufacturing industries such as the car industry. In the 1990s and early 2000s, the Rover Car Group (which has since been bankrupted) struggled to survive in the UK car industry. Rover was unable to compete with Japanese car makers such as Nissan and Toyota. Nissan had invested in a state-of-the-art factory near Sunderland. Labour productivity in the ramshackle Rover factories amounted to only 33 cars per worker per year. By contrast, Nissan produced 98 cars per worker in its brand new factory. Given these figures, it is not surprising that the Rover Group was forced to stop production.

Specialisation and the division of labour

Over 200 years ago, the great classical economist, Adam Smith, first explained how, within a single production unit or firm (he took the example of a pin

factory), output could be increased if workers specialise at different tasks in the manufacturing process.

Smith had established one of the most fundamental of all economic principles: the benefits of **specialisation** or the **division of labour**. According to Adam Smith, there are three main reasons why a factory's total output can be increased if workers perform specialist tasks rather than if each worker attempts all the tasks himself or herself. These are:

- a worker will not need to switch between tasks so time will be saved;
- more and better machinery or capital can be employed (we now call this **capital widening** and **capital deepening**); and
- the 'practice makes perfect' argument that workers become more efficient or productive at the task they are doing, the greater the time spent on the specialist task, though this latter advantage can easily become a disadvantage if it involves 'de-skilling' and the creation of boredom and alienation among workers.

Trade and exchange

For specialisation to be economically worthwhile for those taking part in the division of labour, a system of **trade** and **exchange** is necessary. This is because workers who completely specialise can't enjoy a reasonable standard of living if forced to consume only what they produce. The obvious solution is to produce more than what the worker actually needs, and then for him or her to trade the surplus for that produced by others.

key terms

Division of labour
This concept goes hand in hand with specialisation. Different workers perform different tasks in the course of producing a good or service. Different workers may also produce different goods or services.

Exchange Specialisation and the division of labour mean that goods and services must be exchanged for each other. Money and the use of barter are mediums of exchange.

Specialisation A worker only performing one task or a narrow range of tasks.

Blacksmiths might exchange services with farmers

Until quite recently, people living in rural communities within the UK could specialise and then trade whatever they produced through **barter**. Thus a farmer might harvest wheat, part of which was then exchanged for services provided by local grain millers and village blacksmiths.

But successful barter requires a **double coincidence of wants**. Not only must the farmer require the services of the blacksmith; the blacksmith must want the wheat produced by the farmer, and a rate of exchange must be agreed for the two products. As this example suggests, it is reasonably easy to achieve the double coincidence of wants in a small community where people live close to each other and where only a few goods and services are produced and exchanged. However, in modern economies in which a vast number of goods are produced, reliance on barter holds back the growth of the economy. In such economies, barter is an extremely inefficient method of exchange.

> **examiner's voice**
> The Unit 1 exam may require knowledge of money's function as a medium of exchange. You don't need to know anything more about money or about banks and building societies for the Unit 1 exam.

These days, when we buy or sell a good or service, we almost always use **money**. We finance the transaction, either with cash, or with a debit card or cheque drawn on a bank or building society deposit. (The cheque or the piece of plastic is not in itself money; all it does is shift ownership of the bank or building society deposit from the person making the payment to the person receiving the payment.)

Using money is much more efficient than bartering. As I have explained, for successful barter there must be a double coincidence of wants. This is not necessary when money is used as a medium of exchange. Suppose I want to buy a television from you and you have a second-hand car you wish to sell. If we barter the goods, you must want my television set and I must want your car. We must also agree that the two goods have the same value. But if we use money rather than barter, you pay for my car with money, which I can then use to buy what ever I want from somebody else, say an MP3 player. I could also save the money rather than spend it. Used in this way, money enables the economy to achieve much greater specialisation and division of labour than is possible if we were to rely on barter.

Box 8.1 The making of a Wimbledon tennis ball

For the whole of the twentieth century, the tennis balls used at Wimbledon were manufactured in a factory in Barnsley, Yorkshire. However, in the early 2000s, Dunlop Slazenger's decision to move tennis ball production to the Philippines provided an example of the changing nature of international specialisation and division of labour. Before the Barnsley factory closure, the workers hoped that the European Union would fund a new automated factory. Although wages are higher in the UK than in the Philippines, increased labour productivity might reduce costs and make production competitive. There would be fewer jobs in Barnsley, but the remaining jobs would be safe. But it was not to be. The factory closed and 134 workers lost their jobs.

Dunlop Slazenger is just one of dozens of companies involved in the making of a tennis

ball. All over the world right now, there are ships chugging across oceans towards Dunlop's factory in the Philippines with a breathtakingly diverse range of ingredients. Clay from South Carolina, sulphur from Korea, silica from mines in Greece, magnesium carbonate from Japan and zinc oxide from Thailand are but a few of the substances used to vulcanise the rubber and give it the right amount of stretch and bounce. The tins come from Indonesia; some of the dyes are shipped from the UK.

Guardian, 24 June 2002

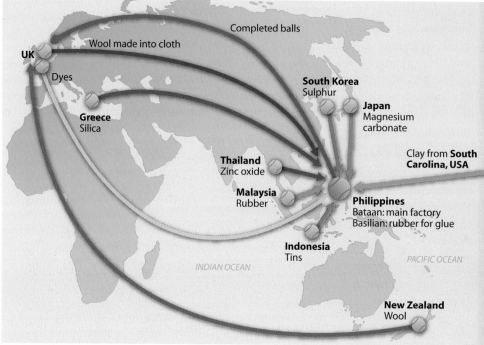

Figure 8.1 *The routes of the parts of a tennis ball*

Follow-up questions

1 Explain the meaning of the division of labour, and give an example of how the information above illustrates the changing nature of international specialisation and division of labour.

2 Explain the meaning of labour productivity and how increased labour productivity affects costs and competitiveness.

Average cost curves

When studying microeconomics, we generally assume that a firm's main business objective is to make the largest possible profit. This is called the profit-maximising objective. Profit depends on both the demand conditions and the supply conditions facing a firm, with the latter depending on whether average costs of production fall or rise as the firm's output increases.

examiner's voice

At AS, you should assume that a firm's average cost curve is 'U' shaped. You will not be asked to explain the shape. However, you should be able to use a 'U' shaped average cost curve to illustrate economies and diseconomies of scale.

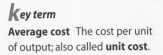

Average cost or unit cost is calculated by dividing the firm's total cost of production by the size of output produced. Average costs for each level of output can be shown on an average cost curve, such as the curve drawn in Figure 8.2.

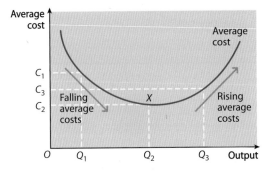

Figure 8.2 A firm's average cost curve

In Figure 8.2, the firm's average costs of production initially fall as the size of output increases. For example, when the firm produces output Q_1, average cost per unit of output is quite high at C_1. But when the firm increases output to Q_2, average cost per unit falls to C_2. However, for higher levels of output, average costs rise, for example to C_3 when output increases to Q_3.

The average cost curve in Figure 8.2 is 'U' shaped, showing average costs falling and then rising as the level of output increases. Point X, which is located in the diagram above level of output Q_2, is the **cost-minimising level of output**. The cost-minimising level of output is also called the **optimum level of output**. Be careful about this. In this context, the word 'optimum' means *best for the whole community*, or *socially optimal*. It does not necessarily mean *best for the firm* that produces the output, since the cost-minimising level of output and the profit-maximising level of output need not be the same.

Productive efficiency

Economic efficiency is one of the most important economic concepts you need to know. There are a number of different types of efficiency, but the only one you need to know at AS is **productive efficiency**. There are two different ways of defining productive efficiency – at the level of a single firm within the economy and at the level of the whole economy.

For a single firm to achieve productive efficiency, the firm must use the techniques and factors of production which are available to produce the cost-minimising or optimum level of output described in the previous section. In Figure 8.3, the productively efficient level of output is Q_1, where the average costs are minimised. Q_1 is located below the lowest point on the 'U' shaped average cost curve. All other levels of output, including Q_2, are productively inefficient because higher average costs are incurred.

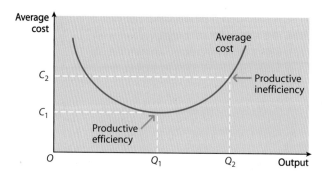

Figure 8.3
Productive efficiency for a firm in the economy

e*xaminer's voice*

If an exam question asks for a definition of productive efficiency, you can use either (or both) of the definitions given in this chapter.

If you have to apply the concept, choose the definition that is most appropriate to the question, i.e. the first definition if you are explaining a firm's costs, and the second definition if you are discussing resource allocation in the economy.

The **whole economy is productively efficient** when production takes place on the economy's production possibility frontier. To illustrate this in Figure 8.4, I have redrawn Figure 2.1 (which in Chapter 2 illustrates scarcity as the economic problem) to show productively efficient and inefficient levels of output for the whole economy.

k*ey term*
Productive efficiency (for the whole economy) The whole economy is productively efficient when producing on its production possibility frontier.

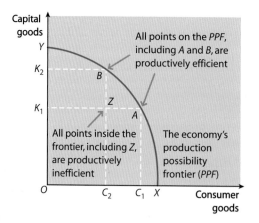

Figure 8.4
Productive efficiency for the whole economy

All points on the economy's production possibility frontier, such as *A* and *B*, show output being maximised from the available inputs or factors of production, given the technology available for the economy to use. Note that, at point *A* for example, it is impossible to increase output of capital goods without reducing production of consumer goods, and vice versa. By contrast, all points inside the frontiers, such as *Z*, are productively inefficient. At *Z*, it is possible to produce more capital goods without reducing output of consumer goods.

Economies of scale

As a firm grows in size by investing in new plant or buildings, it can benefit from **economies of scale**. However, beyond a certain size, the firm may eventually suffer from **diseconomies of scale**. Economies of scale are defined as falling average costs of production that result from an *increase* in the size or scale of the firm.

key term
Economy of scale
Falling average or unit costs as a firm increases its size or scale.

Figure 8.5 illustrates the nature of economies of scale. In the diagram, I assume initially that the size or scale of the business is shown by firm size 1. If there is spare capacity, the firm can increase output to meet an increase in demand by taking on more workers and employing more variable capital. Increasing production in this way is shown by the movement along horizontal arrow A, drawn to the right of firm size 1. Eventually, however, the firm runs into a capacity constraint, which means that it can't produce any more output solely by employing more workers and machines. In order to produce more output, the firm must expand by investing in new fixed capacity. In Figure 8.5, this is depicted by the movement along vertical arrow X to firm size 2.

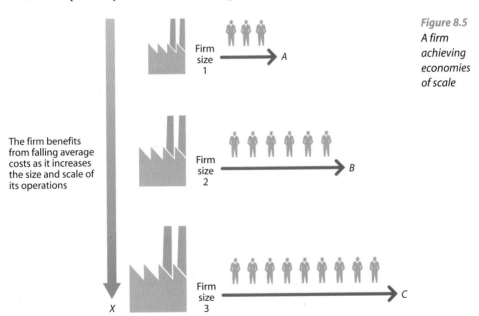

The firm benefits from falling average costs as it increases the size and scale of its operations

Figure 8.5
A firm achieving economies of scale

Once it has reached firm size 2, the firm meets any further increase in demand, in the first instance, by moving along horizontal arrow B. Then, when full capacity has again been reached, the firm meets further increases in demand by investing in new capacity, which takes the business to firm size 3.

examiner's voice
At AS, you don't need to know the difference between variable and fixed capital. Nevertheless, knowledge of the difference is useful. As the name implies, fixed capital, such as a firm's buildings, cannot quickly be changed. By contrast, variable capital, such as raw materials, can be quickly changed.

Types of economy of scale

There are various types or causes of economy of scale, the main ones being technical economies of scale, managerial economies of scale, marketing economies of scale, financial economies of scale and risk-bearing economies of scale.

Technical economies of scale

The main types of technical economy of scale are listed below.

- **Indivisibilities.** Many types of plant or machinery are indivisible in the sense that there is a certain minimum size below which they cannot efficiently operate. A firm requiring only a small level of output must, therefore, choose between installing plant or machinery which it will be unable to use continuously, buying from an outside supplier, or using a different but less efficient method to produce the smaller required level of output.

- **The spreading of research and development costs.** Research and development (R&D) costs associated with new products also tend to be indivisible and independent of the size of output to be produced. With large plants, R&D costs can be spread over a much longer production run, reducing unit costs in the long run.

- **Volume economies.** These are also known as **economies of increased dimensions**. With many types of capital equipment (for example metal smelters, transport containers, storage tanks and warehouses), costs increase less rapidly than capacity. When a storage tank or boiler is doubled in dimension, its storage capacity actually increases eight-fold. And since heat loss depends on the area of the container's walls (which will only have increased four-fold) and not upon volume, a large smelter or boiler is technically more efficient than a small one. Volume economies are thus very important in industries such as transport, storage and warehousing, as well as in metal and chemical industries where an increase in the scale of plant provides scope for the conservation of heat and energy.

- **Economies of massed resources.** The operation of a number of identical machines in a large plant means that proportionately fewer spare parts need be kept than when fewer machines are involved. This is an application of the 'law of large numbers', since we can assume that not all the machines will develop a fault at the same time. (The massing of resources also allows for firm-level economies of scale. A multi-product multi-plant firm may also benefit from the cross-fertilisation of experience and ideas between its various subsidiaries.)

- **Economies of vertically linked processes.** Much manufacturing activity involves a large number of vertically related tasks and processes, from the initial purchase of raw materials, components and energy through to the completion

examiner's voice

You may be required to explain two or three types of economy of scale and two or three causes of diseconomies of scale.

examiner's voice

You may be required to link economies of scale to the growth of monopolies. In the case of a 'natural' monopoly (explained in Chapter 12), there is only room in the market for one firm (i.e. a monopoly) benefiting from full economies of scale.

and sale of the finished product. Within a single firm, these processes may be integrated through the linkages between the various plants owned by the firm — with the output of one plant providing an input or source of component supply for another plant further along the route to the finished product. Alternatively, the tasks or processes may be integrated within the workshops of a single large plant, enabling the plant to benefit from substantial economies of scale. The linking of processes in a single plant can lead to a saving in time, transport costs and energy, and the close physical proximity of specialist workshops within the plant may allow a subsequent stage in the production process to be sure of obtaining exactly the supplies it needs in the right quantity and technical specification at the right time.

Managerial economies of scale

The larger the scale of a firm, the greater the ability to benefit from specialisation and the division of labour within management as well as within the ordinary labour force. A large firm can benefit from a functional division of labour, namely the employment of specialist managers, for example in the fields of production, personnel and sales. Detail can be delegated to junior managers and supervisors.

Marketing economies of scale

Marketing economies of scale are of two types: **bulk-buying** and **bulk-marketing economies**. Large firms may be able to use their market power both to buy supplies at lower prices and also to market their products on better terms negotiated with wholesalers and retailers.

Financial or capital-raising economies of scale

Financial or capital-raising economies of scale are similar to the bulk-buying economies just described, except that they relate to the 'bulk-buying' or the bulk-borrowing of funds required to finance the business's expansion. Large firms can often borrow from banks and other financial institutions at a lower rate of interest and on better terms than those available to small firms.

Risk-bearing economies of scale

Large firms are usually less exposed to risk than small firms, because risks can be grouped and spread. Large firms can spread risks by diversifying their output, their markets, their sources of supply and finance and the processes by which they manufacture their output. Such economies of diversification or risk-bearing can make the firm less vulnerable to sudden changes in demand or conditions of supply that might severely harm a smaller less-diversified business.

Diseconomies of scale

In contrast to economies of scale, **diseconomies of scale** occur when average costs (or unit costs) rise as the scale or size of the firm grows. Managerial diseconomies of scale are particularly important. They can be caused by communication failure, which occurs when a firm becomes too large and there are many layers

Key term
Diseconomy of scale Rising average or unit cost as a firm increases its size or scale.

of management between the top managers and ordinary production workers. In this situation, decision making and the ability to respond to customers' needs or to problems arising in the course of production both suffer. As a result, the resources the business uses are not allocated as effectively as they could be. Top management loses touch with junior managers and employees and with the problems facing the business.

Economies and diseconomies of scale and the firm's average cost curve

Figure 8.6 shows how a firm's 'U' shaped average cost curve can illustrate economies and diseconomies of scale. The curve has been drawn under the assumption that average costs change as the firm changes the scale of its operations, i.e. changes its overall size. Economies of scale are shown by the downward-sloping section of the curve, while the upward-sloping section (at a higher level of output) illustrates diseconomies of scale. This particular average cost curve also contains a flat middle section, lying between the downward-sloping and upward-sloping sections of the curve. The flat section depicts a range of output in which there are no economies or diseconomies of scale. This can certainly happen in real life. However, the middle (flat) section is possible but not inevitable. Graphs which show economies and diseconomies of scale often do not have a flat middle section.

> **examiner's voice**
>
> You may be required to illustrate economies and/or diseconomies of scale on a firm's average cost curve.

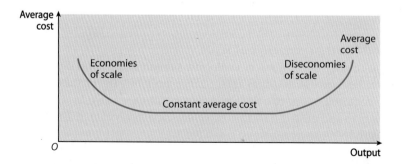

Figure 8.6
Economies and diseconomies of scale

Extension material

You will come across average cost curves again when studying Unit 3 at A2. At this level, it is necessary to know and understand the difference between short-run cost curves and long-run cost curves. Strictly, because economies and diseconomies of scale occur when the scale or size of a firm changes, the cost curve in Figure 8.6 is a *long-run* cost curve. The long run is defined as the time period in which all the factors of production can be changed. By contrast, a short-run cost curve depicts a situation in which at least one factor of production — usually assumed to be capital — is held fixed.

However, because knowledge of short-run and long-run cost curves is not required at AS, you will not be tested at this level on the difference between the two types of cost curve.

Internal and external economies and diseconomies of scale

All the economies and diseconomies of scale so far described are examples of **internal economies and diseconomies of scale**. These occur when a firm grows and changes its scale and size.

By contrast, **external economies of scale** occur when a firm's average or unit costs of production fall, not because of the growth of the firm itself, but because of the growth of the industry or market of which the firm is a part. Very often, external economies of scale are produced by cluster effects, which occur when a lot of firms in the same industry are located close to each other, providing markets, sources of supply and a pool of trained labour for each other.

External diseconomies of scale occur in a similar way, with the growth of the whole market raising the average costs of all the firms in the industry. As with external economies of scale, external diseconomies can arise from cluster effects. When a large number of similar firms locate close to each other, not only do they create benefits which aid all the firms in the cluster; they may also get in each other's way. Competition for labour amongst the firms may raise local wages, which while being good for workers, increases the unit wage costs of their employers. There may also be an increase in local and regional traffic congestion, which lengthens delivery times and raises delivery costs both for firms and for their customers.

> ***e*xaminer's voice**
> The Unit 1 specification only asks for knowledge of economies and diseconomies of scale. Because the specification does not mention external economies or diseconomies of scale, exam questions will only require knowledge of *internal* economies and diseconomies. Nevertheless, it is useful to know about external economies and diseconomies of scale.

Box 8.2 Are economies of scale now less important in the car industry?

A century ago the car industry more or less invented modern industrial capitalism. The car started life in Germany, and early development of the industry began in France, but it was in the USA that it came of age. Henry Ford's adaptation for car-making of the <u>moving assembly line</u> he had seen in Chicago slaughterhouses marked the birth of <u>mass production</u>.

The car industry's long-standing obsession with scale arose from the needs of its manufacturing processes. Garel Rhys, director of the Centre for Automotive Industry Research at Cardiff University, has calculated that <u>economies of scale</u> reach their peak at 250,000 cars a year in an assembly plant, although for the body panels the figure could be as high as 2 million.

Today, the motor car is the epitome of mass production. For most households in rich countries, it is the second-biggest purchase after a house or flat. Few other consumer-goods industries depend so heavily on a thriving second-hand market for their products.

And yet there are powerful forces at work that could profoundly change the car industry. One is <u>market fragmentation</u>, leading to <u>lower production runs</u>. Another is dissatisfaction with the costly system of building cars for stock, not to order. A third is innovative modular construction, in which more of the car

is put together by parts suppliers. And further ahead, a fourth force could be a switch to electric cars with electronic and electrical rather than mechanical controls.

Some of the alternative business models currently being touted would, in effect, attempt another revolution, with companies outsourcing more and more of the car.

If consumers are demanding an ever wider choice of vehicles, it follows in a mature market that production runs have to get smaller. Car companies are already reconciling themselves to this trend. That increases the appeal of more flexible manufacturing methods.

As the industry's products begin to change, so will the way they are made. In time, there will be less need for huge, capital-intensive factories, so the barriers to entry will come down. Start-up companies could take business away from established traditional manufacturers. Low-cost carmakers could swoop in, rather as low-cost airlines have done in aviation.

The Economist's Survey of the Car Industry,
2 September 2004

Follow-up questions

1 Explain the meaning of each of the concepts underlined in the passage.
2 Describe some of the economies of scale that have contributed to lower average costs in the UK car industry.

How internal economies and diseconomies of scale affect particular industries

Boxes 8.3 and 8.4 contain two case studies of industries or markets that are affected by economies and diseconomies of scale. Study the two case studies, and then consider the following questions.

■ Using the concepts of economies and diseconomies of scale, discuss the advantages and disadvantages of bendy buses, first for Transport for London, the organisation that provides the buses, and second for members of the general public.
■ How could the oil tanker industry be organised to get round the problem mentioned in Box 8.4 about the disadvantages of large super-tankers?

Box 8.3 London's bendy buses

Articulated buses, also known as bendy buses in the UK, are a type of bus with an enhanced passenger capacity. The main benefits of a bendy bus over the double-decker bus are increased stability from a lower centre of gravity, lower road wheel pressure and higher maximum speed. Bendy buses also have an accessibility advantage over double-decker buses: people in wheelchairs, those with baby buggies or those who are otherwise unable to climb stairs can access the whole bus, and are not limited to only a downstairs deck.

One disadvantage is the effective power available for moving the bendy bus. Bendy buses often use the same engine as ordinary buses, and this leads to reduced acceleration, due to an increase of weight. The vehicles are prone to overheating. During 2004 in the early stages of deployment of bendy buses in London there were several fires, which required the temporary withdrawal and modification of the entire fleet. In London, another disadvantage to the introduction of bendy buses is increased fare evasion. Articulated buses in London have three separate entrances, and passengers are expected to pay for their journey in advance. Passengers can do this by validating a pre-paid card called 'Oyster', or by

using pre-purchased tickets. Since the introduction of this bus type, many people have opted to evade their fare and not pay for their journeys. Such passengers simply board the bus via the middle or rear doors. This increase in fare evasion has resulted in Transport for London recruiting an extra 150 Revenue Protection Inspectors, to police revenue collection on the bus network.

A further disadvantage comes with difficulties caused by the length of bendy buses, and the turning radius they require in order to negotiate corners. In London, many roads, even in central areas, lack sufficient lane width and space, and this had led to difficulties with bendy buses blocking junctions when at bus stops, or having difficulty turning at tight intersections.

Box 8.4 Super-tankers and volume economies of scale

The large super-tankers that are used to transport crude oil across seas and oceans from oil fields to industrial markets benefit significantly from volume economies of scale. However, super-tankers can also suffer from a diseconomy of scale. This is because large super-tankers cannot enter shallow ports. A wider tanker with a shallow draught does not yield as many economies of scale as a conventional super-tanker, but is more flexible and can enter more ports.

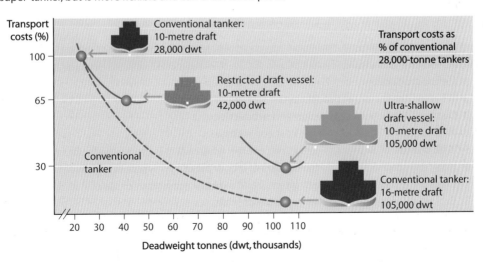

Figure 8.7

Summary

- Production is a process, or set of processes, that converts inputs into outputs.
- Productivity is measured by output per unit of input.
- Labour productivity, or output per worker, is the most commonly used measure of productivity.
- The division of labour means that different workers do different jobs.
- The division of labour and specialisation occur together.
- Specialisation and the division of labour require trade and exchange.
- Money is the main medium of exchange in modern economies, though barter still sometimes takes place.
- Average cost is cost per unit of output.
- A firm's average cost curve is typically 'U' shaped, showing average costs first falling and then rising as output increases.
- A firm is productively efficient when producing the cost-minimising level of output.
- For the whole economy, all points on the economy's production possibility frontier are productively efficient.
- Economies of scale mean that a firm's average costs fall as the scale or size of the firm increases.
- There are a number of different types of economy of scale, e.g. technical economies.
- Diseconomies of scale mean that a firm's average costs rise as the scale or size of the firm increases.
- Economies and diseconomies of scale can be shown on a 'U' shaped average cost curve, drawn to show average costs changing as the size of the firm increases.
- External economies and diseconomies of scale result from the growth of the industry rather than from the growth of a firm within the industry.

Questions

1 Define production.
2 What are the factors of production?
3 Distinguish between production and productivity.
4 What does a 'U' shaped average cost curve show?
5 With the use of an average cost curve, explain when a firm is productively efficient.
6 How may specialisation and the division of labour make a firm more productively efficient?
7 Explain the difference between internal and external economies of scale.
8 Explain three types of internal economy of scale.
9 Explain three examples of internal economy of scale.
10 How are economies and diseconomies of scale likely to affect the size of a firm?

Chapter 9

Introducing market failures

In earlier chapters, I have explained how markets work. This is the first of four chapters that explain how markets fail. In this short introductory chapter on market failure, I introduce you to the general idea of market failure. Specific market failures, such as public goods and monopoly, are then explored in detail in Chapters 10, 11 and 12.

examiner's voice

Because the title of Unit 1 is Markets and Market Failure, you should expect one of the two data-response questions in the Unit 1 exam to be mostly on market failure.

Learning outcomes

This chapter will:
- explain the meaning of market failure, distinguishing between complete and partial market failure
- relate market failure to the important economic concepts of efficiency and equity
- discuss market failure in terms of the breakdown of the three functions of prices
- examine three introductory case studies of market failure

The meaning of market failure

Market failure occurs whenever the market mechanism or price mechanism performs badly or unsatisfactorily, or fails to perform at all. There are two main ways in which markets fail.
- Markets can function inequitably.
- Markets can function inefficiently.

It is also useful to distinguish between complete market failure, when the market simply does not exist, and partial market failure, when the market functions, but produces the wrong quantity of a good or service. In the former case, there is a missing market. In the latter case, the good or service may be provided too cheaply, in

key term

Market failure A market completely failing to provide a good or service, or providing the wrong quantity, i.e. a quantity that leads to a misallocation of resources in the economy.

which case it is over-produced and over-consumed. Alternatively, as in monopoly, the good may be too expensive, in which case under-production and under-consumption results.

Markets functioning inequitably

Equity means fairness or justice (though in other contexts, such as the housing market, equity has a very different meaning, namely wealth). As soon as equitable considerations are introduced into economic analysis, nor-mative or value judgements are being made, 'socially fair' distributions of income and wealth are discussed, and questions are raised about the goods and services people *ought* to produce and consume.

> **key term**
> **Equity** Fairness or justness.

As the experience of many poor countries shows, unregulated market forces tend to produce highly unequal distributions of income and wealth. Some economists, usually of a free-market persuasion, dispute whether this is a market failure. Some argue that the people who end up being rich deserve to be rich and that the people who end up being poor deserve to be poor. According to this view, the market has not failed — it merely creates incentives which, if followed, cause people to generate more income and wealth.

However, most economists reject as too extreme the view that the market contains its own morality with regard to the distributions of income and wealth. They argue that markets are 'value-neutral' with regard to the social and ethical desirability or undesirability of the distributions of income and wealth resulting from the way the market functions. Few economists now believe that markets should be replaced by the command mechanism. There is, however, much more agreement that, instead of *replacing* the market, governments should *modify* the market so that it operates in a more equitable way than would be the case without government intervention. Taxing the better-off and re-distributing tax revenues as transfers to the less well-off is the obvious way of correcting the market failure to ensure an equitable distri-bution of income and wealth. (However, as Chapter 14 explains, redistributative policies can promote new types of inefficiency and distortion within the economy.)

Markets functioning inefficiently

Monopoly and other forms of imperfect competition provide examples of market failure resulting from markets performing inefficiently. The *wrong* quantity is produced in monopoly, particularly when there are no economies of scale, and the *wrong* price is charged. *Too little* is produced and is sold at *too high* a price. Scarce resources are not utilised in the most efficient way, and a misallocation of resources results.

The next three chapters

In the next three chapters, I examine six causes of market failure that result from inefficient functioning of markets. These occur in the context of:

- **public goods** (which are compared to *private goods*) and **externalities** in Chapter 10
- **merit goods** and **demerit goods** in Chapter 11
- **monopoly** and the **immobility of labour** in Chapter 12

(Chapter 11 also returns to the market failure resulting from the inequitable functioning of markets, namely **income and wealth inequalities**, that I mentioned earlier.)

Market failure and the three functions of prices

In Chapter 5, when explaining how the price mechanism distributes scarce resources between alternative uses in a market or mixed economy, I introduced you to the three functions prices perform in such economies. The functions involve:
- signalling information
- creating incentives for people and firms to respond to
- allocating and rationing resources between competing uses, as a result of the way economic agents respond to the information signalled by changing prices

As a generalisation, we can say that when all three of these functions perform well, markets also work well, and market failure either does not occur, or, if it occurs, its effects are relatively trivial. However, when one or more of the three functions of prices significantly breaks down, market failure occurs. In Chapter 10, I explain how in the case of pure public goods and externalities, the price mechanism breaks down completely. If an alternative method of provision is unavailable, complete market breakdown means that markets fail completely to provide public goods such as national defence. A useful service for which there is a need is not provided — hence the market failure. In the case of an externality such as pollution, firms (and indeed consumers) that generate pollution simply dump it on other people (whom we call **third parties**). There is no market in which the unwilling consumers of pollution can charge a price, and thence create an incentive for the polluter to pollute less. Hence, again, the market failure.

> **examiner's voice**
> Market failure can also be defined as a situation in which one or more of the three functions of prices breaks down, either partially or completely.

Three case studies to introduce you to possible market failures

I shall conclude this chapter by introducing you to three case studies that illustrate market failures I explain in greater depth in the next chapters.

The first of my case studies (Box 9.1) relates to the first of the alleged market failures we look at in Chapter 10, namely public goods. National defence and the police are often regarded as **pure public goods**, which, for reasons I explain in the next chapter, markets cannot provide. However, as you read through the first case study, which describes how worried neighbours have set up their own private police force in the state of Georgia in the USA, you should question whether in fact markets are

unable to provide police services. The employment of private security guards at UK shopping malls could provide a similar example.

Box 9.1 Paying for protection

For many Atlanta residents, it seems having a mower stolen, car radio taken or home broken into is a rite of passage.

For Muffie Michaelson of Druid Hills, her welcome to Atlanta came 4 years ago. About 11 p.m., Michaelson went to the door of her Oakdale Road home to make sure it was secure. As she looked outside, she was shocked to see a man rifling through her car. The thief smashed her car window and took the stereo.

Three other neighbours reported car break-ins that night. 'We don't get any patrolling in our neighborhood,' Ms Michaelson said.

In response, Atlanta residents frustrated with chronically understaffed city police are piecing together their own private police force neighborhood by neighborhood.

Dozens of Atlanta neighborhoods such as East Lake supplement Atlanta police with their own private patrols. In some cases, businesses are paying extra taxes to create a private agency they control. In others, homeowners are selling memberships to their own neighborhood police departments using off-duty Atlanta officers to tackle street-level crime like burglary, car break-ins and thefts from tool sheds.

East Lake's new service costs members $200 a year. They have 130 paying members from among about 1,200 households.

Atlanta Journal-Constitution, 13 July 2007

Atlanta residents have formed a private police force

Follow-up questions

1 Should the provision of police services be classified as a pure public good, as a non-pure public good, or as a private good? Justify your answer.

2 Why may some Atlanta households decide to 'free-ride'? How would they do it?

My second case study (Box 9.2) centres on the other example of market failure I shall discuss in Chapter 10. Many of you will be familiar with the debate that has taken place in recent years about 4×4 vehicles such a sports utility vehicles (SUVs) and their alleged contribution to global warming pollution and traffic accidents (both of which are negative externalities or external costs).

In the March 2006 budget, Gordon Brown, then the UK Chancellor of the Exchequer and the country's most important economics minister, introduced higher road taxes for 4×4 vehicles such as Land Rovers and other allegedly higher polluting vehicles, popularly known as 'Chelsea tractors'.

Box 9.2 Drive one of these?

You're crass and irresponsible, says minister on warpath

Drivers of gas-guzzling cars are to be penalised under measures being developed to tackle climate change. Ministers are particularly keen to target the growing number of people who drive large 4×4s around cities and venture off tarmac only when parking on grass verges.

A record 187,000 4×4s were sold last year, up from 80,000 a decade ago. Small cars accounted for the smallest proportion of new cars since 1999. British and European manufacturers have been too slow to develop hybrid cars, such as the Toyota Prius, which have both a petrol or diesel engine and an electric motor, and use energy normally lost in braking to recharge their batteries.

Malcolm Wicks, the Energy Minister, said that the small measures the government had adopted so far, such as offering £1,000 grants to people buying a Prius, were no longer enough.

'We are going to need more than just a series of marginal changes. We are going to need a step change. We will have to ask "is it environmentally responsible to be producing cars which are a serious part of the problem?" There will come a time when it will be irresponsible for those to be on sale.'

In the short term, the government is considering raising vehicle excise duty for gas guzzlers.

Ben Webster, *The Times*, 26 February 2006

Follow-up questions

1 Explain the economic factors that may be responsible for the increase in sales of 4×4 vehicles.
2 Given the large increase in sales of 4×4 vehicles, with the use of a demand and supply diagram assess whether taxation can reverse the trend back to sales of small cars.

The last of my three case studies (Box 9.3) switches attention to demerit goods, which I explain in Chapter 11. A demerit good, such as an alcoholic drink, for example whisky, is both bad for the wider community and possibly also, in the long run, for the person consuming it.

The case study article is not on alcohol, but on a rather similar demerit good, tobacco. But, as the article indicates, there may be a case for encouraging people to consume demerit goods — so that they die early and thus save the taxpayer the cost of paying pensions and keeping them alive into extreme old age.

Box 9.3 Smoking for Britain

Kicking the habit is good for you and the NHS. Right?

Pity the British smoker: cast on to the pavement to face the elements, just to light up. High cigarette taxes are supposed to wean Britons off tobacco and raise money for the NHS.

But smokers tend to die younger than non-smokers, who require, on average, even greater spending than smokers for other chronic ailments. So by reducing smokers' life expectancy, tobacco saves government money, even without considering the pension benefits that go unclaimed by dead puffers. So the lower classes, who do most of the smoking, are probably subsidising the healthcare of the better-off, who have largely given up.

The Economist, 2 May 2002

Follow-up questions

1 Taking account of the information in the extract, should cigarettes be classified as a demerit good or as a merit good?
2 Discuss the effects of tobacco taxes on the real incomes of different groups in society.

I chose the three market failure case studies to try to get you to approach the various market failures you need to know about in a sceptical frame of mind. Not all economists agree that the market failures included in the AQA AS specification are indeed failures of the market. But, whatever views you form, don't rest on blind assertion. An important skill to learn at both AS and A2 is that of justifying your arguments.

Summary

- Market failure occurs whenever the market mechanism or price mechanism performs badly or unsatisfactorily, or fails to perform at all.
- Complete market failure (and missing markets) should be distinguished from partial market failure.
- Markets can fail because they are inefficient or inequitable.
- Public goods, externalities, merit and demerit goods, monopoly, and the immobility of factors of production are the main examples of microeconomic market failure resulting from the inefficient functioning of markets.
- The unequal distribution of income and wealth is the main market failure resulting from the inequitable functioning of markets.

Questions

1 What is meant by market failure?
2 Distinguish between complete and partial market failure.
3 Link market failure to the three functions of prices.
4 Explain how markets can function inefficiently.
5 What is the difference between equality and equity?
6 What is a 'missing market'?

Chapter 10

Private goods, public goods and externalities

Chapter 9 explained how market failure occurs whenever a market does not function very well or, in extreme cases, does not function at all. This chapter explains two of the market failures briefly mentioned in Chapter 9: public goods and externalities. By way of establishing a clear understanding of the nature of public goods, the chapter starts by explaining their opposite, namely private goods. The chapter also explains how public goods and externalities provide examples of complete market failure or missing markets.

Learning outcomes

This chapter will:

- explain the difference between a private good and a public good
- distinguish between public 'goods' and public 'bads'
- show how an externality is a form of public 'good' or public 'bad'
- distinguish between negative and positive externalities
- introduce the concept of the margin and use marginal analysis to explain why market failure occurs when negative and positive externalities are generated

Private goods

I am using my laptop computer to write this paragraph. A few minutes ago, a window cleaner came into my study. Suppose he had said to me: 'That's a nice computer; I'm going to steal it.' Not surprisingly, I would try to stop the theft. The computer is mine and not his. It is my **private good**.

> **Key term**
>
> **Private good** A good, such as an orange, that is excludable and rival.

Most goods, such as my laptop computer, are private goods which possess two defining characteristics. The owners can exercise **private property rights**, preventing other people from using the good or consuming its benefits. This property is

called **excludability**. The second property is called **rivalry**, though this is better illustrated by a good such as a sweet rather than by my computer. If I eat the sweet, you, or anyone else, cannot. In this sense, we are rivals. (Rivalry is sometimes called **diminishability**. When one person consumes a private good such as a sweet or a banana, the quantity available diminishes.)

Public goods

A **public good** exhibits the opposite characteristics of **non-excludability** and **non-rivalry** or **non-diminishability**. It is these characteristics that lead to market failure.

A lighthouse, or rather the beam of light provided by a lighthouse, is an example of a public good. Suppose an entrepreneur builds the lighthouse shown in Figure 10.1, and then tries to charge each ship that passes in the night and benefits from the beam of light. Providing ships pay up, the service can be provided commercially through the market.

key term

Public good A good, such as a radio programme, that is non-excludable and non-rival.

Ships may be tempted to free-ride to avoid paying the lighthouse for its services

The beam of light is a public good

Stormy ocean

Dangerous rocks

Figure 10.1 A lighthouse as a public good

However, the market is likely to fail because the *incentive* function of prices breaks down. Because it is impossible to exclude **free-riders** (in this case, ships that benefit without paying), it may be impossible to collect enough revenue to cover costs. If too many ships decide to 'free-ride', profits cannot be made and the incentive to provide the service through the market disappears. The market thus fails to provide a service for which there is an obvious need. There is then a need for alternative provision by the government in its public spending programme, or possibly by a charity (such as Trinity House in the UK).

key term

Free-rider Somebody who benefits from a good or service without paying for it.

examiner's voice

Make sure you understand the difference between a private good and a public good, and can give examples of both.

Other examples of public goods

Other examples of public goods include national defence, police, street lighting, roads and television and radio programmes. Consider a situation in which the state does not provide national defence. Instead, the government lets individual

citizens purchase in the market the defence or protection they want. But markets only provide defence when entrepreneurs can successfully charge prices for the services they supply. Suppose an aspiring citizen, who believes a fortune can be made in the defence industry, sets up a company, Nuclear Defence Services Ltd, with the aim of persuading the country's residents to purchase the services of nuclear missiles strategically located around the country. After estimating the money value of the defence received by each individual, Nuclear Defence Services bills each household accordingly and waits for the payments to flow in....

But the payments may never arrive. As long as the service is provided, every household can benefit without paying. Nuclear Defence Services Ltd cannot provide nuclear defence only to the country's inhabitants who are prepared to pay while excluding the benefit from those who are not prepared to pay. Withdrawing the benefit from one means withdrawing it from all. But all individuals face the temptation to consume without paying, or to free-ride. If enough people choose to free-ride, Nuclear Defence Services Ltd makes a loss. The incentive to provide the service through the market thus disappears. Assuming, of course, that the majority of the country's inhabitants believe nuclear defence to be necessary (i.e. a good rather than a 'bad') the market fails because it fails to provide a service for which there is a need. The result is a **missing market**.

Box 10.1 What is a public good?

We know that markets generally provide private goods, but markets may not be able to provide public goods. Public goods are recognised for having benefits that cannot easily be confined to a single buyer (or set of buyers). Yet, once public goods are provided, many people can enjoy them for free. For an individual pursuing his or her self-interest, it is often the best and most rational strategy to let others provide the good and then to enjoy it, free of charge.

Adapted from Kaul, I., Grunberg, I. and
Stern, M.A. (1999) Global Public Goods:
International Cooperation in the 21st Century

Follow-up question

Distinguish between a public good, a free good and an economic good.

Goods and 'bads'

A **good** such as a loaf of bread provides benefits to the person or persons who consume it. Consumer goods yield usefulness or utility, and sometimes pleasure and satisfaction. (Using economic jargon, we say that consumer goods increase economic welfare.)

> **Key term**
> A **good** yields utility, unlike a 'bad' which yields disutility.

In everyday language, we generally use the word 'bad' as an adjective, e.g. a bad film or a bad football match. However, economists also use the word as a *noun*. In this usage, an economic 'bad' is the opposite of a good, yielding disutility, dissatisfaction or displeasure. For most people, consumption of a bad such as rotten meat *reduces* rather than *increases* economic welfare.

Public bads

The free-rider problem which I have explained in the context of public goods also affects a group of bads which are known as public bads. An example of a public bad is rubbish or garbage. However, the free-rider problem is a little different in the case of public bads. People are generally prepared to pay for the *removal* of an economic bad, to avoid the unpleasantness otherwise experienced. But in the case of rubbish or garbage, payment can be avoided by dumping the bad in a public place or on someone else's property.

In the UK, local authorities generally empty dustbins without charging for each bin emptied. Suppose this service is not provided, and private contractors remove rubbish and charge households £1 for each dustbin emptied. To avoid paying £1, some households may decide to dump their waste in the road or in neighbours' dustbins. (Builders' skips provide a good example of this practice. A household hiring a skip is well advised to fill the skip as quickly as possible, before the rest of the street takes advantage of the facility.) If too many households free-ride, it is impossible for the private contractor to make a profit, and a service for which there is a need is no longer provided. Hence the case for free local authority provision, financed through taxation.

Free-riding can be a problem with public bads

Extension material

Public goods can be divided into **pure public goods** and non-pure public goods. National defence and police are examples of pure public goods — defined as public goods for which it is impossible to exclude free-riders. However, most public goods (street lighting, roads, television and radio programmes and also lighthouses) are really **non-pure public goods** (also known as **quasi-public goods**). Methods can be devised for converting the goods into private goods by excluding free-riders (for example, electronic pricing of road use). Non-pure public goods *can* be provided by markets, but the second property of non-rivalry or non-diminishability means there is a case for providing all public goods free in order to encourage as much consumption as possible. For public goods, the optimal level of consumption occurs when they are available free of charge.

Public goods and government goods

Public goods are goods for which there is a need. But because of the missing market problem, markets may fail to provide public goods. This means (as I shall explain in greater detail in Chapter 13) there is a case for the state providing public goods at zero price to the consumer.

Students often wrongly define a public good as a good that is provided by the government, i.e. as a government good. This is confusing *cause* with *effect*. The word *public* in public good refers to the fact that members of the general public cannot be excluded from enjoying the good's benefits. It is this that *causes* market failure. To try to correct the market failure, governments provide public goods. This is the *effect*. Government goods include public goods such as defence, police and roads, but they include also merit goods such as education and healthcare, which are explained in the next chapter.

> **examiner's voice**
> Don't confuse a public good with a government good.

Box 10.2 Rational herdsmen?

In 1968, Garrett Harding published 'The Tragedy of the Commons' in *Science* (the journal of the American Association for the Advancement of Sciences).

The Tragedy of the Commons

Picture a pasture open to all. Each herdsman will try to keep as many cattle as possible on the commons. Such an arrangement may work reasonably well for centuries because tribal wars, poaching and disease keep the numbers of both man and beast well below the carrying capacity of the land. Finally, however, comes the day of reckoning...

As a rational human being, each herdsman seeks to maximise his gain. He asks, 'What is the utility to me of adding one more animal to my herd?' This utility has one negative and one positive component. The positive component is a function of the increment of one animal. Since the herdsman receives all the proceeds from the sale of the additional animal, the positive utility is nearly +1. The negative component is a function of the additional over-grazing created by one more animal. Since, however, the effects of over-grazing are shared by all the herdsmen, the negative utility of any particular decision-making herdsman is only a fraction of −1.

Adding together the component partial utilities, the rational herdsman concludes that the only sensible course for him to pursue is to add another animal to his herd. And another. But this is the conclusion reached by each and every rational herdsman sharing a commons. Therein is the tragedy. Each man is locked into a system that compels him to increase his herd without limit — in a world that is limited. Ruin is the destination toward which all men rush, each pursuing his own best interest in a society that believes in the freedom of the commons. Freedom of the commons brings ruin to all.

Follow-up question

Do you agree that over-fishing of North Sea cod and global warming are the result of the Tragedy of the Commons? Justify your answer.

Externalities

An **externality** is a special type of public good or public 'bad' which is 'dumped' by those who produce it on other people (known as third parties) who receive or consume it, whether or not they choose to. The key feature of an externality is that

there is no market in which it can be bought or sold — externalities are produced and received *outside* the market, providing another example of a missing market.

As with the public goods and public bads, externalities provide examples of the free-rider problem. The provider of an external benefit (or positive externality), such as a beautiful view, cannot charge a market price to any willing free-riders who enjoy it, while conversely, the unwilling free-riders who receive or consume external costs (or negative externalities), such as pollution and noise, cannot charge a price to the polluter for the bad they reluctantly consume.

Negative externalities or external costs

Consider the power station illustrated in Figure 10.2, which discharges pollution into the atmosphere in the course of producing electricity. We can view a negative production externality (or external cost) such as pollution as being that part of the *true* or *real* costs of production which the power station evades by dumping the bad on others, e.g. the people living in the houses and the businesses in the commercial forestry industry. The price that the consumer pays for the good (electricity) reflects only the *money* costs of production, and not all the *real* costs, which include the external costs (including the eyesore or visual pollution also

> ### key term
> **Externality** A public good, in the case of an external benefit, or a public bad, in the case of an external cost, that is 'dumped' on third parties outside the market.

> ### examiner's voice
> Candidates often fail to understand that externalities are generated and received outside the market. Remember that both public goods and externalities provide examples of missing markets.

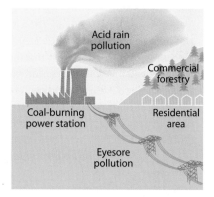

Figure 10.2 The discharge of negative externalities by a power station

shown in the diagram). In a market situation, the power station's output of electricity is thus under-priced. The incentive function of prices has once again broken down — under-pricing encourages too much consumption of electricity, and therefore over-production of both electricity and the spin-off, pollution.

Positive externalities or external benefits

Figure 10.3 shows the power station illustrated in Figure 10.2 again, but I have assumed that the production of electricity yields positive externalities (or external benefits) rather than negative externalities. I have assumed that the power station discharges warm (but clean) water into the lake adjacent to the power station. Warmer temperatures increase fish stocks and commercial fishing boats and private anglers then benefit. Unless it owns the lake, the power station company cannot charge the fishermen for the benefits they are receiving. (You might of course query my assumption that the water discharge creates positive rather than

negative externalities. In all likelihood, disruption of a local ecosystem might cause negative externalities, for example, algae pollution.)

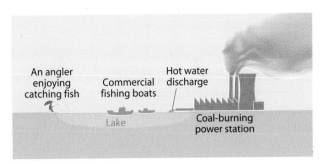

Figure 10.3 The production of positive externalities by a power station

Different types of externalities

As I have explained, externalities divide into external costs and external benefits (which are also known as negative externalities and positive externalities). However, it is possible to go a stage further and identify pure production externalities, pure consumption externalities and externalities involving a mix of production and consumption. Table 10.1 illustrates both these methods of classifying externalities. The two columns to the right of the table depict external costs and external benefits, while the rows in the table show the various forms of production and consumption externalities.

Table 10.1 Examples of the different types of externality

Types of externality	External costs	External benefits
Pure production externalities (generated and received in production)	Acid rain pollution discharged by a power station which harms a nearby commercially run forest	A farmer benefiting from drainage undertaken by a neighbouring farmer
Mixed production externalities (generated in production but received in consumption)	Dust pollution discharged by a brickworks breathed by asthmatic children living nearby	Commercially owned bees pollinating fruit trees in neighbouring gardens
Pure consumption externalities (generated and received in consumption)	Noisy music at a party disturbing neighbouring households	Households benefiting from the beauty of neighbouring gardens
Mixed consumption externalities (generated in consumption but received in production)	Congestion caused by private motorists increasing firms' transport and delivery costs	Commercial beekeepers benefiting from the private gardens of nearby houses

Using marginal analysis to analyse externalities

The last part of this chapter introduces a method of economic analysis which becomes very important in the microeconomics you will study at A2. This is called **marginal** analysis. However, at AS, you are only required to know about, and to

apply, marginal analysis in two contexts. These are externalities (the second of the two topics in this chapter), and merit and demerit goods, which are explained and analysed in the next chapter.

The meaning of the 'margin'

As I said earlier in the chapter, I am writing this book by typing on my laptop computer, alone in my study. Being the only human being in the room, I am the marginal person, namely the last person to have entered the room. But I can hear footsteps — it's my window cleaner returning. As soon as he enters the room, my window cleaner becomes the marginal person. He wants to be paid, but I have no money with me. (Maybe he'll think again about stealing my computer.) Fortunately, my son Tom has heard what's going on and runs into the room with my wallet. Tom is now the marginal person, though I wish he'd brought his own money rather than mine. However, that indeed is wishful thinking.

I hope that this little story gives you a grasp of what is meant by the 'margin'. Whichever economic activity we are investigating, the marginal unit is always the *last* unit of the activity undertaken. If one more unit of the activity is now added, the previous unit, which, up to that point had been the marginal unit, can no longer be classified in this way.

Marginal costs and marginal benefits

Let us turn again to the coal-burning power station illustrated in Figures 10.2 and 10.3. If we focus to start with on negative externalities (and ignore for the time being the possibility of positive externalities), then as I have already explained, the power station incurs the private costs of electricity production, but also discharges external costs which are suffered by other people. I shall now introduce another cost concept: **social cost**. Social cost is defined as **private cost** plus **external cost**:

key terms

Marginal benefit The benefit resulting from the last unit of a good.

Marginal cost The cost of the last unit of a good.

Social cost The total cost of an activity, including the external cost as well as the private cost.

  social cost = private cost + external cost

At the next stage, we bring the concept of the **margin** into the analysis. **Marginal private cost** is the extra cost incurred by the power station when producing the last unit of electricity. Likewise, **marginal external cost** is the extra cost dumped on the wider community when the power station produces the last unit of electricity. And finally, **marginal social cost** is the extra cost (private plus external) borne by everybody, as a result of producing the last unit of electricity. Bringing these together, we get the following relationship:

  marginal social cost = marginal private cost + marginal external cost

or:

  $MSC = MPC + MEC$

Turning now to positive externalities, and using similar reasoning, we arrive at:

social benefit = private benefit + external benefit

and

marginal social benefit = marginal private benefit + marginal external benefit

or:

$MSB = MPB + MEB$

Bringing together marginal costs and marginal benefits

At the heart of microeconomic theory lies the assumption that, in a market situation, an economic agent considers only the private costs and benefits resulting from its market actions, ignoring any costs and benefits imposed on others. For the agent, **private benefit maximisation** occurs when:

marginal private cost = marginal private benefit

or

$MPC = MPB$

However, **social benefit maximisation**, which maximises the public interest or the welfare of the whole community, occurs when:

marginal social cost = marginal social benefit

or

$MSC = MSB$

The important point to understand is that households and firms seek to maximise private benefit or private self-interest, and not the wider social interest of the whole community. They ignore the effects of their actions on other people. However, when externalities are generated, costs and benefits are inevitably imposed on others, so private benefit maximisation no longer coincides with social benefit maximisation.

Using marginal analysis to show how negative externalities cause market failure

At this point, I shall return to a simplification I made earlier in the chapter, when I assumed that when a coal-burning power station generates electricity, only negative externalities are discharged and there are no positive externalities. Given this simplification, the marginal private benefit accruing to the power station from the production of electricity, and the marginal social benefit received by the whole community, are the same and shown by the downward-sloping curve in Figure 10.4. But, because pollution is

key terms
Private benefit maximisation occurs when $MPC = MPB$.

Social benefit The total benefit of an activity, including the external benefit as well as the private benefit.

Social benefit maximisation occurs when $MSC = MSB$.

examiner's voice
At AS, Unit 1 examination questions require use of marginal analysis, but only for externalities and for merit and demerit goods, which are explained in the next chapter.

discharged in the course of production, the marginal social cost of electricity production exceeds the marginal private cost incurred by the power station. In the diagram, the *MSC* curve is positioned above the *MPC* curve. The vertical distance between two curves shows the marginal external cost (*MEC*) at each level of electricity production.

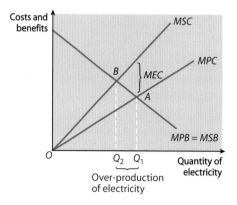

Figure 10.4 A coal-burning power station discharging pollution

The power station maximises private benefit by producing output Q_1, where *MPC* = *MPB*. Q_1 is immediately below point *A* in Figure 10.4. However, the socially optimal level of output is Q_2, where *MSC* = *MSB*. Q_2 is immediately below point *B* in Figure 10.4. The privately optimal level of output is thus above the socially optimal level of production. To put it another way, market forces over-produce electricity by the amount Q_1 minus Q_2. The market fails because the power station produces the *wrong* quantity of the good, namely too much electricity. Over-production has occurred.

Using marginal analysis to show how positive externalities cause market failure

I shall now reverse the simplifying assumption I made at the beginning of the previous section, when I assumed that electricity production yields only negative externalities and not positive externalities. I shall consider an economic activity (tree planting) which generates positive externalities but not negative externalities.

Figure 10.5 illustrates the costs incurred and the benefits generated when a commercial forestry company plants trees. Given that there are no negative externalities, the marginal social cost of tree production is the same as the marginal private cost incurred by the forestry company. This is shown by the upward-sloping marginal cost curve in the diagram. However, tree planting produces a number of positive externalities or external benefits. These include improved water retention in the soil and a carbon sink effect, whereby trees absorb greenhouse or global-warming gases from the atmosphere. Positive externalities such as these mean that the marginal social benefit of tree-growing is greater than the marginal private benefit accruing to the forestry company. In the diagram, the *MSB* curve is positioned above the *MPB* curve. The vertical distance between the two curves shows marginal external benefit (*MEB*) at each level of tree planting.

In order to maximise its private benefit, the commercial forestry plants Q_1 trees. Q_1 is immediately below point X, where $MPC = MPB$. However, Q_1 is less than the socially optimal level of output Q_2, located below point Y, where $MSC = MSB$. Figure 10.5 illustrates the fact that, when positive production externalities are generated, the market fails because too little of the good is produced and consumed. Under-production and under-consumption are depicted by the distance $Q_2 - Q_1$.

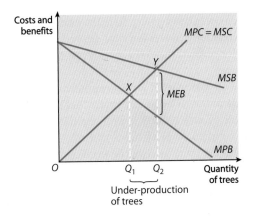

Figure 10.5 Under-production of a positive externality

Government policy and externalities

There are two main ways in which governments can intervene to try to correct the market failure caused by externalities. To eliminate or reduce production of negative externalities such as pollution and traffic congestion, governments can use quantity controls (or regulation), including in the extreme, prohibition of the externality. Governments can also tax the polluter. Regulation directly influences the quantity of the externality that a firm or household can generate. By contrast, taxation adjusts the market price at which a good is sold and creates an incentive for less of the negative externality to be generated.

And just as governments *discourage* the production of negative externalities, in much the same way they try to *encourage* the production of positive externalities. As with negative externalities, the government can choose to regulate and/or to try to change the prices of goods and activities that yield external benefits. In the latter case, subsidies rather than taxes are used to encourage production and consumption. These government policies are fully explained in Chapter 13.

Extension material

In this chapter, I have asserted that public goods and externalities result in missing markets. While this assertion is completely acceptable at AS (and also at A2), many economists now dispute the view that missing markets mean that public goods should be provided by the state, and that externalities must be regulated by the state. I have included below an extract from an article published in *The Economist* in 1991 commenting on the work of Professor Ronald Coase, a British economist working in the UK, who in 1960 published a paper that first started this debate.

Of bees and lighthouses

The crucial question for government policy-makers is this: how common are public goods and externalities? For years it seemed they were common enough. Standard examples were drummed into students' heads. The favourite illustration of a public good was the lighthouse: the conditions of non-excludability and non-rivalrous consumption were both met, and it was obvious that if governments did not provide lighthouses nobody would. The favourite example of an externality, odd as it might seem, was bee-keeping. Here the externality was a benefit, not a cost: bee-keepers provide pollination services for local growers of flowers and fruit. Because they are not paid for this service, there may be a socially less-than-optimal amount of bee-keeping.

Theory concerned itself mainly with asking what form government intervention should take. For instance, part of the trouble in the clean air example is that nobody owns the air; if somebody did, polluters would not be able to dirty it with impunity. Traditional micro-economic theory stressed this link between property rights and efficiency. It is part of the government's job, on this view, to allocate property rights in an efficiency promoting way.

Then, in 1960, Ronald Coase of the University of Virginia published 'The Problem of Social Cost'. Mr Coase argued that, as a rule, no form of government action is required to deal with externalities or public goods. There is no need for taxes, subsidies and public provision; and so long as property rights already exist, there is no need for energetic policies aimed at shifting them around.

The article caused a rethink in microeconomics, a rethink that is still going on. It spurred the growth of a distinct new branch of the subject, called law and economics. And it converted many more economists to the liberal, anti-interventionist wing of their trade.

Choo Choo

Mr Coase's favourite case of externality was an American icon, the wood-burning locomotive whose sparks, regrettably, were prone to set fire to farmers' fields. According to the conventional thinking, what matters in such a case is the allocation of property rights.

Suppose farmers have a right in law to enjoin the railway company not to set fire to their fields: the result is that the company will fit spark-suppressing equipment to their trains, and there will be less damage to the farmers' fields. Alternatively, if the company has an unfettered right to spray as many sparks as it likes, there will be plenty of damage to fields.

Mr Coase asked if this analysis was good economics, and showed that it was not. His main point was simply that legal entitlements — property rights — can be bought and sold. They are commodities whose exchange can be analysed like that of any other. If farmers can legally insist that locomotives are spark-free, they can sell this right to the railway. If the railway is free to spark as much as it likes, farmers can pay them to reduce the sparks that locomotives emit. Not only that, but the outcome will be the same in either case. Suppose farmers have a right to stop the sparks. If this right to emit sparks is worth more to the railway than stopping the sparks is to the farmers (because suppressing sparks is costly, say), then the railway will buy the right to emit sparks from the farmers, and the damage will continue. Suppose instead that the railway is entitled to emit sparks but that this right is still worth more to the railway than to the farmers, in that case, the right will not be sold, and the damage will continue.

The Economist, 23 February 1991

Summary

- A private good, such as a car, is excludable and rival.
- A public good, such as national defence, is non-excludable and non-rival.
- In the case of a public good, people free-ride by benefiting without paying for the good.
- In the case of a public 'bad' such as garbage, people free-ride by dumping it on others, e.g. by fly-tipping.
- A negative externality (external cost) such as pollution is a public 'bad' dumped on others.
- A positive externality (external benefit) such as a beautiful view is a public good that benefits others.
- The margin refers to the last unit undertaken of an activity.
- Private benefit maximisation occurs when $MPC = MPB$.
- Social benefit maximisation occurs when $MSC = MSB$.
- When an activity generates only negative externalities, $MSC > MPC$ and the socially optimal level of the activity is less than the privately optimal level.
- When an activity generates only positive externalities, $MSB > MPB$ and the socially optimal level of the activity is greater than the privately optimal level.
- Governments use regulations, including prohibition and taxation, to prevent or reduce production of negative externalities.
- Governments use regulations, including compulsory consumption, and subsidies to enforce or encourage production of positive externalities.

Questions

1 What is a public good?
2 Define a public good and explain the free-rider problem.
3 With examples, explain the difference between a pure and a non-pure public good.
4 Distinguish between a public good and a government good.
5 Define an externality.
6 Distinguish between, and give examples of, positive and negative externalities.
7 How can a government reduce negative externalities?
8 Use marginal analysis to explain the difference between the privately optimal and the socially optimal level of production of a good when externalities are generated.

Chapter 11

Merit goods and demerit goods

Chapter 10 explained how market failure occurs when externalities are produced by firms, households and, indeed, by the government. A negative externality causes too much of an activity to be undertaken, while conversely a positive externality leads to the opposite outcome, namely too little of the activity. This chapter develops the analysis of externalities, showing how consumption of a demerit good such as tobacco harms both the smoker and other people who breathe the tobacco fumes, while consumption of a merit good such as healthcare benefits both the patient and the wider community.

Learning outcomes

This chapter will:
- explain the difference between a merit good and a public good
- distinguish between a merit good and a demerit good
- explain how externalities lead to market failure in the case of merit and demerit goods
- use marginal analysis to illustrate how externalities lead to market failure
- introduce information problems to explain under-consumption of merit goods and over-consumption of demerit goods
- explain the importance of value judgement when deciding whether a good is a merit or demerit good

The difference between a merit good and a public good

Students often confuse merit goods with public goods, largely because both types of good are often provided by the state, with the provision funded through the tax system. Indeed, both merit goods and public goods provide examples of government goods, which were defined in the previous chapter.

examiner's voice
Make sure you don't confuse merit goods with public goods.

However, merit goods are not the same as public goods. As we saw in the last chapter, a public good is defined by two characteristics: they are non-excludable and non-diminishable. Because of these characteristics, a market may fail to provide a pure public good such as national defence. By contrast, markets can and do provide merit goods such as healthcare and education, but arguably, they under-provide. While public goods can result in a missing market or complete market failure, merit goods (and also their opposite, demerit goods) lead to partial market failure. As goods such as private healthcare and private education clearly show, markets provide merit goods, but they provide the 'wrong' quantity. Likewise, markets provide demerit goods such as tobacco, alcoholic drink and hard drugs such as cocaine, but, by over-providing, they again provide the 'wrong' quantity.

Merit goods, demerit goods and externalities

A **merit good**, such as education or healthcare, is a good or service for which the social benefits of consumption enjoyed by the whole community exceed the private benefits received by the consumer. Consumption by an individual produces positive externalities that benefit the wider community.

As their name suggests, **demerit goods** are the opposite of merit goods. The social costs to the whole community which result from the consumption of a demerit good, such as tobacco or alcohol, exceed the private costs incurred by the consumer. This is because consumption by an individual produces negative externalities that harm the wider community. The private cost can be measured by the money cost of purchasing the good, together with any health damage suffered by the person consuming the good. But the social costs of consumption also include the cost of the negative externalities.

Healthcare is a merit good

key terms

Demerit good A good, such as tobacco, for which the social costs of consumption exceed the private costs.

Merit good A good, such as healthcare, for which the social benefits of consumption exceed the private benefits.

examiner's voice

Many exam candidates assert that any good that is 'good for you' is a merit good. This assertion is wrong.

Examples of merit goods

Education and healthcare are the most well-known examples of merit goods. However, many goods can be classified as merit goods, though you must avoid the temptation that many students succumb to, to define any good that is 'good for you' as a merit good. Most if not all consumer goods are good for you, but economists don't classify them as merit goods. Besides education and healthcare, other examples of merit goods are car seat belts, crash helmets, public parks and museums.

Box 11.1 Museums as merit goods

In 2001 the UK government abolished admission charges in major UK museums, arguing that museums are merit goods that everybody should enjoy without having to pay an entry charge. The text below, taken from the website of an organisation representing the museum industry, was written 5 years later in 2006 and describes the effect of free entry on museum attendance.

Culture Minister David Lammy has signalled the government's intention to continue its policy of free entry to our national museums with the release of figures showing a 5 million rise in visitors since entry fees were scrapped in December 2001.

Despite an 11% drop in visits to all government-sponsored museums and galleries in London since the terrorist bombings on 7 July 2005, figures show that visits to former charging London museums were up by 66% since December 2001.

Of the former charging museums in London, the V&A registered the highest rise in visitor numbers with 94%, the Natural History Museum clocked 83% while the Science Museum saw its visitor figures rise by 54%. However, the largest rise was enjoyed outside the capital, at National Museums Liverpool, which recorded a dramatic increase in visitors of 129% across the period.

'We strongly believe museums should be free to everyone, whatever their background, and should provide visitors with a great experience,' said David Fleming, Director of National Museums Liverpool.

Overall, the regional museums registered a rise of 72% with the Museum of Science and Industry in Manchester recording a healthy rise of 48% and the National Railway Museum in York 43%. The national museums that have always been free, such as the British Museum, National Gallery and Tate, rose by an overall 2% over the same period.

Of the free admission policy, Mr Lammy seemed to indicate continued government support when he added: 'It is a cornerstone of this government's cultural policy. And we can be proud of its continuing success and what it means for our country's museums and galleries, and our tourism industry.'

www.24hourmuseum.org.uk

Follow-up questions

1 Do you agree that a museum is a merit good? Justify your answer.
2 Using the concept of price elasticity of demand, analyse the effect of free admissions on the success or otherwise of the decision to allow free admission to museums located within the UK.

How positive externalities lead to under-consumption of a merit good

As just noted, consumption of merit goods such as education or healthcare produces positive externalities which benefit the whole community. As a result, the social benefit of consumption exceeds the private benefit enjoyed by the consumer. The community benefits from an educated (and civilised) population, and a healthy population means there are fewer people to catch diseases from.

As Figure 11.1 shows, when education is available only through the market, at prices unadjusted by subsidy, too little of the merit good ends up being consumed. Many people (especially the poor) end up uneducated, or at least relatively uneducated. The privately optimal level of consumption is Q_1, where $MPC = MPB$. But this is below the socially optimal level of consumption, Q_2, located where $MSC = MSB$. Free-market provision of merit goods therefore leads to under-consumption, and hence to under-production. In a free market, too few scarce resources are used to produce merit goods.

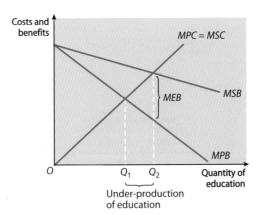

Figure 11.1 A market under-producing a merit good

Note that Figure 11.1 is very similar to Figure 10.5 in the previous chapter. This is not surprising, because the diagrams show how positive externalities result in the planting of too few trees (in Figure 10.5) and in under-consumption of education (in Figure 11.1).

How negative externalities lead to over-consumption of a demerit good

The social costs to the whole community resulting from the consumption of a demerit good such as tobacco or alcohol exceed the private costs incurred by the consumer. The private cost can be measured by the money cost of purchasing the good, together with any health damage suffered by the person consuming the good. However, the social costs of consumption include the costs of damage and injury inflicted on other people, resulting, for example, from passive smoking and road accidents caused by drunken drivers. The social costs also include the costs imposed on other people through taxation to pay for the care of victims of tobacco- and alcohol-related diseases.

*e*xaminer's voice

Make sure you don't confuse a demerit good with an economic 'bad', which was explained in the last chapter. When consumed, a 'bad' yields disutility, whereas a demerit good provides utility to the consumer, at least in the short run.

In the same way as the consumption of merit goods generates positive externalities which benefit the wider community, the consumption of demerit goods leads to the dumping of negative externalities on others. Figure 11.2 shows that too much of a demerit good is consumed when bought at market prices. At least in the short-term, the privately optimal level of consumption is Q_1, where $MPC = MPB$. This is greater than the socially optimal level of consumption, Q_2, located where $MSC = MSB$. Free-market provision of demerit goods therefore leads to over-consumption, and hence over-production. In a free market, too many scarce resources are used to produce demerit goods.

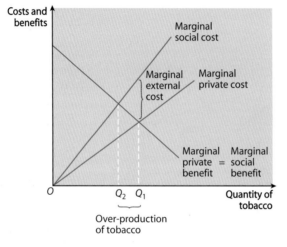

Figure 11.2 How a free market over-provides tobacco

Again, note the similarity between Figure 10.4 in the previous chapter and Figure 11.2. The two diagrams show how negative externalities result in over-consumption of electricity (in Figure 10.4) and tobacco (in Figure 11.2). In each case, over-consumption results from the fact that, at market prices, both goods are too cheap.

Figure 11.2 indicates that some smoking is socially optimal. There may of course be more extreme situations in which the social costs resulting from the consumption of demerit goods are so severe that the good should be banned. But, because of the addictive or habit-forming nature of the consumption of demerit goods such as heroin and cocaine, attempts to ban their use are often counter-productive. Consumption is not abolished; the market is simply driven underground. Indeed, the social costs of consumption in an illegal and completely unregulated market may well exceed the social costs occurring when consumption is legal but closely regulated. Because of this, as I explain in Chapter 13, governments often prefer to discourage or limit consumption of demerit goods by taxation and regulations, which stop short of an outright ban. Examples include spatial limits on where the demerit good can legally be consumed, for example no-smoking areas and licensed premises for the sale of alcohol, restrictions on young people consuming the good, and limits on times of day when alcohol can be consumed in a public place.

Examples of demerit goods

Box 11.2 Smoking yourself 'fit'

Strange as it seems, early cigarette ads, such as the Kensitas ad from 1929, often boasted the 'health benefits' of smoking, claiming 'relief' for asthma, wheezing, hay fever and obesity. In 1946 the American tobacco company Camel ran a series of adverts claiming that Camel were the 'doctor's choice'.

By the 1950s, research began to link smoking to cancer. Today, in developed countries, an estimated four million people a year die from smoking-related diseases.

BBC: Goodbye Tobacco ads

1929 Kensitas magazine advert (left) and 1946 Camels magazine advert (right)

Follow-up questions

1 Most economists agree that tobacco is a demerit good. Why is this so?
2 Why do governments in countries such as the UK and USA now ban advertisements like these?

Cigarettes, and other tobacco products, and alcoholic drink are the two best-known examples of demerit goods. These days, governments in countries such as the UK either ban tobacco and drinks advertising, or severely regulate what the adverts can show. This has not always been the case, as the examples of advertisements for Kensitas and Camel cigarettes show.

Tobacco and drinks companies want to make their products appealing to young people, possibly in the hope that if teenagers develop the habit, they will be hooked on cigarettes and alcohol for the rest of their lives. To combat claims that the

industry has been acting in an irresponsible way, the UK firms that produce alcoholic drinks have set up a public relations organisation, the Portman Group, to monitor adverts that might bring the drinks industry into disrepute. Here is an example of a recent drinks advert that was banned, not directly by the Portman Group, but by a local Trading Standards office.

Box 11.3 Scratch-off label 'too sexy' for UK

A beer bottle featuring a busty model wearing a removable swimsuit on the label has been banned by watchdogs for being too sexy. Labels of 'Rubbel Sexy Lager' featured a curvy blonde in a blue swimsuit which could be scratched off to show her naked.

The beer, brewed in Belgium, has been banned from British shelves. David Poley, chief executive of the Portman Group, said that linking alcohol to sexual success was responsible for problems including the rise in teenage pregnancies and sexually transmitted diseases. The industry has set itself strict marketing rules and this drink has fallen short of those high standards.

However, Geoff Cook, general manager of Beer Paradise Ltd, said that no-one had complained before in the 7 years they had imported the beer. He said: 'The beer has been made an example of. They told us if we carry on selling it we'll be warned and they'll take the licence away, but I don't agree with it at all.'

Website of Realbeer.com, posted 11 April 2007

Follow-up questions

1 With the use of a demand and supply diagram, explain the possible effect of the advertising campaign described in the extract on the quantity of 'Rubbel Sexy Lager' sold in the UK.

2 Should the regulation of advertising be left to self-regulatory bodies such as the Portman Group (an organisation set up by the drinks industry in the UK), or should the government intervene to regulate the advertising of demerit goods such as alcoholic drinks? Justify your answer.

Merit and demerit goods and the information problem

Some economists argue that under-consumption of merit goods and over-consumption of demerit goods stems not so much from the externalities that consumption generates, but from an information problem. Many people become addicted to demerit goods in their teenage years. Because of peer-group pressure and related factors, teenagers are heavily influenced by factors relating to lifestyle and personal circumstances, while at the same time ignoring or downplaying information about how their addictions may affect them many years ahead.

For a merit good, the *long-term private benefit* of consumption exceeds the *short-term* private benefit of consumption. But when deciding how much to consume, individuals take account of short-term costs and benefits, but ignore or undervalue the long-term private cost and benefit. Preventative dentistry provides a good example. Many people ignore the long-term benefit of dental check-ups, and decide, because of the short-term unpleasantness of

key term

An **information problem** occurs when people make wrong decisions because they don't possess or they ignore relevant information.

the experience, not to consume the service. Unfortunately, these people can end up later in life with rotten teeth or gum disease, saying: 'If only I had visited the dentist more often when I was younger.'

In the case of demerit goods, it is the *long-run private costs* rather than the long-run private benefits that are significant. For a demerit good, the long-term private cost of consumption exceeds the short-term private cost of consumption. A person who started smoking at a young age may regret the decision later in life when affected by a smoking-related illness. But when a person starts to smoke and gradually becomes addicted to tobacco, private costs that will only appear many years into the future are often ignored. This means that, because of the information problem, even in the short run a demerit good is likely to be over-consumed.

Merit goods, demerit goods and value judgements

The left-hand and right-hand columns of Table 11.1 list a number of goods that are accepted by most people as clear-cut examples of merit goods or demerit goods. However, for the goods listed in the middle panel — for example, contraception — the position is less clear. Because people have different values and ethics (often related to their religions), contraception is viewed by some people as a merit good, but by others as a demerit good. Whether a good is classified as a merit good or a demerit good, or indeed as neither, thus depends crucially on the value judgements of the person making the classification. This provides an important example of the distinction between **positive statements** and **normative statements**, a distinction first explained in Chapter 1. A positive statement is a statement of fact or a statement that can be tested to see if it is right or wrong. For example, statements that the earth is round and that the earth is flat are both positive statements, though scientific evidence shows that the second statement is wrong. By contrast, a normative statement is a statement of opinion, involving a value judgement. Thus, a statement that the earth *ought* to be flat is normative.

> *k*ey terms
>
> **Normative statement**
> A statement of opinion based on a value judgement.
>
> **Positive statement**
> A statement of fact, or one that can be scientifically tested.

Table 11.1 Merit and demerit goods, and less clear-cut cases

Merit goods	Merit or demerit goods?	Demerit goods
Education	Contraception	Tobacco
Healthcare (e.g. vaccination, preventative dental care, AIDS testing)	Abortion	Alcohol
Crash helmets	Sterilisation	Narcotic drugs, such as heroin and crack cocaine
Car seat belts		Pornography
Museums and public parks		Prostitution

Government policy and merit goods and demerit goods

As in other situations in which positive externalities occur, governments can use regulation (including making consumption compulsory), subsidy or both to enforce or encourage consumption of merit goods. Likewise, governments can use

regulation (including making consumption illegal), taxation or both to prevent or discourage consumption of demerit goods. These government policies are fully explained in Chapter 13.

Vaccination as a merit good

Vaccination, which is a form of healthcare, is listed as a merit good in Table 11.1. But as well as being a merit good in the conventional sense, vaccination also illustrates the free-rider problem, which I explained in the previous chapter in the context of public goods. Suppose that, for a serious infectious disease, vaccination is 100% effective in preventing people catching the disease. The vaccination has no adverse side-effects, but the market price of vaccination is £50. The disease is contagious and will spread rapidly through the country if a significant number of people in the population choose to remain unvaccinated. Given this information, we might conclude that everybody chooses to purchase vaccination for themselves and for their children, believing that complete immunisation is well worth spending £50.

However, some people may choose to remain unvaccinated. This is because for each individual, the best possible solution is to remain unvaccinated — provided everyone else chooses vaccination. In this way, the person saves £50 and free-rides on the rest of the community. If everyone else is vaccinated, there is nobody from whom to catch the disease. However, other people will make their choices in exactly the same way, and if too many people choose to free-ride, the 'best solution' for the individual breaks down. Vaccination becomes under-consumed at market prices and an epidemic occurs. Therefore, it makes sense to subsidise the provision of vaccination, and possibly make it compulsory, to ensure that everyone benefits from the merit good.

Merit goods and uncertainty, moral hazard and adverse selection

Uncertainty about future long-term benefits and costs contributes to under-consumption of merit goods. For example, a person usually does not know in advance when, if ever, the services of a specialist surgeon might be needed. Sudden illness may lead to a situation in which a person cannot afford to pay for costly surgery, if provided solely through a conventional market. One market-orientated solution is for private medical insurance to pay for the cost of treatment at the time when it is needed. However, private medical insurance often fails to pay for treatment for the chronically ill or for the poor. Private insurance may also fail to provide medical care for **risk-takers** in society who decide not to buy insurance, as distinct from **risk-averters**, who are always the most ready customers for insurance.

Like all private insurance schemes, healthcare insurance suffers from two further problems, both of which lead to market failure. These are the problems of moral hazard and adverse selection. **Moral hazard** is demonstrated by the tendency of people covered by health insurance to be less careful about their health because they know that the insurance company will pick up the bill in the event of

examiner's voice
You don't need to know about moral hazard and adverse selection at AS. However, understanding these concepts can add depth to an AS answer on merit goods.

accident or illness. **Adverse selection** relates to the fact that people whose health risks are greatest are also the people most likely to try to buy insurance policies. Insurance companies react by refusing to sell health policies to those who most need private health insurance. For those to whom they do sell policies, premium levels are set sufficiently high to enable the companies to remain profitable when settling the claims of customers facing moral hazard or who have been adversely selected.

Public collective provision, perhaps organised by private sector companies but guaranteed by the state and funded by compulsory insurance, may be a better solution. Both private and public collective provision schemes are a response to the fact that the demand or need for medical care is much more predictable for a large group of people than for an individual.

Summary

- Along with public goods, merit goods such as education are often provided by governments.
- Although both are often government goods, a merit good should not be confused with a public good.
- A merit good is a good that yields positive externalities that benefit the wider community.
- The privately optimal level of consumption of a merit good where $MPC = MPB$ is less than the socially optimal level where $MSC = MSB$.
- A demerit good is a good that yields negative externalities that harm the wider community.
- The privately optimal level of consumption of a demerit good where $MPC = MPB$ is greater than the socially optimal level where $MSC = MSB$.
- Information problems also contribute to under-consumption of merit goods and over-consumption of demerit goods.
- Governments encourage consumption of merit goods through state provision and subsidy.
- Governments discourage consumption of demerit goods through regulation and taxation.
- Private provision of a merit good such as healthcare may be affected by moral hazard and adverse selection.

Questions

1 With examples, explain the difference between a merit good and a public good.
2 Using the concept of positive externalities, define a merit good.
3 Using the concept of negative externalities, define a demerit good.
4 What is an information problem?
5 Use the concept of an information problem to define a merit good and a demerit good.
6 Outline the policies a government can use to promote the optimal level of consumption of merit and demerit goods.
7 What is the difference between a positive statement and a normative statement?
8 How do merit and demerit goods reflect normative views of human behaviour?
9 Explain the concepts of moral hazard and adverse selection.

Chapter 12

Monopoly and other market failures

Much of the earlier part of this book focused on how scarce resources are allocated between different uses by the forces of supply and demand in the competitive markets that were assumed to make up the economy. This chapter switches the focus away from competitive markets to monopoly, examining the extent to which monopoly is a market failure, together with circumstances in which monopoly may improve resource allocation. The chapter also surveys two other possible causes of market failure: the immobility of factors of production and inequalities in the distribution of income and wealth.

Learning outcomes

This chapter will:
- define monopoly and provide examples of monopoly
- survey the causes of monopoly and market concentration
- explain how monopoly may lead to market failure and resource misallocation
- explain the potential benefits of monopoly, including economies of scale
- examine causes of immobility of factors of production
- consider whether income and wealth inequalities lead to market failure

The meaning of monopoly

Economists use the word **monopoly** in two rather different ways, in terms of a *strict* definition and in terms of a rather *looser* definition. The strict definition refers to **pure monopoly**, which occurs when a single firm produces the whole of the output of a market or a pure monopolist faces no competition at all since there are no other firms to compete against. The looser definition refers to a market in which there is a

key terms

Monopoly A market dominated by one firm.

Pure monopoly One firm only in a market.

dominant firm, but there are also some other firms in the market. According to this second meaning, monopoly is a *relative* rather than an *absolute* concept.

An effective monopoly must be able to exclude rivals from the market through **barriers to entry**. However, even when a firm is a monopoly producer of a particular good or service, the monopoly position is weak if close substitutes exist produced by other firms in other industries. The closer the substitutes available, the weaker the monopoly position. A monopoly is therefore strongest when it produces an essential good for which there are no substitutes — or when demand is relatively inelastic.

Examples of monopoly

The US company Microsoft provides a very good example of a monopoly in the second, looser, meaning of the word. Microsoft is the dominant producer in both the US and the world markets of personal computer operating systems. Microsoft is also the largest producer of computer software applications. Its products, Word and Excel, dominate the word processor and spreadsheet markets. Earlier versions of Microsoft's operating system were called Windows, though the latest version has been re-branded as Vista. However, although Microsoft controls over 90% of the PC operating system market, it faces some competition, notably from Linux and Apple.

Pure monopolies, by contrast, are extremely rare. Usually pure monopoly exists only when a government outlaws competition. Until about 20 years ago, **nationalised industries** (industries owned by the state) were more or less pure monopolies. However, this is no longer the case, as all the previously nationalised industries, such as British Gas and BT, have been privatised and exposed to competition. The Royal Mail has been the last nationalised industry to be exposed to competition, recently losing its monopoly over the first class letter post. However, the water industry, which was privatised more than 10 years ago, continues to provide a good example of a pure monopoly. If you live in a town, though possibly not if you live in the countryside, bottled water provides the only substitute to the tap water sold to you by a monopoly water company.

Box 12.1 Is Microsoft a monopoly?

In the late 1990s and early 2000s, Microsoft defended a case in the US courts, in which it was accused of abusing its market power as a monopoly. Although Microsoft eventually lost the case and had to pay a heavy fine, the company was not forced to break up and form smaller separate companies. Arguably, therefore, Microsoft has remained a monopoly to the present day. The following commentary has been adapted from a policy debate, *Is Microsoft a Monopoly?*, conducted during the court case.

The current popularity of Windows does not mean that its market position is unassailable. The potential financial reward for building the 'next Windows' is so great that there will never be a shortage of new technologies seeking to challenge it. Powerful competitors such as IBM, Sun Microsystems and Oracle are spending hundreds of millions of dollars annually to develop new software aimed squarely at replacing Windows. That is one reason why we price Windows so

low. If we increased prices, failed to innovate, or stopped incorporating the features consumers want (such as support for the internet), we would rapidly lose market share.

Bill Gates, quoted in The Economist, 13 June 1998

Everyone who uses a computer or depends on computers has an interest in seeing Microsoft's anti-competitive and anti-consumer practices curtailed. Microsoft's claim that it is defending its right to innovate is a cruel joke in an industry that sees its best innovators attacked by the company's anti-competitive actions. Microsoft's agenda isn't innovation, it's imitation, as well as the imposition of suffocating control over user choices and an ever-widening monopoly.

Ralph Nader and James Love, Computer World, 11 September 1998

Microsoft operating systems account for approximately 90–95% of microcomputer computer operating systems. Microsoft's Windows has become the standard operating system for home and business computer applications. It is fairly clear that Microsoft is the dominant firm in the market for computer operating systems. The question is whether or not the computer firm has used its market dominance to reduce competition.

Follow-up questions

1 Do you agree that Microsoft is a monopoly? Justify your answer.
2 Assess whether personal computer users would benefit if Microsoft is broken up into about ten smaller independent companies.

Natural monopoly

In the past, **utility industries** such as water, gas, electricity and the telephone industries were regarded as **natural monopolies**. Because of the nature of their product, utility industries experience a particular marketing problem. The industries produce a service that is delivered through a distribution network or grid of pipes or cables into millions of separate businesses and homes. Competition in the provision of distribution grids is extremely wasteful, since it requires the duplication of fixed capacity, therefore causing each supplier to incur unnecessarily high fixed costs or overheads. Until quite recently, utility industries were generally monopolies. However, governments had to choose whether utilities should be publicly owned monopolies or nationalised industries, or privately owned monopolies, possibly subject to public regulation. For historical reasons until the 1980s, most UK utility industries were nationalised industries. In the 1980s and early 1990s, utilities such as the British Gas Corporation and BT were privatised, becoming privately owned utilities. Immediately following privatisation, they remained monopolies, protected from competition, though subject to a certain amount of state regulation, for example OFCOM regulating British Telecom.

> **key terms**
>
> **Natural monopoly**
> A market in which there is only room for one firm benefiting to the full from economies of scale.
>
> **Utility industry** An industry, such as the post, which delivers its service to millions of separate customers.

Box 12.2 Opening up the Royal Mail to competition

On 1 January 2006, the Royal Mail became the final UK <u>nationalised industry</u>, and, with the exception of water, the final <u>utility industry</u>, to be exposed to the full force of competition. The two extracts that follow look at this in different ways.

The first extract, published just before 1 January 2006, shows the worries expressed by a group of MPs on whether the Royal Mail Group can continue to offer a '<u>universal service</u>'.

The second extract, published a year later by Postcomm, the recently established industry regulator, is much more upbeat, lauding the success of the policy to expose the Royal Mail to competition.

House of Commons Trade and Industry Committee Report on the Royal Mail Group

A month before the privatisation of the Royal Mail on 1 January 2006, an influential group of MPs, the House of Commons Trade and Industry Committee, stated that the decision to open up the postal market to full competition is 'untimely' and could threaten Royal Mail's ability to deliver to every UK address.

The MPs warned that intense competition in the market will make it harder to adhere to the 'universal service' commitment to deliver post to all addresses for the same price.

Committee chairman Peter Luff said: 'The committee is really anxious to protect a universal service similar to the one we have at present. If competition is more intense than people are expecting, that service could be threatened in all kinds of ways, particularly as private sector operators cream off more profitable parts of the market.'

Postcomm News Release, December 2006

Postcomm, the independent postal services regulator, has hailed the first year of full competition as a promising start, but warned there are more challenging times ahead for postal operators.

Although the competitive market is only a year old and Royal Mail still has more than 96% of the addressed letters market, the regulator has found that competition has prompted major mailers to look more closely at their mail costs and to take advantage of the choices now available to them.

In the face of full competition, Royal Mail has dramatically improved its service quality.

Postcomm Chairman Nigel Stapleton said: 'Everybody has benefited because, in response to competition, Royal Mail has delivered record service levels. But the Royal Mail must continue to modernise in order to succeed in a competitive market.'

Competition in delivery — the 'final mile' — has thus far been slow to develop, due mainly to the difficulty of competing with Royal Mail's economies of scale.

Follow-up questions

1 Explain the meaning of the underlined terms: nationalised industry, utility industry, universal service.

2 Why is it difficult to expose the Royal Mail to competition in delivering letters over the 'final mile', i.e. to customers' front doors?

Other causes of monopoly

Geographical causes of monopoly

A pure natural monopoly would be rather different to the natural monopolies described in the previous section, occurring when for climatic or geological reasons a particular country or location is the only source of supply of a raw material or foodstuff. Monopolies of this type are quite rare, but geographical or spatial factors quite commonly give rise to another type of monopoly. Consider the case of a single grocery store in an isolated village or of a petrol company that owns all the land around a busy road junction on which it has built a filling station. In the former case, entry to the market by a second store is restricted by the fact that the local market is too small, while in the second example the oil company uses private property rights to exclude immediate competition. In both these examples, no monopoly exists in an absolute sense, since the villagers can travel to the nearest town to buy their groceries, or motorists can drive on to the next convenient filling station. Nevertheless, the grocery store and the petrol station still exercise considerable market power, stemming from the fact that for many villagers and motorists it is both costly and inconvenient to shop elsewhere. Prices charged are likely to be higher than they would be if competition existed in the immediate neighbourhood.

Village shops exercise considerable market power

Economies of scale

Many manufacturing industries, for example the aircraft building industry, benefit from economies of large-scale production. However, the size of the national market, and in extreme cases the world market, limits the number of firms

AQA AS Economics

that can coexist in an industry and continue to benefit from full economies of scale. **Economies of scale** thus help to explain the existence of a natural monopoly; a natural monopoly occurs when there is room in the market for only one firm benefiting from full economies of scale.

> **key term**
>
> **Economy of scale** Falling average or unit cost as a firm increases its size or scale (see Chapter 8).

Government-created monopolies

Governments sometimes create monopoly in industries other than utility industries or natural monopolies. In the UK industries such as coal, rail and steel were nationalised in the 1940s by a Labour government and turned into state-owned monopolies. At the time, the Labour government believed on the one hand that these industries were the commanding heights of the economy, and were essential for the well being and planning of the whole economy. At the same time, the government believed that, on the other hand, state ownership was required for the industries to operate in the public interest, rather than in the narrower interest of their previous private owners.

In other instances, government may deliberately create a private monopoly. Examples include the granting of a broadcasting franchise to a commercial television company or a gambling franchise to a casino. Both these are examples of the state using monopoly to regulate the consumption of a good or service. State monopolies can ensure standards of supply of merit goods such as public service broadcasting, or prevent the worst excesses of consumption of a demerit good such as gambling.

Patent law provides another example of government-created monopoly. Patents and other forms of **intellectual copyright** give businesses, writers and musicians exclusive right to innovations or creative work (such as a novel or a piece of music) for several years, though the right may be difficult or impossible to enforce.

Control of market outlets and raw materials

Firms may try to obtain exclusive control over market outlets in order to deny access to their competitors. UK examples have included oil companies buying up garages and petrol stations and breweries acquiring public houses. In a similar way, firms may obtain exclusive control over sources of raw materials or components for their products, starving their competitors of a source of supply or charging artificially high prices.

Advertising as a barrier to entry

Monopolies and other large firms can prevent small firms entering the market with devices such as saturation advertising. The small firms are unable to enter the industry because they cannot afford the minimum level of advertising and other forms of promotion for their goods which are necessary to persuade retailers to stock their products. The mass-advertising, brand-imaging and other marketing strategies of large established firms effectively crowd-out the newcomers from the market place.

How monopoly may lead to market failure and resource misallocation

Figure 12.1 illustrates how a monopoly may lead to market failure. If the market is competitive, all the firms in the market produce output Q_1, which they sell at price P_1. Suppose a monopoly now replaces the competitive firms. The monopoly uses its market power to restrict output to Q_2 and to hike the price up to P_2. Market failure and resource misallocation occur because, compared to the competitive market, output falls and the price rises, leading to under-consumption of the good the monopoly produces.

examiner's voice

At AS, exam questions may require analysis and evaluation of the case against monopoly and the case justifying monopoly. The two diagrams you need to know are Figures 12.1 and 12.2.

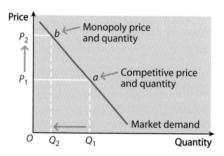

Figure 12.1 A monopoly restricting output and raising the price

The absence of competitive pressure in monopoly, which in competitive markets serves to reduce the profit that firms make, means that a monopoly may be able to enjoy an easy life, incurring unnecessary production costs and thus making satisfactory rather than the highest possible profit. This can occur because the monopoly is protected by entry barriers. As a result, the absence or weakness of competitive forces means there is no mechanism in monopoly to eliminate unnecessarily high costs of production. This is a further reason for resource misallocation.

How entry barriers protect monopolies

Monopolies and firms in concentrated markets use entry barriers to protect the firm's position in the market. There are two main types of entry barrier: natural barriers and artificial or man-made barriers.

examiner's voice

Make sure you understand the meaning of entry barriers and are able to give at least two examples.

Natural barriers, which are also known as innocent barriers, are barriers such as economies of scale and indivisibilities, which have not been created by firms already in the market (i.e. by incumbent firms) to deter new firms from entering the market. Economies of scale mean that established large firms produce at a lower average cost, and are more productively efficient, than smaller new entrants, who suffer from higher average costs of production. Indivisibilities prevent certain goods and services being produced in plant below a certain size. Indivisibilities occur in metal smelting and oil refining industries.

Artificial or **man-made entry barriers**, which are also known as strategic barriers, are the result of deliberate action by incumbent firms to prevent new firms from entering the market. Strategic entry barriers include:

- **Patents** — incumbent firms acquire patents for all the variants of a product that they develop.
- **Setting prices deliberately low** to deter entry by new firms or to kill off small firms which have already entered the market.
- **Deliberately building excess capacity** — firms considering entering a market may be put off by excess capacity owned by firms already in the market. Excess capacity allows incumbent firms to step up production in order to drive down the price to a level at which new entrants cannot compete.

The potential benefits of monopoly

The conclusion that a competitive market produces a better resource allocation than monopoly depends on an assumption that no or few economies of scale are possible in the market in which the firms produce. When substantial economies of scale are possible in an industry, monopoly may lead to a better outcome than competition. Figure 12.2 illustrates a natural monopoly where, because of limited market size, there is insufficient room in the market for more than one firm benefiting from full economies of scale.

> **examiner's voice**
>
> Chapter 8 provides more detail about a firm's average cost curve.

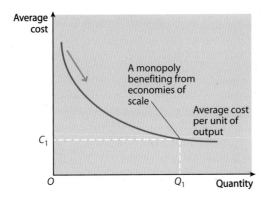

Figure 12.2
How economies of scale may justify a monopoly

In Figure 12.2, economies of scale are shown by the downward-sloping average cost curve. By assumption, a monopoly is able to produce output Q_1 at an average cost (or unit cost) of C_1, whereas competitive firms are unable to produce this output without destroying the competitive market.

A monopoly may also benefit from a second advantage possibly denied to firms in a competitive market. For example, protected by a patent that prevents competitors from free-riding on its success, a monopoly may be able to use high monopoly profit to finance product innovation. Monopoly profit can fund research and development (R&D), which leads to better ways of making existing products and to the development of completely new products.

Factor immobility as a cause of market failure

As I explained in earlier chapters, the price mechanism allocates scarce resources between competing uses in a market economy. (The price mechanism also performs this function in a mixed economy, though in such an economy, the planning mechanism also has an important role.) In both market and mixed economies, the price mechanism operates in two different types of market: the economy's **goods markets** (or **product markets**) and the economy's **factor markets**, including **labour markets**.

As Figure 12.3 shows, households and firms function simultaneously in both sets of markets, but their roles are reversed. Whereas firms are the source of supply in goods markets, in the factor markets firms exercise demand for factor services supplied by households. It is the incomes received by households from the sale and supply of factor services that contributes in large measure to the households' ability to demand the output supplied by the firms in the goods market. Indeed, the relationship between households and firms in the two sets of markets is essentially circular. In goods markets, output or finished goods flow from firms to households in return for money revenues. In factor markets, the money revenues received enable the firms to purchase factor services supplied by the households. The circle is complete when households spend this income on the goods produced by the firms.

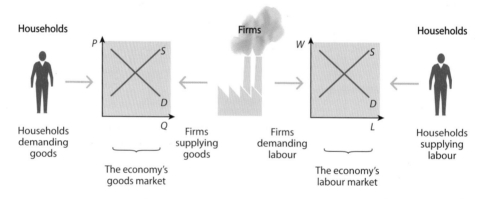

Figure 12.3 *The relationship between goods markets and labour markets*

Usually when economists talk of market failure, they refer to failures occurring in goods markets, such as over-production of demerit goods, a failure to produce public goods and under-production of merit goods. However, market failure can also occur in factor markets and especially in labour markets. Whereas in a fully developed market economy or mixed economy, markets are pretty good at arranging the efficient exchange of goods for money, **labour immobility** means this is often not the case for

> **key term**
>
> **Immobility of labour**
> The inability of labour to move from one job to another, either for occupational reasons, e.g. the need for training, or for geographical reasons, e.g. the cost of moving to another part of the country.

workers. Occupational and geographical immobility of labour mean that economic resources are not fully utilised in areas of high unemployment, while at the same time economic growth is held back by labour shortages in areas, regions and countries benefiting from full employment.

Box 12.3 Polish plumbers

Labour immobility has an international dimension as well as a regional dimension within a nation state such as the UK. As the extract below argues, one of the reasons for the economic success of the USA has been labour mobility across a continent. In earlier times, there was a mass migration of people who wished to escape from poverty and repression in Europe in order to start a new life in America.

Since 1 May 2004, workers in countries such as Poland and Hungary have had a similar opportunity to migrate to the richer countries of western Europe. Arguably, the resulting 'Polish plumber' phenomenon has eased labour shortages and helped to create more flexible labour markets in countries such as the UK, while mopping up unemployment in the poorer countries of the east. However, as the article states, Europe still has a very long way to go to match the labour mobility of North America.

Europe needs more mobility, not less

Britain has been traumatised in recent months by stories about a tidal wave of Polish and Lithuanian workers coming to the UK.

In the USA it is far more common for workers to cross state lines in search of jobs. In fact, such labour mobility is a vital part of the US economy's success.

Just 2% of Europeans live and work in a foreign EU country. Amazingly, that percentage has hardly changed over the last 30 years. It compares with a figure of 8% of Americans who live and work outside their home state.

Whatever the headlines say – Europe needs more mobility, not less.

George Parker, *Financial Times*, 20 December 2006

Follow-up questions

1 Do you agree that labour immobility is an example of a market failure? Justify your answer.
2 Evaluate how UK markets have been affected by the migration of labour from EU countries in central and eastern Europe.

Occupational immobility of labour occurs when workers are prevented by either natural or artificial barriers from moving between different types of jobs. Workers are obviously not homogeneous or uniform, so differences in natural ability may prevent or restrict movement between jobs. Some types of work require an innate ability, such as physical strength or perfect eyesight, which prevent a worker immediately switching between labour markets. Examples of artificial barriers include membership qualifications imposed by professional bodies such as accountancy associations, and trade union restrictive practices which restrict employment to those already belonging to the union. Various forms of racial, religious and gender discrimination are also artificial causes of occupational immobility of labour.

Geographical immobility of labour occurs when factors such as ignorance of job opportunities, family and cultural ties and the financial costs of moving or travel,

prevent a worker from filling a job vacancy located at a distance from his or her present place of residence or work. Perhaps the most significant cause of geographical immobility within the UK in recent years has been the state of the housing market, which itself reflects imperfections in other factor markets. During house price booms, low-paid and unemployed workers in the northern half of Britain have found it difficult or impossible to move south to fill job vacancies in the more prosperous southeast of England. The prices of owner-occupied housing had soared out of reach and there was very little housing available at affordable rents in either the private or the public sectors. At the same time, workers living in their own houses in the southeast may be reluctant to apply for jobs elsewhere in the country, for fear that they can never again afford to move back to southern England.

The distribution of income and wealth

In Chapter 9, when I introduced the concept of market failure, I explained that there are two main ways in which markets fail. Markets can function inefficiently or they can function inequitably. So far, in Chapters 10 and 11, and also earlier in this chapter, I have been focusing on the first of these two types of market failure, with the partial exception of merit and demerit goods. However, the final type of market failure you need to consider results from the inequitable functioning of markets.

Equity means fairness or justness (though in other contexts, such as the housing market, equity has a very different meaning, namely wealth). As soon as equitable considerations are introduced into economic analysis, normative or value judgements are being made about a 'socially fair' distribution of income and wealth, and about the goods and services people ought to produce and consume.

Income is a *flow*, received per week, per month or per year, whereas **wealth** is a *stock*, which for rich people tends to accumulate over time. Examples of income are wages, salaries, rents and the dividend income received by shareholders. Shares themselves, together with other financial assets such as money deposited in banks, are forms of wealth. People also keep their wealth in physical assets, notably property or housing.

In the UK, as in most other countries, the distributions of income and wealth are both unequal, but the distribution of wealth is significantly more unequal than the distribution of income. The link between wealth and income partly explains this. For the better-off, wealth generates investment income, part of which, being saved, then adds to wealth and generates even more income. The poor, by contrast, who possess little or no wealth, have incomes (from low-paid jobs and/or welfare benefits) that are too low to allow saving and the accumulation of wealth. The tax system also hits income harder than wealth. In the UK income is usually taxed, but wealth is largely untaxed (except through inheritance tax and capital gains tax which, for the wealthy, are quite easy to avoid).

Box 12.4 Growing wealth inequality in the UK

In the past, UK governments have used **progressive taxation** and **welfare benefits** directed at the low-income families to redistribute income (but not really wealth) from the rich to the poor. From the 1940s to the 1970s, such policies narrowed inequalities in income distribution. Since the 1970s, however, income and wealth inequalities have widened. As the extract below, from a report by the Joseph Rowntree Foundation, describes, Britain is now more unequal than at any time in the last 40 years. It has been argued that the country was more equal at the beginning of the Victorian era, over 150 years ago. The main causes of recently growing inequality have been a rapid rise in top incomes, for example, City incomes fuelled by huge annual bonuses, and in the case of wealth, the growth of house and share prices.

*k*ey terms

Progressive taxation
A tax that taxes the rich proportionately more than the poor.

Welfare benefits
Transfers of money by the government to people in low income groups or with special needs, e.g. disabled people.

Wealth gap 'widest in 40 years'

Since 1970, area rates of poverty and wealth in Britain have changed significantly. Britain is moving back towards levels of inequality in wealth and poverty last seen more than 40 years ago.

Over the last 15 years, more households have become poor, but fewer are very poor. Even though there was less extreme poverty, the overall number of 'breadline poor' households increased — households where people live below the standard poverty line. This number has consistently been above 17%, peaking at 27% in 2001.

Already wealthy areas have tended to become disproportionately wealthier. There is

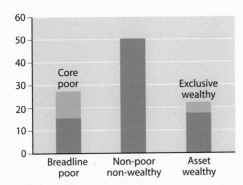

Figure 12.4 The percentage of households that are 'breadline poor', 'non-poor but non-wealthy' and 'asset wealthy'

evidence of increasing polarisation, where rich and poor now live further apart. In areas of some cities over half of all households are now breadline poor.

There has been slower change in wealth patterns overall. The national percentage of 'asset wealthy' households fell slightly in the early 1990s but rose dramatically between 1999 and 2003 — 23% of households are now wealthy in terms of housing assets.

The general pattern is of increases in social equality during the 1970s, followed by rising inequality in the 1980s and 1990s. Changes since 2000 are less clear.

Urban clustering of poverty has increased, while wealthy households have concentrated in the outskirts and surrounds of major cities, especially those classified as 'exclusive wealthy', which have been steadily concentrating around London.

Both poor and wealthy households have become more and more geographically segregated from the rest of society.

'Average' households (neither poor nor wealthy) have been diminishing in number and gradually disappearing from London and the southeast.

Joseph Rowntree Foundation (2007)
Poverty and Health across Britain, 1968 to 2005

Follow-up questions

1 Explain the difference between income and wealth.

2 Why is the distribution of wealth in the UK more unequal than the distribution of income?

Unregulated market forces tend to produce a highly unequal distribution of income and wealth. Some economists, usually of a free-market persuasion, dispute whether this is a market failure. They argue that people who end up being rich deserve to be rich, and that people who end up being poor deserve to be poor. According to this view, the market has not failed — it merely creates incentives which, if followed, cause people to generate more income and wealth, which, via a trickle-down effect, will also benefit the poor.

A version of this argument has recently been used to justify low or non-existent UK taxation for those of the world's super-rich who choose to live in London. If the super-rich, or 'non-doms', are taxed as if they are ordinary UK citizens, then, so the argument goes, they will move to tax havens outside the UK.

However, most economists reject as too extreme the view that the market contains its own morality with regard to the distributions of income and wealth. They argue that markets are 'value-neutral' with regard to the social and ethical desirability or undesirability of the distributions of income and wealth resulting from the way the market functions.

Few economists believe that markets should be replaced by the command mechanism. There is, however, much more agreement that, instead of *replacing* the market, governments should *modify* the market so that it operates in a more equitable way than would be the case without government intervention. Taxing the better-off and re-distributing tax revenues as transfers to the less well-off is the obvious way of correcting the market failure to ensure an equitable distribution of income and wealth.

However, as Chapter 14 explains, redistributative policies can promote new types of inefficiency and distortion within the economy.

> **examiner's voice**
> Make sure you don't confuse *equality* and *equity*. Equality is a positive term that can be measured. Equity is a normative term based on what is considered to be fair or just.

Summary

- Pure monopoly means only one firm in a market.

- A concentrated market dominated by one firm can also be regarded as a monopoly.

- In the past, utility industries were natural monopolies.

- Economies of scale can also lead to monopoly.

- Monopoly leads to market failure if it restricts output and raises prices, compared to the situation in a competitive market.

■ Entry barriers protect monopolies and enable a monopoly to exploit consumers.

■ Monopoly can be justified if economies of scale allow a monopoly to cut prices.

■ Monopoly can be justified if it uses its profit to finance R&D and innovation.

■ Immobility of labour leads to the inefficient use of productive resources.

■ An unequal distribution of income and wealth can be regarded as a market failure because it is inequitable.

Questions

1 Explain two different ways of defining monopoly.
2 Using examples, explain the meaning of natural monopoly.
3 State four causes of monopoly.
4 Explain how monopoly may lead to market failure.
5 Evaluate the case for and against monopoly.
6 Explain how the immobility of labour may lead to market failure.
7 Do you agree that a highly unequal distribution of income is a market failure?
8 Distinguish between equality and equity.

Chapter 13

Government intervention in the economy

When people think of government intervention in the economy, they often focus on the government's budget, in which decisions are made about overall levels of taxation and government spending in the whole of the economy, and on interest rate changes made by the Bank of England. However, these provide examples of government intervention in the macroeconomy, which is part of the subject matter of Unit 2 and Chapters 23 to 25 in particular. The content of this and the next chapter is rather different, examining government intervention at the microeconomic level, in the individual markets that make up the total economy.

Learning outcomes

This chapter will:
- survey the reasons against and for government intervention in markets
- link government intervention in the economy to the correction of market failure
- explain why governments often intervene to provide public goods
- describe how regulation and taxation are used to improve resource allocation in the cases of negative externalities and demerit goods
- describe how regulation and subsidy are used to improve resource allocation in the cases of positive externalities and merit goods
- explain permits to pollute
- describe how government intervention may deal with the problems posed by monopoly
- examine government policies to reduce income and wealth inequalities

The reasons against and for government intervention in markets

To understand why governments intervene in markets in mixed economies such as the UK, it is useful to divide economists (and politicians) into two different groups, those that believe that unregulated markets generally work well, and those who argue that markets are prone to market failure. The former group are non-interventionists who want to leave as much as possible to market forces, while the latter group believe that government intervention can make markets work better.

Pro-free market economists see a market economy as a calm and orderly place in which the market mechanism, working through incentives transmitted by price signals in competitive markets, achieves a better or more optimal outcome than can be attained through government intervention. In essence, risk-taking business men and women who will gain or lose through the correctness of their decisions in the market place know better what to produce than civil servants and planners cocooned by risk-free salaries and secured pensions. And providing that markets are sufficiently competitive, what is produced is ultimately decided by the wishes of consumers who know better than governments what is good for them. According to this philosophy, the correct economic function of government is to act as 'night-watchman' by maintaining law and order, providing public goods and possibly merit goods when the market fails, and generally ensuring a suitable environment in which 'wealth-creating' firms can function in competitive markets, subject to minimum interference and regulation.

> ### *e*xaminer's voice
> *Consumer sovereignty* means the consumer is king. Households and individuals ultimately decide what is produced. *Producer sovereignty* means the producer is king. Firms use monopoly power to exploit consumers.

By contrast, **interventionist economists** believe that all too often markets are uncompetitive, characterised by monopoly power and producer sovereignty, and prone to other forms of market failure. Additionally, uncertainty about the future and lack of correct market information are destabilising forces. By intervening in the economy, especially to correct market failures, the government 'knows better' than unregulated market forces. It can anticipate and counter the destabilising forces existent in markets, achieving a better outcome than is likely in an economy subject to market forces alone.

Correcting market failures

There are various methods open to a government for correcting, or at least reducing, market failures. At one extreme, the government can **abolish the market**, using instead the command or planning mechanism, financed from general taxation, for providing goods and services. At the other extreme, the government can try to influence market behaviour by providing information, and by exhorting firms and consumers to behave in certain ways, e.g. not to use plastic bags. Between these extremes, governments can **impose regulations** to limit people's freedom of action in the market place, and use **taxes** and **subsidies** to alter prices in the market in order to change incentives and economic behaviour.

Government provision of public goods

Because of the free-rider problem (explained in Chapter 9), markets may fail to provide pure public goods such as national defence and police services. When free-riding occurs, the incentive function of prices breaks down. If provided by a market, people can free-ride rather than pay a price, so the firms that are trying to sell the goods can't make a profit. Given that there is a need for public goods, governments often step into the gap and provide the goods, financing the provision out of general taxation.

However, with many so-called public goods (non-pure public goods or quasi-public goods) such as roads, free-riders can be excluded — in this case by toll gates or electronic pricing — and prices can be charged successfully. There may still be a case for free provision by the government outside the market. Provided the road is uncongested, the socially optimal level of road use occurs when motorists can drive their cars without having to pay to use the road. But once congestion occurs, there is a case for road pricing.

examiner's voice
Refer back to Chapters 5 and 9 to make sure that you understand the functions of prices and the meaning of market failure. When the signalling, incentive and allocative functions of prices work well, markets do too, and there is little need for government intervention. But, if one or more of the functions of prices breaks down, market failure occurs. This leads to resource misallocation in the economy, which means that the economy fails to make best use of resources.

Box 13.1 Police services: public good or private good?

The passage below has been adapted from a past Unit 1 examination data-response question. The question asked candidates to evaluate the case for and against the government providing public goods such as national defence or policing.

Should governments provide police services?

Policing is normally considered to be a form of public good which the market can, in principle, provide, but which it would under-provide. However, certain aspects of policing are a private good rather than a public good. The specific task of guarding a particular property, such as a shopping mall, can be done by private security firms such as Securicor. Since the private benefits in such cases are large, there is a strong case for charging the person or business receiving the private benefits.

As an alternative to private security firms, the police could provide specific guard duties and charge for the service. They already charge for providing security inside football grounds. If private security firms were not allowed to operate, the police would have a monopoly and might charge very high prices. Also the quality of the service might be poorer than that provided by private security companies who are competing against each other for business. But on the other hand, the police are likely to have greater experience, and there are economies of scale to be gained from the police providing security services.

Follow-up question

Give your own views on whether policing is a public good, a private good or some form of 'mixed good'.

Government intervention, negative externalities and demerit goods

There are two main ways in which governments can intervene to try to correct the market failures caused by negative externalities and demerit goods. The government can use quantity controls (or **regulation**) or it can use **taxation**. Regulation directly influences the quantity of the externality that a firm or household can generate, and the level of consumption of a demerit good such as tobacco. By contrast, taxation adjusts the market price at which a good that generates the externality is sold, or the price of the demerit good. For example, taxing pollution discharged by power stations and taxing tobacco creates incentives for less pollution to be generated and less tobacco to be consumed.

Regulation or quantity controls

In its most extreme form, regulation can be used to ban completely, or criminalise, the generation of negative externalities such as pollution or the sale and consumption of a demerit good as heroin. However, it may be impossible to produce a good or service such as electricity in a coal-burning power station without generating at least some of a negative externality. In this situation, banning the externality has the perverse effect of preventing production of a good (e.g. electricity) as well as the bad (pollution). Because of this, quantity controls that fall short of a complete ban may be more appropriate. These include maximum emission limits and restrictions on the time of day or year during which the negative externality can legally be emitted. In the case of 'milder' demerit goods, smoking can be banned in public places, while shops would break the law by selling alcohol to younger teenagers.

Taxation

Completely banning negative externalities and demerit goods is a form of market replacement rather than market adjustment. By contrast, because taxes placed on goods affect incentives which consumers and firms face, they provide a market-orientated solution to the problems posed by negative externalities and demerit goods. Taxation compensates for the fact that there is a missing market in the externality. In the case of pollution, the government calculates the money value of the negative externality, and imposes this on the firm as a pollution tax. This is known as the **polluter must pay** principle. The pollution tax creates an incentive, which was previously lacking, for less of the bad to be dumped on others. By so doing, the tax **internalises the externality**. The polluting firm must now cover all the costs of production, including the cost of negative externalities, and include these in the price charged to customers. By setting the tax so that the price the consumer pays equals the marginal social cost of production ($P = MSC$), resource

allocation in the economy is improved. However, a pollution tax, like any tax, itself introduces new inefficiencies and distortions into the market, associated with the costs of collecting the tax and with creating incentives to evade the tax illegally, for example by dumping pollution at night to escape detection. This is an example of **government failure**. Government failures are explained in Chapter 14.

Until recently governments have been much more likely to use regulation rather than taxation to reduce negative externalities such as pollution and congestion. Indeed in the past, it has been difficult to find examples of pollution taxes outside the pages of economics textbooks, possibly because politicians have feared that pollution taxes would be too unpopular. But in recent years, governments have become much more prepared to use congestion and pollution taxes. This reflects growing concern, by governments and public opinion alike, of environmental issues such as global warming and the problems posed by fossil fuel emissions and other pollutants. It may also reflect the growing influence both of green or environment pressure groups such as Friends of the Earth, and of a growing preference to tackle environmental problems with market solutions rather than through regulation. For example, read Box 13.2 — which includes some of the advice given to the UK government by Sir Nicholas Stern about the need for carbon pricing in the *Stern Review on The Economics of Climate Change*, published by the UK Treasury in October 2006.

To analyse how the imposition of a tax on a demerit good such as tobacco affects consumption of the good, refer back at this stage to Figure 6.9 in Chapter 6. The diagram shows that imposing an expenditure tax on a good in fairly elastic demand is effective in reducing demand for the product. However, because of their addictive properties, the demand for demerit goods such as alcohol, tobacco and hard drugs can be inelastic. Taxing demerit goods can raise lots of revenue for the government, but not do much to reduce consumption. And if the tax is set at a very high rate, it may lead to smuggling and to black market activity.

Climate change may be caused by industrial emissions

Extension material

Climate change and market failure

Many people living in advanced developed economies such as the UK agree with Sir Nicholas Stern, whom I quote in Box 13.2, for stating that climate change provides the greatest market failure facing humankind. Governments have not as yet taken sufficient action to reduce the rate at which climate change is taking place, let alone to reduce the total adverse effect of climate change.

An explanation for this, which is provided in the extract below, is that individual governments take too little action because they are victims of what economists call a *prisoner's dilemma game*. You should come across the prisoner's dilemma game, and possibly other examples of *game theory*, in your A2 course next year. However, it is possible, at least in theory, to escape the prisoner's dilemma if governments co-operate to introduce policies to tackle climate change.

Playing games with the planet

At any given summit on climate change, it is never long before some politician declares how 'urgent' or 'vital' or 'imperative' it is to stop the planet from overheating. And yet few governments are willing to tackle the problem by themselves.

That is natural enough. After all, all countries will enjoy the benefits of a stable climate whether they have helped to bring it about or not. So a government that can persuade others to cut their greenhouse gas emissions without doing so itself gets the best of both worlds: it avoids all the expense and self-denial involved, and yet still escapes catastrophe. The most obvious free-riders of this sort are the USA and Australia, the only rich countries that refuse to put a limit on their emissions.

The problem, of course, is that if everyone is counting on others to act, no-one will. Game theorists call a simplified version of this scenario the 'prisoner's dilemma'. In it, two prisoners accused of the same crime find themselves in separate cells, unable to communicate. Their jailers try to persuade them to implicate one another. If neither goes along with the guards, they will both receive a sentence of just one year. If one accepts the deal and the other keeps quiet, then the turncoat goes free while the patsy gets ten years. And if they both denounce one another, they both get five years.

If the first prisoner is planning to keep quiet, then the second has an incentive to denounce him, and so get off scot-free rather than spend a year in prison. A rational, self-interested person would always betray his fellow prisoner. Yet that leaves them both mouldering in jail for five years, when they could have cut their sentences to a year if they had both kept quiet.

Pessimistic souls assume that the international response to climate change will go the way of the prisoner's dilemma. Rational leaders will always neglect the problem, on the grounds that others will either solve it, allowing their country to become a free-rider, or let it fester, making it a doomed cause anyway. So the world is condemned to a slow roasting, even though global warming could be averted if everyone co-operated.

The Economist, 27 September 2007

Box 13.2 The economics of climate change

Climate change presents a unique challenge for economics: it is the greatest and widest-ranging market failure ever seen. The economic analysis must therefore be global, deal with long time horizons and have the economics of risk and uncertainty at centre stage.

Policy to reduce emissions should be based on three essential elements: carbon pricing, technology policy and removal of barriers to behavioural change. Leaving out any one of these elements will significantly increase the costs of action.

The first element of policy is carbon pricing. Greenhouse gases are, in economic terms, an externality: those who produce greenhouse gas emissions are bringing about climate change, thereby imposing costs on the world and on future generations, but they do not face the full consequences of their actions themselves.

Putting an appropriate price on carbon — explicitly through tax or trading, or implicitly through regulation — means that people are faced with the full social cost of their actions. This will lead individuals and businesses to switch away from high-carbon goods and services, and to invest in low-carbon alternatives. Trading schemes can be an effective way to equalise carbon prices across countries and sectors, and the EU Emissions Trading Scheme is now the centrepiece of European efforts to cut emissions.

The second element of climate-change policy is technology policy. The development and deployment of a wide range of low-carbon technologies is essential in achieving the deep cuts in emissions that are needed. Public spending on research and development has fallen significantly in the last two decades and is now too low.

The third element is the removal of barriers to behavioural change. Information policies, including labelling and the sharing of best practice, can encourage behavioural change. They can help consumers and businesses make sound decisions, and stimulate competitive markets for low-carbon and high-efficiency goods and services.

Governments have a role in providing a policy framework to guide effective adaptation by individuals and firms in the medium and longer term. There are four key areas:

- High-quality climate information and tools for risk management will help to drive efficient markets.
- Land-use planning and performance standards should encourage both private and public investment in buildings and other long-lived infrastructure to take account of climate change.
- Governments can contribute through long-term policies for climate-sensitive public goods, including natural resources protection, coastal protection and emergency preparedness.
- A financial safety net may be required for the poorest in society, who are likely to be the most vulnerable to the impacts and least able to afford protection (including insurance).

Follow-up question

What action, if any, has been taken by national governments and by international organisations to implement Sir Nicholas Stern's recommendations since the publication of his report?

Pollution permits

Until recently, the main choice of policy for dealing with the problem of pollution was between regulation and taxation. As I have explained, the former is an *interventionist solution* whereas taxation, based on the principle the polluter must pay, has been seen as a more *market-orientated solution*, but nevertheless one which required the government to levy and collect the pollution tax. In the 1990s, another market-orientated solution started in the USA, based on a trading market in **permits** or **licences to pollute**. And as the Stern Review notes (see Box 13.2), the 'EU **Emissions Trading** Scheme is now the centrepiece of European efforts to cut emissions'.

A permits to pollute scheme (for electricity) still involves regulation, for example, the imposition of maximum limits on the amount of pollution that coal-burning power stations are allowed to emit, followed by the steady reduction in each subsequent year (say by 5%) in these ceilings. But once this regulatory framework has been established, a market in traded pollution permits takes over, creating market-orientated incentives for the power station companies to reduce pollution because they can make money out of it.

A tradable market in permits to pollute works in the following way. Energy companies able to reduce pollution by more than the law requires sell their spare permits to other power stations that, for technical or other reasons, decide not to, or cannot, reduce pollution below the maximum limit. The latter still comply with the law, even when exceeding the maximum emission limit, because they buy the spare permits sold by the first group of power stations. But in the long run, even power stations that find it difficult to comply with the law have an incentive to reduce pollution, so as to avoid the extra cost of production created by the need to buy pollution permits.

Government intervention, positive externalities and merit goods

Just as governments discourage the production and consumption of negative externalities and demerit goods, in much the same way they try to encourage the production and consumption of positive externalities and merit goods. Again, the government can choose to regulate, or to try to change the prices of merit goods and other goods and activities which yield external benefits. In the latter case, **subsidies** rather than taxes are used to encourage production and consumption.

Regulation can force firms and consumers to generate positive externalities. For example, local authority bylaws can require households to maintain the appearance of properties, and the state may order landowners to plant trees. In this situation, it is illegal not to provide external benefits for others. In the case of merit goods, the government may require people to be vaccinated against disease and to wear seat belts in cars and crash helmets on motor bikes.

key term

Emissions trading Emissions trading systems allow policy-makers to set a pollution target, and then issue tradable permits corresponding to that amount. Companies that wish to pollute must hold permits equal to their emissions.

examiner's voice

The introduction of a pollution permit system is an attempt to work with the market and provide a market-orientated way of reducing market failure caused by negative externalities.

examiner's voice

At this stage you should refer back to Chapter 4 to refresh your knowledge of the effect of a subsidy on the supply curve of a good.

key term

A **subsidy** is a payment made by government, usually to producers, for each unit of the subsidised good that they produce. Consumers can also be subsidised, e.g. bus passes given to children to enable them to travel on buses free or at a reduced price.

In the UK, education is both compulsory and completely subsidised, at least for children between the ages of 5 and 16. Low-income families would be in an impossible situation if required to pay for education as well as to send their children to school. Subsidies can of course be paid to private providers of education and healthcare, namely to private schools and private hospitals. However, in the UK, education and healthcare are also provided by the state, forming an important part of public spending. Nevertheless, private sector provision is growing. One reason for growing private sector provision of merit goods lies in the fact that state provision does not necessarily mean *good quality* provision.

Box 13.3 Regulating BAA's monopoly over UK airports

The UK government's monopoly policy is implemented by a number of government agencies, which are responsible to a government department, the Department for Business, Enterprise and Regulatory Reform (until recently called the Department of Trade and Industry). The agencies are the Office of Fair Trading (OFT), the Competition Commission (CC) and various industry-specific regulatory agencies such as the Office of Communications (OFCOM), which can regulate the prices charged by the privatised industries they oversee.

The news item below is extracted from a BBC News Report on the OFT's decision to refer the British Airports Authority (BAA) to the Competition Commission. After the referral was made, the Commission's job was to investigate whether BAA's monopoly power over airports has resulted in anti-competitive business practices.

Commission outlines BAA inquiry
The Competition Commission (CC) says its study into the market domination of airport operator BAA will focus on the firm's level of customer service. The commission said it would look at whether BAA's market domination affected its willingness to invest in, develop and operate its airports.

BAA was referred to the commission by the Office of Fair Trading in March, amid calls for BAA to be broken up. BAA says lack of capacity is the issue, not its ownership of seven UK airports. 'BAA accepts that the experience of too many passengers using London airports is unsatisfactory,' said the firm. 'But the problems of congestion and delay which affect passengers have their roots in lack of terminal and runway capacity, not the ownership structure of BAA.'

Follow-up questions
1 How does the British Airports Authority (BAA) allegedly exercise its monopoly power?
2 Do you agree that passengers will benefit if BAA's monopoly over UK airports is broken up? Justify your answer.

The government and monopolies

In the previous chapter, I explained how monopoly can be both good and bad. Arguably, by restricting output and choice, and by raising the price, monopoly is bad more often than it is good. However,

examiner's voice
Knowledge of the different policies governments can use to deal with a monopoly will also be useful in your A2 studies.

monopoly can be justified in certain circumstances, especially in the case of natural monopoly where economies of scale can reduce the firm's costs.

For this reason, a government may adopt a 'cost–benefit' approach to monopoly, investigating each case on its merits if its advantages outweigh its disadvantages. Other approaches to monopoly are possible, however.

- The **compulsory breaking up** of all monopolies, or 'monopoly busting'. Many free-market economists believe that the advantages of a free-market economy, namely economic efficiency and consumer sovereignty, can only be achieved when the economy is fully competitive. Monopoly, as such, is bad, and impossible to justify. On this line of reasoning, the government should follow an automatic policy rule to break up monopolies wherever they are found to exist. UK policymakers have rarely adopted such a monopoly-busting approach, though powers do exist that allow the government to order the break-up of an established monopoly.

- The use of **price controls** to restrict monopoly abuse. These have been used by regulatory agencies set up by UK governments, to regulate industries that were privatised in the 1980 and 1990s. For example OFGEM regulates energy industries such as gas and electricity, though price controls have mostly been dropped.

- **Taxing monopoly profits**. As well as controlling prices directly, the government can tax monopoly profit to create an incentive for monopolies to reduce prices and profits. Monopoly taxes have not generally been used in the UK, except on a few occasions when a tax has been imposed on the windfall gain landlords receive when the land they own is made available for property development, and when windfall profits received by banks from high interest rates have been subject to a special tax. Also, in the late 1990s, the incoming Labour government imposed a windfall profit tax on the privatised utilities.

- **Rate of return regulation**. In the USA, the regulators have imposed maximum rates of return on the capital that the energy companies employ. This is meant to act as a price cap, as the utilities are fined if they set prices too high and earn excessive rates of return. However, in practice, instead of increasing productive efficiency, rate of return regulation often has the opposite effect, having the unintended consequence of encouraging energy companies to raise costs (knowing they are protected by entry barriers), rather than to cut prices to comply with the rate of return regulation.

- **Changing monopoly ownership**. This can work in one of two ways. Either the government can **nationalise** and take into public ownership large firms or whole industries in the private sector of the economy, changing them into state-owned monopolies. Or the government can sell back to the private sector, or **privatise**, previously state-owned monopolies. I shall explain the choice further in Chapter 14, in the context of government failure.

key terms

Nationalisation The state taking over firms or industries previously in the private sector.

Privatisation The state selling nationalised firms or industries to the private sector.

- **Deregulation** and the **removal of barriers to entry**. Nevertheless, most economists believe that privatisation alone cannot eliminate the problem of monopoly abuse, since it merely changes the nature of the problem back to private monopoly and the commercial exploitation of a monopoly position. The fact that the privatisation of the telecommunication and gas monopolies was accompanied by the setting up of regulatory bodies (originally known as OFTEL and OFGAS) is a recognition of this problem. One method of exposing monopolies – including the privatised utility industries – to increased competition, is to use deregulatory policies to remove artificial barriers to entry.

Government policy and the distribution of income and wealth

The UK government has sometimes tried to make the distribution of income and wealth less unequal and arguably more equitable but not always with success. The main policy that governments use to achieve this end is **fiscal policy**. Fiscal policy is explained in detail in Chapter 24. However, for discussing how economic policy can be used to make the distribution of income and wealth more equal, I shall introduce at this stage just two elements of fiscal policy: **progressive taxation** and **government transfers**.

In a progressive tax system the proportion of a person's income paid in tax increases as income rises, while in a regressive tax system, the proportion paid in tax falls. A tax is proportionate (or a flat tax) if exactly the same proportion of income is paid in tax at all levels of income. The word progressive is value-neutral, implying nothing about how the revenue raised by the government is spent. Nevertheless, progressive taxation is used by governments to achieve the social aim of a 'fairer' distribution of income. But progressive taxation cannot by itself redistribute income or wealth. Progressive taxation used on its own merely reduces post-tax income differentials compared to pre-tax income differentials.

For redistribution to take place, transfers in the government's public expenditure programme are required. The government *transfers* income when paying tax revenue collected from certain groups in society to other groups, without the latter producing any goods or services in return. Although transfers are not always directed to the poor and are not always used to reduce income inequalities, usually they are, at least in countries such as the UK. When used in this way, transfers are also called welfare benefits, for example income support and housing benefit paid to poor families and households in the UK.

key terms

Fiscal policy is government policy that uses the fiscal instruments of taxation, government spending and the government's budgetary position to achieve particular policy objectives.

Government transfers
A payment of money from a government to an individual for which no good or service is given in return.

Progressive taxation
A progressive tax is a tax imposed with the tax rate increasing as income rises. As a result, the rich pay a larger proportion of their income in tax than the poor.

Summary

■ Governments intervene in the economy to try to correct or reduce market failures.

■ Governments often provide public goods directly, arguably because markets fail to supply them.

■ Regulation and taxation are used to discourage the production of negative externalities such as pollution, and to discourage production and consumption of demerit goods.

■ Governments are now using emissions trading or markets in permission to pollute as an extra approach to the problem of pollution.

■ Along with subsidy, regulation is also used to encourage the production of positive externalities such as a beautiful view, and to encourage production and consumption of merit goods.

■ UK governments generally use a cost–benefit approach to reduce the problems caused by monopoly, though other methods of intervention can also be used.

■ Progressive taxation and transfers are used to make the distribution of income and wealth more equal.

Questions

1 Why do governments intervene in markets to provide public goods?

2 How can regulation be used to prevent the discharge of negative externalities?

3 How does a market in tradable pollution permits function?

4 Explain how subsidies and taxes may be used to promote the consumption of merit goods or deter the consumption of demerit goods.

5 Using the concept of elasticity, explain why taxing demerit goods may be relatively ineffective in reducing their consumption.

6 Why do governments rarely ban the consumption of demerit goods such as alcoholic drink?

7 What are the advantages and disadvantages of using a cost–benefit approach to deal with the problems posed by monopolies?

8 'Progressive taxation can help in the redistribution of income and wealth, but it does not actually redistribute.' Explain.

Chapter 14

Government price controls and the problem of government failure

This final chapter on markets and market failure continues and completes the coverage of government intervention in markets. The chapter starts by looking at government intervention to influence or indeed to control prices in competitive or relatively competitive markets. The last part of the chapter completes my coverage of the specification content of Unit 1 by examining the nature of government failures in the economy.

Learning outcomes

This chapter will:

- compare price ceilings or maximum price laws with price floors or minimum price laws
- explain how buffer stock intervention attempts to stabilise the prices of agricultural products
- discuss the problems that buffer stock intervention leads to
- relate buffer stock intervention to the European Union's Common Agricultural Policy
- explain the meaning of government failure
- compare government failure with market failure
- introduce the 'law of unintended consequences'
- provide examples of possible government failures

Price ceilings or maximum price laws

Perhaps the simplest ways in which a government can impose a price control is through the use of a price ceiling or a price floor. Suppose, for example, that in a particular market, say the market for bread, the government imposes a **price ceiling** or **maximum legal**

Key term

Price ceiling A price *above* which it is illegal to trade. Price ceilings, or maximum legal prices, can distort markets by creating excess demand.

price, shown as P_1 in Figure 14.1. Because the price ceiling has been imposed *below* the free market equilibrium price of P^*, it creates excess demand, shown by the distance between Q_1 and Q_2. In a free market, market forces would raise the price and eliminate the excess demand. But, because the price ceiling prevents this happening, there is no mechanism in the market for getting rid of excess demand. Rather than **rationing by price**, households are **rationed by quantity**. Queues and waiting lists occur, and possibly bribery and corruption through which favoured customers buy the good, but others do not.

examiner's voice

Exam questions often ask for a description and an explanation of ways in which government intervention can affect the price of a good or service.

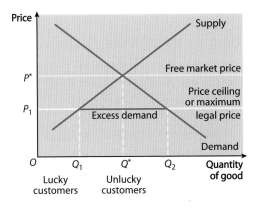

Figure 14.1 The effect of a maximum price law or price ceiling

The emergence of a **secondary market** (sometimes called a black market) is also likely. Secondary markets emerge when primary markets (or free markets) are prevented from working properly. A secondary market is a meeting place for lucky and unlucky customers. In the secondary market, some lucky customers, who bought the good at price P_1, resell at a higher price to unlucky customers unable to purchase the good in the primary market. (Note: later in the chapter I discuss whether a black market provides an example of government failure.)

Price floors or minimum legal prices

Sometimes governments impose **minimum price laws** or **price floors**. For a minimum price law to affect a market, the price floor *must* be set *below* the free market price. Figure 14.2 illustrates the possible effect of the national minimum wage imposed in UK labour markets. A **national minimum wage** rate set at W_1 (which is *above* the free market wage rate of W^*) creates an excess supply

key terms

Price floor A price *below* which it is illegal to trade. Price floors, or minimum legal prices, can distort markets by creating excess supply.

Secondary market A market that comes into existence when the primary market is not allowed to function properly.

of labour, thereby causing unemployment equal to the distance between L_1 and L_2. It may also cause rogue employers to break the law, for example paying 'poverty wages' to vulnerable workers such as illegal immigrants. Note also that whereas a price ceiling imposed *above* the free market price in Figure 14.1 would have no effect on the price at which bread is traded in the market, a national minimum wage set *below* the free market wage rate in Figure 14.2 would have no effect on unemployment. This is the situation in many UK labour markets.

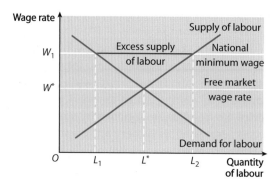

Figure 14.2 The possible effect of the UK national minimum wage

Buffer stock intervention to stabilise agricultural prices

At this point, you should refer back to the reasons given in Chapter 7 to explain why the prices of agricultural goods are often unstable and fluctuate wildly from year to year. To remind you, agricultural prices fluctuate because supply curves shift leftward or rightward in response to factors outside farmers' control, namely climate, weather and the resulting state of the harvest. This cause of price instability is illustrated in Figure 7.2 in Chapter 7.

Because a completely unregulated free market can lead to price volatility, governments, or their agencies, often intervene in agricultural markets to try to stabilise prices. They believe intervention is in the interest of farmers, or consumers, or possibly both groups.

key term

Buffer stock A store of an agricultural good or primary product which is added to in the event of a surplus and released onto the market in the event of a shortage.

examiner's voice

Unit 1 exam questions often require knowledge and analysis of buffer stock intervention.

Agricultural prices are unstable

Buffer stock intervention is one method of stabilising farm prices. Two forms of buffer stock intervention are illustrated in Figures 14.3 and 14.4. The first diagram is similar to Figure 7.2, except that a third supply curve, the 'normal harvest' supply curve, is located mid-way between the 'bad harvest' and the 'good harvest' supply curves. Suppose that the government, or an agency of farmers, decides to stabilise the good's price at the 'normal' year price, P^*. If no intervention takes place, the quantity of the good available on the free market is Q_1 in the event of a good harvest. However, the glut of supply means the free market price has fallen to P_1. But to prevent the price falling so low, and to stabilise the price at P^*, the government buys quantity Q_3 minus Q^*. (Note that farmers wish to supply Q_3 at price P^*, so the difference between Q_3 and Q^* has to be bought by the government and stored in a buffer stock.)

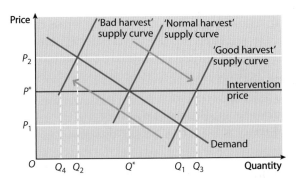

Figure 14.3 Buffer stock intervention to completely stabilise the price of an agricultural commodity

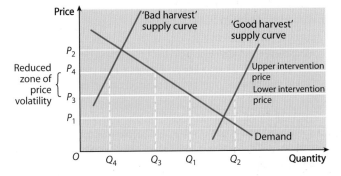

Figure 14.4 A buffer stock policy based on upper and lower intervention prices

Suppose that next year, following a bad harvest, the free market quantity (assuming there is no intervention) falls to Q_2, with the price rising to P_2. To prevent the price rising above P^*, the government supplements supply by releasing from its buffer stock quantity Q^* minus Q_4. The sale of Q^* minus Q_4 prevents the price rising to P_2, and stabilises the price at P^*. (Note, in this case, Q_4 is the maximum quantity farmers are willing to supply at the intervention price P^*, so quantity equal to Q^* minus Q_4 has to be sold by the government to keep the price at P^*.)

Summarising, the government, or an association of producers, accumulates a buffer stock when the harvest is good and releases this onto the market in the event of a crop failure.

Lower and upper intervention prices

Figure 14.4 illustrates a slightly different form of buffer stock intervention. In this case, rather than completely stabilising the price, support buying and selling *reduces* rather than *eliminates* the fluctuations resulting from free market forces. Two **intervention prices** are set — a **lower intervention price** at P_3 and an **upper intervention price** at P_4. Following a bumper crop, the supply curve shifts to the 'good harvest', causing the market price to fall toward P_1. As the price falls through P_3, the support-buying agency steps into the market and purchases a buffer stock. This prevents any further fall in the price, which stabilises at P_3.

> **Key term**
>
> **Intervention price** A price at which a buffer stock agency starts to buy or sell a good, thereby adding to or depleting the buffer stock.

Suppose that next year, following a bad harvest, market forces cause the price to rise toward P_2. When the price reaches the upper intervention price of P_4, the government once again steps into the market, selling Q_3 minus Q_4 from the buffer stock. The release of the buffer stock prevents the price rising above P_4.

By purchasing a buffer stock when the price falls to the lower intervention price of P_3, and selling from the buffer stock when the price rises to the upper intervention price of P_4, support buying is meant to be self-financing. In theory, costs of management and administration are financed from the margin between the lower and upper intervention prices. In practice, however, buffer stock intervention leads to a number of problems, as I explain in the next section.

> **examiner's voice**
>
> Exam candidates sometimes confuse the decision to hold back the supply of a good i.e. a retention policy with buffer stock intervention. The EU's set-aside policy was a form of retention policy and a response to the over-production that resulted from setting support prices too high.

Box 14.1 The EU's Common Agricultural Policy and support buying

For many years after its creation in 1962, the support buying of commodities such as butter, wheat and wine was one of the most important parts of the EU's Common Agricultural Policy (CAP). However, the prices at which the CAP intervened and began to buy up agricultural goods were set too high. Attracted by the high guaranteed prices, too many farmers (usually those owning very large farms) switched into producing the supported products. As a result, grain and butter 'mountains' and a wine 'lake' accumulated. Some of the CAP's main features are explained below in the extract from a BBC News item.

Grain 'mountains' accumulated

The Common Agricultural Policy

The CAP is regarded by some as one of the EU's most successful policies, and by others as a scandalous waste of money.

The objectives of the CAP are:

- to increase productivity
- to ensure fair living standards for the agricultural community
- to stabilise markets
- to ensure availability of food
- to provide food at reasonable prices

Agriculture has been one of the flagship areas of European collaboration since the early days of the European Economic Community. In negotiations on the creation of a Common Market, France insisted on a system of agricultural subsidies as its price for agreeing to free trade in industrial goods.

The CAP began operating in 1962, with the European Economic Community intervening to buy farm output when the market price fell below an agreed target level. This helped reduce Europe's reliance on imported food but led before long to over-production, and the creation of 'mountains' and 'lakes' of surplus food and drink.

France is by far the biggest recipient of CAP funds — in 2004 it received 22% of the total.

Most of the CAP money goes to the biggest farmers — large agribusinesses and hereditary landowners. The sugar company Tate & Lyle was the biggest recipient of CAP funds in the UK in 2005, receiving £127m (€186m). It has been calculated that 80% of the funds go to just 20% of EU farmers, while at the other end of the scale, 40% of farmers share just 8% of the funds.

Until 1992, most of the CAP budget was spent on price support: farmers were guaranteed a minimum price for their crop and the more they produced, the bigger the subsidy they received.

Critics argue that the CAP costs too much and benefits relatively few people. Only 5% of EU citizens — 10 million people — work in agriculture, and the sector generates just 1.6% of EU GDP.

CAP reforms include:

- 1992: direct payments and set-aside introduced
- 1995: rural development aid phased in
- 2002: subsidy ceiling frozen until 2013
- 2003: subsidies decoupled from production levels and made dependent on animal welfare and environmental protection
- 2005: sugar reform tabled

Follow-up questions

1 In recent years and with varying degrees of success, the EU has reformed the CAP and its system of support buying. Why has reform been necessary?

2 Has the CAP been 'one of the EU's most successful policies', or has it been 'a scandalous waste of money'? Justify your answer

Problems resulting from buffer stock policies

Buffer stock policies can cause a number of problems, which harm and can ultimately undermine both the policy and the agricultural economy. The problems include:

- Good and bad harvests may not alternate. A succession of bad harvests could lead to a situation in which the government's buffer stock was exhausted and it could no longer prevent the price from rising.
- However, the opposite problem of over-production is more likely. A succession of good harvests could result in continuous

examiner's voice

Buffer stock intervention can lead to government failure. It is important to understand the problems that buffer stock intervention causes.

over-production, with the government or support agency accumulating an ever-growing buffer stock.

- As a result, the fund used to finance the purchase of the buffer stock may run out. A few years ago, the tin-producers support-buying scheme collapsed, basically because it ran out of money.
- Over-production occurs if farmers stop producing crops which lack government support, and start producing crops which are supported. The supply curve of these crops will shift permanently to the right as more farmers enter the market, leading to permanent over-production.

Farm support policies in the UK and the European Union

In 1973 the UK joined what is now called the European Union (EU), and a fundamental change took place in British agricultural policy. UK farmers are relatively high-cost producers when compared to farmers in such countries as the USA, Canada and Australia, but they are efficient within the constraints imposed by the British climate and average farm size. Compared with many European farmers employed on even smaller and less mechanised farms, British farmers are relatively low-cost producers.

Before the UK joined the EU, **deficiency payments**, which were a form of producer subsidy, were the main form of agricultural support. Deficiency payments provided cheap food for the British population, while ensuring the incomes of domestic farmers. Imports of food were allowed into the UK at the world price and subsidies were paid to British farmers to keep them in business.

By contrast, the EU's Common Agricultural Policy (CAP) results in relatively expensive food for consumers. The CAP imposes an **external tariff** or **levy**, which brings the price of imported food up to the level of European costs of production. The levy has increased EU food production, but at the expense of cheap food imports.

The levy on food imports is tied in with a support-buying policy based on the intervention prices similar to the one I described earlier. However, as I have already explained, lower intervention prices have often been set too high, resulting in the accumulation of butter and wheat mountains, wine lakes and over-production in general. Prices can only be sustained if the CAP intervenes continuously to purchase excess supply. So far, the political power of farmers, particularly in France, has prevented significant reform of the system. Over-production continues, at great expense to EU taxpayers who finance the CAP. Poor developing countries outside the EU also suffer. They are denied free access to the rich EU export market, and they also suffer from the EU dumping or selling below cost surplus production in their markets, which destroys indigenous agriculture in poor countries.

Government failure

When studying market failure, we assumed that market failure can be reduced or completely eliminated, once identified, through appropriate government intervention, for example by imposing taxes, controls and regulation. But there is another possibility. When the government intervenes to try to deal with a problem, far from curing or ameliorating the problem, intervention actually makes matters worse. When this happens, the problem of **government failure** replaces the problem of market failure.

Government failure versus market failure

Students often confuse government failure with market failure, usually by wrongly arguing that a failed or ineffective government policy is an example of market failure. As Chapter 9 explains, market failure occurs when markets perform unsatisfactorily or badly. As I have noted in the last paragraph, having identified a case of market failure, the government may then intervene to try to reduce or indeed eliminate the market failure.

Government failure, by contrast, occurs when government intervention to correct market failure, or to try to achieve the government's policy objectives, is ineffective and possibly damaging.

key term

Government failure occurs when government intervention in the economy is ineffective, or wasteful or damaging.

examiner's voice

Government failure often results from the failure of interventionist policies to correct market failure.

Extension material

Public interest theory versus public choice theory

The rather benign view of the role of government in the economy — centring on the use of public policy to correct market failure wherever it is found to exist — is part of the **public interest theory** of government behaviour. Public interest theory argues that governments intervene in a benevolent fashion in the economy in order to eliminate waste and to achieve an efficient and socially desirable resource allocation.

Public interest theory was extremely influential in the UK from the end of the Second World War (in 1945) until around 1979. Then interventionist government policies gave way to a revival in the belief in free market forces. At that time, the influence of public interest theory gave way to a growing influence of public choice theory. According to **public choice theory**, not only can *market failure* arise in the situations described in Chapter 9; there is also the possibility — perhaps even the likelihood — of government failure occurring whenever the state attempts to improve on the working of the market. As I explained in Chapter 13, pro-free market economists regard a market economy as a calm and orderly place in which the price mechanism, working through the incentives signalled by price changes in competitive markets, achieves a more optimal and efficient outcome than could result from a policy of government intervention.

The 'law of unintended consequences'

This 'law', which has become very fashionable in recent years, predicts that, whenever the government intervenes in the market economy, effects will be unleashed which the policymakers had not foreseen or intended. Sometimes of

course, the unintended effects may be advantageous to the economy, while in other instances, they may be harmful but relatively innocuous. In either of these circumstances, government intervention can be justified on the grounds that the social benefits of intervention exceed the social costs and therefore contribute to a net gain in economic welfare. But if government activity — however well intentioned — triggers harmful consequences which are greater than the benefits that the government intervention is supposed to promote, then government failure results.

Some examples of possible government failure

Black markets

Earlier in the chapter, I explained how a price ceiling or maximum price law can create excess demand in a market, which is then relieved through trading in a secondary market or **black market**. Price ceilings are normally put in place to protect consumers from high prices. However, the rising price of a product may simply reflect market forces and the changing nature of supply or demand in the market. A higher price might be needed to create incentives for consumers to economise and for firms to divert more scarce resources into producing the good. The price ceiling may prevent this happening. The controlled price can send out the wrong signals and create the wrong incentives, thus contributing to resource mis-allocation. And since it may be a criminal activity to break the price law, black markets are sometimes characterised by corruption and the threat of the use of illegal force.

> **e*xaminer's voice**
>
> There are various forms of black markets or secondary markets. One type results from government-imposed price ceilings, a second from under-pricing of tickets for sport and entertainment events, a third from a government-imposed price floor, and a fourth from banning consumption of a demerit good such as a hard drug.

However, economists of a free market persuasion often justify black markets on the ground that they do the job that the primary market should do, i.e. equate demand with supply. A price ceiling prevents the primary or 'over-ground' market from working properly. Arguably, the touts, spivs and dealers who act as middle men in the black market or underground economy, contribute to better resource allocation, though their contribution would not be needed if there were no price controls. A black market or secondary market only comes into existence because price controls distort the primary market.

Merit and demerit goods

Various examples of government failure possibly occur when the state provides merit goods such as education free or at zero price for the consumer, or taxes or bans production and consumption of demerit goods. When education is provided free by the state, shortages emerge for places in so-called 'good' schools. Parents who are unable to get their children into these schools sometimes lie about where they live, in the hope of winning places in the 'post code lottery' through which the local education authority offers places to the children living nearest to the school.

In the case of demerit goods, the imposition of high taxes on goods such as alcohol and tobacco has encouraged 'booze cruise' trips to France to buy beer, wine, spirits and cigarettes at lower French prices. Not only does this erode the UK government's tax base, it also unnecessarily diverts productive resources into car and van journeys that would not otherwise take place, which in turn leads to unnecessary carbon pollution. And, however worthy it is, banning the production and consumption of demerit goods such as cocaine and heroin creates black markets characterised by crime and racketeering.

> **examiner's voice**
> Merit goods, demerit goods and externalities provide a link between market failure and government failure.

Box 14.2 The landfill tax and government failure

Government policies that aim to reduce the discharge of negative externalities can also lead to government failure. Almost every economic activity produces waste, for example household rubbish and the waste created by building and construction. A large fraction of UK waste is either incinerated (which discharges pollutants into the atmosphere) or collected by local government and placed in landfill sites. Landfill also causes pollution, and a further problem arises as all the available landfill sites fill up.

In 1996, the UK government imposed a landfill tax which it hoped would create jobs and reduce waste. But as the following extract shows, to evade the tax, rogue building contractors and some households began to fly-tip and to dump rubbish in public places and on other people's land. This was an unintended and adverse consequence of a tax that was intended to improve the environment.

We protested, but the lorries kept coming

Millions of tons of rubbish are being dumped illegally in the countryside and, apparently, little is being done to stop it. In the past 3 years, rogue companies have sprung up to take advantage of a loophole in the law.

The government and back-bench MPs blame the Environment Agency, the country's leading pollution watchdog, for not being 'tough enough'. The Agency is asking for the law to be changed and for more money to enforce it.

Many blame the controversial landfill tax, introduced 3 years ago, for the rise in organised unauthorised dumping. The tax increased the costs of taking waste to licensed sites by up to a third. The cost of getting rid of one truck-load of rubble could be as high as £400. Finding alternative dumping grounds, where off-loading a lorry costs little or nothing, allows the unscrupulous to make a fortune. But the cost to the environment is immense.

Villagers in Gloucestershire woke early one morning to the sound of heavy lorries. People were horrified to discover that a local landowner was allowing his land to be used for unauthorised tipping. 'For weeks, the lanes were blocked by big lorries and the noise was terrible,' says Maureen Diss, the chairwoman of the parish council. 'We protested, but the lorries kept coming.'

The Environment Agency says that there are scores of companies dumping waste at more than 1,000 unauthorised sites all over the country. 'At the extreme end of the scale, it is little more than organised crime,' says Steve Lee, the head of waste management policy at the Environment Agency.

Rupert Segar, *Daily Telegraph*, 19 August 2000

Follow-up questions

1 Distinguish between market failure and government failure.
2 How does landfill illustrate both market failure and government failure?

Box 14.3 The growing inequality of income in the UK

An example of government failure?

Over the last 40 or so years, the distribution of income has become more unequal. Some people believe that this is an example of market failure, but others argue that government policies to make the distribution more equal lead to government failure by causing poverty. John Grieve Smith, the author of the extract below (which has been taken from a longer article in the *Guardian*), queries the effectiveness of the policy implemented by the Labour government in the early 2000s. Grieve argues that the UK tax system should be made more progressive. However, a counter argument can be made, that if the rich are taxed more heavily, the incentives to take financial risks and to be entrepreneurial will be weakened. Economic growth then slows down. As a result, the poor end up less unequal (compared to the rich) but also poorer than they would be if greater inequality was allowed to persist.

Agenda for a fairer Britain

This week's revelation that the earnings of chief executives are now almost 100 times that of their average employee comes hard on the heels of a study by the Joseph Rowntree Foundation pointing to widespread dissatisfaction with the current gap between those at the top of the income scale and those at the bottom. It is time the government took more vigorous action to achieve a fairer and more equal society.

The government's tax and benefit policies have stemmed the growth in inequality inherited from the Thatcher years, but have not reversed it. Were it not for the more progressive tax and benefit regime, inequality would have continued increasing. The introduction of the minimum wage has helped the lowest paid, but top salaries have reached levels once regarded as unthinkable. There could be considerable public support for curbing the excessively high salaries and bonuses of company directors.

While the introduction of tax credits has helped many people financially, this has been at a quite excessive cost in worry and frustration, and many people have lost out by not taking up the benefits to which they are entitled. In 2004/05, 18% of those entitled to child tax credits did not claim them. The spread of means-testing means that we are now in the paradoxical position that large numbers of people on low incomes are subject to higher 'withdrawal' (in effect tax) rates on any increase in their income than those at the top of the scale.

John Grieve Smith, fellow of Robinson College, Cambridge, *Guardian*, 31 August 2007

Follow-up questions
1 How can progressive taxation help to make the distribution of income more equal?
2 Do you agree that the high salaries paid to company directors and top managers should be reduced? Justify your answer.

Government failure and monopoly

In Chapter 13, I mentioned that a government could attempt to deal with the problems posed by private monopolies (namely restricting output and choice and hiking up prices) by nationalising the firm or taking it into public ownership. Some 40 and more years ago, British Labour governments nationalised industries such as coal mining in the belief that monopoly problems only arise when the monopoly is privately owned.

However, opponents of nationalisation argued that state ownership produces particular forms of abuse that would not be experienced if the industries were privately owned. These include a general inefficiency and resistance to change which stem from the belief by workers and management in the state-run monopolies that they will always be baled out by government in the event of a loss.

According to this view, monopoly abuse occurs in nationalised industries, not from the pursuit of private profit, but because the industries are run in the interest of a feather-bedded workforce which is protected from any form of market discipline.

In the 1980s and 1990s, the Conservative governments that were opposed to nationalisation decided to denationalise or privatise previously state-owned industries such as coal, gas and electricity. But because the governments realised that, once back in the private sector, a privatised monopoly might use its market power to raise prices at the expense of consumers, government agencies such as OFGEM were set up to regulate and police the privatised industries.

But some critics argue that the regulatory agencies have been weak and ineffective, and that they have lacked sufficient knowledge of technical conditions in the industries they regulate to do their job properly.

Summary

- Governments impose price ceilings or maximum legal prices to prevent prices rising above desired levels.
- A price ceiling imposed *below* the free market price distorts the market and creates excess demand.
- In this situation, a secondary market or black market is likely to emerge.
- Black markets can perform the useful economic function of dealing with shortages and equating demand with supply.

■ Governments impose price floors or minimum legal prices, such as the national minimum wage, to prevent prices falling below desired levels.

■ Buffer stock intervention is used to try to stabilise the prices of agricultural goods and primary products.

■ Support buying of buffer stocks has been an important part of the EU's Common Agricultural Policy.

■ Buffer stock intervention can lead to government failure, generally through the accumulation of unwanted stocks of surplus goods, e.g. butter mountains and wine lakes.

■ Government failure occurs when government intervention in markets leads to unsatisfactory or bad results.

■ There are many different forms of government failure.

Questions

1 Explain how a maximum legal price (a price ceiling) may distort a market.
2 Using a supply and demand diagram, explain how a national minimum wage may increase unemployment in labour markets.
3 What is a buffer stock scheme?
4 Explain why buffer stock intervention often fails.
5 Distinguish between government failure and market failure.
6 Describe three examples of government failure.
7 Outline one way in which government policy towards externalities may result in government failure.
8 How may a government's monopoly policy lead to government failure?
9 In what ways may progressive taxation lead to government failure?

Unit 2

The national economy

Chapter 15

Introducing macroeconomics

This is the first chapter covering the macroeconomic topics in Unit 2. It is important to note that examination questions may be set on the national economies of countries other than the UK. For example, in past examinations, questions have required analysis of the French and Irish economies. On some occasions, questions have asked for a comparison of numerical data taken from a range of industrialised countries, such as European Union (EU) countries, Japan and the USA.

For the most part, future questions are likely to be on the UK economy. If a question is set on a non-UK economy, the data in the question will provide all the necessary information about that economy.

Data-response questions usually test the skills of application, analysis and evaluation, rather than just the display of knowledge. Nevertheless, some knowledge of events that have taken place in the UK economy over the decade or so before your examination is required. Knowledge of the structure of overseas economies is not generally expected. However, the Unit 2 specification does require awareness of the fact that UK economic performance is influenced by the country's membership of the EU, and by external events in the international economy.

examiner's voice

The Unit 2 specification states that: 'Candidates should have a good knowledge of developments in the UK economy over the past 10 years, but should be able to illustrate the economic cycle from UK experience, taking as a starting point the boom of the late 1980s.'

Learning outcomes

This chapter will:
- review the difference between microeconomics and macroeconomics
- introduce different macroeconomic 'schools of thought', such as free-market economics and Keynesianism
- explain how the influences of free-market economics and Keynesian economics have changed over time
- introduce the main topics covered in the rest of Section 3

The difference between microeconomics and macroeconomics

In Chapter 1, I briefly explained the difference between **micro-economics** and **macroeconomics**. In this chapter, I explain the nature of macroeconomics, and its difference from micro-economics, in another way. My starting point is three light bulb jokes about economists. The first joke highlights a key difference between microeconomics and macroeconomics, while the others introduce two opposing schools of thought, each with a very different view on how the macroeconomy functions. The first, and older, school is the free-market or neoclassical school. Free-market economists believe that economic problems can and should largely be solved at the microeconomic level and that government intervention in markets is generally not necessary. The second school is the Keynesian school, named after the economist John Maynard Keynes, who more or less invented macroeconomics. Keynesian economists often justify government intervention in the economy to achieve the government's macroeconomic objectives.

key term

Macroeconomics involves the study of the *whole* economy at the *aggregate* level.

examiner's voice

At this stage, you should go back to Chapter 1 and re-read the brief explanation of the difference between microeconomics and macro-economics, as well as the section on shifts of demand and the extension material in Chapter 3, where ceteris paribus is explained.

Joke 1

Question: How many economists does it take to change a light bulb?
Answer: Eight. One to screw it in and seven to hold everything else constant.

Joke 2

Question: How many free-market economists does it take to change a light bulb?
Answer: None. The invisible hand does it.

Joke 3

Question: How many Keynesian economists does it take to change a light bulb?
Answer: All of them. Changing the light bulb will generate employment, which will increase consumption, which will increase the demand for light bulbs, which will increase the need to change light bulbs...

So what message am I trying to convey with these light bulb jokes? The first joke reminds us of the **ceteris paribus** assumption, important to much of what we study in microeconomics.

key term

Ceteris paribus means holding all other factors in the economy constant when examining one part of the economy. It is an important assumption in microeconomics, but not generally in macro-economics.

By contrast, macroeconomics looks at the *whole economy*, or the economy *in aggregate*. This means that the ceteris paribus assumption seldom holds. For example, if wages are cut in large parts of the economy, we cannot assume there will be no effect on total spending or aggregate demand in the economy.

The second and third jokes relate to the two main schools of economic thought introduced above. In order to understand macroeconomics with any degree of

sophistication, it is important to appreciate how economists from different schools have held very different views on macroeconomic problems and on the type of government policy needed to reduce or solve the problems.

At the macroeconomic level, economists divide into **free-market** and **Keynesian economists**. Free-market economists generally believe that the economy is self adjusting, with the market mechanism automatically bringing about full employment and economic growth — providing that at the microeconomic level, markets are allowed to function freely and are sufficiently competitive. Hence, the message conveyed by the second light bulb joke is that decentralised decision making and the market's 'invisible hand' can achieve optimal resource allocation in a competitive market economy, without the need for government intervention in the economy.

> **k**ey terms
>
> **Free-market economists** are also known as neo-classical economists.
>
> **Keynesian economists** are followers of the economist John Maynard Keynes.

The third light bulb joke, by contrast, gets to the heart of what Keynesian economics is all about. As I explain below, Keynes believed that in a modern economy, people may save too much and spend too little of their incomes. This means unemployment persists in the economy as long as people continue to spend too little.

Keynes's approach to the cause of large-scale persistent unemployment is illustrated in Figure 15.1. Keynes believed that too little spending and too much saving mean the economy produces at a point such as *X*, which lies inside the economy's production possibility frontier. By contrast, free-market economists (as illustrated in the second light bulb joke) believe that in competitive markets, the market mechanism automatically ensures the economy is on its production possibility frontier, producing at a point such as *A* or *B*. According to the free-market view, competitive market forces bring about a full employment equilibrium in the economy (which occurs *on* the production possibility frontier). By contrast, Keynes argued that too little spending in the economy can result in an under-full employment equilibrium, at a point *inside* the production possibility frontier such as *X*.

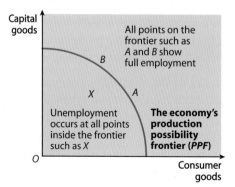

Figure 15.1 Using a production possibility curve diagram to show full employment and unemployment in the economy

Hence the Keynesian message in the third joke: if everybody (including Keynesian economists) were to change light bulbs, spending would increase in the economy (because new replacement bulbs have to be produced and then bought). The initial increase in spending would generate further increases, and so on until full employment is reached.

Don't worry too much if, on first reading, a lot of the information above seems difficult to understand. It has introduced the theme of competing schools of economic thought that I shall now put into a historical context, and return to in some of the remaining chapters of this book. I hope that when you re-read my commentary on the three light bulb jokes after you have completed the macro-economic part of your course, and just before the Unit 2 examination, you will have got the message.

Free-market and Keynesian economics and the history of macroeconomics

The interwar years and the Great Depression of the 1930s

To understand modern macroeconomics, we have to go back to the 1920s and 1930s, when the word 'macroeconomics' hardly existed. Economics was dominated by the free-market or neoclassical orthodoxy mentioned in the previous section. Free-market economists at this time believed that in a competitive market economy, market forces would automatically deliver full employment and economic growth.

The problem was, however, that in the UK economy in the 1920s, and in the wider world economy (especially the USA) in the 1930s, free-market forces did *not* deliver full employment and economic growth. Instead, unregulated market forces produced economic stagnation and mass unemployment. The seminal event of the time was the **Great Depression**, which began around 1930 and lasted for much of the next decade. During the Great Depression, unemployment rose in 1933 to almost 25% in the USA, and in 1931 to 24% in the UK. Regional unemployment in towns such as Jarrow in northeast England rose to as high as 70%, though London, the southeast and the midlands fared much better.

> **Key terms**
>
> The term **depression** has no generally agreed definition. It is best to think of it as a long and deep recession. In the UK, a **recession** is defined as a period of negative economic growth lasting at least 6 months.

Free-market economists responded to the Great Depression by arguing that markets were not to blame for persistent large-scale unemployment. Instead, they argued that mass unemployment was caused by institutional and governmental factors that prevented markets from operating freely. In particular, they blamed trade unions for using monopoly power to prevent the wage cuts deemed necessary to price the unemployed into jobs.

Box 15.1 The Great Depression in the 1930s

These days, a recession is defined in the UK (though not in the USA) as a fall in national output which lasts for at least 6 months. However, a depression or slump are vaguer terms, though they can be thought of as very deep and long recessions. (According to an old joke, a recession is when your neighbour loses his job, a depression is when you lose your own job.)

The 1920s was a period of growing national prosperity in the USA. Nevertheless, the Great Depression, when it arrived in 1929–30, was steeper and more protracted in the USA than in other industrial countries. The US unemployment rate rose higher and remained higher longer than in any other Western country. US GNP fell by 9.4% in 1930 and the US unemployment rate climbed from 3.2% to 8.7%. In 1931, US GNP fell by another 8.5% and unemployment rose to 15.9%. 1932 and 1933 were the worst years of the Great Depression. In 1932, US GNP fell by a record 13.4% and unemployment rose to 23.6%. In total, GNP had fallen in the USA by 31% since 1929 and over 13 million Americans had lost their jobs. Output and employment continued to fall in 1933, but by much less. US GNP dipped by only 2.1% and unemployment rose only slightly, to 24.9%. The US economy began the first stage of a long recovery in 1934: GNP rose by 7.7% and unemployment fell to 21.7%.

A soup kitchen in Chicago during the Great Depression

Follow-up questions

1 Find out how a recession is defined in the USA. Access the article 'Economists who make the recession call' by Stephen Foley in the *Independent*, 8 January 2008.

2 Research whether the US economy entered recession in 2008, and in later years.

In the 1920s and 1930s, free-market economists argued that persistent mass unemployment was caused by wage rates being too high. This explanation is illustrated in Figure 15.2, which shows the economy's aggregate labour market. The aggregate demand curve for labour (labelled AD_L) in Figure 15.2 shows how many workers all the employers in the economy are willing to hire at different real wage rates. Likewise, the aggregate supply curve of labour (labelled AS_L) shows how much labour all the economy's workers are willing to supply at different real wage rates.

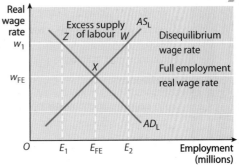

Figure 15.2 The free-market explanation of large-scale unemployment

In the 1920s, free-market economists believed that, provided labour markets were sufficiently competitive, market forces would deliver full employment through eliminating any excess supply of labour in the economy's aggregate labour market. Once the market-clearing wage of W_{FE} was achieved, full employment would occur at E_{FE}. At W_{FE}, the number of workers firms wished to hire exactly equals the number of workers who wished to work. The aggregate labour market would be in equilibrium: there would be no excess supply of labour, and hence no unemployment.

Suppose, however, that trade unions had restricted the supply of labour in order to fix the real wage rage at W_1, which was higher than W_{FE}. In this situation, E_2 workers wished to work, but there were only jobs available for E_1. Free-market economists believed that if wage rates could be cut, the unemployed would be priced into jobs. However, labour market imperfections, notably the monopoly power of trade unions, prevented this from happening. In modern parlance, **wage rates were inflexible**, or **'sticky' downward**. Thus, in the 1920s and 1930s, free-market economists believed that trade unions and excessive and inflexible wage rates were perhaps the most important cause of mass unemployment, and governments were not to blame for unemployment or for the Great Depression.

Keynes's explanation of mass unemployment and the Great Depression

In the late 1920s, John Maynard Keynes, who started his academic career as a free-market economist, began to change his view on the main cause of unemployment. In response to an accusation of inconsistency, Keynes is reported to have said, 'When the facts change, I change my mind — what do you do, sir?'

Whereas Keynes's predecessors explained large-scale mass unemployment and economic stagnation from the point of view of 'don't blame markets or the government for unemployment, blame trade unions', Keynes came to believe that 'if orthodox economic theory is inadequate, a better and more general theory is needed to explain mass unemployment'. Keynes completed his new theory in 1936 with the publication of *The General Theory of Employment, Interest and Money*, commonly referred to as Keynes's *General Theory*.

Keynes's *General Theory* marks the beginning of modern macroeconomics. For over a generation, until approximately 1979, 'Keynesian economics was macroeconomics' and 'macroeconomics was Keynesian economics'. In the years after the Second World War, **Keynesianism** became the new economic orthodoxy.

To capture the flavour of Keynes's view on how the economy works, read Box 15.2, which is adapted from a radio talk given by Keynes in 1934, entitled 'Poverty in Plenty'.

Box 15.2 Keynes on 'Poverty in Plenty'

In 1934, in the depth of the Great Depression, and 2 years before he published his *General Theory*, John Maynard Keynes gave a radio talk in which he expressed his view on the causes of unemployment. Keynes's talk was one of a series, entitled 'Poverty in Plenty', in which a number of economists and public figures gave their views on the title theme. At this time, the UK unemployment rate was 16.7%. Keynes started by summarising the common ground between himself and the other contributors. He then outlined what he saw as the main difference between the various contributors, before arguing that, in his view, the economic system was not self-adjusting.

Is the economic system self-adjusting?

We must not regard the conditions of supply, our ability to produce, as the fundamental source of our troubles. It is the conditions of demand which our diagnosis must search and probe for explanation. All the contributors to these talks meet to this extent on common ground. But every one of us has a somewhat different explanation of what is wrong with demand, and, consequently, a different idea of the right remedy.

Though we all start out in the same direction, we soon part company into two main groups. On one side are those who believe that the existing economic system is, in the long run, a self-adjusting system, though with creaks and groans and jerks, and interrupted by time lags, outside interference and mistakes.

On the other side of the gulf are those who reject the idea that the existing economic system

is, in any significant sense, self-adjusting. They believe that the failure of effective demand to reach the full potential of supply, in spite of human psychological demand being far from satisfied for the vast majority of individuals, is due to much more fundamental causes.

The strength of the self-adjusting school depends on it having behind it almost the whole body of organised economic thinking and doctrine of the last hundred years. Now, I range myself with the heretics on the other side of the gulf. There is, I am convinced, a fatal flaw in that part of the orthodox reasoning which deals with the theory of what determines the level of effective demand and the volume of aggregate employment. The system is not self-adjusting, and, without purposive direction, it is incapable of translating our actual poverty into our potential plenty.

Follow-up questions

1 What is meant by 'effective aggregate demand'?
2 Suggest why there may be too little effective aggregate demand in an economy.

Macroeconomics in the Keynesian era

The **Keynesian era** extended from the late 1940s and early 1950s to the late 1970s. During these decades, governments in the UK, the Netherlands and Scandinavia implemented Keynesian economic policies. Economic policy in the USA also eventually became Keynesian, with the Republican president, Richard Nixon, famously stating in 1971 that 'we are all Keynesians now'. As mentioned previously, the **Keynesian revolution** of the 1930s led to Keynesianism becoming the new orthodoxy, replacing the free-market economics of earlier years.

The Keynesian era covered the decades after Keynes's death in 1946, when economists and politicians who claimed to have inherited the mantle of the now-deceased British economist implemented policies they believed he would have supported.

I shall explain much more about Keynesian economics in the next few chapters. For the moment, I shall restrict myself to saying, at the risk of gross over-simplification, that Keynesian economic policy centred on **managing the level of aggregate demand** in the economy, in order to prevent large-scale unemployment and inflation (a rising price level). For more than two decades after the late 1940s, UK governments used **fiscal policy** and sometimes **monetary policy** to increase aggregate demand. They did this to get rid of demand-deficient unemployment, the type of unem-ployment that Keynes identified at the time of the Great Depression. Sometimes, however, expansionary policies created too much demand, which led to inflation. This meant the government had to reduce aggregate demand to relieve infla-tionary pressures in the economy.

> **k**ey terms
>
> **Fiscal policy** is the use of government spending and taxation to achieve the government's policy objectives.
>
> **Monetary policy** is the use of interest rates to achieve the government's policy objectives.

The free-market counter-revolution

An economic orthodoxy can remain dominant and resistant to being replaced, as long as its theories appear to explain how the economy operates or functions, and the policies based on those theories appear to work. If its theories fail to explain adequately events taking place in the real economy, and if the policies based on those theories are ineffective or don't work at all, the orthodoxy becomes extremely vulnerable to attack.

This happened in the 1930s when free-market economics gave way to the Keynesian revolution. After the Second World War, Keynesianism dominated as long as Keynesian demand-management policies delivered full employment and economic growth, combined with a relatively stable price level. In the 1970s, the same fate befell Keynesian economics as had afflicted free-market economics 40 years earlier. As I shall explain in the next chapter, in the 1970s there was simul-taneous failure to achieve any of the standard objectives of macroeconomic policy, such as full employment and control of inflation. The 1970s became the decade of the **crisis in Keynesian economics**.

Perhaps not surprisingly, therefore, the failure of Keynesianism led to the **free-market counter-revolution**, or revival. In the 1970s and 1980s, an important part of the free-market revival was known as **monetarism**. Monetarists believe that inflation (or a rising price level) is caused by a prior increase in the money supply. It follows that if a government wishes to control inflation, it must first control the rate of growth of the money supply. In the **monetarist era**, monetary policy was elevated to become the main plank of macroeconomic policy. However, monetary policy was used not to manage aggregate demand (demand management was disparaged by the monetarists), but solely to control the rate of growth of the money supply, and thence the rate of inflation.

> **k**ey term
>
> **Monetarism** is the belief that as inflation is assumed to be caused by excessive growth of the money supply, monetary policy should be used to control its growth.

Box 15.3 The ascendancy of monetarism

The following extract shows vividly how monetarism and free-market economics were replacing Keynesianism as the dominant economic orthodoxy in the 1970s and 1980s.

We are all monetarists now

From time to time a revolution in political ideas takes place. The trouble is that the process is so slow and so subtle that hardly anybody notices until it has happened. But if you can spot the thing immediately it is worth noting and discussing. In the end, the country, indeed the world, is governed by ideas and hardly anything else.

In the management of the British economy for the last 20 years or so, the prevailing idea has been a doctrine called 'Keynesianism'. Most of us get a bit impatient when people start going on about various 'isms', but this particular one matters to you. If you have the misfortune to be out of work, if you are a housewife appalled by the constantly rising cost of living, or if you are angry when you look at your wage-packet or salary cheque and see how much has gone in tax, then you

ought to know that all this is a product, not of chance or of the stars, but of an idea.

The big-spending, high-taxing governments we have had have largely created the inflation, unemployment and falling living standards that you now suffer. They did this because they thought Keynes was the 'Great Economist', and this was what he advised. Through unpleasant experience, Keynesianism has been discredited, and Callaghan and Healey are now talking a different language. It is the old language of controlling the money supply, trying to hold back public spending and balancing the budget.

If you think this is just common sense, then you are right. And of course this is excellent news for Britain.

Daily Express, 19 August 1977

Follow-up questions

1 What is monetarism?

2 Why do monetarists believe that it is necessary to control the growth of the money supply?

Supply-side economics

To begin with, monetarism was perhaps the most important part of the free-market revival. However, the UK government largely abandoned monetarist policies in 1985, on the grounds that they hadn't worked. The relationship between the growth of the money supply and the subsequent rise of the price level, which had appeared to be stable *before* monetarist policies were implemented, broke down *after* the UK government attempted to tightly control the growth of the money supply. On 18 October 1985, the *Financial Times* ran the headline 'Monetarism is dead — official' in response to the UK government's admission that targeting the money supply would no longer be practised in any meaningful way.

> **k*ey term***
>
> **Supply-side economics**
> is a branch of free-market economics arguing that government policy should be used to improve the competitiveness and efficiency of markets.

However, monetarism's alleged 'death' did not mean free-market economists immediately reverted to Keynesianism. Instead, free-market theories continued to dominate the macroeconomic agenda, but were now re-branded as **supply-side theory**. These days, Keynesian demand-management policies are often called demand-side policies, to separate them from the **supply-side policies** advocated by free-market economists. Supply-side policies aim to improve national economic performance by creating competitive and more efficient markets. Arguably, for this reason, supply-side policies are more microeconomic than macroeconomic. Indeed, in the early days of supply-side economics, the UK government argued that a redefinition was needed of the respective roles of macroeconomic and microeconomic policies. The government argued that macro policy should be restricted to the limited role of controlling inflation, while micro policy would be used to promote growth and employment. This would be the new orthodoxy.

Where are we now?

In recent years, conflicts between free-market and Keynesian economists have to some extent disappeared, or at least have been downplayed. Members of both schools now agree about the importance of supply-side economics and the need at the macro level to control inflation — a need that to some extent was ignored during the Keynesian era. In the other direction, many free-market economists now accept the Keynesian argument that governments should manage the level of aggregate demand. However, unlike in the Keynesian era, when fiscal policy rather than monetary policy was used to manage aggregate demand, since 1992 monetary policy has been used for this purpose. Interest rates, the main instrument of modern monetary policy, are raised or lowered to try to achieve the inflation rate objective set by the government.

Fiscal policy is now used primarily to achieve supply-side objectives, and to promote the macroeconomic stability deemed necessary for markets to be competitive and efficient. Perhaps the best way to sum up the current consensus

between the free-market and Keynesian traditions is to say that the policy aim is to allow aggregate demand to expand (via monetary policy) so that there is just sufficient demand in the economy to absorb the extra output that successful supply-side policies enable the economy to produce. In a nut shell, demand-side policies now supplement supply-side policies.

The main macroeconomic topics

This chapter has explained where macroeconomics comes from and how it has developed, by placing it in a historical context. It briefly mentions some of the macroeconomic topics, problems and policies in the AQA National Economy specification, which I explore in more detail in the remaining chapters of this book. Chapter 16 explains the objectives of government macroeconomic policy, three of which — full employment, economic growth and the control of inflation — I have touched on briefly in this chapter. Chapters 18 and 19 cover the main body of macroeconomic theory you need to know. Chapters 17, 20, 21 and 22 look in greater detail at the policy objectives of economic growth, full employment, control of inflation and a satisfactory balance of payments. Chapters 23–25 then investigate the policy instruments that governments use to try to 'hit' or achieve the policy objectives. These instruments are: monetary policy (Chapter 23), fiscal policy (Chapter 24) and supply-side policy (Chapter 25).

Summary

- Modern macroeconomics came into existence between the two world wars.
- Free-market or neoclassical economists generally believe that at the macro level, the economy is self-regulating or self-adjusting.
- John Maynard Keynes disputed this view.
- Keynes believed that an unregulated market economy can settle into an under-full employment equilibrium.
- Keynes also believed that large-scale unemployment is caused by deficient aggregate demand.
- The Keynesian revolution in the 1930s led to the Keynesian era in the post-Second World War years.
- The crisis in Keynesian economics in the 1970s led to the free-market counter-revolution in the next decade.
- Monetarism was an early feature of the renewed dominance of free-market economics.
- The decline of monetarism was followed by the growth of supply-side economics.
- In recent years, there have been areas of agreement between free-market and Keynesian economists.

Questions

1 Explain the meaning of macroeconomics.
2 What is another name for the free-market school of economists?
3 How might the macroeconomy be self-adjusting?
4 Illustrate and explain unemployment with the use of a production possibility diagram.
5 Explain why the Keynesian revolution occurred.
6 Why and when was there a crisis in Keynesian economics?
7 What is monetarism?
8 Why did monetarism fail?
9 Relate monetarism to supply-side economics.
10 Explain the difference between demand management in the Keynesian era and at the present day.

Chapter 16

The objectives and instruments of macroeconomic policy

A fruitful way of developing an understanding of how government activity affects the economy at the aggregate level is to approach the macroeconomic role of the government by distinguishing between macroeconomic policy objectives, policy instruments and policy indicators. This chapter provides an overview of what these concepts mean and the linkages between them. Later chapters will examine particular policy objectives such as full employment, economic growth and control of inflation, and the three main groups of policy instrument: monetary policy, fiscal policy and supply-side policy.

> **e*xaminer's voice***
> Examination questions are often set on particular policy objectives or policy instruments.

Learning outcomes

This chapter will:
- distinguish between policy objectives and policy instruments
- outline the five main objectives of macroeconomic policy
- explain how the ranking of the policy objectives has changed over time
- discuss policy trade-offs and conflicts
- briefly explain each of the five main policy objectives
- explain how a 'policy indicator' differs from policy objectives and instruments

Policy objectives versus policy instruments

A **policy objective** is a target or goal that a government wishes to achieve or 'hit'. By contrast, a **policy instrument** is a tool, or set of tools, that the government uses to try to hit one or more of the government's policy objectives.

There are three main sets of policy instruments that UK governments have used in recent years to try to achieve their policy objectives: **monetary policy**, **fiscal policy** and **supply-side policy**. The rate of interest (the cost of borrowing money and the reward for lending money) is the main monetary policy instrument. Taxes, levels of government spending and the government's budgetary position are fiscal policy instruments. Supply-side policy instruments, which are often microeconomic rather than macroeconomic, centre on the methods the government uses to try to make individual markets and industries more competitive and efficient.

A policy objective is a target or goal

TOPFOTO

Since 1997, monetary policy has been implemented by the UK government's agent, the **Bank of England**, rather than by the government itself, though the government sets the policy objective (control of inflation) that the Bank of England has to try to achieve. Fiscal policy is implemented by the government,

> *k***ey terms**
> A **policy instrument** is a tool or set of tools used to try to achieve a policy objective.
>
> A **policy objective** is a target or goal that policy makers aim to 'hit'.

through the government's finance ministry, the **Treasury**. The chancellor of the exchequer, who is in charge of the Treasury, is the government minister (or secretary of state) ultimately responsible for implementing fiscal policy. These days, much of fiscal policy is an important part of supply-side policy. Supply-side policies are implemented by a number of government ministries or departments, the main one being the **Department for Business, Enterprise and Regulatory Reform**, which before 2007 was called the Department of Trade and Industry (DTI).

To find out more about the various policy instruments the UK government uses to try to achieve its policy objectives, refer to Chapters 23 to 25.

The five main macroeconomic policy objectives

Since the Second World War, governments in mixed economies such as the UK have faced the same broad range of objectives. These are:

- to create and maintain full **employment** or low unemployment
- to achieve **economic growth** and improved living standards and levels of economic welfare
- to achieve an acceptable or **fair distribution of income and wealth** between regions and different income groups in society
- to limit or control **inflation**, or to achieve some measure of price stability
- to attain a satisfactory **balance of payments**, usually defined as the avoidance of an external deficit which might create an exchange rate crisis

examiner's voice

Examiners may expect you to appreciate how Keynesian and free-market economists rank policy objectives in different ways.

Keynesian economists also tend to be interventionist, whereas free-market economists are non-interventionist, wishing to minimise government intervention in the economy.

How the ranking of the policy objectives has changed over time

The order in which I have listed the five main objectives of macroeconomic policy shows a broadly Keynesian ranking of priorities. Before the free-market counter-revolution in macroeconomics, Keynesian economists believed that economic policy should be used to achieve full employment, economic growth and a generally acceptable or fair distribution of income and wealth. For Keynesians, these were the prime policy objectives, which had to be achieved in order to increase human happiness and economic welfare – the ultimate policy objective. Keynesians regarded the fourth and fifth objectives as intermediate objectives or possibly constraints, in the sense that an unsatisfactory performance in controlling inflation or the balance of payments could prevent the attainment of full employment, growth and a satisfactory income distribution.

In the early 1980s, things changed. At the time, and partly in response to the fact that inflation had threatened to escalate out of control, free-market economists placed control of inflation in pole position, relegating full employment to a much lower economic priority. This was the era of monetarism, the period of a few years when UK macroeconomic policy revolved around controlling the growth of the money supply in order to control inflation.

Although monetarist policies lasted for only a few years, since the 'death of monetarism' in the mid-1980s, UK governments have continued to give much more attention to the need to control inflation than was the case in the Keynesian era. Indeed, in 1993, the Conservative chancellor Norman Lamont stated that high unemployment was a 'price well worth paying' for keeping inflation under control. This view was echoed in 1998, when under a Labour government, the Governor of the Bank of England argued that 'job losses in the north were an acceptable price to pay for curbing inflation in the south'.

As I shall explain in the next chapter, in recent years the argument about whether controlling inflation is more important than reducing unemployment has to a certain extent been overtaken by events. This is because, up until the time of writing, unemployment has for the most part fallen year by year since 1993, while the rate of inflation has almost always been below 3%. Free-market economists believe that the concurrence of low inflation and low unemployment supports their view that, in order to maintain a high and sustainable level of employment, inflation must first be brought under control.

Trade-offs and policy conflicts

Before the recent success in combining high employment with low inflation, many economists, particularly Keynesians, argued that it was difficult, if not impossible, to 'hit' all five macroeconomic objectives at the same time. Believing they couldn't achieve the impossible, policy makers generally settled for the lesser goal of **'trading off' between policy objectives**. A trade-off exists when two or more desirable objectives are mutually exclusive. Because the government thinks it cannot achieve, for example, full employment and zero inflation, it aims for *less than full* employment combined with an *acceptably low* and sustainable rate of inflation.

In the Keynesian era, UK macro-policy was influenced and constrained by four significant **conflicts** between policy objectives. Governments often tried to resolve these conflicts by trading off between the competing policy objectives. The main conflicts were:

- between internal policy objectives of full employment and growth and the external objective of achieving a satisfactory balance of payments (or possibly supporting a particular exchange rate)

- between achieving full employment and controlling inflation (this is often called the Phillips curve trade-off)

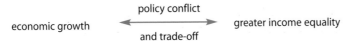

- between increasing the rate of economic growth and achieving a more equal distribution of income and wealth. During the Keynesian era, progressive taxation and transfers to the poor were used (as part of fiscal policy) to reduce inequalities between rich and poor. In recent years, free-market supply-side economists have argued that such policies reduce entrepreneurial and personal incentives in labour markets, which make the economy less competitive and the growth rate slower. In the free-market view, greater inequalities are necessary to promote the conditions in which rapid and sustainable economic growth can take place

```
                       policy conflict
economic growth   <------------------->   greater income equality
                       and trade-off
```

- between higher living standards *now* and higher living standards in the *future*. In the short term, the easiest way to increase living standards is to boost consumption. However, this 'live now, pay later' approach means sacrificing saving and investment, which reduces economic growth.

key terms

A **policy conflict** occurs when two policy objectives cannot both be achieved at the same time: the better the performance in achieving one objective, the worse the performance in achieving the other.

Governments often **trade off between policy objectives** because it may be impossible to achieve two or more objectives simultaneously. They aim for a satisfactory combination.

examiner's voice

You don't need to learn about the Phillips Curve at AS; it is an A2 concept.

policy conflict

current living standards ⟷ future living standards

and trade-off

Developing your understanding of policy objectives and policy instruments

At AS, you need only an elementary understanding of macroeconomic policy objectives and policy instruments. However, as you proceed through the 2-year course leading to the A-level qualification, you should develop a more sophisticated understanding of the two sets of concepts. Figure 16.1 illustrates what you may eventually learn.

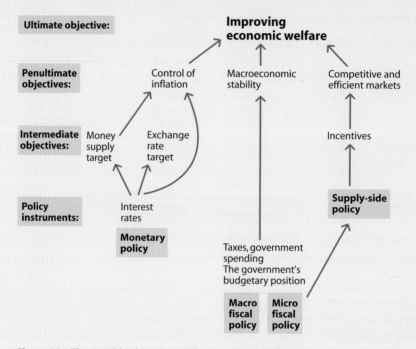

Figure 16.1 The possible objectives and instruments of government economic policy

The figure sets out some of the possible linkages between monetary policy, fiscal policy and supply-side policy instruments and the objectives they may be intended to 'hit'.

The left side of the flow chart shows the instruments and objectives of monetary policy, whereas the right side allows us to relate monetary policy to fiscal policy and supply-side policy. The left side shows control of inflation as the principal objective of monetary policy. However, control of inflation is best regarded as a penultimate policy objective, since improving economic welfare (shown at the top of the flow chart) should be regarded as the true ultimate policy objective.

At this stage of your course, you should not expect to understand all the nuances of the flow chart. Return to the figure towards the end of the AS course, or next year when you are studying A2 macroeconomics.

A closer look at the main policy objectives

Full employment

Although the financial journalist Ed Crooks, quoted in Box 16.1, states that economists don't have a formal definition of full employment, there are at least two definitions commonly used by economists and politicians. The first is often called the **Beveridge definition**. In 1944, a famous White Paper on employment policy, inspired by Keynes but largely written by William Beveridge (an economist at the London School of Economics, who later became Lord Beveridge), effectively committed postwar governments to achieving full employment. In the White Paper, Beveridge defined full employment as occurring when unemployment falls to 3% of the labour force.

> ***e*xaminer's voice**
>
> In Chapter 20, I define full employment in a different way. Either way will do in an exam, provided the definition is accurate and clear.

Box 16.1 What is meant by full employment?

Economists don't have a formal definition of full employment, although they know it when they see it. In the UK, post-war unemployment hit its lowest point in July 1955. Just 215,000 people were out of work — a mere 1% of the available labour force.

That was full employment by anyone's standards. There will always be some people who are unemployed for a little while as they move between jobs, but everyone who wants a job can have one.

According to many economists, 'full employment' translates to 'a level of unemployment that puts no upward pressure on inflation'. In other words, an economy with full employment is an economy where employment is as high as it can be, without labour shortages appearing that lead to rising wages, and hence rising prices.

Ed Crooks, BBC News,
27 September 1999

Follow-up questions

1 What are the different types of unemployment? (See Chapter 20.)
2 Why may the rate of inflation be expected to increase as unemployment falls?

During the 1950s and 1960s, UK unemployment was always below 3%, so full employment, according to Beveridge's definition, was achieved during the postwar Keynesian decades.

However, during and after the crisis in Keynesian economics in the 1970s, UK unemployment rose considerably above 3%, peaking at 11.3% (and over 3 million workers unemployed) in 1986. High unemployment in the mid-1980s was the aftermath to recession at the beginning of the decade. Likewise, the second recession suffered by the UK economy, from 1990 to 1992, led to unemployment rising to peak at 9.9% (and 2.9 million unemployed) in 1993. (Recessions are explained in the next chapter.) Since 1997, UK unemployment has always been less than 5%, falling to meet Beveridge's definition of full employment (at 2.8%) in 2007. However in early 2008 many commentators feared that UK unemployment would

begin to rise again, as economic growth slowed down and the economy teetered on the brink of another recession.

Partly because they regard Beveridge's 3% definition as too arbitrary and lacking any theoretical underpinning, free-market economists favour a second definition of full employment. For them, full employment occurs in the economy's aggregate labour market at the market-clearing real wage rate at which the number of workers willing to work equals the number of workers employers wish to hire. I shall develop the implications of this way of defining unemployment in Chapter 20.

Economic growth and rising living standards

There isn't much point in achieving full employment if everybody with a job then experiences a very low standard of living. Thus, as well as aiming to reduce unemployment, a government must try to achieve an acceptable and sustainable rate of economic growth. Growth facilitates higher living standards, and usually also creates more jobs. As policy objectives, lower unemployment and economic growth generally go hand-in-hand, though some free-market economists argue that a certain level of unemployment is needed to create the supply-side conditions in which growth is best fostered.

Box 16.2 UK GDP growth in 2007

To be a good economist, you need to undertake your own research. A good source to use at AS is the Office for National Statistics (ONS) website (**www.statistics.gov.uk**). Recent figures, accompanied by graphs and written details, are presented in a neat and clear way. Figure 16.2 is an example of the information about economic growth in the UK that was available at the end of 2007.

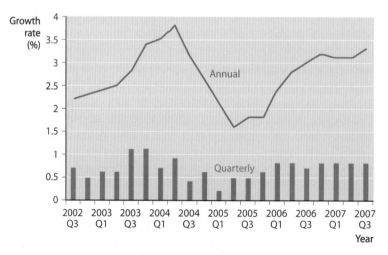

*Figure 16.2
Real GDP annual
and quarterly
growth rates*

GDP rose by 0.8% in the third quarter of 2007, the same rate of growth as in the previous quarter. A slight acceleration in total services was offset by slower growth in production. Total production rose by 0.2% in the third quarter of 2007, compared with an increase of 0.7% in the previous quarter. The deceleration in growth comes mainly from manufacturing, which rose by 0.2% in the third quarter, compared with a rise of 0.8% in the second quarter. Mining and quarrying also contributed to the

slower growth, falling by 0.3% compared with a 1.3% rise in the previous quarter. Electricity, gas and water showed growth of 1.0%, compared with a 0.4% fall in the second quarter.

Total services rose by 1.0% in the third quarter of 2007, compared with a rise of 0.9% in the previous quarter. There was stronger growth in distribution, hotels and restaurants, and transport, storage and communication, partly offset by weaker growth in government and other services.

Follow-up questions

1 Why is economic growth usually considered to be good for an economy?

2 What are the economic disadvantages of economic growth?

A fair distribution of income and wealth

As well as targeting full employment and an acceptable and sustainable rate of economic growth as policy objectives, most governments, especially those in countries where people vote, want to avoid unacceptably unfair or inequitable distribution of income and wealth. For example, most people would agree that a distribution in which 1% of the population received 99% of income, while the other 99% of the population earned hardly anything, is not politically acceptable. But as I first stated in Chapter 12, as soon as equitable considerations are introduced into economic analysis, normative judgments are made about what is a 'socially fair' distribution of income and wealth, and about what *ought* to happen in the economy. To recap on this, refer to the section in Chapter 12 on 'The distribution of income and wealth'. This describes the link between distributional issues and the role of markets in the economy, and also the link to market failure.

> **examiner's voice**
>
> Inequalities in the distribution of income and wealth can also be viewed as a form of market failure and tested as such in the Unit 1 exam.

In a macroeconomic context, a possible conflict also exists between greater equality in the distribution of income and wealth and the policy objective of faster economic growth. Free-market economists argue that people must be incentivised for faster and sustained growth to be achieved. However, this may require greater income inequality to create the conditions in which people are prepared to take financial risks, knowing that if successful, they, rather than other people, will enjoy the fruits of their efforts.

Box 16.3 What is inflation?

Inflation is a general rise in prices across the economy. This is distinct from a rise in the price of a particular good or service. Individual prices rise and fall all the time in a market economy, reflecting consumer choices and preferences, and changing costs. If the price of one item — say a particular model of car — increases because demand for it is high, this is not inflation. Inflation occurs when most prices are rising by some degree across the whole economy.

In September 2007, the UK inflation rate was 1.8%, when measured by the consumer prices index (CPI) (see Chapter 21 to find out about the CPI). The inflation rate is a measure of the average change in prices across the economy over a specified period, usually a year (the annual rate of inflation). If the annual inflation rate measured in March 2007 was 3.1% (see Figure 16.3), then prices on average were

3.1% higher than they had been in March 2006. A typical basket of goods and services costing £100 in March 2006 would cost £103.10 in March 2007.

The reason why I have quoted the UK's inflation rate for March 2007 is interesting. In Chapter 21, I explain how the UK government requires the Bank of England to keep the inflation rate between 1% above and 1% below a target rate of inflation set by the government of 2%. A glance at Figure 16.3 shows that over the period of nearly 10 years (the data in the graph end in September 2007) inflation rose above the 3% ceiling only once, in March 2007.

Inflation then quickly fell back to less than 3%. Any one individual price change could cause the measured rate of inflation to change, particularly if it is large or if the item has a significant weight in the price index. For example, the large recent rise in the price of petrol raised the overall rate of inflation. However, unless the price of petrol continues to rise, the annual rate of inflation will eventually fall back again — providing the prices of other 'big ticket' items such as food do not rise by significantly more than the old (lower) rate of inflation.

Source of data: **www.bankofengland.co.uk/education/targettwopointzero**

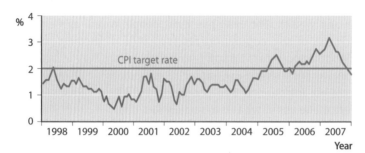

Figure 16.3 Changes in the annual UK inflation rate, 1998–2007

Follow-up questions

1 Do you think that the CPI rate of inflation measures 'true' inflation as experienced by ordinary people?

2 What has happened to the UK rate of inflation since 2007?

Controlling inflation

People sometimes regard controlling inflation as an end in itself and believe that price stability (i.e. zero inflation) or a steady rate of inflation of, say, 2% is a 'good thing'. However, as I explain in Chapter 21, under certain circumstances, inflation can yield benefits. For example, a steady but low rate of inflation may be associated with a climate of consumer and business optimism. If this is the case, then trying to achieve absolutely stable prices may be a bit like 'killing the goose that lays the golden egg'. The deflationary policies needed to remove inflation from the economic system completely may

A steady but low rate of inflation could be viewed as the golden situation

create economic stagnation and highly depressed economic conditions. It is better to live with a degree of inflation (albeit controlled) than to try to bleed inflation completely out of the economy.

To extend this argument a stage further, controlling inflation should be regarded not as an ultimate objective of macroeconomic policy, but as an intermediate objective, or a necessary condition that must be achieved in order to create the efficient and competitive markets that are required, in the long run, for the main policy objectives of full employment and sustained growth to be achieved. Even these don't form the *true* ultimate policy objective, increasing human happiness or economic welfare.

A satisfactory balance of payments

As is the case with the word 'fair' in the context of a fair distribution of income, the word 'satisfactory' can be interpreted in different ways. People sometimes assume that a satisfactory balance of payments only occurs when the government achieves the biggest possible current account surplus (i.e. the value of exports exceeding the value of imports by the greatest amount). However, a country can only enjoy a trading surplus if at least one other country suffers a trading deficit. It is mathematically impossible for *all* countries to have a current account surplus at the same time. Therefore, most economists take the view that a 'satisfactory' balance of payments is a situation in which the current account is in equilibrium, or when there is a small surplus or a small but sustainable deficit.

The **current account of the balance of payments** contains two main items: the monetary value of **exports** (of both goods and services), and the monetary value of **imports**. If we ignore one or two other items in the current account, which I shall explain in Chapter 22, current account equilibrium occurs when the monetary value of exports equals the monetary value of imports. If the value of imports exceeds the value of exports, there is a **current account deficit**; if the value of imports is less than the value of exports, there is a **current account surplus**.

In the mid-1970s, huge current account deficits caused the UK to suffer two massive balance of payments crises. To try to reduce the deficits, UK governments had to contract or deflate the economy, which meant that unemployment grew and economic growth slowed down. Internal policy objectives were sacrificed in order to achieve the external objective of a satisfactory balance of payments. In the early 2000s, however, the UK's current account deficit has been much larger, both in absolute size and as a ratio of UK output, without the newspapers being full of stories of balance of payments crises. A large payments deficit is no longer necessarily regarded as a problem, partly because modern governments are generally prepared to allow market forces to determine the exchange rate. By contrast, 30–40 years ago, a large balance of payments deficit forced the government to deflate the economy in order to support the exchange rate to which it was committed. I explain this in greater detail in Chapter 22.

Box 16.4 Changes in the current account of the UK balance of payments, 1976–2008

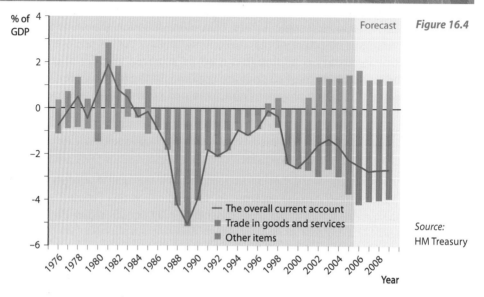

Figure 16.4

Source: HM Treasury

At AS, examination questions are set on the current account of the balance of payments, which mainly records the value of trade in goods and services (exports minus imports).

Questions are not set directly on the other main part of the balance of payments, capital flows into and out of the UK. However, Chapters 22 and 23 explain how some knowledge of capital flows will help you to understand the link between monetary policy and changes in the current account of the balance of payments.

Figure 16.4 shows that the UK's current account has been in deficit in recent years, with the trade deficit rising to 4% of GDP in 2006. The issues you have to consider centre on the extent to which a current account deficit poses problems for the UK economy, and the policies the government can and possibly ought to use to try to reduce the size of the deficit. These issues are explored in Chapter 22.

Follow-up questions
1 What is the difference between a 'budget deficit' and a 'balance of payments deficit'?
2 Research figures for the size of the UK balance of payments deficit since 2006.

Policy indicators

I am finishing this chapter with a short explanation of the difference between a **policy indicator** and policy instruments and objectives. Whereas a policy objective is a target or goal that a government wishes to 'hit', and a policy instrument is a tool used to achieve this end, a policy indicator simply provides the government with

key term

A **policy indicator** provides information about what is happening in the economy.

information about the state of the economy and/or whether current policy is on course to achieve the government's objectives.

The **money supply** provides a good example of a policy indicator. In the monetarist era of the late 1970s and the early 1980s, the money supply (or stock of money circulating round the economy) was treated both as a policy objective and as a policy instrument. Under the influence of monetarist theory, governments attempted to control the rate of growth of the money supply in order to control inflation. In this sense, the money supply was the policy instrument, while control of inflation was the policy objective. However, for various technical reasons centring on what money is (for example, is it just cash, or are bank deposits money?), the Bank of England was unable to control the rate of growth of the money supply *directly*. Because of this, interest rates were raised or lowered to try to control the growth of the money supply *indirectly*. For a time, the Bank of England used its interest rate, or lending rate, as the policy instrument, while the rate of growth of the money supply became the (intermediate) policy objective.

All this is now history. After the 'death' of monetarism, the money supply ceased to be either a policy objective or a policy instrument. These days, the money supply indicates whether or not there is plenty of liquidity (spending power) in the UK's financial system. Along with other economic indicators, such as surveys of business and consumer confidence and information about new houses being built and summer holidays booked, changes in the money supply provide the government and the Bank of England with information about what is happening, and what is likely to happen, in the UK economy.

Summary

- A policy objective is a target or goal which a government aims to achieve or 'hit'.

- A policy instrument is a tool or set of tools used to try to achieve an objective or objectives.

- Policy instruments can be grouped under the headings of monetary policy, fiscal policy and supply-side policy.

- The main macroeconomic policy objectives are full employment, economic growth, a fair distribution of income and wealth, control of inflation and a satisfactory balance of payments on current account.

- Full employment and economic growth are the prime policy objectives, but many free-market and monetarist economists place control of inflation in pole position.

- Whatever the ranking of policy objectives, Keynesian or monetarist, improving economic welfare or human happiness is the ultimate policy objective.

- The main policy objectives and policy instruments are explained in more depth in later chapters.

- A policy indicator provides information about the state of the economy, and on how best policy instruments may be used to achieve particular policy objectives.

Questions

1 What are the objectives of macroeconomic policy?
2 Compare the ways in which Keynesian and free-market economists rank policy objectives.
3 How are monetary and fiscal policy (a) similar and (b) different?
4 State the main conflicts affecting macroeconomic policy.
5 What is a policy trade-off?
6 Why do governments wish to achieve full employment and economic growth?
7 Why is it important to achieve a low and stable rate of inflation?
8 Discuss whether it is a good idea for a government to aim for the biggest possible current account surplus.
9 Compare policy indicators with policy objectives and instruments.

Chapter 17

Economic growth and the economic cycle

In Chapter 16, I explained how achieving a satisfactory, sustainable (and implicitly faster) rate of economic growth, along with other policy objectives such as reducing unemployment and controlling inflation, is an important target for governments. This chapter examines the nature of economic growth, both in the short run and in the long run, before explaining the ups and downs of economic growth in the various phases of the economic cycle.

Learning outcomes

This chapter will:

- define economic growth and distinguish between short-run and long-run growth
- explain how economic growth is measured
- distinguish between the real and the nominal values of economic variables
- relate economic growth to capital, wealth and national income or output
- explain the causes of short-run and long-run economic growth
- explain the difference between economic growth and economic development
- relate economic growth to sustainability and the trade-off with environmental objectives
- describe the different phases of the economic cycle and explain its causes
- explain how UK growth may have speeded up and how the economic cycle has become milder
- relate output gaps to the economic cycle and to the difference between actual and trend growth

What is economic growth?

Economic growth is defined as the increase in the *potential* level of *real* output the economy can produce over a period of time, for example a year. Strictly, this is **long-run economic growth**, which is not the same as **short-run economic growth** (both are illustrated in Figure 17.1). If the economy's production possibility frontier is PPF_1 initially, short-run economic growth is shown by the movement from point C *inside* the frontier to point A *on* the frontier. Long-run economic growth is shown by the outward movement of the frontier to PPF_2. The movement from point A to point B depicts long-run economic growth. Short-run growth makes use of spare capacity and takes up the slack in the economy, whereas long-run growth increases total productive capacity.

How economic growth is measured

Economic growth is measured by the percentage annual increase in real national output. For example, a 3% growth rate means that the aggregate level of real output (actual goods and services) produced in the economy over the last year is 3% higher than it was when measured a year ago for the previous 12 months.

Real national output is the total of all the goods and services produced in an economy over a particular time period. As Box 1 explains, an increase in real national output can be calculated by subtracting the rate of inflation from the increase in nominal national output over the period in question.

key term

Economic growth is an increase in the economy's potential level of real output, and an outward movement of the economy's production possibility frontier.

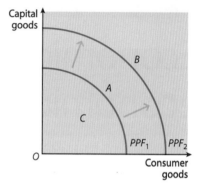

Figure 17.1 Short-run and long-run economic growth

examiner's voice

It is important to understand the difference between short-run and long-run economic growth and the causes of the two forms of growth.

examiner's voice

Economic growth is always measured in real rather than in nominal terms. You must understand the difference between real national output and nominal national output.

Box 17.1 Real and nominal

It is important to avoid confusing *real* national income or output with *nominal* national income or output. (Nominal national output is also called *money* national output.)

The photograph shows a number of cheeses on display in a delicatessen in Oxfordshire. The cheeses contributed in a small way to the UK's real national output in 2007 — a contribution made even smaller because all the cheeses on display were imported.

Nominal national income or output is real national income or output multiplied by the average price level for the year in question. Two of the cheeses on display in the Oxfordshire delicatessen were priced

at £1.80 and £1.99 per 100 grams. Estimates for the level of UK nominal national output in 2007 were based on information about the prices charged for all goods produced in the UK, including cheeses sold by market stalls, delis and supermarkets. However, with imports, only the contribution to output added in the UK is included in the real and nominal values of UK national output.

The equation below shows how the rate of change of real national income or output can be calculated:

rate of growth of real national output = rate of growth of nominal national output – inflation rate

Nominal national income or output rose by 4.76% in the UK in 2006. However, this figure over-estimates the rate of economic growth in the country. Prices rose on average by 1.9% in 2007. Based on these figures, the growth rate of UK real national income or output was therefore 2.86% in 2007.

There are many other examples of differences between the real and the nominal values of economic variables. Chapter 15 referred to the real wage rate and the nominal wage rate. The nominal wage rate is the money paid to workers for working a particular period. From a worker's point of view, the real wage is the purchasing power of the nominal wage, i.e. the goods and services the money wage can buy. We can calculate a change in the real wage rate by using the following equation:

increase in the real wage rate = increase in the money wage rate – the inflation rate

The annual rate of inflation recorded in the UK for the 12 months up to August 2007 was 1.8%. Over the same period, the nominal or money earnings of UK employees had increased on average by 3.7%. Real earnings per worker had therefore risen by 1.9% over the year — providing that the statistics were accurate. As I explain in Chapter 21, the 'true' rate of inflation experienced by many workers may be considerably more than that officially recorded in the consumer prices index (CPI), from which the figure of 1.8% has been taken.

Follow-up questions

1 Why do domestically produced cheeses such as British cheddar contribute more to UK national output than imported cheeses such as brie?

2 How may an increase in the real wage rate affect businesses?

National output, national income and economic growth

Before exploring economic growth in more detail, I shall explain how long-term growth relates to the concepts of **national output** and **national income**.

Economists use the terms national output (also called national product) and national income interchangeably. To produce the flow of national output, the economy must possess a stock of physical capital goods (the **national capital stock**) and a **stock of human capital**.

The national capital stock is part of the **stock of national wealth**, which comprises all physical assets owned by the nation's residents that have value. The national capital stock includes capital goods and raw materials, together with **social capital** such as the roads, hospitals and schools which are owned by the state. However, the national capital stock excludes consumer goods, which are a part of national *wealth* but not part of national *capital*. All capital is wealth, but not all wealth is capital.

key term

National income or **national output** is the *flow* of new output produced by the economy in a particular period, e.g. a year.

examiner's voice

Make sure you understand the difference between stocks and flows.

The national capital stock is the *stock* of capital goods that has accumulated over time in the economy. By contrast, national income is the *flow* of new output produced by the stocks of physical and human capital.

Figure 17.2 shows how we can relate a country's national income or output (for example in 2009) to the national capital stock and the human capital stock. In the figure, national income in 2009 is shown as the area contained by the three rectangles *A*, *B* and *C*. I shall now assume that at the beginning of 2009, the economy operates on its production possibility frontier. This means there is no unemployed labour, and the economy is working at full capacity to produce the flow of national income shown by *A* + *B* + *C*.

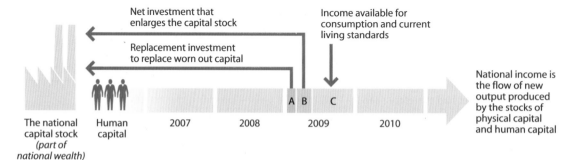

Figure 17.2 National income and the stocks of physical and human capital

However, part of the national capital stock wears out in the course of producing 2009's national income. Worn-out capital (or the **depreciation** of the national capital stock) reflects **capital consumption**. To maintain the size of the capital stock,

AQA AS Economics

so that (in the absence of population growth and technical progress) the stock is capable of producing exactly the same size of national income in 2010 as in 2009, part of 2009's national output must be replacement capital goods. The spending on replacement investment is shown by area *A*. If this investment doesn't take place, the national capital stock shrinks in size. **Negative economic growth** occurs and the economy's production possibility frontier shifts inward.

Positive economic growth generally requires that investment takes place, over and above the replacement investment shown by rectangle *A* in Figure 17.2. The extra investment needed to enlarge the capital stock is shown by rectangle *B*. This is called net investment. **Gross investment** (shown by *A* + *B*) is the sum of **replacement investment** and **net investment**. Only net investment increases the size of the capital stock, thereby facilitating long-run (positive) economic growth.

Rectangle *C* shows the fraction of national income available for consumption in 2009. As I explained in the last chapter, a decision to sacrifice *current* consumption in favour of a higher level of *future* consumption means that more of society's scarce resources go into investment or the production of capital goods, enabling the national capital stock to increase in size. However, in the short term, the easiest way to increase living standards is to boost current consumption. This 'live now, pay later' approach sacrifices saving and investment, which ultimately reduces long-term economic growth.

Gross national product and gross domestic product

Two of the most commonly used measures of national income or output are **gross national product (GNP)** and **gross domestic product (GDP)**. Gross national product measures the total value of national output, including that produced in other countries. (UK residents and UK-based multinational companies (MNCs) receive profit and interest payments from the capital assets they own but which are located overseas.) Likewise, overseas-owned MNCs such as IBM and Nissan receive profit from assets they own in the UK. The difference between inward and outward profit flows is called **net income from abroad**. Net income from abroad is included in GNP, but is excluded from GDP.

examiner's voice
The specification states: 'candidates are *not* expected to have a detailed knowledge of the construction of national income accounts'. Nevertheless, data-response questions often include GDP data, so it is necessary to understand the concept.

Box 17.2 GNP, GDP and living standards

Because it measures all the income available to spend in the UK, GNP is a better measure than GDP of the standard of living currently enjoyed by UK residents. However, GDP is a better measure of the productivity of industries located within the UK. As Table 17.1 shows, for the UK, net income from abroad is usually positive, reflecting the fact that the country has invested in and accumulated assets in other countries over time. As a result, UK GNP is generally larger than UK GDP. Unfortunately, for most developing countries, GDP usually exceeds GNP. Profit outflows and interest payments to developed world MNCs and banks explain why this is the case.

Table 17.1

	£million		
	UK gross national product at market prices	UK net income from abroad	UK gross domestic product at market prices
1995	720,319	−2,761	723,080
1996	766,606	−2,299	768,905
1997	816,484	603	815,881
1998	874,620	8,910	865,710
1999	910,115	−1,830	911,945
2000	959,708	777	958,931
2001	1,011,623	8,326	1,003,297
2002	1,076,865	21,072	1,055,793
2003	1,140,887	22,642	1,118,245
2004	1,209,844	25,548	1,184,296
2005	1,258,722	24,746	1,233,976
2006	1,319,025	17,111	1,301,914

Source: Monthly Digest of Statistics, October 2007

Extension material

The causes of economic growth

Investment and technical progress: the two main factors leading to economic growth

Economic growth results from investment in new capital goods (physical capital), which enlarges the national capital stock, and investment in human beings (human capital). Although investment is an important factor in the growth process, it may not be as important as technical progress.

Until recently, economists had little to say about the causes of technical progress, treating it as manna from heaven which falls upon the economy, triggering economic growth. However, an important relatively new theory, known as endogenous growth theory, incorporates the causes of technical progress into the theoretical explanation of the growth process. New growth theory suggests that governments can create supply-side conditions that favour investment and technical progress. These conditions include external economies for businesses, often in the form of infrastructure, and a judicial system which protects patents and other intellectual property rights, and which enforces the law of contract.

The difference between economic growth and economic development

Economic growth measures changes in the physical quantity of goods and services an economy actually produces, or has the potential to produce, but growth does not necessarily improve the economic welfare of all or most of the people living in a country. Economic development is a better indicator of improved human happiness, and the ability to continue to improve happiness, than economic growth. **Economic development**, which includes the *quality* and not just the *quantity* of growth, is measured by:

- a general improvement in living standards that reduce poverty and human suffering
- greater access to resources such as food and housing required for basic human needs
- greater access to opportunities for human development, for example through education and training
- environmental sustainability and regeneration, through reducing resource depletion and resource degradation

examiner's voice
For the most part, AQA exam questions test knowledge of economic growth rather than knowledge of economic development.

Resource depletion occurs when finite resources such as oil are used up, and when soil fertility or fish stocks irreversibly decline. By contrast, **resource degradation** is best illustrated by pollution of air, water and land. To benefit people in the long run, growth (and development) must be sustainable.

Sustainable economic growth means the use of:

- renewable rather than non-renewable resources
- technologies that minimise pollution and other forms of resource degradation

The trade-off between faster economic growth and achieving environmental objectives

Governments continuously face a trade-off between the two policy objectives of maintaining and improving environmental quality, and maximising the economy's growth rate, measured by GDP growth.

Before explaining this trade-off, it is useful to identify three main components in standards of living and economic welfare:

$$\text{standard of living} = \text{economic welfare derived from goods and services purchased in the market economy} + \text{economic welfare derived from public goods and merit goods collectively provided by the state} + \text{economic welfare derived from quality of life factors, including external benefits and intangibles minus external costs and intangibles}$$

GDP and GNP statistics are often used to measure standards of living and economic growth, but they usually only capture the first two of the components of the standard of living: the material goods and services. Intangible factors, the third element in people's living standards, are ignored. These intangible factors include the value people place on leisure time and living close to work, and the externalities generated from the production and consumption of national income, which affect people's welfare and quality of life.

The environment provides us with many positive externalities which add to the quality of life, but also many negative externalities which do the opposite. Beautiful views, clean air, and the water-retaining and carbon dioxide-absorbing properties of forests provide examples of positive externalities (or external benefits). Conversely, traffic congestion, acid rain pollution, and rising sea levels and climatic deterioration caused by global warming are examples of negative externalities (or external costs), which are likely to have growing adverse effects on the quality of life. If the pursuit of economic growth leads to the destruction of beautiful views and other external benefits conveyed by the environment, while simultaneously creating more pollution and congestion, there is a conflict between the government's growth objective and its environmental objectives.

examiner's voice

This section of the chapter relates to the concept of negative externalities in the Unit 1 specification.

Insofar as externalities are taken into account in the measurement of GNP and GDP growth, what is in effect a welfare loss may be shown as an increase in national output, falsely indicating an apparent welfare gain. For example, the stresses and strains of producing an ever higher national output may not only lead to a loss of leisure time; it may make people ill more often, showing up in the national accounts as extra consumption of healthcare. Likewise, the extra time motorists spend in traffic jams caused by increased traffic congestion apparently contributes to economic growth through increased expenditure on petrol and garage services. (Goods such as flood protection barriers and breathing masks, which fend off some of the adverse effects of a deteriorating environment, are sometimes called 'regrettables'.)

Extension material

The environment and the sustainability of economic growth
Nearly 40 years ago, the first oil crisis, in which the price of crude oil more than doubled, led to British people becoming aware of how the environment — in the guise of raw material and energy shortages — might severely limit a government's ability to achieve high employment levels and continuing economic growth.

Fuel shortages and increased energy prices drew people's attention to two publications of the new but fast-growing ecology or environmentalist movement. The first of these was a document called 'Blueprint for Survival', published in the January 1972 issue of the British journal *The Ecologist*. According to the authors:

The principal defect of the industrial way of life with its ethos of expansion is that it is not sustainable. Its termination within the lifetime of someone born today is inevitable — unless it continues to be sustained for a while longer by an entrenched minority at the cost of imposing great suffering on the rest of mankind. Our task is to create a society which is sustainable and which will give the fullest possible satisfaction to its members. Such a society by definition would not depend on expansion but on stability.

The Limits to Growth: A Report for the Club of Rome's Project on the Predicament of Mankind, an influential book published a few months later in 1973, suggested that humanity would soon face a threefold dilemma: the impending exhaustion of the world's non-renewable natural resources, the world's pollution problem becoming so acute that the capacity for self-cleaning and regeneration is exhausted, and continued population growth leading to humankind destroying itself through sheer weight of numbers. One reviewer of this publication wrote:

> Man is heading for disaster if, overall, mankind does not learn to limit economic growth. That such a thesis would be unpopular with economists was to be expected. All their training, their research and their ethos has been concerned with ways in which the economy can be stimulated and expanded. Practically no economist has given thought to the problems of economic stability. For one thing stability is read as stagnation, and for another it is hard for an economist to find anyone to employ him who is interested in economic equilibrium. It has no appeal to governments, board chairmen, company presidents or even to used-car salesmen.

The authors of these two publications based much of their forecasts and predictions on the assumption of accelerating rates of population growth and resource use. This is known as exponential growth. Figure 17.3 illustrates the forecast made in 'Blueprint for Survival' of exponential growth in demand for crude oil or petroleum and exponential decline in petroleum reserves. The dashed lines show the total world oil reserves that the authors estimated would be available for extraction in 1975.

The forecasts of resource use and depletion made in *The Limits to Growth: A Report for the Club of Rome's Project on the Predicament of Mankind* were more sophisticated, but they were still based on the assumption of exponential rates of growth of use and depletion. In their most optimistic scenario, the authors argued that it might be possible to achieve a state of equilibrium — providing restrictions were placed on population growth and industrialisation, the two elements limiting growth which they argued are the principle causes of resource exhaustion and pollution.

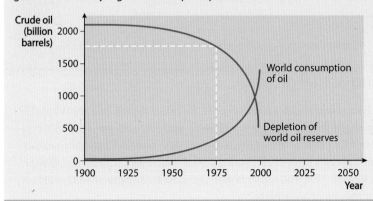

Figure 17.3
The 1970s gloomy prediction that exponential growth of oil consumption, matched by exponential depletion of known oil reserves, would lead to the world running out of oil by 2000

Fluctuations in economic activity and the economic cycle

Fluctuations in economic activity occur in two main ways: through **seasonal fluctuations**, and through **cyclical fluctuations** taking place over a number of years. Seasonal fluctuations are largely caused by changes in climate and weather. Examples include the effect of very cold winters closing down the building trade and seasonal employment in travel and tourism.

key term
The **economic cycle** is the fluctuation of real output above and below the trend line of economic growth.

Cyclical fluctuations, which are longer than seasonal ones, divide into the **short economic cycle** (also called the **business cycle** and the **trade cycle**), which lasts for just a few years, and **long cycles** (or long waves), which arguably extend over approximately 60 years. In an economic cycle, the economy's growth rate fluctuates considerably from year to year. Economic cycles, which can be between approximately 4 and 12 years long, are caused primarily by fluctuations in aggregate demand (I explain the nature of aggregate demand in the next chapter). In recent years, supply-side factors such as supply-shocks hitting the economy have also been recognised as causes of economic cycles.

The causes of long cycles lie on the supply-side of the economy. Significant improvements in technical progress cause firms to invest in new technology, which triggers a long period of boom. Electrification and the automobile have had this effect. In recent years, information and communication technology (ICT) may be having a similar effect, possibly creating a **new economy**. In the past, long booms have run out of steam when the innovating technology becomes fully used — until the next burst of technical activity creates another boom.

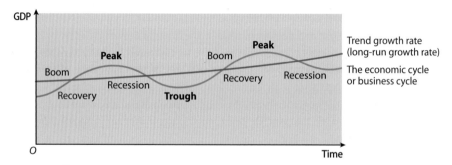

Figure 17.4 Economic growth and the economic cycle (or business cycle)

Trend growth and actual growth

Figure 17.4 shows two complete economic cycles, together with a line showing the economy's **trend growth rate** or **long-term growth rate**. **Actual growth**, which is usually measured by the percentage change in real GDP over a 12-month period, varies in the different phases of the economic cycle. In the cycle's upswing, growth is positive, but as Figure 17.4 shows, 'growth' becomes negative if and when a recession occurs in the cyclical downturn.

The economy's trend (or potential) growth rate is the rate at which output can grow, on a sustained basis, without putting upward or downward pressure on inflation. The trend growth rate is measured over a period covering more than one (and preferably several) economic cycles. Until recently, the UK's trend growth rate was judged to be about 2.25% per year. At first sight, this growth rate appears low, especially when compared with higher trend growth rates in **newly-industrialising countries (NICs)** such as China. Nevertheless, the UK's trend growth rate is similar to the long-run growth rates of other developed economies in western

Europe and North America. The absolute increase in real output delivered by a 2.25% growth rate may also exceed that delivered by a 10% growth rate in a much poorer country. Because of the compound interest effect, a 2.25% growth rate means that average UK living standards double every generation or so. (The compound interest effect also explains why the trend growth rate line in Figure 17.5 becomes steeper from year to year, moving along the line. For example, 2.25% of £1,000 billion is a larger annual increase in GDP than 2.25% of £800 billion.)

Recessions

A **recession** is defined in the UK as negative economic growth (or falling real GDP) for 6 months or more (i.e. two quarters or more). There have been two recessions in the UK during approximately the last 30 years. The first occurred between 1979 and 1981, and the second between 1990 and 1992. Both recessions (which raised unemployment to around 3 million) were followed by longer periods of recovery and boom in the rest of the 1980s and 1990s.

> **key term**
> A **recession** is a fall in real output for 6 months or more.

Box 17.3 The alphabet of recessions and hard and soft landings

The world's stock markets are signalling a recession, with no one able to determine whether there will be a hard or soft landing, or whether the recession will be U-shaped or V-shaped or, worst of all, Japanese L-shaped.

Marketing and communication group WPP, 2001

To make economics as interesting as possible, journalists like to use slang. This is certainly true when they cover recessions, particularly when predicting the length and depth of a recession that might occur in the future.

The USA feared recession in 2001

In 2001, amid fears that the US economy was about to suffer a recession, the fashion was to write about V-shaped, U-shaped and W-shaped recessions. A V-shaped recession can be described as 'quickly in, quickly out', in the sense that recovery occurs soon after the recession starts. A V-shaped recession is really a 'blip' in an otherwise continuing growth process. A W-shaped recession, or 'double-dip' recession, describes a situation in which an economy appears to be recovering from recession, but is quickly dragged into another downturn. A U-shaped recession is long, deep and nasty, for example the recessions suffered by the UK at the beginning of the 1980s and 1990s. Finally, as the quotation above indicates, Japan experienced what was described as an L-shaped recession in the 1990s — in the sense that the country appeared to be going through a never-ending recession, though recovery did eventually take place in the early 2000s.

In a similar way, economics journalists are prone to write about the likelihood of the economy suffering a 'hard landing', or possibly benefiting from a 'soft landing'. The possibility of a 'hard landing' conjures up the fear of a U-shaped recession. By contrast, when predicting a 'soft landing', journalists

---

believe that growth will slow down but just about remain positive, or, if a recession occurs, the downturn will be short and mild.

Follow-up questions

1 In the 1990s Japan was often said to be in recession. Did real output actually fall in Japan during the 1990s?

2 In 2008 some economists feared that the UK would suffer recession. What actually happened in 2008 and in subsequent years?

Recent UK economic cycles

From the late 1970s until the mid-1990s, UK economic cycles were much more volatile and unstable than in the Keynesian years of the 1950s and 1960s. As I have explained, there were deep recessions in the cycle's downswings. However, since the last deep recession ended in 1992, the economic cycle has been much milder and recession-free, at least up to mid-2008. Since 1992, the annual growth rate has fallen in the economic cycle's downturn, but has still remained positive.

The recent change in the UK economic cycle is illustrated in Figure 17.5. In the earlier years shown by the graph, recessions occurred in the downturn of volatile economic cycles. However, the milder and recession-free cycles I have just described are shown for more recent years.

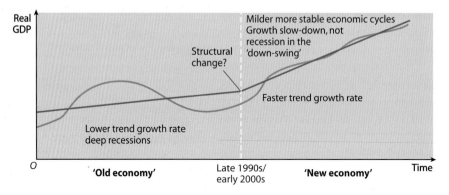

Figure 17.5 Recent changes in the economic cycle and in the UK's trend growth rate

Box 17.4 The UK economic cycle

According to the government, the UK economic cycle is defined as 'a period between two points when the economy is identified as being on-trend and which includes both a period when the economy is above trend and a period when it is below trend'.

The government has stated that the last economic cycle lasted almost exactly 10 years, starting in 1997 and ending in March 2007. However, during this period, the government revised the dates at which it thought the cycle had started, and at which it believed the cycle would end.

The choice of dates is significant, because the government's ability to meet its fiscal policy rules (which I explain in Chapter 24) depends to some extent on when the cycle begins and ends. Changing the dates at which economic cycles start and finish slightly can affect whether fiscal rules are met or broken. Indeed, the Labour government would not have met its fiscal rules if it had stuck to its original dates for the start and end of the last cycle. Cynics might argue that changing the dates is like moving the goal posts during a rugby or soccer match.

Follow-up questions
1 'Economic cycles can also be defined in terms of output gaps.' Explain this statement (see p. 206).
2 Why does 'moving the goal posts' reduce the credibility of the government's fiscal policy?

The recent increase in the UK's trend growth rate

Figure 17.6 shows another significant change that may have occurred in the UK economy in recent years. Since 1997, the UK economy has grown at an annual per capita rate of 2.4% a year, which is better than the average for the previous half century, of 2.1%.

In 2002, the Office of National Statistics (ONS) estimated that the UK's trend or long-term growth rate had increased from approximately 2.25% a year to 2.75%. If the trend growth rate has increased, it could be the result of structural change in the UK economy. Faster growth may have resulted, in part at least, from the benign effect on UK productivity of new technologies, most notably ICT, and in particular the effect of the internet on cheaper and faster communication.

The UK government accepted the ONS's estimate immediately, but was more cautious, building a 2.5% projected growth rate into the information it uses when deciding on economic policy. The government hoped that faster trend growth could deliver sufficient extra tax revenue to finance increased government spending on healthcare and education, without tax rates being raised. However, by 2007, estimates of future growth were more pessimistic, and tax revenues were less than had been expected. If the growth rate reverts back to the previous lower figure, which is possible, tax rates will probably have to rise to pay for increases in public spending on social capital, such as schools and hospitals, which were announced when the optimistic growth forecasts were made.

Some explanations of the economic cycle

In the 1930s, John Maynard Keynes argued that economic recessions are caused by fluctuations in aggregate demand, which are caused by consumer and business confidence giving way to pessimism, and vice versa. However, it is now recognised that supply-side factors can also trigger economic cycles. Edward Prescott and Finn Kydland, the 2004 Nobel Laureates in economics, have recently developed a theory of 'real business cycles', which argues that changes in technology on the supply side of the economy might be as important as changes

in aggregate demand in explaining economic cycles. Other factors that may cause or contribute to economic cycles include:

- **The role of speculative bubbles.** Rapid economic growth leads to a rapid rise and speculative bubble in asset prices. When people realise that house prices and/or share prices rise far above the assets' real values, asset selling replaces asset buying. This causes the speculative bubble to burst, which in turn destroys consumer and/or business confidence. People stop spending and the economy falls into recession.

- **Political business cycle theory.** In democratic countries, general elections usually have to take place every 4 or 5 years. As an election approaches, the political party in power may 'buy votes' by engineering a pre-election boom. After the election, the party in power deflates aggregate demand to prevent the economy from overheating, but when the next general election approaches, demand is once again expanded.

- **Outside shocks hitting the economy.** These divide into 'demand shocks' which affect aggregate demand, and 'supply shocks' which impact on aggregate supply. In some cases, an outside shock hitting the economy may affect both aggregate demand and aggregate supply. Thus, the outbreak of a war in the Middle East may affect demand by causing a sudden collapse in consumer and business confidence, and aggregate supply via its effect on the supply and price of crude oil.

Extension material: Other explanations of the economic cycle

At AS, it is a good idea to stick to learning two or three simple explanations of the economic cycle. However, there are other explanations that could give depth to your answers at A2:

- **Climatic cycles.** Stanley Jevons, a nineteenth-century neoclassical economist, was one of the first economists to recognise the economic cycle. Perhaps taking note of the Bible's reference to '7 years of plenty' followed by '7 years of famine', Jevons believed a connection exists between the timing of economic crises and the solar cycle. Variations in sunspots affect the power of the sun's rays, influencing the quality of harvests and thus the price of grain, which, in turn, affects business confidence and gives rise to trade cycles.

  Although Jevons's sunspot theory was never widely accepted, there is no doubt that climate changes affect economic activity. The effect named 'El Niño' has renewed interest in Jevons's theory. This is a severe atmospheric and oceanic disturbance in the Pacific Ocean, occurring every 7–14 years. The disturbance leads to a fall in the number of plankton, upsetting the entire ocean food chain and devastating the fishing industry. The effect leads to a complete reversal of trade winds, bringing torrential rain, flooding, and mud slides to the otherwise dry Pacific coastal areas of countries such as Chile and Peru. By contrast, droughts occur in much of Asia and in areas of Africa and central North America. In 2008, El Niño occurred again.

- **Changes in inventories.** Besides investing in fixed capital, firms also invest in stocks of raw materials, and in stocks of finished goods waiting to be sold. This type of investment is called inventory investment or stock-building. Although stock-building accounts for less than 1% of GDP in a typical year, swings in inventories are often the single most important determinant of recessions. Firms hold stocks of raw materials and finished goods in order to smooth production to cope with swings in demand. However, paradoxically, changes in stocks tend to trigger and exacerbate economic cycles. Stocks of unsold finished goods build up when firms over-anticipate demand for finished goods. As the stocks accumulate, firms are forced to cut production by more than the original fall in demand. The resultant destocking turns a slowdown into a recession. In the USA, swings in inventory investment account for about half of the fall in GDP in its past nine recessions. Destocking has also made UK recessions worse.

■ **Marxist theory.** Marxist economists explain economic cycles as part of a restructuring process that increases the rate of profit in capitalist economies. Under normal production conditions, a fall in the rate of profit caused by competitive pressure threatens to bankrupt weaker capitalist firms. Marxists believe that recessions create conditions in which stronger firms either take over weaker competitors, or buy the assets of rivals that have been forced out of business at rock-bottom prices. Either way, restructuring by takeover or bankruptcy means that the 'fittest' capitalist firms survive. In Marxist analysis, economic cycles are deemed necessary for the regeneration and survival of capitalism.

■ **Multiplier/accelerator interaction.** Keynesian economists have argued that business cycles may be caused by the interaction of two dynamic processes: the multiplier process, through which an increase in investment leads to multiple increases in national income, and the accelerator, through which the increase in income induces a change in the level of investment. (These processes are explained more fully in the next chapter.)

Stabilising the economic cycle

Demand management policies can be used to try to reduce fluctuations in the business cycle. In the Keynesian era, fiscal policy was used in this way in the UK. However, during the monetarist era, in the late 1970s and early 1980s, demand management was abandoned. Arguably, this deepened and lengthened the recession the UK suffered at the beginning of the 1980s.

Since the end of the last recession in 1992, monetary policy has been used successfully to stabilise the economic cycle. In a boom, when the economy is overheating, the Bank of England raises interest rates to contract or deflate aggregate demand. By contrast, in a downturn the Bank of England cuts interest rates to reflate or boost aggregate demand.

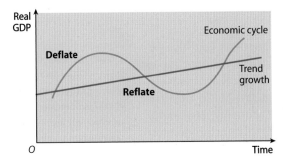

Figure 17.6 Getting the timing right when stabilising the economic cycle

Successful stabilisation of the economic cycle requires accurate timing. If monetary policy is used to stabilise the economic cycle, interest rates should be raised *before* output would otherwise peak in the boom phase of the economic cycle. Likewise, interest rates should be cut *before* output bottoms out in the downturn that follows.

The danger is that bad timing will destabilise the economic cycle and make the fluctuations more volatile. Also, by causing long-term risky investments to be abandoned in favour of less risky short-term projects, unexpected interest rate (or tax) changes may adversely affect competitiveness and long-term growth.

Output gaps

If the economy's *actual* growth rate was always to equal the *trend* growth rate, there would be no **output gaps**. (In this situation, there would also be no economic cycles.) An output gap measures the difference between the level of real output of GDP the economy is actually producing and the level it would be producing, were the economy to grow continuously at the trend rate of growth at which inflation is stable. As Figure 17.7 shows, output gaps can be negative or positive. Negative output gaps occur when actual output is *below* the trend growth rate level of output. The vertical line drawn from point *A* to point *B* illustrates a negative output gap. As well as occurring in the cycle's downturn, negative output gaps can occur in the recovery phase of the economic cycle when output is growing, but the level of output is still *below* the trend line. By contrast, positive output gaps occur when actual output is *above* trend growth rate output, both in the cycle's boom phase and when the downturn has started, but the level of output still lies *above* the trend line. The vertical line drawn from point *C* to point *D* depicts a positive output gap.

> **key term**
>
> The **output gap** is the difference between actual output and the trend growth level of output.

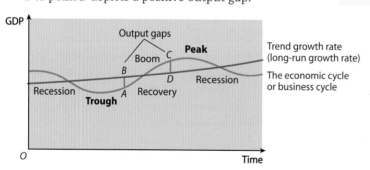

Figure 17.7 A negative and a positive output gap

Production possibility frontier diagrams can also be used to illustrate output gaps. A negative output gap is illustrated by a point *inside* the production possibility frontier (such as point *C* in Figure 17.1). A positive output gap can be shown by the economy *temporarily* producing at a point outside its current production possibility frontier. Because it represents overuse of

> **examiner's voice**
>
> Don't confuse an output gap with a productivity gap, which is the gap between the productivity levels of two countries.

capacity, such a point cannot be sustained for long, though long-run economic growth should eventually shift the frontier outward.

Summary

- Long-run economic growth is an increase in an economy's potential level of output, whereas short-term economic growth is a movement from a point inside the economy's production possibility frontier to a point on the frontier.

- Economic growth is measured as a change in *real* output rather than as a change in *nominal* output.

- National income or output is the *flow* of new output produced by an economy in a year.

- Investment and technical progress are two of the causes of economic growth.

- The economic cycle or business cycle reflects actual growth fluctuating around trend growth.

- Economic cycles are usually caused by changes in aggregate demand, though supply-side factors can also cause recessions.

- A recession occurs in the UK when real national output falls for 6 months (two quarters) or more.

- Recent UK economic cycles have exhibited a slowdown in the rate of growth in the downturn rather than a recession.

- An output gap is the difference between actual output and the level of output associated with trend growth.

Questions

1 Illustrate short-term and long-term economic growth on a *PPF* diagram.
2 Distinguish between income, wealth and capital.
3 Distinguish between nominal national income and real national income.
4 Explain the difference between GNP and GDP.
5 Outline possible causes of long-term economic growth.
6 State two benefits and two costs of economic growth.
7 What is meant by sustainable economic growth?
8 State three ways in which economic activity fluctuates.
9 Briefly explain three possible causes of economic cycles.
10 What is a recession?
11 Distinguish between a positive and a negative output gap.

Chapter 18

Aggregate demand and the circular flow of income

I have mentioned aggregate demand, in previous chapters, without explaining in any detail what the concept means. In this chapter, I start by defining aggregate demand, before focusing on two of the components of aggregate demand, consumption and investment, and relating both to the nature of saving. The coverage of investment provides a brief explanation of the accelerator concept. The last part of the chapter links aggregate demand to the circular flow model of the macroeconomy and to the multiplier process, through which a change in aggregate demand leads to a larger decrease or increase in national income.

Learning outcomes

This chapter will:
- explain the meaning of aggregate demand
- introduce the aggregate demand equation and the components of aggregate demand
- explain the determinants of the aggregate levels of consumption and saving in the economy
- briefly explain the personal saving ratio and the household saving ratio
- explain the determinants of the aggregate level of investment in the economy
- link investment to the concept of the accelerator
- relate aggregate demand to the circular flow of income in the economy
- explain the equilibrium level of national income in the context of the circular flow model
- introduce and explain the national income multiplier

The meaning of aggregate demand

Aggregate demand comprises total planned spending on goods and services produced by the economy. (The closely-related concept of national expenditure measures realised or actual spending, which has already taken place.) Four types of spending are included in aggregate demand, each type originating in a different sector of the economy: households, firms, the government sector and the overseas sector. The four sources of aggregate demand are shown in the following equation and identity:

aggregate demand = consumption + investment + government spending + exports (net of imports)

or: $AD = C + I + G + (X - M)$

where C, I, G, X and M are the symbols used respectively for consumption, investment, government spending, and net export demand, i.e. exports minus imports.

key term

Aggregate demand is the total planned spending on real output produced within the economy.

examiner's voice

Aggregate demand is a macroeconomic example of an *ex ante* concept: it is a measure of what people plan or intend to do.

The components of aggregate demand

Consumption, **investment**, **government spending** and **net export demand** (spending on UK exports by residents of other countries minus spending on imports by UK residents) form the components of aggregate demand. If any of the components change, aggregate demand increases or deceases. The next sections of this chapter examine two of the components of aggregate demand, consumption and investment, and their relationship to saving. The remaining components of aggregate demand, government spending and net export demand, are explained in Chapters 24 and 22.

Aggregate consumption and saving

Aggregate **consumption** is spending by all the households in the economy on consumer goods and services produced within the economy. Aggregate consumption does not include spending by households on imports, which are part of the goods and services produced in other countries.

If we assume a **closed economy** — pretending that there are no exports or imports — and that there is no taxation, then at any level of income, households can only do two things with their income: spend it or not spend it. Spending income is consumption, whereas not spending income is saving.

The difference between saving and investment

Economists make a clear separation between **saving** and **investment**, even though in everyday language the two terms are often used interchangeably. Whereas saving is simply income that is not spent on consumption, investment is spending by firms on capital goods such as machines and office equipment. Investment also includes spending by firms on raw materials and energy.

examiner's voice

It is important not to confuse consumption, saving and investment.

key terms

Consumption is total planned spending by households on real output produced within the economy.

Investment is total planned spending by firms on real output produced within the economy.

Saving is income which is not spent.

As a simplification, economists often assume that households make saving decisions, while firms make investment decisions. There are, however, exceptions to this rule. An important example occurs when a firm makes a decision to plough back or retain profits rather than to distribute them as income to the owners of the business. In this situation, the firm is simultaneously saving and investing. If a business were simply to store these profits as a cash reserve — usually on deposit in a bank — then the firm would only be saving and not investing.

The determinants of consumption and household saving

Whenever members of households make decisions about whether or not to spend on consumer goods, they are simultaneously deciding whether or not to save. A determinant of consumption is also a determinant of household saving. In the next sub-sections, I explain a number of factors influencing consumption and saving. These are: **interest rates** (the reward for saving), the **level of income**, **expected future income**, **wealth**, **consumer confidence**, and the **availability of credit**.

Interest rates

Before Keynes, economists generally gave little attention to explaining how the level of aggregate consumption spending is determined in the economy. Some attention was, however, given to the determination of saving. Economists assumed that interest rates are the main determinant of saving. The rate of interest rewards savers for sacrificing current consumption, and the higher the rate of interest, the greater the reward. Thus, at any particular level of income, the amount saved will increase as the real rate of interest rises and the amount consumed will fall.

The level of income

In his 'General Theory', Keynes explained his theory of aggregate consumption in the following way:

> The fundamental psychological law, upon which we are entitled to depend with great confidence...is that men are disposed, as a rule and on average, to increase their consumption as their income increases, but not by as much as the increase in their income.

Keynes believed that, although aggregate planned consumption rises as income rises, it rises at a slower rate than income, so that at high levels of income planned consumption is less than income, and planned saving is positive.

Extension material

Keynes's theory of consumption and saving
In the 1930s, Keynes argued that interest rates have little affect on *aggregate* saving and consumption decisions, though they do affect how people move their savings, for example

between a bank and a building society. During the Great Depression, Keynes doubted whether a fall in interest rates could allow market forces to adjust automatically to eliminate the deficient demand plaguing the world's depressed economies. This caused Keynes to focus on the level of income as the main determinant of consumption and saving decisions.

In contrast to his predecessors, Keynes argued that the level of income (Y) is the most important single determinant of consumption: consumption is largely a function of the level of income. Using functional notation, we may state the Keynesian consumption theory in the following equation:

$$C = f(Y)$$

Autonomous consumption and income-induced consumption

The equation $C = f(Y)$ is general, telling us no more than that consumption is assumed to be determined mainly by income, and is some (as yet) unspecified function of the level of income. We can write the consumption function in more detail as:

$$C = a + cY$$

Written in this way, the equation for the consumption function shows aggregate consumption as comprising two elements: autonomous consumption and income-induced consumption.

Autonomous consumption (represented by the symbol a) is the part of total consumption which is unaffected by the level of income, i.e. it is constant at all levels of income. The value of autonomous consumption is thus determined by influences on income other than the level of income. These influences will include the rate of interest (which I have already covered) and others such as wealth and the availability of credit (which I shall discuss shortly).

Income-induced consumption is measured by (cY), c being the slope of the consumption function. As the name suggests, income-induced consumption is the part of consumption that varies with the level of income.

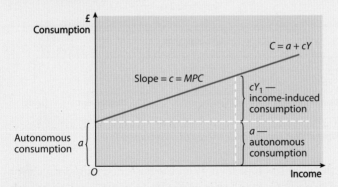

If consumption increases as incomes rise, but at a *slower* rate than income, it follows that household saving also increases as incomes rise, but at a *faster* rate than income.

Saving can be positive or negative. People on very low incomes borrow, or dissave, in order to spend more than their incomes. By contrast, rich people spend less than their incomes, even though their total spending is greater than that of the poor. The rich spend more and save more than the poor, and the rich are positive savers.

Expected future income and the 'life-cycle' theory of consumption

The Keynesian consumption theory explained above is sometimes also called the **'absolute income' consumption theory**, because it assumes that the most important influence on consumption is the *current* level of income. However, the current level of income in a particular year may have much less influence on a person's planned consumption than some notion of 'expected income' over a much longer time period, perhaps extending over the individual's remaining lifetime or life cycle.

> **examiner's voice**
>
> You should appreciate that people's economic behaviour is influenced by their expectations of what might happen in the future.

In order to understand the **'life-cycle' theory**, which is illustrated in Figure 18.2, it is useful to distinguish between two different types of saving: 'non-contractual' and 'contractual' saving. **Non-contractual saving** takes place when a person sets income aside, for example in a building society deposit. Such saving is usually short term, for example saving to pay for a summer holiday. **Contractual saving**, by contrast, occurs when an individual makes a contract to save regularly with a financial institution such as a pension fund. This type of saving is usually undertaken with a long-term motive in mind. Many people sign savings contracts, especially early in their working lives, to finance a house purchase, and then continue to save to finance retirement or to protect dependents against the financial problems that would result from the saver's early death. Thus, with contractual saving, saving takes place at regular intervals over a number of years, to be followed in later years by dissaving when a house is purchased or on retirement.

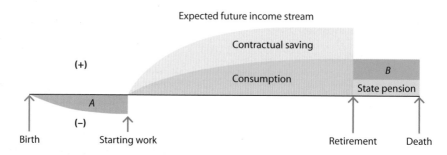

Figure 18.2 The life-cycle theory of consumption

People therefore plan their contractual savings on the basis of a long-term view of their expected life-time or permanent income, and of likely spending plans over the remaining length of an expected life cycle. Temporary fluctuations in yearly income generally have little effect on the contractual savings that are regularly contributed to pension schemes and to the purchase of life insurance policies.

Wealth

The stock of personal wealth, as well as the flow of income, influences consumption and saving decisions. In countries such as the UK and USA, houses and shares

are the two main forms of wealth asset that people own. An increase in house prices usually causes home-owners to consume more and to save less from their current flow of income, partly because the wealth increase 'does their saving for them'. The same is true when share prices rise, though the effect is less noticeable in the UK, where houses rather than shares are the main household wealth asset. Rising house prices induce a feel-good factor among owner-occupiers of houses, which leads to a consumer spending spree in the shops. Conversely, falling house prices have the opposite effect, increasing uncertainty and precautionary saving via a 'feel-bad' factor.

> ***e*xaminer's voice**
> Make sure you don't confuse **wealth**, which is a stock, with income, which is a flow.

> ***k*ey term**
> **Wealth** is the stock of assets, or things that have value, which people own.

The stock market crash in 2000, which centred on the collapse of the share prices of dot.com and high-tech companies, reduced the wealth of shareholders, and thence their consumption. In the summer of 2007, share prices also fell at the time of a financial crisis in the USA resulting from US banks lending unwisely to poorer American families to finance house purchase (these are known as sub-prime loans). In early 2008, pessimistic commentators feared that a simultaneous crash in house and share markets, caused in part by the growth of sub-prime loans, might usher in a new world recession.

Box 18.1 The UK house price crash, quiet before the fall (2007)

We are now experiencing the quiet before the storm. For some UK residents, the battle for financial survival appears to have already begun. Of 179 properties recently up for auction in Covent Garden, 52 were repossessions.

In the last 8 weeks, banks have stopped lending to each other. Investors aren't buying up commercial debt. There's a rush to sell investments in house-builders, commercial property funds and any mortgage lenders suspected of being exposed to sub-prime loans.

Confidence in the UK financial sector is at its lowest since 1990 — when UK house prices last went into freefall. We've just seen the first run on a British bank since the 1800s. Queues of savers waited outside Northern Rock branches, and both Alliance & Leicester and Bradford & Bingley took hits on their share prices. Our personal savings are at a 47-year low, and twice as many Brits are missing mortgage repayments as in 2006.

Sixty per cent of the UK's wealth is tied up in housing, so the increase in speculative buy-to-let ownership (up by a factor of at least 33 in the last 10 years) doesn't inspire confidence. Following a series of interest-rate hikes, landlords' rental incomes have fallen below their own mortgage repayments, forcing them to sell.

Record numbers of Brits are seeking debt advice. In London, where property prices peaked at 15 times average earnings, some young couples are spending 50% of their post-tax income on mortgage repayments.

We should be worried. Talk of a 1989-style house price correction would be understating how bad today's bust could be. Our disposable income has fallen below 1990 levels. Outstanding household loans currently stand at £1.3 trillion in the UK, double the outstanding debt in 2000. That's a lot of money to pay back, particularly when people have negative equity.

So how should we be preparing for the worst? First, we need to recognise that now isn't the time to be buying a house or taking on debt. Second, things could get really bad, like losing your job. Jobs are already being shed in the financial and building sectors, and the retail sector is about to feel the effect on Christmas sales. Third, the demand for cash isn't about to dry up. If the banks are crying out for cash today, the rest of us will be crying out for it tomorrow. Make sure you can lay your hands on enough cash.

Adapted from **www.ablemesh.co.uk**, November 2007

Follow-up questions

1 Explain the difference between a 'sub-prime' mortgage and a 'prime' mortgage.

2 Summarise how the UK housing market has fared since the above article was written.

Consumer confidence

The state of consumer confidence is closely linked to people's views on expected income and to changes in personal wealth. When consumer optimism increases, households generally spend more and save less, whereas a fall in optimism (or a growth in pessimism) has the opposite effect.

Governments try to boost consumer (and business) optimism to ward off the fear of a collapse in confidence by 'talking the economy up' and by trying to enhance the credibility of government economic policy. If the government is optimistic about the future, and people believe there are good grounds for this optimism, then the general public will be optimistic and confident about the future. However, if people believe the government has 'lost the plot', or if an adverse economic shock hits the economy in a way that the government can't control, confidence can quickly dissipate.

The availability of credit

Besides the rate of interest, other aspects of monetary policy, such as controls on bank lending and hire-purchase controls, affect consumption. If credit is available easily and cheaply, consumption increases as people supplement current income by borrowing on credit created by the banking system. Conversely, a tight monetary policy reduces consumption. The financial crisis that occurred in 2007 and 2008, which arose from bad debts in the US sub-prime market, had this effect in the UK and the USA. Interest rates rose and the supply of credit dried up, with banks refusing to supply applicants with new credit cards or mortgages.

Other influences on consumption and saving

The distribution of income

Rich people save a greater proportion of their income than the poor. Redistribution of income from rich to poor therefore increases consumption and reduces saving.

Expectations of future inflation

Uncertainty caused by fears of rising inflation increases precautionary saving and reduces consumption. It may also, however, have the opposite effect. Households may decide to bring forward consumption decisions by spending now on consumer durables such as cars or television sets, thereby avoiding expected future price increases. People may also decide to borrow to finance the purchase of houses if they expect property prices to appreciate at a rate faster than general inflation. In this situation, and particularly if the real rate of interest is low or negative, people often decide to buy land, property and other physical assets such as fine art and antiques as a 'hedge' against inflation, in preference to saving through the purchase of financial assets.

Speculative demand for housing occurs because house prices rise faster than general inflation

The personal saving ratio and the household saving ratio

The personal saving ratio measures the *actual* or *realised* saving of the personal sector as a ratio of total personal sector disposal income:

$$\text{personal saving ratio} = \frac{\text{realised or actual personal saving}}{\text{personal disposable income}}$$

The household saving ratio is used in a similar way. It measures households' realised saving as a ratio of their disposable income. However, the personal saving ratio and the household saving ratio are not the same. The personal sector is more than just households, including unincorporated businesses such as partnerships and charitable organisations such as independent schools.

Economists and the government are interested in how much of their incomes people *plan* to save and to consume in the near future, as this provides important information about what lies ahead for the state of aggregate demand. Because it is difficult to measure accurately people's plans, the personal saving ratio calculated for the most recent past period is generally used as an indicator of what people wish to do in the future.

Box 18.2 Changes in the UK household saving ratio

Figure 18.3 shows that the UK household savings ratio fell rapidly between the end of 2005 and the first quarter of 2007, when it bottomed out at the extremely low figure of 2.0% of household income.

Consumer spending remained high in this period because households were raiding their savings in order to maintain spending levels, partly through credit card borrowing (borrowing is negative saving or dissaving). Owner-occupiers of houses also engaged in equity release by taking out extra mortgages on houses in order to convert wealth previously locked up in 'bricks and mortar' into money and spending power.

Figure 18.3 shows the saving ratio beginning to rise again in the second quarter of 2007. The financial crisis in the summer and autumn of 2007 might result in people saving more of their incomes, particularly if worries about the future increase. Time will tell.

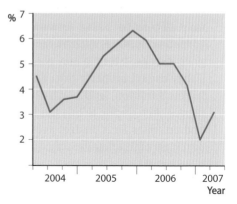

Figure 18.3 Changes in the UK household saving ratio, second quarter 2004 to second quarter 2007

Source: ONS quarterly national accounts, 2nd quarter 2007

Follow-up questions

1 Explain how a fall in the saving ratio may affect investment by businesses.
2 How might a fall in interest rates affect the saving ratio?

Investment

Investment is the second of the components of aggregate demand covered in this chapter. In everyday speech, investment is often used to describe a situation in which a person invests in stocks or shares, paintings or antiques. In economic theory, the term has the narrower and more specific meaning explained earlier in this chapter. In the aggregate demand equation, investment is *planned* demand for capital goods, which must not be confused with demand for financial assets such as shares and bonds. The latter is called financial investment, but is not the same as demand for physical capital needed for the production of other goods and services. Finally, by providing or improving education and training, firms and the government can invest in human capital.

It is important to remember that capital is a stock concept, but investment is a flow. We can measure the national capital stock at any particular point of time. It represents the total of all the nation's capital goods, of all types, which are still in existence and capable of production. By contrast, we measure the flow of investment over a period, usually a year. A country's **gross investment** includes two parts: **replacement investment** (to make good depreciation or capital consumption), which simply maintains the size of the existing capital stock by replacing worn-out capital, and **net investment**, which adds to the capital stock, thereby increasing

productive potential. Along with **technical progress**, net investment is one of the engines of economic growth.

Investment in physical capital goods can be of two types:
- **investment in fixed capital**, such as new factories or plant and social capital such as roads and socially-owned hospitals
- **inventory investment** in stocks of raw materials or variable capital

Determinants of investment in fixed capital

Entrepreneurs' expectations of an investment's *future* yield or rate of return and the cost of borrowing funds to finance the purchase of capital goods are two of the main determinants of investment in fixed capital. Suppose that a firm expects an investment to yield a return of 8% on average for each year of the investment's expected future life. If the cost of borrowing the funds to finance the investment (i.e. the rate of interest) is 6%, the investment is worthwhile, since it is expected to be profitable. An expected rate of return of only 4% would render the investment unprofitable.

Extension material

The marginal efficiency of capital

The expected future rate of return of capital and the rate of interest or cost of borrowing are part of a theory of investment first explained by John Maynard Keynes in his marginal efficiency of capital theory (part of his General Theory) of 1936.

At any point in time, there are thousands of potential investment projects not yet undertaken in the economy. Each *potential* project has its own expected future income stream and expected future rate of return, represented in Figure 18.4 by the symbol i. If the expected future productivity was calculated for each and every possible capital project available to all the business enterprises in the economy, we could, in principle, rank the investments in descending order of expected future yields. Plotted on a graph, the resulting function is known as the marginal efficiency of capital curve. This is the downward-sloping line in Figure 18.4.

Taking the rate of interest as given at r_1, the equilibrium level of aggregate investment (I_1) is determined on the graph at the point where the marginal efficiency of capital equals the cost of borrowing. This is where $i = r$. The investment I_1 is the marginal investment. This investment is expected to be only just worthwhile, since the value of its future returns are expected to match exactly the cost of borrowing the funds to finance the investment. However, all investments to the left of I_1 in the graph are supra-marginal or worthwhile. For them, $i > r$. Investments to the right of I_1 are sub-marginal and should not be undertaken. Future returns are expected to be less than the interest payments needed to finance the investments.

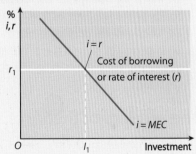

Figure 18.4 The marginal efficiency of capital theory

Other determinants of investment, besides expected future rates of return and the rate of interest, include the relative prices of capital and labour, the nature of technical progress, the adequacy of financial institutions in the supply of investment funds and the impact of government policies and activities on investment by the private sector.

When the price of capital rises (for example when the prices of capital goods or rates of interest rise), in the long run firms adopt more labour-intensive methods of production, substituting labour for capital. A decrease in the relative prices of capital goods has the opposite effect. If the price of capital goods or interest rates fall, firms switch to capital-intensive methods of production, so investment increases.

Technical progress can make machinery obsolete or out-of-date. When this happens, a machine's business life becomes shorter than its technical life, i.e. the number of years before the machine wears out. A sudden burst of technical progress may cause firms to replace capital goods early, long before the end of the equipment's technical life.

Many investments in fixed capital goods are long-term investments that yield most of their expected income several years into the future. These investments may be difficult to finance because of the inadequacy of the financial institutions that provide investment funds. Banks have been criticised for favouring short-term investments and being reluctant to provide the finance for long-term investments. Likewise, the stock market may favour short-termism over long-termism, though in recent years, the growth of private equity finance has emerged to provide an important source of medium to longer-term finance.

> **key term**
>
> **Technical progress** is improvements in methods of production resulting from invention, innovation and research and development. It often leads to the production of new types of goods and better quality goods.

Governments can also provide funds for firms to borrow to finance investment projects. Arguably, however, when choosing whether to invest in or support investment projects, governments may be better at picking losers than picking winners. In the past, UK governments have sometimes provided investment funds to rescue jobs in loss-making and uncompetitive industries that ought to be allowed to continue their decline. As government ministers and their civil servants do not face the risk of being bankrupted by wrong investment decisions, they don't face the financial incentives to make optimal investment decisions.

The accelerator theory of investment

The **accelerator theory** stems from a simple and mechanical assumption that firms wish to keep a relatively fixed ratio, known as the **capital–output ratio**, between the output they are currently producing and their existing stock of fixed capital assets. If output grows by a constant amount each year, firms invest

in exactly the same amount of new capital each year to enlarge their capital stock so as to maintain the desired capital–output ratio. From year to year, the level of investment is therefore constant. When the rate of growth of output accelerates, investment also increases as firms take action to enlarge the stock of capital to a level sufficient to maintain the desired capital–output ratio. When the rate of growth of output decelerates, investment declines.

> **key terms**
>
> The **accelerator** is a change in the level of investment in new capital goods induced by a change in national income or output. The size of the accelerator depends on the economy's **capital–output ratio**.

Extension material

A numerical example of the accelerator

To illustrate the accelerator principle, I shall assume the economy's capital–output ratio is 4:1, or simply 4. This means that 4 units of capital are required to produce 1 unit of output. I shall also assume that the level of *current* net investment in fixed capital depends on the change in income or output in the *previous* year:

$$I = v(\Delta Y)$$

$$\text{or } I_t = v(Y_t - Y_{t-1})$$

where I_t is net investment this year, Y is current national income, Y_{t-1} is national income last year and v is the capital-output ratio. The capital–output ratio, v, is also known as the accelerator coefficient, or simply as the accelerator. I shall also assume no replacement investment is needed, and that the average capital–output ratio in the economy stays at 4.

Given these assumptions, consider the following numerical example of the accelerator principle.

Table 18.1

Year	Net investment		Current income		Last year's income
t = 2008	£40bn	=	4 x (£100bn	–	£90bn)
t = 2009	£40bn	=	4 x (£110bn	–	£100bn)
t = 2010	£80bn	=	4 x (£130bn	–	£110bn)
t = 2011	£40bn	=	4 x (£140bn	–	£130bn)

In each of the years from 2008 to 2011, national income grows. Between 2007 (the year preceding the data in the table) and 2008, income grows by £10 billion. Via the capital–output ratio, the £10 billion income growth induces net investment of £40 billion in 2008. The size of the capital stock increases by £40 billion, which enables the desired capital–output ratio to be maintained at the now higher level of income. In the second row, income continues to grow by £10 billion, so investment in 2009 remains at £40 billion. However, the next year is different. In 2010, shown in the third row, the growth of income accelerates, doubling from £10 billion to £20 billion. Investment also doubles from £40 billion to £80 billion to maintain the value of the capital–output ratio. Thus, a £10 billion increase in income induces a £40 billion increase in investment. But in the fourth row, the growth of income falls back to £10 billion in 2011. Although income is still growing, net investment falls back to £40 billion.

This example shows how the accelerator gets its name. The data show the rate of growth of income and output determining whether investment grows, falls, or remains at a constant level. In summary:

- If income grows by the same amount each year, net investment is constant.
- If income growth speeds up or *accelerates*, net investment increases.
- If income growth slows down or *decelerates*, net investment declines.

As firms adjust the stock of capital to the desired level, relatively slight changes in the rate of growth of income or output cause large absolute rises and falls in investment. The acceleration theory therefore provides a second explanation (the MEC theory provides the first explanation) of why investment in capital goods is a more volatile or unstable component of aggregate demand than consumption.

The circular flow of income and aggregate demand

The first version of the circular flow model, illustrated in Figures 18.5 and 18.6, is based on the simplifying assumption that there are just two sets of economic agents in the economy: households and firms (I am pretending that the government and foreign trade don't exist). Figures 18.5 and 18.6 assume a two-sector economy, or a closed economy with no government sector. The dashed flow lines in the figures show the real flows occurring in the economy between households and firms. Households supply labour and other factor services in exchange for goods and services produced by the firms. These *real flows* generate money flows of income and expenditure, shown by the solid flow lines.

> ℮**xaminer's voice**
>
> Refresh your memory on the difference between real and nominal or money flows taking place in the economy.

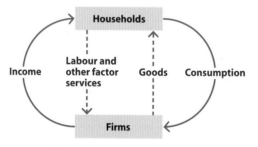

Figure 18.5 A simplified circular flow diagram of a two-sector economy

Aggregate demand in this simplified economy is represented by the equation and identity:

$$AD = C + I$$

There is no saving, but also no investment by firms. All the income received by households (shown by the left-hand flow curve of the diagram) is spent on consumption (shown by the right-hand flow curve). **Deficient aggregate demand** (and likewise **excess aggregate**

> ℮**xaminer's voice**
>
> The circular flow model is one of the two macro-economic models of how the economy works that you need to know. The second model, the *AD/AS* model, is explained in Chapter 19.

demand) cannot occur in this economy — as long as the assumption that all income is spent on consumption holds. At the current price level, spending is just sufficient to purchase the real output produced.

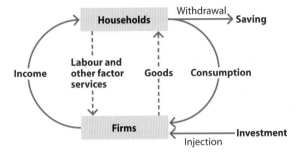

Figure 18.6 Introducing saving and investment into the circular flow of income

Figure 18.6 is more realistic than Figure 18.5, because it shows households saving as well as consuming, and firms investing in capital goods. When households save part of their incomes, people are spending less than their incomes. Saving, which is an example of a **leakage** or **withdrawal from the circular flow of income**, is depicted by the upper of the two horizontal arrows in Figure 18.6. The lower of the two horizontal arrows shows investment, or spending by firms on raw materials, machinery and other capital goods, which is an **injection of demand** into the economy.

The equilibrium level of national income

If planned saving (or the planned *withdrawal* of spending) equals planned investment (or the planned injection of spending into the flow), **national income is in equilibrium**, tending neither to rise nor fall. However, if the withdrawal exceeds the injection, the resulting net leakage of spending from the circular flow causes output and income to fall.

Savings can be hoarded, or the funds being saved can be lent for others to spend. Hoarding, for example keeping money under the mattress, means that a fraction of income is not spent. However, if all savings are lent, via financial intermediaries such as banks, for firms and other consumers to spend, planned saving may end up equalling planned investment. With this outcome, national income remains in equilibrium and there is no reason why the level of income should fall.

In the two-sector circular flow model, national income is in equilibrium when:

planned saving = planned investment

or: $S = I$

However, because households and firms have different motives for making their respective saving and investment decisions, there is no reason why, initially,

household saving should exactly equal the amount firms plan to spend on capital goods (i.e. investment). Let us consider a situation in which planned saving is greater than planned investment ($S > I$). In this situation, the national income or output circulating round the economy is in disequilibrium, with leakages out of the system exceeding injections of spending into the flow of income.

Keynes and deficient aggregate demand

If planned saving by households exceeds planned investment by firms, there is a danger that deficient aggregate demand may cause the economy to sink into a recession. In the 1930s, during the Great Depression, John Maynard Keynes argued that if household savings are not lent to finance spending by others, particularly investment by firms, the level of income or output circulating round the economy falls. This reduces saving, until planned saving equals planned investment and equilibrium is restored, albeit at a significantly lower level of national income. The economy ends up in recession.

examiner's voice

Whether or not deficient aggregate demand exists in the economy, except temporarily, is one of the issues separating Keynesian and free-market economists.

The free-market view of deficient aggregate demand

Keynes's opponents believed that deficient aggregate demand only exists as a *temporary* and self-correcting phenomenon. They argued that when deficient aggregate demand occurs, the rate of interest, rather than the level of income or output, falls, quickly restoring equality between saving and investment intentions. When interest rates fall, people save less because saving becomes less attractive. At the same time, firms invest more in new capital goods because the cost of borrowing has fallen.

Keynes agreed that a fall in interest rates can bring about equality between saving and investment but he believed the process to be slow. In the very long run it may work, but, as in Keynes's memorable phrase, 'in the long run we are all dead'. Keynes argued that when planned leakages of demand from the circular flow of income exceed planned injections of demand into the flow, the level of income or output falls to restore equilibrium. According to Keynes, deficient aggregate demand is the cause of recessions.

Introducing the government sector and the overseas sector into the circular flow model

Figure 18.7 illustrates a four-sector model of the economy, incorporating the full aggregate demand equation introduced at the beginning of the chapter:

$$AD = C + I + G + (X - M)$$

key terms

A **closed economy** is an economy with no international trade.

An **open economy** is an economy with exports and imports.

I have now extended the circular flow model to show an **open economy** with a government sector. The government and overseas sectors have been added to the two demand sectors, households and firms, included in the simplified, circular flow model.

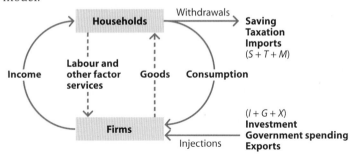

Figure 18.7

The components of aggregate demand and the circular flow of income in an open economy with a government sector

To recap, in the two-sector circular flow model, national income is in equilibrium when:

planned saving = planned investment

or: $S = I$

In the extended circular flow model, national income is in equilibrium, tending neither to rise nor to fall, when:

saving + taxation + imports = investment + government spending + exports

or: $S + T + M = I + G + X$

However, whenever:

$S + T + M > I + G + X$

a net leakage of demand out of the circular flow occurs, which in Keynesian analysis causes the equilibrium level of national income to fall.

If:

$S + T + M < I + G + X$

a net injection of demand into the circular flow occurs, which for Keynesians causes the equilibrium level of national income to rise.

Summary

- Aggregate demand is total *planned* spending on real output of all the economic agents in the economy.
- Consumption by households and investment by firms are two components of aggregate demand.
- Saving, or income which is not consumed, must not be confused with investment.
- Consumption and saving are determined by the same factors.
- Aggregate consumption and saving are determined by the rate of interest, the levels of current and future income, wealth, consumer confidence and the availability of credit.

- The household savings ratio measures *realised* saving as a ratio of household income.
- Investment is determined by factors such as the rate of interest, expected returns on capital, technical progress ,the availability of finance, and the acceleration theory.
- The nature of aggregate demand can be illustrated in a circular flow model of the economy.
- The circular flow model can illustrate injections into and leakages from income circulating round the economy and equilibrium national income.

Questions

1 What is aggregate demand?
2 Distinguish between consumption, saving and investment.
3 What is the personal saving ratio?
4 How may the rate of interest affect consumption and saving?
5 Outline Keynes's theory of consumption.
6 Briefly describe the life-cycle theory of consumption.
7 List other influences on consumption.
8 What is the relationship between capital and investment?
9 What is the marginal efficiency of capital (*MEC*)?
10 How is the level of investment determined in the *MEC* theory?
11 What is the circular flow of income?
12 How does saving affect the circular flow of income?

Chapter 19

The aggregate demand and aggregate supply macroeconomic model

In Chapter 18, I introduced the concept of aggregate demand, and explained the determinants of two of the components of aggregate demand: consumption and investment. Chapter 18 also related aggregate demand to the circular flow of income, and explained that when injections of spending into the circular flow equal leakages or withdrawals from the flow, national income is in equilibrium. In this chapter, I extend the analysis to aggregate supply, and examine the interaction of aggregate demand and supply in the AD/AS macroeconomic model of the economy.

Learning outcomes

This chapter will:

- introduce the *AD/AS* model and use the model to explain macroeconomic equilibrium
- distinguish between macroeconomic equilibrium and microeconomic equilibrium
- relate *AD* curves to the explanation of aggregate demand provided in Chapter 18
- explain the meaning of aggregate supply
- explain the slope of the short-run aggregate supply (*SRAS*) curve and discuss its significance
- distinguish between increases and decreases in aggregate demand and aggregate supply and adjustments or movements along *AD* and *AS* curves in response to changes in the price level
- introduce the long-run aggregate supply (*LRAS*) curve
- explain how the vertical free-market *LRAS* curve differs from the Keynesian *LRAS* curve

Introducing the *AD/AS* macroeconomic model of the economy

In recent years, the *AD/AS* model has become the preferred theoretical framework for the investigation of macroeconomic issues. The model is particularly useful for analysing the effect of an increase in aggregate demand on the economy. It does this by addressing the following question: will expansionary fiscal policy and/or monetary policy increase real output and jobs (i.e. will the policy be **reflationary**), or will the price level increase instead (i.e. will the policy be **inflationary**)? The answer to this key macroeconomic question depends on the shape of the aggregate supply (*AS*) curve, in the short run and the long run.

Macroeconomic equilibrium

Macroeconomic equilibrium occurs in an economy's aggregate goods market when the aggregate demand for real output equals the aggregate supply of real output i.e. where *AD* = *AS*. At this point, households, firms, the government and the overseas sector plan to spend in real terms within the economy an amount exactly equal to the level of real output that firms are willing to produce. In Figure 19.1, macroeconomic equilibrium occurs at point *X*, where the *AD* curve intersects the *AS* curve. The equilibrium level of real output is y_1, and the equilibrium price level is P_1.

key *term*

Macroeconomic equilibrium is the level of real national output at which *AD* = *AS or* at which planned injections into the circular flow of income equal planned withdrawals from the flow.

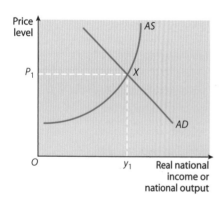

Figure 19.1 *Macroeconomic equilibrium*

INGRAM

The economy is in equilibrium when firms are willing to produce an amount equal to aggregate demand

Box 19.1 The danger of confusing macroeconomic and microeconomic equilibrium

A common mistake students make when answering examination questions is to confuse macroeconomic equilibrium and microeconomic equilibrium. When this confusion occurs, examiners cannot give candidates the full marks that would be available for a correct and relevant diagram.

To avoid this confusion, you should compare the following diagrams:

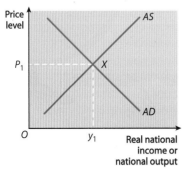

Figure 19.2 *Macroeconomic equilibrium*

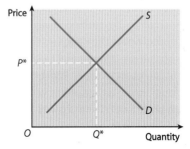

Figure 19.3 *Microeconomic equilibrium*

Figure 19.2, which is the same as Figure 19.1 (except that it depicts a linear (straight-line) rather than a non-linear *AS* curve), shows macroeconomic equilibrium. Figure 19.3, which is similar to Figure 5.2 in Chapter 5 showing equilibrium in the tomato market, illustrates microeconomic equilibrium. Although the figures appear to be similar, they have different meanings. Macroeconomic equilibrium relates to the whole economy, or the economy in aggregate. Microeconomic equilibrium occurs in a particular market *within* the economy, under the assumption that everything else in the economy is held fixed (the ceteris paribus assumption). The price shown in Figure 19.3 is the good's price *relative* to all other prices in the economy (which are held fixed under the ceteris paribus assumption). Don't confuse the *relative* price of a good (microeconomics) with the *average price level* for all goods (macroeconomics). As a general rule, when answering exam questions for Unit 2, only use an *AD/AS* diagram. Likewise, only use a micro diagram when answering a Unit 1 question.

Follow-up questions

1 What is the difference between macroeconomics and microeconomics?
2 What is the difference between the price of a good and the average price level?

Extension material

Building and using economic models

This chapter introduces you to the *AD/AS* macroeconomic model. Model-building is one of the most fundamental analytical techniques used by economists. Economic theory is based on developing economic models which describe particular aspects of the economic behaviour of individuals, groups of individuals, and in a macro context, the whole economy.

A model is a small-scale replica of real-world phenomena, often incorporating a number of simplifications. An economic model simplifies the real world in such a way that the essential

features of an economic relationship or set of relationships are explained using diagrams, words and often algebra. Models are used by economists, first to understand and explain the working of the economy and second, to predict what might happen in the future.

A good economic model simplifies reality sufficiently to allow important and often otherwise obscure economic relationships to be studied, away from irrelevant detail or 'background noise'. The danger is that reality can be oversimplified, with the resulting model failing to reflect in a useful way the world it seeks to explain. Economic modelling involves the art of making strong assumptions about human behaviour so as to concentrate attention and analysis on key economic relationships in a clear and tractable way, while avoiding an excessive oversimplification of the problem or relationship to be explained.

This globe is a small-scale replica of the Earth

The ultimate purpose of model-building is to derive predictions about economic behaviour, such as the prediction of demand theory that demand will increase when price falls. Economic controversy often exists when models generate conflicting predictions about what will happen in a given set of circumstances. For example, a model of the labour market which predicts that the supply of labour increases as wages rise carries the policy-making implication that a cut in income tax, being equivalent to a wage rise, creates an incentive to effort and hard work. Under alternative assumptions, the model could predict the opposite, that as wages rise workers begin to prefer leisure to work and react to the tax cut by working less.

It may often be possible to accept or dismiss a model of economic behaviour on the basis of common sense or casual observation of the world around us. Economists now usually go further, using sophisticated statistical tests to evaluate empirically the model's predictions. Good economic models or theories survive the process of empirical testing (which is part of a branch of the subject called 'econometrics'), whereas models or theories shown to be at odds with observed behaviour must be revised or discarded.

Aggregate demand

The **aggregate demand** (*AD*) curve illustrated in Figure 19.1 shows the total quantities of real output that all economic agents — households, firms, the government and the overseas sector — *plan* to purchase *at different price levels* within the economy, when all the factors influencing aggregate demand, other than the price level, are held constant. If any of the determinants of aggregate demand change (apart from the price level), the *AD* curve shifts right or left, depending on whether there has been an increase or a decrease in aggregate demand. For example, an increase in consumer or business confidence shifts

*e*xaminer's voice

The slope of the *AD* curve tells us what happens to aggregate demand when the price level changes. Don't make the mistake of asserting that a change in the price level shifts the *AD* curve.

*k*ey term

Aggregate demand is the total planned spending on real output produced within the economy.

the *AD* curve right, via the effect on consumption or investment. Likewise, expansionary monetary policy and expansionary fiscal policy both shift the *AD* curve right. Contractionary monetary or fiscal policy, or a collapse in consumer or business confidence, shift the *AD* curve left.

Demand can also originate in the overseas sector of the economy. Spending by residents of other countries on UK output (i.e. exports) is an injection into the circular flow of UK income. Conversely, spending by UK residents on goods produced in other countries (i.e. imports) is demand for their output rather than demand for UK output. Imports are a withdrawal or leakage from the circular flow of UK income. Thus, net export demand (exports minus imports or $X - M$) is a component of aggregate demand. If exports increase, the *AD* curve shifts right, but if imports increase, it shifts left.

Extension material

Explaining the shape of the *AD* curve

At AS, you must understand that the *AD* curve slopes down to the right, showing that all the economic agents in the economy *plan* to demand more real output as the average price level falls. You are unlikely to be asked to explain why an *AD* curve slopes down, but the explanations are useful to know.

A number of factors explain the slope of the *AD* curve, as distinct from a shift of the curve.

One explanation lies in a wealth effect or real balance effect. Assuming a given *nominal* stock of money (or money supply) in the economy, a decrease in the price level increases people's *real*

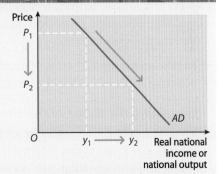

Figure 19.4 Aggregate demand for real output expands from y_1 to y_2, following a fall in the average price level from P_1 to P_2

money balances, i.e. the same amount of money buys more goods and services. Because money is a part of people's wealth, an increase in real money balances makes people wealthier. As we saw in Chapter 18, when wealth increases, consumption also increases, which means that the demand for real output increases following a fall in the price level.

The increase in real money balances also means that the real money supply has increased, relative to people's demand or desire to hold money, for example in cash or in bank deposits. Basic supply and demand analysis tells us that when the supply of any commodity increases relative to demand for the commodity, its price tends to fall. Now, the rate of interest is the price of money. The increase in the supply of real money balances relative to demand reduces real interest rates, which leads to higher levels of consumption and investment.

A third factor relates to exports and imports. When the domestic price level falls (and assuming the exchange rate remains unchanged), demand increases for the country's exports. At the same time, consumers buy domestically-produced goods instead of imports because the latter have become relatively more expensive.

Aggregate supply

Just as the *AD* curve shows the total quantities of real output that economic agents plan to purchase at different levels of domestic prices, so the *AS* curve shows the quantities of real output that businesses plan to produce and sell at different price levels.

> **key term**
>
> **Aggregate supply** is the level of real national output that producers are prepared to supply at different average price levels.

The position of the *AS* curve

Just as with the *AD* curve, if one of the factors determining the position of the *AS* curve changes, the curve shifts right or left.

The factors determining the position of the *AS* curve are virtually the same as those fixing the position of a market supply curve in a particular microeconomic market, such as those studied in Chapter 4. The main determinants are costs of production, taxes firms have to pay, technology, productivity, attitudes, enterprise, factor mobility, economic incentives facing workers and firms, and the institutional structure of the economy.

To take an example, if costs of production increase at all levels of real output, the *AS* curve shifts left. A fall in costs of production shifts the *AS* curve right.

Explaining the shape of the short-run *AS* curve

While it is seldom necessary at AS for students to explain the shape and slope of the *AD* curve, this is not true for the *AS* curve, because there are two aggregate supply curves: the **short-run aggregate supply (SRAS) curve** and the **long-run aggregate supply (LRAS) curve**.

> **examiner's voice**
>
> You must know the difference between short-run and long-run *AS* curves, and the different contexts in which to use the curves to analyse economic problems and issues.

The *AS* curve drawn in Figure 19.1 is an *SRAS* curve, even though I did not label it as such, being more concerned at the beginning of the chapter with introducing you to aggregate supply than with distinguishing between the short run and the long run.

Nowadays, there is general agreement that, in the short run, *AS* curves slope upward. An upward-sloping *SRAS* curve is illustrated in Figure 19.5.

The upward-slope of the *SRAS* curve is explained by two microeconomic assumptions about the nature of firms:

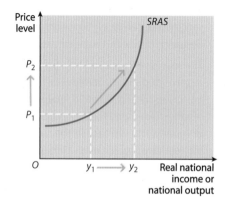

Figure 19.5 An upward-sloping SRAS *curve*

- all firms aim to maximise profits
- in the short run, the cost of producing extra units of output increases as firms produce more output

At the average price level P_1 in Figure 19.5, the level of real output that all the economy's firms are willing to produce and sell is y_1. To persuade the firms it is in their interest to produce the larger output of y_2, the price level must rise. This is because higher prices are needed to create the higher sales revenues needed to offset the higher production costs firms incur as they increase output, so that profits do not fall. In Figure 19.5, the average price level has to rise to P_2 in order to create conditions in which profit-maximising firms are willing and able to supply more output. If the prices firms could charge were not to rise, it would not be profitable to increase supply. Without a higher price level, profit-maximising firms, taken in aggregate, will not voluntarily increase the supply of real output.

Extension material

The slope of the *SRAS* curve

At AS you need to know that in the short run the cost of producing an extra unit of output increases as more output is produced. At A2 you will learn about an important economic 'law' known as the law of diminishing returns.

In the short run, firms cannot change some of the capital equipment they use, for example buildings and machines. These are examples of fixed capital, which, as the name indicates, comprises capital goods that cannot be added to or reduced in size in the short run. It follows that the only way firms can increase output in the short run is by adding increasing numbers of variable factors of production to their fixed capital assets.

Labour is usually classified as a variable factor of production. However, as more workers are added to a fixed quantity of capital, a point is reached beyond which extra workers add less to total output than previous workers added to the firms' labour forces. This results in diminishing returns to labour.

At any given money wage rate paid to workers, diminishing returns to labour mean that in the short run, output rises at a slower rate than the cost of hiring more workers. This means that as output increases, the cost of producing an extra unit of output also increases.

This brings us back to the shape of the *SRAS* curve. The *SRAS* curve slopes upward because profit-maximising firms are only willing to produce more output if sales revenues rise to compensate for the rising average costs of production the firms experience as their output increases.

A cautionary note

Different textbooks and teachers hold different views on the shape and slope of the *SRAS* curve. As a result, the explanations in this chapter may differ from

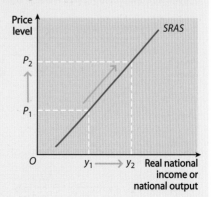

Figure 19.6 *A linear* SRAS *curve*

those you come across elsewhere. Some textbooks assume that the *SRAS* curve is linear (an upward-sloping straight line, see Figure 19.6).

In an AQA exam, it does not matter whether you draw a curved (Figure 19.5) or linear (Figure 19.6) *SRAS* curve. However, you will lose marks if you confuse an *SRAS* with an *AD* curve, or if you confuse the short-run aggregate supply curve with a long-run aggregate supply (*LRAS*) curve.

Increases and decreases in aggregate demand or aggregate supply

Increases and decreases of aggregate demand refer respectively to shifts of the *AD* curve to the left and the right. Likewise, increases and decreases of aggregate supply refer to similar shifts of the *SRAS* curve.

> ### examiner's voice
>
> In microeconomics, exam candidates often confuse an increase or decrease in demand (or supply) with the resulting expansion or contraction along the curve that hasn't shifted. Similar mistakes are made in macroeconomic exams, when, for example, a candidate confuses a decrease in *AD* with the resulting contraction of aggregate supply.

A shift of the *AD* curve, such as that illustrated in Figure 19.7 (a), must not be confused with the adjustment that follows along the *SRAS* curve. In this case, the adjustment is called an expansion or extension of aggregate supply.

Figure 19.7 (b) shows a shift of the *SRAS* curve to the left, followed by a movement or adjustment up the *AD* curve. This time, the adjustment is called a contraction of aggregate demand. Other possibilities not shown in the diagram are a decrease in aggregate demand (or shift of the *AD* curve to the left) followed by a contraction of aggregate supply, and an increase in aggregate supply (shift of the *SRAS* curve to the right) followed by an expansion or extension of aggregate demand. As a practice exercise, try drawing diagrams to illustrate these events.

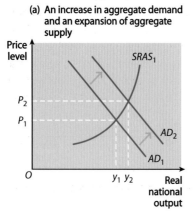

(a) An increase in aggregate demand and an expansion of aggregate supply

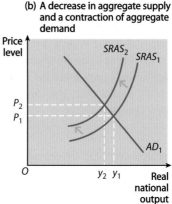

(b) A decrease in aggregate supply and a contraction of aggregate demand

Figure 19.7
Shifts of, and adjustment along, AD and AS curves

Applying the *AD/AS* macroeconomic model in the short run

At the beginning of the chapter, I stated that the *AD/AS* macroeconomic model of the economy is particularly useful for analysing the effect of an increase in aggregate demand on the economy. I shall now illustrate this proposition with the aid of Figure 19.8, which shows an upward-sloping *SRAS* curve, together with a number of *AD* curves.

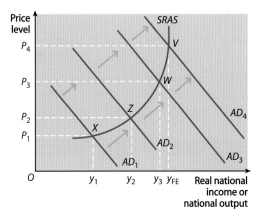

Figure 19.8 The effect of a rightward shift of AD on the economy

Figure 19.8 tells us that, with an upward-sloping *SRAS* curve, an increase in aggregate demand simultaneously **reflates** real output and creates jobs, and **inflates** the price level. The extent to which the demand increase is reflationary or inflationary depends on the steepness of the *SRAS* curve to the right of the initial macroeconomic equilibrium. Suppose that macroeconomic equilibrium initially is at point *X* in Figure 19.8, with the aggregate demand curve in position AD_1. In this situation, which depicts a recessionary economy suffering significant demand deficiency, an increase in aggregate demand to AD_2 increases both real output and the price level. The increase in aggregate demand simultaneously reflates and inflates the economy, though the reflationary effect is greater as long as the *SRAS* curve is gently-sloped. Real output and the price level both increase, respectively to y_2 and P_2, to bring about a new macroeconomic equilibrium at point *Z*.

*k*ey terms
Inflation is a persistent or continuing rise in the average price level.
Reflation is an increase in the level of real output following an increase in aggregate demand.

However, as the *SRAS* curve becomes steeper, any further increase in aggregate demand, for example to AD_3, is more inflationary than reflationary. The increase in aggregate demand to AD_3 moves macroeconomic equilibrium to point *W*. Real output has increased to y_3, and the price level has risen to P_3.

Thus, for any given shift of the *AD* curve to the right along an ever-steeper *SRAS* curve, the reflationary effect of the increase in demand becomes smaller and the inflationary effect becomes greater, particularly as the economy approaches full employment. The shift of the *AD* curve to the right from AD_3 to AD_4 illustrates this. Following the move from AD_3 to AD_4, the new macroeconomic equilibrium occurs at point *V*. Real output is now the full employment level of output (y_{FE}). Figure 19.8 shows that any further increase in aggregate demand to the right of AD_4 solely causes inflation. As the economy is producing at full capacity (being on its production possibility frontier), real output cannot increase any further, except perhaps temporarily.

The difference between long-run and short-run aggregate supply

The aggregate supply curves considered so far in this chapter are short-run *AS* curves. I shall now extend my analysis to explain the economy's long-run aggregate supply (*LRAS*) curve. Many economists believe that the *LRAS* curve is vertical, as illustrated in Figure 19.9.

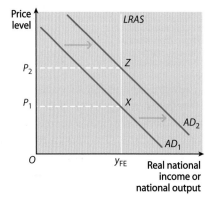

Figure 19.9
The vertical long-run aggregate supply curve

In the short run, the aggregate supply or real output depends on the average price level in the economy. Other things remaining constant, firms are only prepared to supply more output if the price level rises. However, in the long run, aggregate supply is *not* influenced by the price level. Long-run supply reflects the economy's production potential. It is the maximum level of output the economy can produce when the economy is on its production possibility frontier.

Producing on the production possibility frontier means the labour force is fully employed. Thus, the vertical *LRAS* curve in Figure 19.9 is located immediately above the full-employment level of output (y_{FE}).

The level of output at y_{FE} is the is a maximum level of physical output that the economy can produce. As Figure 19.9 shows, once the economy produces the full employment level of real output, an increase in aggregate demand from AD_1 to AD_2 increases the price level from P_1 to P_2, but real output remains unchanged.

Extension material

Producing to the right of the full-employment level of real output

If you refer to the section covering output gaps in Chapter 17, you will see that the economy can temporarily produce at a point outside its current production possibility frontier. However, because this represents overuse of capacity, such a point cannot be sustained for long.

In the context of the *AD/AS* model, this means that the economy can produce *temporarily* in a position to the right of the *LRAS* curve and above the full-employment level of output, for example at point *W* in Figure 19.10. Note that in this diagram the *SRAS* curve extends to the right of the full-employment level of output (y_{FE}), without becoming vertical at point *X*. For a short period, output can rise above y_{FE} to y_1, but as the arrow at the bottom of the figure shows, eventually output falls back to the full-employment level.

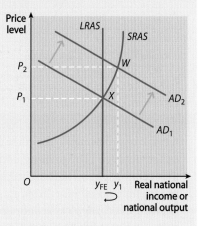

Figure 19.10 A temporary increase in output above the full-employment level of output

The position of the *LRAS* curve, shifts of the *LRAS* curve, and economic growth

The position of the *LRAS* curve is determined by the same factors that determine the position of the economy's production possibility frontier: the quantities of capital and labour and other factors of production in the economy, and technical progress.

Chapter 17 explains how an *increase* in the quantity of available factors of production, and improvements in technology that

increase the productivity of labour, capital or land, shift the economy's production possibility frontier outward. For the same reasons, the economy's *LRAS* curve shifts right. The shifts of the production possibility frontier and the *LRAS* curve to the right are both illustrated in Figure 19.11.

examiner's voice

You can illustrate long-term economic growth, either by shifting the *LRAS* curve right, by shifting the economy's production possibility frontier right, or by drawing a diagram to show the economy's trend growth rate.

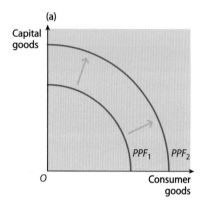
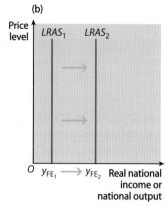

Figure 19.11 Linking an outward movement of the economy's production possibility frontier to a shift of the LRAS *curve to the right*

A final way of bringing together the economy's production possibility frontier and its *LRAS* curve is by relating both to the process of economic growth. Remember that economic growth (long-run) involves an outward movement of the economy's production possibility frontier. This is shown in Figure 19.11 (a). Meanwhile, Figure 19.11 (b) depicts economic growth in terms of a shift of the economy's *LRAS* curve to the right. The shift from $LRAS_1$ to $LRAS_2$ increases the full-employment level of real output, from y_{FE1} to y_{FE2}.

Free-market and Keynesian long-run aggregate supply curves

The AQA Unit 2 specification states that: 'emphasis should be given to the assumption that the *LRAS* curve is vertical but candidates should also have an understanding of the Keynesian *LRAS* curve'.

The vertical *LRAS* curve described in this chapter is sometimes called the free-market *LRAS* curve. This label reflects the view commonly expressed by free-market economists that, provided markets function competitively and efficiently, the economy always operates at or close to full capacity. In the short run, real output is influenced by the average price level, but in the long run, aggregate supply is determined by maximum production capacity (though as the Extension material on page 235 explains, an economy can *temporarily* produce above full capacity, when there is a positive output gap).

AQA AS Economics

Most modern Keynesians (who are often called New Keynesians) agree that the *LRAS* curve is vertical. However, in the past, some Keynesians have been associated with a different *LRAS* curve illustrated in Figure 19.12. This curve is derived from Keynes's own views on how the economy operates.

The Keynesian *LRAS* curve is based on Keynes's explanation of the Great Depression in the UK and US economies in the 1930s. Keynes argued that a depressed economy can settle into an under-full employment equilibrium, shown for example by point *A* on the horizontal section of the *LRAS* curve. At point *A* in Figure 19.12, the level of real national output is y_1. Keynes argued that without purposeful intervention by the government, an economy could display more or less permanent demand-deficiency. Market forces would fail to adjust automatically and achieve full employment. If the government could shift *AD* to the right along the horizontal section of the *LRAS* curve (mainly through expansionary fiscal policy), the existence of huge amounts of spare capacity would lead, in Keynes's view, to a growth in real output (and employment), without an increase in the price level.

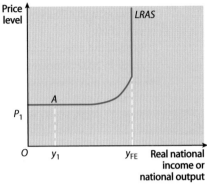

Figure 19.12
The Keynesian LRAS *curve*

Box 19.2 Applying *AD/AS* analysis to the US economy

Unit 2 data-response examination questions usually include information about the state of a national economy (not necessarily the UK). Below is some information about the US economy from 2000 to 2004. Think how you might use *AD/AS* diagrams and analysis to answer the questions that follow.

Two years ago, at the peak of the late-1990s boom, the US economy was slightly overheated. As the unemployment rate fell to 4% and below, inflation began to creep upwards, rising by between a quarter and half a percentage point each year. By late 2000 it was clear that America's gross domestic product was 1–2 percentage points above potential output — above the level at which aggregate demand balanced aggregate supply, at least in the sense that there was neither upward nor downward pressure on inflation.

Today, in 2002, things are very different. The USA's level of real GDP is running 2 percentage

points higher than it was in the summer of 2000. However, there is an extremely strong underlying productivity growth trend driven by technological revolutions in data processing and data communications. These technological revolutions have boosted potential output by perhaps 7% over the past 2 years. Thus, today the USA's real GDP is not 1–2% above, but 3–4% below potential output.

Bradford DeLong, professor of economics at the University of California at Berkeley, *Financial Times*, 22 August 2002

Follow-up questions

1 Using *AD* and *AS* curves, illustrate how the US economy may have become 'overheated' in the year 2000.

2 Explain the effect of changes in technology and productivity on the position of the *LRAS* curve in 2002 compared with its position in 2000.

Summary

- The *AD/AS* model can be used to show macroeconomic equilibrium in the economy.

- Don't confuse macroeconomic equilibrium and microeconomic equilibrium.

- Make sure you can relate the *AD* curve to the explanation of aggregate demand in Chapter 18.

- The *AD* curve shows total planned spending on real national output at different price levels.

- Likewise, the *SRAS* curve shows how much output producers are prepared to supply at different price levels.

- It is important to distinguish between a *shift* of an *AD* or *AS* curve and the resulting *adjustment* along the curve that doesn't shift.

- A shift of the *AD* curve to the right is known as an increase in aggregate demand.

- The resulting movement up the *SRAS* curve is known as an expansion or extension of aggregate supply.

- Similar labelling is used with respect to other shifts of, and adjustment along, the *AD* and *SRAS* curves.

- The *LRAS* curve, which should not be confused with *SRAS* curves, is vertical because it is determined by the maximum potential output the economy can produce.

- The economy can produce to the left of the *LRAS* curve, in which case there is unused capacity and unemployment, *temporarily* to the right of the *LRAS* curve, or above the potential level of output.

- A rightward movement of the *LRAS* curve illustrates long-term economic growth.

- In the past, and as a result of their interpretation of Keynes's 'General Theory' written at the time of the Great Depression in the 1930s, some Keynesian economists have argued that the *LRAS* curve is horizontal to the left of the full-employment level of real output, becoming vertical at the full-employment level of output.

Questions

1 What is macroeconomic equilibrium?

2 Explain the shape of the aggregate demand curve.

3 Define aggregate supply.

4 Explain the shape and slope of a short-run aggregate supply curve.

5 Considering only the *SRAS* curve and not the *LRAS* curve, explain how an increase in aggregate demand may affect output and the price level.

6 Distinguish between short-run and long-run aggregate supply.

7 Why is the *LRAS* curve vertical?

8 Relate the vertical *LRAS* curve to the economy's production possibility curve and to output gaps.

9 Explain the shape of the Keynesian *LRAS* curve.

Chapter 20

Full employment and unemployment

In Chapter 16 I stated how achieving full employment, or at least reducing the level and rate of unemployment, is arguably one of the government's two main policy objectives, the other being an acceptable and sustainable rate of long-term economic growth. I also defined full employment using Lord Beveridge's approach, set out in the 1944 White Paper on Employment Policy. Beveridge stated that an economy with 3% unemployment is more or less is fully employed.

Having explained the two ways in which unemployment is measured in the UK, this chapter offers an alternative definition of full employment, in terms of the aggregate demand for, and the aggregate supply of, labour. It surveys the main causes of un-employment, and the government policies appropriate to reduce unemployment. The chapter concludes by considering the costs of unemployment, for the economy as a whole and for the unemployed and their families.

Learning outcomes

This chapter will:

- explain how unemployment is measured in the UK
- define full employment
- illustrate full employment on a graph showing the economy's aggregate labour market
- explain the main causes of unemployment
- discuss the government policies appropriate for reducing unemployment
- assess the costs of unemployment, both for individuals and for the wider economy

How unemployment is measured in the UK

Unemployment is officially measured or estimated by the UK government in two ways: through the use of the claimant count and the Labour Force Survey.

The claimant count

Until recently, the main measure of unemployment officially used in the UK was the monthly **claimant count**. This is a by-product of the administrative system for paying unemployment-related benefits — the main benefit currently being the Jobseeker's Allowance.

Many economists believe that the claimant count provides an inaccurate measure of true unemployment. Free-market economists in particular argue that the claimant count overstates unemployment because many claimants are either (a) not genuinely looking for work, or (b) not genuinely unemployed because they work in undeclared jobs in the underground or informal economy.

In other respects, however, the claimant count understates true unemployment. The toughening up of eligibility requirements or tests for the availability for work in the 1980s and early 1990s reduced the claimant count without reducing unemployment. Various groups of unemployed, such as young workers on government training schemes and unemployed workers approaching retirement (who were reclassified as 'early retired'), have also been removed from the register, even though some of them would like full-time jobs.

The Labour Force Survey

The UK government now recognises a second measure of unemployment, based on the **Labour Force Survey** (LFS) of households. The LFS method uses standard, internationally-recognised definitions recommended by the International Labour Organisation (ILO). It is a quarterly survey of 60,000 households that counts people as unemployed if they are actively seeking work (they have been looking for a job in the last 4 weeks) and have not had a job during the week in question.

*e*xaminer's voice

Exam questions might be set on how unemployment is measured in the UK. You must also be able to interpret claimant count or LFS data.

*k*ey terms

The **claimant count** is the method of measuring unemployment according to those people who are claiming unemployment-related benefits (Jobseeker's Allowance).

The **Labour Force Survey** is a quarterly sample survey of households in the UK. Its purpose is to provide information on the UK labour market. The survey seeks information on respondents' personal circumstances and their labour market status during a period of 1–4 weeks.

When the LFS method of measuring unemployment is used, the unemployment total is significantly larger than the claimant count total. One of the reasons for this stems from the fact that many people without jobs who are actively looking for work are not registered as unemployed at Job Centres. Take the example of a family in which the father is employed full-time, but the mother stays at home bringing up the couple's children. When their youngest child becomes a teenager, the mother decides to look for a job that allows her to take time off during school holidays or if her children are ill. Because such jobs are few and far between, the mother is prepared to wait until such a vacancy appears. As she is actively looking for work but not claiming benefit, the mother is unemployed according to the LFS measure of unemployment, but not according to the claimant count.

Although the LFS measure is higher than the claimant count, both measures may understate true unemployment because they ignore 'discouraged workers' – people who have given up hope of finding a job even though they would take one if it were offered – and roughly half a million people who are classified as 'economically inactive'.

Box 20.1 Britain has three times the official number of jobless, study finds

The real level of unemployment in Britain is almost three times as high as the official claimant count and has remained unchanged at 2.6 million in the second half of Tony Blair's time in Downing Street, according to a report released today.

A study by researchers at Sheffield Hallam University found that in addition to the 900,000 people out of work and claiming benefit, Britain had another 1.7 million 'hidden jobless'.

According to the report, the main reason for the discrepancy was that the official unemployment figures failed to count those diverted on to other benefits or out of the welfare system altogether. In particular, 1 million of the 2.7 million people on incapacity benefit should be regarded as being in hidden unemployment, the researchers said.

Professor Steve Fothergill, who led the study, said: 'This does not mean that 1 million incapacity claims are fraudulent, but these men and women would almost certainly have been in work in a genuinely fully employed economy.'

The figures show that hidden unemployment is particularly concentrated in the older industrial areas of the north, Scotland and Wales. The estimated real rate of

Official unemployment figures underestimate the size of the problem

unemployment is well above 10% in a number of cities, including Liverpool, Glasgow and Middlesbrough, and in several former coal-mining areas, whereas much of the south of England outside London is at, or close to, full employment.

Larry Elliott, *Guardian*, 13 June 2007

Follow-up questions

1 Relate the 'hidden unemployed' to the causes of unemployment described later in the chapter.
2 How does the informal or underground economy (sometimes called the black economy) affect hidden unemployment?

Making sense of employment and unemployment data

Table 20.1 UK employment and unemployment, 1990–2007

	Employment (millions) (LFS count)	Unemployment (millions) (claimant count)	Unemployment (millions) (LFS count)
1990	26.92	1.65	1.97
1991	26.37	2.27	2.40
1992	25.63	2.74	2.76
1993	25.28	2.88	2.92
1994	25.45	2.60	2.75
1995	25.73	2.29	2.43
1996	26.00	2.09	2.32
1997	26.45	1.58	2.02
1998	26.71	1.35	1.76
1999	27.05	1.25	1.74
2000	27.43	1.09	1.62
2001	27.69	0.97	1.42
2002	27.87	0.95	1.51
2003	28.17	0.93	1.46
2004	28.42	0.85	1.41
2005	28.70	0.86	1.41
2006	28.95	0.95	1.63
2007	29.46	0.86	1.67

Source: ONS website

Table 20.1 shows how employment and unemployment levels changed in the UK over the period from 1990 to 2007. The most important points to be aware of are:

■ Employment rose continuously throughout the 1990s and early 2000s, except for the period 1991–93.

■ The data on unemployment mirror the changes in the level of employment. Thus, unemployment increased from 1990 to 1993, and then fell until the early 2000s. By 2001, unemployment had fallen below the psychologically important level of 1 million, at least when measured by the claimant count.

■ The employment and unemployment data for the early 1990s show the impact of recession on the UK economy.

■ In the decade following the recession of 1990–92, continuous economic growth occurred. Despite occasional slow downs, there was no return to recession, and economic growth increased employment and reduced unemployment. By the early 2000s, many communities in the UK, particularly in southeast England, could be said to be fully employed. However, other regions in the north and west of the UK were not so fortunate, and there are continuing pockets of unemployment in parts of London such as Hackney.

■ By 2005, the UK job market was turning for the worse. The claimant count showed a small increase in both 2005 and 2006, and the LFS measure increased

in 2006. By the third quarter of 2007, the claimant count measure of un-employment was falling again, though the LFS measure was still rising. The general feeling among economists was that slower economic growth would lead to rising unemployment totals over the remaining years of the decade.

■ Much of the increase in employment in recent years results from growth of the public sector. Private sector growth has been weaker and has not created many jobs. However, public sector growth is now weakening and job cuts have been announced, for example in the civil service.

■ The figures also reflect a more deep-seated and perhaps intractable feature of British society: the gap between households in which every adult works, apart from those still in education or retired; and those in which nobody works, but live on welfare benefits instead.

■ In 2006, both unemployment (according to the claimant count and the LFS measure) and employment were growing. This can happen when the number of people available for work grows faster than the number of jobs. Recent immi-gration into the UK provides part of the explanation for this.

■ The gap between unemployment measured by the claimant count and un-employment measured by the LFS occurred in all the years shown in the table. However, the gap has increased in size. By the third quarter of 2007, the LFS measure (at 1.68 million) was just over twice the size of the claimant count measure (at 834,700).

The meaning of full employment

Full employment does not necessarily mean that every single member of the working population is in work. Rather, it is a situation in which the number of people wishing to work at the going market real wage rate equals the number of workers that employers wish to hire at this real wage rate. Figure 20.1 reflects the free-market view that full employment occurs at the level of employment E_{FE}, where the aggregate demand for labour equals the aggregate supply of labour at real wage rate W_{FE}.

key term

According to Beveridge's definition, **full employment** means 3% or less of the labour force unemployed. According to the free-market definition, it is the level of employment occurring at the market-clearing real wage rate at which the number of workers employers wish to hire equals the number of workers wanting to work.

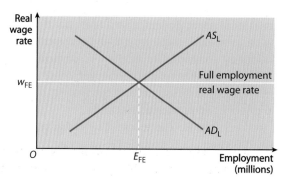

Figure 20.1 Full employment in the economy

Equilibrium employment and unemployment

At AS, it is not necessary to understand the meaning of equilibrium employment and un-employment, but the concepts will be useful at A2. In Figure 20.1, the full employment level of employment E_{FE} occurs when the economy's aggregate labour market is in equilibrium. Free-market economists also call this the natural level of employment.

On first sight, Figure 20.1 suggests that there is *no* unemployment when labour market equilibrium occurs, but as Figure 20.2 shows, this is not the case. There can be unemployment in the economy even when the aggregate labour market clears.

Frictional and structural unemployment (which are explained below and on page 248) are the two forms of equilibrium unemployment. In Figure 20.2, the AS_{LN} curve shows *all* the workers available for work, and not just those willing to work at different real wage rates. The AS_{LN} curve is located to the right of the AS_L curve. Although full employment occurs at E_{FE}, depicted where the AD_L and AS_L curves intersect at point X, equilibrium unemployment is measured by the distance from X to Z, or E_1 minus E_{FE}. Free-market economists call the equilibrium level of unemployment the natural level of unemployment.

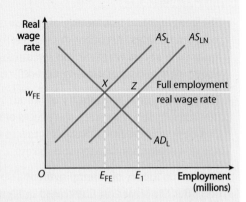

Figure 20.2 Equilibrium unemployment

The causes of unemployment

Full employment does not necessarily mean that every member of the working population is in work. Rather, as I have explained, it means a situation in which the number of people wishing to work at the going market real wage rate equals the number of workers that employers wish to hire at this real wage rate.

However, even this definition needs qualifying, since in a dynamic economy, change is constantly taking place, with some industries declining and others growing. Workers moving between jobs may decide to take a break between the two employments. This is called **frictional unemployment**. As new products are developed and demand and cost conditions change, firms demand more of some labour skills while the demand for other types of labour declines. This leads to **structural unemployment**.

> **key term**
>
> **Frictional unemployment** is voluntary unemployment, occurring when a worker switches between jobs.

Frictional unemployment

Frictional unemployment, also known as **transitional unemployment**, is essentially 'between jobs' unemployment. As its name suggests, this type of unemployment

results from frictions in the labour market which create a delay, or time-lag, during which a worker is unemployed when moving from one job to another. Note that the definition of frictional unemployment assumes a job vacancy exists and that a friction in the job market, caused by the immobility of labour, prevents an unemployed worker from filling the vacancy. It follows that the number of unfilled job vacancies existent in the economy can be used as a measure of the level of frictional unemployment.

Among the causes of frictional unemployment are geographical and occupational immobilities of labour, which prevent workers who are laid off from immediately filling job vacancies.

*e**xaminer's voice*

Do not confuse the *causes* and *effects* of unemployment.

The **geographical immobility of labour** is caused by factors such as family ties and local friendships discouraging people from moving to other parts of the country, ignorance about whether job vacancies exist in other parts of the country, and above all, the cost of moving and difficulties of obtaining housing.

The **occupational immobility of labour** results from difficulties in training for jobs that require different skills, the effects of restrictive practices such as a requirement that new workers must possess unnecessary qualifications, and racial, gender, and age discrimination in labour markets.

The **search theory of unemployment** also helps to explain frictional unemployment. Consider the situation illustrated in Figure 20.3. A worker earning £1,000 a week in a skilled professional occupation loses her job. Although no vacancies apparently exist at present in her current line of work, there are plenty of vacancies for low-skilled office workers earning around £300 a week. Given this information, if on the day of her job loss, the newly-unemployed worker sets the weekly wage she aspires to at £1,000, she will *choose* to be unemployed, at least to start with, because she doesn't wish to fill a lower-paid vacancy. The lower weekly wage on offer, and perhaps poorer conditions of work and status associated with the lower-paid job, fail to meet her aspirations. She may also realise that she possesses imperfect information about the state of the job market. This means she needs to search the labour market to find out whether better-paid and higher status vacancies exist, but which she does not know about currently.

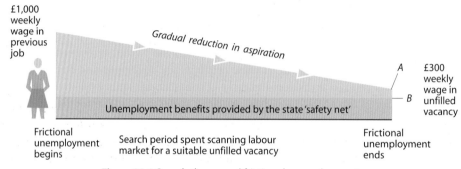

Figure 20.3 Search theory and frictional unemployment

Approached in this way, frictional unemployment can be viewed as a *voluntary* search period in which newly-unemployed workers scan the labour market, searching for vacancies which meet their aspirations.

There are a number of ways in which a voluntary search period can end. First, in the example I have described, the woman may eventually learn of a vacancy for which she is qualified, and which meets her initial aspiration. Indeed, the vacancy might have been there all the time but, until she searched the job market, she was unaware of its existence. Second, the vacancy may have arisen during her search period, perhaps because of a general improvement in the condition of labour markets. Third, she may end her voluntary unemployment if she decides, on the basis of her lack of success in getting a job, that her initial aspirations were unrealistically high and that she must settle for a lower-paid, less attractive job.

Long search periods, which increase the amount of frictional unemployment in the economy, result in part from the welfare benefit system. Without the receipt of welfare benefits, search periods would have to be financed by running down stocks of saving, or through the charity of family and friends. In this situation, the threat of poverty creates an incentive to search the job market more vigorously and to reduce the aspirational wage levels of the unemployed.

The availability of a state safety net provided by unemployment benefits and other income-related welfare benefits, together in some cases with redundancy payments, enable unemployed workers to finance long voluntary search periods. Because of this, many free-market economists support a reduction in the real value of unemployment benefits, together with restricting benefits to those who can prove they are genuinely looking for work. Free-market economists believe these policies create incentives for the unemployed to reduce aspirations quickly, which shortens search periods.

Box 20.2 The replacement ratio

The replacement ratio is a factor influencing the length of periods of voluntary frictional unemployment. It is defined in the following equation:

$$\frac{\text{replacement}}{\text{ratio}} = \frac{\text{disposable income out of work}}{\text{disposable income in work}}$$

The size of the replacement ratio is largely determined by the level of welfare benefits claimable when unemployed, relative to income after taxation and receipt of benefits when in work. A replacement ratio of 100% means that a worker is no better off in work than out of work and living off the state. Even for low-paid workers, replacement ratios are seldom as high as 100%. Nonetheless, high replacement ratios approaching 100% destroy the incentive to work, at least in the 'official' or formal economy. For people with poor job prospects, high replacement ratios create an unemployment trap. Those caught in the unemployment trap are out of work — at least in terms of officially declared employment. The trap contains un-waged social security claimants who 'choose' unemployment over paid work because they are better-off out of work living on benefits, than in low-paid jobs paying income tax and National Insurance Contributions (NIC) and losing some or all of their right to claim means-tested benefits.

In Figure 20.3, for a worker earning £300 a week, points *A* and *B* could be used to calculate the replacement ratio. Point *A* shows the weekly wage (though income tax and receipt of any benefits available to the worker in work also need to be taken into account to calculate weekly disposable income). Point *B* shows the level of welfare benefit claimable out of work.

Follow-up questions

1 Do you agree that all unemployment caused by the geographical and occupational immobility of labour is voluntary? Justify your answer.
2 Can you think of any other reasons, apart from that explained in the passage, for a worker being 'trapped in unemployment'?

Structural unemployment

Structural unemployment results from the structural decline of industries, unable to compete or adapt in the face of changing demand or new products, and the emergence of more efficient competitors in other countries. Structural unemployment is also caused by changing skill requirements as industries change ways of producing their products. In the latter case, the structural unemployment is often called technological unemployment. Technological unemployment results from the successful growth of new industries using labour-saving technology such as **automation**.

In contrast to **mechanisation** (workers operating machines) which has usually increased the overall demand for labour, automation can lessen the demand

> **k**ey term
> **Structural unemployment** is caused by structural change in the economy, for example when industries decline without being replaced by new industries.

Automation can lead to technological unemployment

TOPFOTO

for labour because it means that machines (such as robots) rather than humans operate other machines. Whereas the growth of mechanised industry increases employment, automation of production can lead to the shedding of labour, even when industry output is expanding.

The growth of international competition has been a particularly important cause of structural unemployment. During the post-Second World War era from the 1950s to the 1970s, structural unemployment in the UK was regionally concentrated in areas where nineteenth-century staple industries such as textiles and shipbuilding were suffering structural decline. This regional unemployment, caused by the decline of 'sunset industries', was more than offset by the growth of employment elsewhere in the UK in 'sunrise industries'.

However, in the severe recessions of the early 1980s and 1990s, structural unemployment affected almost all regions in the UK as the de-industrialisation process spread across the manufacturing base. However, the UK economy has benefited from continuous economic growth since the end of the last recession in 1992, though this may not continue. It is difficult to say whether structural unemployment has grown or fallen in this period, as it is not easy to separate changes in structural unemployment from other causes of falling unemployment. In many years, manufacturing output has grown, but manufacturing employment has fallen. There is a danger of exaggerating the growth of unemployment in manufacturing employment, because many activities, ranging from cleaning to IT maintenance, which were previously undertaken in house by manufacturing firms, have been out-sourced to external service sector providers. Structural unemployment has also occurred within the service sector, partly due to the increasing use of ICT and automated services. Call centre employment has grown significantly in the service sector in recent years. However, a decline has been forecast, partly due to call centres moving overseas, but also because companies employ automated communication software rather than human beings to provide customer service and answer telephone and internet queries.

Casual and seasonal unemployment

Casual unemployment is a special case of frictional unemployment, which occurs when workers are laid-off on a short-term basis in trades such as tourism, agriculture, catering and building. When casual unemployment results from regular fluctuations in weather conditions or demand, it is called **seasonal unemployment**.

Cyclical, Keynesian or demand-deficient unemployment

I introduced the possibility of **demand-deficient unemployment** in Chapter 15. Keynes — but not his opponents — believed that deficient aggregate demand was a major cause of persistent mass unemployment between the First and Second World Wars. Free-market economists generally agree that temporary

key terms

Cyclical unemployment is also known as Keynesian and **demand-deficient unemployment**. As this name suggests, it is unemployment caused by a lack of aggregate demand in the economy.

Seasonal unemployment is caused by factors such as the weather and the end of the Christmas shopping period.

unemployment (called **cyclical unemployment**) may be caused by a lack of demand in the downswing of the business cycle. However, Keynes went further, arguing that the economy could settle into an under-full employment equilibrium, caused by a continuing lack of effective aggregate demand. In contrast to frictional unemployment, which is voluntary, Keynes believed that cyclical unemployment is involuntary, i.e. not caused by the workers themselves. As a result, the unemployed should not be blamed for their idleness and lack of work opportunities.

Figure 20.4 illustrates cyclical unemployment in the context of the economy's *AD/AS* diagram. A collapse in business and consumer confidence causes the *AD* curve to shift left from AD_1 to AD_2. If goods and labour markets are competitive, the average price level should then fall from P_1 to P_2. If this happens, real output only falls from y_1 to y_2.

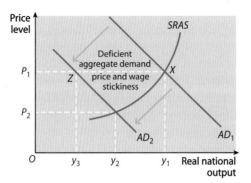

Figure 20.4 Cyclical unemployment caused by a shift of aggregate demand to the left

However, price (and wage) stickiness (or inflexibility) can prevent this happening. If prices (and wages) don't fall, real output falls to y_3 rather than y_2. Deficient aggregate demand, shown by the distance between points X and Z, leads to severe cyclical unemployment.

Figure 20.5, which shows the economy's production possibility frontier (*PPF*), illustrates another way of showing cyclical unemployment. All points on the production possibility frontier, including point X, show the economy using all its productive capacity, including labour. There is no demand deficiency and thus no cyclical unemployment. By contrast, deficient aggregate demand can lead to the economy producing inside its production possibility, for example at point Z. When this is the case, cyclical unemployment exists in the economy.

e*xaminer's voice*

This is an example of applying *AD/AS* analysis to illustrate an important aspect of macroeconomics. There are many other economic problems and issues that can be analysed in similar ways.

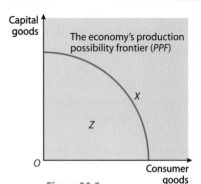

Figure 20.5
Cyclical unemployment and the economy's production possibility frontier

examiner's voice

This is another example of how to use a production possibility curve diagram to illustrate your point. Remember its other applications: scarcity, opportunity cost, choice, productive efficiency and economic growth.

Extension material

Other causes of unemployment

The AQA specification requires knowledge of cyclical, frictional, seasonal and structural unemployment. Unemployment can, however, have causes other than those that lead to the four types of unemployment listed in the AS specification. It is useful, though not essential, to be aware of some of these other causes, particularly if you intend to study economics at A2.

Classical or real-wage unemployment

Before the Keynesian era, economists believed that a large part of the high level of unemployment in the 1920s and 1930s was caused by excessively high real wages in labour markets, which were insufficiently competitive for market forces to eliminate the problem. In recent years, the view that a large part of modern unemployment in the UK, especially youth unemployment, has been caused by too high a level of real wages has been revived by free-market and supply-side economists.

Figure 20.6 is similar to Figure 20.1, with the exception that I am now assuming the average real wage rate in the economy is w_1 rather than w_{FE}. At this wage, employers wish to hire E_1 workers, but a greater number of workers (E_2) wish to supply their labour. This results in an excess supply of labour in the labour market. The pre-Keynesians believed that, as long as the labour market was competitive, this classical or real-wage unemployment could only be temporary. Market forces operating in the labour market would cure the problem, bidding down the real wage rate to w_{FE} to get rid of excess supply of labour. Full employment would be restored when the number of workers willing to work equalled the number that firms wished to hire.

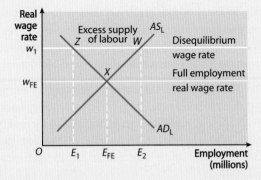

Figure 20.6

Suppose labour market rigidity, perhaps caused by trade unions, prevents the real wage rate falling below w_1. In this situation, the market mechanism fails to work properly, the excess supply of labour persists, and real-wage or classical unemployment occurs. Using modern terminology, unemployment is caused by wage stickiness or wage inflexibility.

Hysteresis

Hysteresis is a cause of unemployment which emerged in the recessions of the early 1980s and 1990s. In these recessions, factories were bulldozed and the firms that owned them disappeared completely. As a result, productive capacity declined. When the economy recovered, demand had to be met by imports.

'Insider/outsider' unemployment

The 'insider/outsider' theory of unemployment argues that trade union members are 'insiders' in the labour market, while the unemployed, especially those who allowed their union membership to lapse on losing their jobs, are 'outsiders'. The theory is based on the assumption that unionised workers enjoy higher wages than non-unionised ones. Unions may care only about the employment prospects of their members who are currently employed (the insiders), and may not really care about the outsiders. The 'insider/outsider' theory suggests that unions may be prepared to push for higher real wages even when unemployment is high, basically because they are unconcerned about unemployment among 'outsiders'.

Queuing unemployment

Queuing unemployment occurs when unemployed workers reject lower-paid jobs in the non-unionised sector of the economy, in the hope that a better-paid unionised job will arise. Continuous turnover in the labour market also contributes to queuing. Every week, some employees retire or leave the labour force, others switch jobs, while simultaneously new jobs are created. Waiting for a suitable vacancy may be a sensible strategy. In this second interpretation, queuing unemployment is closely related to the search theory of voluntary frictional unemployment, explained earlier in the chapter.

Government policies to reduce unemployment

When governments intervene to reduce unemployment, the appropriate policy depends on identifying correctly the underlying cause of unemployment. For example, if unemployment is incorrectly diagnosed in terms of demand deficiency, when the true cause is structural, a policy of fiscal or monetary expansion to stimulate aggregate demand will be ineffective and inappropriate. Indeed, reflation of demand in such circumstances would probably create excess demand, which raises the price level in a demand-pull inflation, with no lasting beneficial effects on employment.

Governments can try to reduce frictional unemployment by improving the geographical and occupational mobility of labour, and by reducing workers' search periods between jobs. Geographical mobility can be improved by making it easier for families to move house from one region to another. However, the widening difference in house prices between south and north are in fact increasing the geographical immobility of labour.

The introduction of the Jobseeker's Allowance in 1996 was an attempt to reduce search periods between jobs. Because the Allowance can only be claimed for the first few months of unemployment, it creates an incentive for the newly-unemployed to accept lower wage rates and to speed up the search for vacancies

that meet their (now reduced) aspirations. However, because Income Support, the other main benefit available to the unemployed, does not 'taper' in this way, the introduction of the Jobseeker's Allowance has had little effect on frictional unemployment. The only really effective way to reduce frictional and structural unemployment is to achieve successful economic growth, which increases firms' demand for new employees.

Governments can improve the occupational mobility of labour by providing retraining schemes and introducing laws to ban professional and trade union restrictive practices that prevent workers moving between jobs. However, government retraining schemes are usually less effective than those run by private sector firms. But a problem is that employers in trades such as plumbing often prefer to free-ride, by poaching workers from the few employers who do train their workers. As a result of this market failure, too few workers end up being trained.

In the past, structural unemployment posed an even more intractable problem in the UK than frictional unemployment. Deindustrialisation, or the decline of manufacturing industries, together with coal mining and fishing, led to large-scale structural unemployment, concentrated in regions of decline such as coal fields and areas previously dominated by heavy industry.

Arguably, structural unemployment is now less significant in the UK, though it still exists, especially in more isolated areas. Many manufacturing industries and the coal industry have now largely disappeared, so there is less scope for further structural decline in these activities. The supply-side reforms of the 1980s and 1990s also created conditions in which service industries grew to replace manufacturing. As a result, more workers were able to move from declining industries into growing ones. However, service industries such as banking can themselves become vulnerable to structural decline and to overseas location.

Unemployment and supply-side economics

It is now widely agreed, by Keynesians as well as by free-market economists, that the cause of most modern unemployment in countries such as the UK lies on the supply-side of the economy rather than on the demand-side. There is much disagreement, however, on the appropriate policies to improve supply-side performance.

Free-market economists argue that poor supply-side performance is the legacy of government interventionism in the Keynesian era in the 1960s and 1970s. Supply-side economists argue that to cut frictional, structural and real wage unemployment, the state's economic role should be reduced rather than extended. Obeying the dictum, 'markets and not governments create full employment', the government's role should be to set markets free, encourage competition, foster private enterprise and the entrepreneurial spirit, so as to create an enterprise culture in which the price mechanism, and not the government, delivers economic growth and reduces unemployment. In the free-market view, the correct role of

government is to create the conditions, through controlling inflation, promoting competitive markets and maintaining the rule of law and social order, in which the market mechanism and private enterprise can function properly.

Many Keynesian economists disagree. They believe that markets are prone to market failure and that unemployment is itself the result of a massive market failure. The failure can only be cured by interventionist policies to modify the market and make it function better.

The costs and consequences of unemployment for the whole economy

Unemployment is bad for the economy as a whole, largely through the waste of human capital. When workers are unemployed, not all the economy's productive resources are used to produce output, which, if produced, could add to the material standards of living and economic welfare of the whole population. Instead, the economy produces inside its production possibility frontier and fails to operate to its potential.

Unemployment is also one of the factors that reduce an economy's international competitiveness. High unemployment can reduce incentives for firms to invest in new state-of-the-art technologies that generally lead to increased export competitiveness. The under-investment associated with high unemployment also results from a reduced need to invest in capital-intensive technologies when there are plenty of unemployed workers who are not only available, but cheap to hire. In these circumstances, employers continue to use labour-intensive but antiquated technologies, particularly when high unemployment accompanies a stagnant economy, low profits and a climate of business pessimism.

Under-investment can also be caused by the higher business taxes firms may have to pay to help finance the welfare benefits paid to unemployed workers. While it is true that the Jobseeker's Allowance can only be claimed in the first months of unemployment, in the UK the state continues to pay Income Support to families in which there is no wage earner, in order to save family members, particularly children, from the effects of absolute poverty.

Economies are particularly badly affected by long-term unemployment. A worker may become effectively unemployable the longer the period he/she is out of work, for example, because of erosion of job-skills and work habits. Long-term unemployment is also made worse by the fact that employers, who might otherwise hire and retrain workers who have been economically inactive for several years, perceive that workers with more recent job experience present fewer risks and are more employable. When inactive workers are seen as unemployable, the economy begins to behave as if it is on its production possibility frontier, even though there are plenty of unemployed workers notionally available for work. An increase in aggregate demand can then lead to inflation rather than to an increase in output and jobs.

Nevertheless, despite the disadvantages of high unemployment for the economy, many free-market economists believe a certain amount of unemployment is necessary to make the economy function better. In particular, by providing downward pressure on wage rates, unemployment can reduce inflationary pressures. Unemployment also contributes to a widening of income differentials between better-paid and low-paid workers. Free-market economists believe that differences in pay are needed to promote incentives which then create the supply-side conditions in which the economy can prosper.

The costs and consequences of unemployment for the unemployed and their families

Unemployment is obviously bad for the unemployed themselves and for their families, largely through the way in which the low incomes that accompany un-employment lead to low standards of living. However, the costs of unemployment for the unemployed go further than this. Apart from situations in which the unemployed enjoy having 24 hours of leisure time each and every day, or when the so-called 'unemployed' are engaged in black economy activity, unemployment destroys hope in the future. The unemployed become marginalised from normal economic and human activity and their self-esteem is reduced. Families suffer increased health risks, greater stress, a reduction in the quality of diet, and an increased risk of marital break-up and social exclusion caused by loss of work and income. The longer the duration of unemployment, the greater the loss of marketable skills in the labour market.

Summary

- In the UK, unemployment is measured by the claimant count and through the Labour Force Survey.
- UK unemployment is much higher when measured by the LFS.
- People may be employed, unemployed or economically inactive.
- Full employment exists when the number of workers firms wish to hire equals the number of workers wanting to work.
- AS exam questions may test knowledge of frictional, structural, cyclical and seasonal unemployment.
- Frictional unemployment is transitional and 'between jobs' unemployment. It is also voluntary.
- Structural unemployment results from the structural decline of industries.
- Cyclical unemployment is also known as Keynesian and demand-deficient unemployment.
- Keynesian economists argue that cyclical unemployment is involuntary, which means that it is not the fault of the unemployed themselves.
- Policies to reduce unemployment will only be effective if the causes of unemployment are correctly diagnosed.
- The costs of unemployment fall on the whole economy and on the unemployed and their families.

Questions

1 Define full employment.
2 What is frictional unemployment?
3 Relate frictional unemployment to search theory.
4 Explain the difference between frictional and structural unemployment.
5 Relate real-wage unemployment to 'sticky' wage rates.
6 Explain demand-deficient unemployment.
7 Why is it important to identify correctly the cause of unemployment?
8 Do you agree that a certain amount of unemployment benefits the economy?

Chapter 21

Price stability and inflation

For three decades from the 1960s to the early 1990s, unacceptably high rates of inflation were perhaps the most serious problem facing UK governments. The inflation rate crept up in the 1960s, before accelerating in the early 1970s to over 15% in each year between 1974 and 1977. Inflation peaked at its highest rate in modern UK history in the mid-1970s, when it hit 25–26%. A further surge, which took inflation to around 18% in 1980, ushered in the modern era in which control of inflation has become arguably the most important single macroeconomic policy objective.

Nevertheless, in recent years, the UK economic climate has changed once again. Inflation was more or less under control from around 1993 until 2008. Recently, however, the rising prices of imported commodities, ranging from crude oil to copper and wheat, together with inflation imported into the UK via the rising prices of manufactured goods produced in China, threaten another surge in UK inflation. UK inflation could once again become difficult to control.

Learning outcomes

This chapter will:

- review the meaning of inflation and related concepts such as deflation and reflation
- describe how inflation is measured
- compare changes in the rate of inflation for goods with changes in the rate of inflation for services
- introduce the main theories of inflation
- apply *AD/AS* analysis to the two main theories of inflation: demand-pull and cost-push
- discuss the benefits and costs of inflation

The meaning of inflation

Inflation is best defined as a persistent or continuing rise in the price level, or as a fall in the value of money. **Deflation** is the opposite, a persistent tendency for the price level to fall, which involves a rise in the value of money. However, because the *overall* price level has seldom fallen in western industrialised countries since the 1930s, the term deflation is usually applied in a looser way to describe a reduction in aggregate demand and levels of economic activity, output and employment. A **deflationary policy** (also known as a disinflationary policy) involves using fiscal and/or monetary policy to reduce aggregate demand. Likewise, **reflation** refers to an increase in economic activity and output, and a reflationary policy stimulates aggregate demand. It is often useful to think of inflation as 'reflation gone wrong', with an increase in aggregate demand stimulating the price level rather than real output and employment.

k*ey terms*

Deflation is a persistent or continuing fall in the average price level.

Inflation is a persistent or continuing rise in the average price level.

Reflation is an increase in the level of real output following an increase in aggregate demand.

The measurement of inflation

Until 2003, the rate of inflation was measured in the UK by changes in the **retail price index (RPI)**. The government still uses the RPI for this purpose, but the **consumer prices index (CPI)** has now become the main measure of inflation. The CPI is based on the method of measuring the price level used in the European Union. As I explain in greater detail in Chapter 23, UK monetary policy now aims to hit an inflation rate target of 2%, measured by the CPI. However, for the time being, the RPI rather than the CPI continues as the measure of inflation used for deciding how much welfare benefits, such as the state pension and unemployment benefits, will rise each year.

Box 21.1 The CPI and the RPI

Measuring inflation: changes to CPI and RPI shopping baskets

It is impossible to measure changes in the prices of all the goods and services on sale in the UK, so the Office for National Statistics (ONS) collects information monthly about 120,000 prices for a 'shopping basket' of approximately 650 goods and services. The change in the prices of those items is used to compile the two main measures of inflation:

the consumer prices index (CPI) and the retail price index (RPI).

The contents of the basket are reviewed every year, and changes can be made for a number of reasons. Some items enter the basket because spending on them has reached a level that demands inclusion to ensure the basket represents typical consumer spending.

Some are included to make collection easier or to improve coverage of particular categories. Similarly, items are dropped for a variety of reasons. For example, diamond solitaire rings have replaced gemstone cluster rings because it is easier to collect prices for them.

Spending on satellite navigation systems has reached a level that demands their inclusion. Digital audio broadcast (DAB) radios replace radio/CD/cassette players, on which expenditure has fallen. The growing popularity of flat-panel televisions is illustrated

The ONS collects information on a 'shopping basket'

by the inclusion of a second, smaller type in the basket, replacing portable televisions, while deeper widescreen televisions drop out.

Digital cameras have been included in the basket since 2004. In 2007, digital processing replaced mail order developing. Recordable DVDs replaced blank VHS tapes, and video cassette recorders dropped out of the basket. Around 77% of households have a mobile phone, and the growing market for services such as ringtones brought downloads into the basket in 2007.

Changes to the basket are often made to improve coverage of a sector where spending has increased. The ONS tracks consumer spending, and uses survey results to ensure that items on which people spend most have the biggest share of the basket. Each is assigned a proportion, or 'weight' of the index. The 'weight' of each category in both the CPI and the RPI is adjusted every year to take account of these changes, giving more prominence to areas whose 'weight' is rising.

Source: Office for National Statistics, 19 March 2007

Follow-up questions

1 Why may changes in a price index such as the CPI or the RPI not provide an accurate measure of the rate of inflation?

2 In recent years, the rate of inflation measured by the RPI has been higher than the rate measured by the CPI. Discuss how pensioners' incomes would change in the future if pension increases are linked to changes in the CPI rather than to changes in the RPI.

A price index such as the RPI or CPI attempts to measure the cost of living of a representative family in the economy. (Other price indices, such as an input price index (producer price index) or a wholesale price index, can be used for other purposes.)

Each month, the prices of all the goods in the national 'shopping basket' are recorded at hundreds of supermarkets, shops and other retail outlets, so that the price index for that month can be calculated. Twelve months earlier, the price index will have been calculated for the same month in that year. The inflation rate covering the 12-month period between these two dates can therefore be calculated using one of the following formulae:

CPI formula

$$\frac{\text{later date CPI} - \text{earlier date CPI}}{\text{earlier date CPI}} \times 100$$

RPI formula

$$\frac{\text{later date RPI} - \text{earlier date RPI}}{\text{earlier date RPI}} \times 100$$

Using these formulae, the annual rate of inflation measured by the CPI was 2.1% for the year ending October 2007. By contrast, the inflation rate measured by the RPI was higher, at 4.2%.

Why the CPI and the RPI may fail to measure the true rate of inflation

A price index can never provide a completely accurate measure of the price level, the cost of living, or the rate of inflation. There are a number of reasons for this. The representative sample of goods in the national shopping basket is never fully representative of all income groups and types of household in the economy. Different income groups and households buy different goods and services, so some will experience higher inflation rates than others. Because it is difficult to accommodate improvements in the quality of goods in a price index, price indices may also tend to slightly overstate the true rate of inflation. In the case of the CPI, however, this may be countered by the exclusion from the index of 'big ticket' high-inflation items such as mortgage costs and the council tax. The way in which goods in the sample are weighted may also be inaccurate, and it is possible that junior government employees who collect raw data that goes into the construction of the index may not record prices accurately.

The RPI and 'index-linking'

In the early days of the RPI, approximately 50 years ago, its main purpose was measurement of the cost of living and the rate of inflation. However, the RPI came to be used in another way: for **index-linking** rates of increase in welfare benefits, for example the state pension and unemployment benefits. The rates at which welfare benefits are paid (and some public sector pay) increase each year in line with annual changes in the RPI.

A significant problem arises when the RPI understates the true rate of inflation, particularly the rate experienced by pensioners and the unemployed. In this situation, the *money* incomes of pensioners and benefit claimants rise at exactly the same rate as the RPI, but by less than the true rate of inflation affecting them. If, at the same time, the incomes of employed people keep up with or exceed the RPI rate of inflation, people on index-linked benefits or pay become *relatively* poorer. The opposite is true when index-linked benefits rise faster than average pay.

Box 21.2 The scandal of the 'true cost of living'

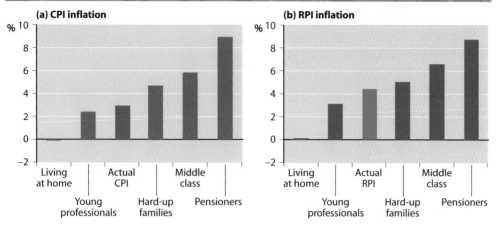

Figure 21.1 The different rates of inflation experienced by different social groups in the second half of 2006

The government's new measure of inflation — the CPI — claims inflation is running at 2.7%, but, for most of us, the true increase in the cost of living is far higher.

According to research carried out by Capital Economics, pensioners and those on fixed incomes faced rises of 8.9% in their living costs over the 12 months to October 2006.

Families with a combined income of £100,000 faced cost of living increases of 5.4%, and those families on lower incomes were hit by rises of around 5.2%. The only people not hit so hard were 'people living with parents' and 'young single professionals'.

What was costing families and pensioners so much more money in 2006 than in 2005? The obvious culprit is the taxman. Gordon Brown is now taking more of our money than a chancellor has for 20 years.

Local government has also increased council tax by 84% in the last 10 years. All this comes as the ONS shows that Britons have less money available to spend than they have had for 50 years, with rail costs up 11% in the year to the third quarter of 2006, healthcare costs up 5% and utility bills surging due to high gas and electricity prices.

Corin Vestey, **www.Everyinvestor.co.uk**,
10 January 2007

Follow-up questions

1 Why might one query the assertion that in 2006 Britons had less money to spend than they had nearly 50 years earlier?

2 Suggest reasons why pensioners experience a higher rate of inflation than students living with their parents.

Changes in the RPI and the CPI

Figure 21.2 shows the changes occurring in the RPI over the period 1971–2006, together with the changes in the CPI over the shorter period since the consumer

prices index was first used as a measure of UK inflation in 1988. Likewise, Figure 21.3 shows changes in the two measures of inflation over the 2-year period between October 2005 and October 2007.

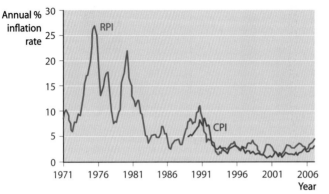

Figure 21.2 Measurement of the UK rate of inflation, 1971–2006

Source: Social Trends 37: 2007 edition

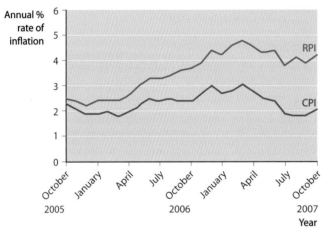

Figure 21.3 Measurement of the UK rate of inflation, October 2005–October 2007

Source: ONS, December 2007

The first of the two graphs shows the UK inflation rate falling after the period of rapid inflation in the 1970s and 1980s. In those decades, the UK inflation rate was also extremely volatile from year to year, as well as being higher than in the 1990s and (so far) in the 2000s.

Comparing the rate of inflation for goods with the rate of inflation for services

The CPI and the RPI both measure average prices of samples of goods and services. However, as Figure 21.4 shows, prices of services rise at a faster rate than the prices of goods. There is a simple explanation for this. Most, though not all, goods produced in the UK compete with imports, and imported manufactured goods are increasingly made in China. In the 1990s and early 2000s, falling prices of imported manufactured goods and commodities brought down the rate of inflation for goods

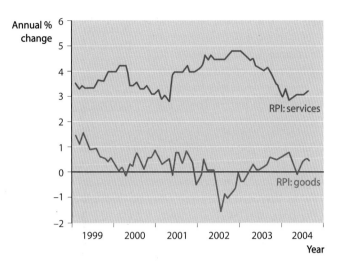

Figure 21.4 The rate of inflation for services and the rate of inflation for goods

Source: ONS

in the UK. As Figure 21.4 shows, in some years, particularly in 2002, price *deflation* occurred for goods, i.e. a *falling* price level for goods.

However, the overall rate of inflation for goods and services, measured by both the RPI and the CPI, remained positive throughout the period covered by the data, largely because prices of services rose from 1999 to 2004, often at an annual rate approaching 5%. Unlike goods, many, though not all, services do not have to compete with imports. Services such as hair cuts, car servicing and restaurant meals are sold in the 'sheltered', or non-internationally traded, economy. By contrast, goods such as cars and food are generally sold in the open, or internationally traded, economy. Service provision also tends to be labour-intensive, and thus less able to benefit from the productivity increases which reduce costs in the manufacturing industry. Note also that, with increasing real incomes, people tend to spend more of their incomes on services and a smaller proportion on manufactured goods.

The data in Figure 21.4 end in 2004. Since then, the prices of many goods, especially commodities and sources of energy such as wheat, copper and oil, have risen rapidly, fuelled by speculative buying, as well as by soaring demand emanating from China, India and Russia. As I explain later in the chapter, by 2007, rising import prices were contributing to cost-push inflation in the UK.

The causes of inflation

There are two basic causes of inflation: excess aggregate demand in the economy, and a general rise in costs of production. The former gives rise to demand-pull inflation (or demand inflation), while the latter is called cost-push inflation (or cost inflation).

As the names imply, demand-pull inflation locates the cause of inflation in the demand-side of the economy, whereas cost-push inflation has supply-side causes.

*e***xaminer's voice**
Don't confuse the *causes* of inflation with the *effects* of inflation.

Demand-pull inflation

Demand-pull inflation is caused by an increase in aggregate demand. Following the shift of the aggregate demand curve to the right, the price level has to rise to persuade firms to produce more output to meet the extra demand.

key term

Demand-pull inflation is a rising price level caused by an increase in aggregate demand, shown by a shift of the *AD* curve to the right.

Demand inflation also occurs when the economy is on its production possibility frontier (and also producing at a point on the vertical *LRAS* curve). In this situation, an increase in aggregate demand creates excess demand that cannot be met in the short run by an increase in output (except through a temporary increase in output above the potential level of output). Excess aggregate demand pulls up the price level.

The equation summarising the different elements of aggregate demand is:

$$AD = C + I + G + (X - M)$$

An increase in *any* of the components of aggregate demand, *C*, *I*, *G*, or (*X* − *M*), can lead to demand-pull inflation. Increases in consumption spending (*C*) by households or current government spending (*G*) on public sector pay and welfare benefits are particularly likely to pull up the price level.

examiner's voice

Investment spending and government spending on capital goods shift the *LRAS* curve right. In the long run, a shift of the *LRAS* curve to the right can offset demand-pull inflationary pressures

Using *AD/AS* diagrams to illustrate demand-pull inflation

Aggregate demand/aggregate supply (*AD/AS*) diagrams can illustrate the main features of demand-pull and cost-push inflation. Figure 21.5 illustrates demand-pull inflation.

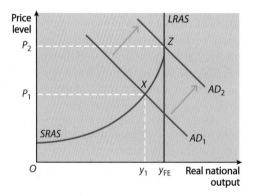

Figure 21.5 Demand-pull inflation illustrated by an AD/AS diagram

In the figure, I am assuming that macroeconomic equilibrium is initially at point *X*. The *AD* curve is in the position AD_1; real output is at level y_1 and the price level is P_1.

Given this initial situation, any event that shifts the AD curve to the right, for example to AD_2, causes the price level to rise, in this case to P_2. In this example, real income increases to its full-employment level at y_{FE}. At the price level P_1, the economy's firms are only prepared to produce an output of y_1. This means that a higher price level is needed to create the conditions in which firms increase output from y_1 to y_{FE}.

Figure 21.5 shows an economy initially close to full employment, and eventually at full employment, once the AD curve has shifted right to AD_2. Following the increase in aggregate demand, macroeconomic equilibrium is at point Z, with the economy also on its long-run aggregate supply (*LRAS*) curve. This means the economy is producing at full capacity, so any further shift of aggregate demand to the right would result solely in demand-pull inflation, with no increase in real output (except on a temporary basis).

Contrast this outcome with what would happen had the AD curve initially been located substantially to the left of AD_1, with the economy in deep recession, suffering demand-deficient or cyclical unemployment. In this situation, a shift of aggregate demand to the right would increase output and employment, but with relatively little effect on inflation. Arguably, the adverse effect of a rising price level would be less significant than the boost to output and employment brought about by an increase in aggregate demand. However, as the increasing slope of the *SRAS* curve suggests, as the AD curve shifts right and moves closer to the *LRAS* curve, increasingly, the reflation of real output (and employment) gives way to demand-pull inflation.

Extension material

Monetarist and Keynesian demand-pull inflation

The monetarist theory of inflation

In the late 1970s and the early 1980s, a group of generally pro-free-market economists became known as monetarists.

Monetarists argue that inflation is caused by excess demand pulling up the price level, but they go one stage further by arguing that excess aggregate demand for output is caused by a prior increase in the money supply. To quote the leading monetarist economist Milton Friedman (who died at the age of 92 in 2006), many monetarists believe that 'inflation is always and everywhere a monetary phenomenon'.

The oldest theory of inflation, the quantity theory of money, lies at the heart of the monetarist theory of inflation. According to the quantity theory, the government creates or condones an expansion of the money supply greater than the increase in real national output. As a result, households and firms hold excess money balances which, when spent, pull up the price level — given the assumption that real output does not expand in line with the increase in spending power.

Cost-push inflation

During the Keynesian era in the 1960s and 1970s, the rate of inflation increased even when there was no evidence of excess demand in the economy. This led to the development of the **cost-push theory of inflation**. Cost theories of inflation locate the cause of inflation in structural and institutional conditions on the supply side of the economy, particularly in the labour market and the wage-bargaining process.

key term

Cost-push inflation is a rising price level caused by an increase in the costs of production, shown by a shift of the SRAS curve to the left.

Causes of cost-push inflation

Cost-push theories generally argue that the growth of monopoly power in the economy's labour market and in its markets for goods and services is responsible for inflation. In labour markets, growing trade union strength in the Keynesian era enabled trade unions to bargain for money wage increases in excess of any rise in labour productivity. Monopoly firms were prepared to pay these wage increases, partly because of the costs of disrupting production, and partly because they believed that they could pass on the increasing costs as price rises when they sold output in the markets for their goods.

Using *AD/AS* diagrams to illustrate cost-push inflation

The *AD/AS* diagram in Figure 21.6 illustrates cost-push inflation. Once again (as is the case in Figure 21.5, which illustrates demand-pull inflation), macroeconomic equilibrium is at point X, with real output and the price level respectively at y_1 and P_1. In this case, the money costs of production that firms incur when they produce output rise, for example because money wages or the price of imported raw materials increase. The increase in production costs causes the *SRAS* curve to shift left and up from $SRAS_1$ to $SRAS_2$.

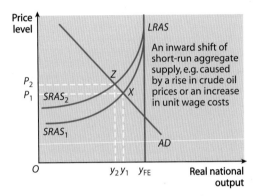

Figure 21.6
Cost-push inflation illustrated on an AD/AS diagram

As a result of the shift of the *SRAS* curve to the left, the price level increases to P_2, but higher production costs have reduced the equilibrium level of output firms are willing to produce to y_2. The new macroeconomic equilibrium is at point Z.

Cost-push inflation and the danger of 'stagflation'

An increase in business costs, which leads to the shift of the *SRAS* curve to the left and the consequent increase in the price level, also causes the level of real output to fall, or at least for its rate of growth to slow down. The 1970s was the last decade in which cost-push inflation was rampant in the UK. At the time, the resulting combination of rising prices and falling output became known as 'stagflation' or 'slumpflation'.

Stagflation was one of the factors that led to free-market policies replacing the Keynesian policies of demand management and intervention in markets. Free-market policies have been dominant since the 1980s.

In early 2008 many economists feared that the danger of stagflation (also called slowflation) was returning to haunt the UK economy and its policy makers.

In 2003, the governor of the Bank of England coined the term 'NICE-ness' to describe the benign years of continuing economic growth, falling unemployment and low inflation that benefited the UK during most of the 1990s and the early 2000s. (The acronym 'NICE' stands for non-inflationary, consistently expansionary.)

As the first decade of the twenty-first century reaches its end, economists now worry that 'NICE-ness' is giving way to 'slowflation', the euphemism for 1970s-style stagflation. Time will tell whether this gloomy prediction is correct or not.

Box 21.3 'NICE-ness' gives way to 'slowflation'

NICE-ness

The ups and downs of the economy were much smaller in the NICE decade than in any previous historical period. Will this stability last?

Mervyn King, governor of the Bank of England,
12 October 2004

Mervyn King

Slowflation

Bank warns of sharp slowdown

The Bank of England did not use the trendy new word 'slowflation' in its Inflation Report yesterday, but it is clearly signalling a combination of slower growth, higher inflation and lower interest rates for the UK next year — 'not an outcome we've seen very often' in the words of the Bank's governor, Mervyn King.

Rachel Lomax, the deputy governor of the Bank of England for monetary policy, last night warned of a combination of such a slowdown in economic growth with higher inflation, the so-called 'slowflation' or 'stagflation' dreaded by observers.

Sean O'Grady, the *Independent*,
15 and 23 November 2007

Follow-up questions

1 Explain two factors that caused the years 1993–2007 to be 'non-inflationary and consistently expansionary'.
2 Explain how cost-push inflation contributes to 'stagflation' or 'slowflation'.

The benefits and costs of inflation

Inflation can have serious adverse effects or costs, and the seriousness of the adverse effects depends on whether inflation is anticipated or unanticipated. If inflation could be anticipated with complete certainty, it would pose few problems. Households and firms would simply build the expected rate of inflation into their economic decisions, which would not be distorted by wrong guesses.

> ***e**xaminer's voice*
> You should discuss the benefits and costs of inflation when explaining the *effects* of inflation on the economy.

When inflation is relatively low, with little variation from year to year, it is relatively easy to anticipate next year's inflation rate. Indeed, creeping inflation, which is associated with growing markets, healthy profits and a general climate of business optimism, greases the wheels of the economy. Viewed in this way, a low rate of inflation — and not absolute price stability or zero inflation — may be a necessary side-effect or cost of expansionary policies to reduce unemployment.

However, some free-market economists argue that inflation acts like sand in the wheels of the economy, making it less efficient and competitive. If the sand-in-the-wheels effect is stronger than the greasing-the-wheels effect, the costs or disadvantages of inflation exceed the benefits or advantages.

A low but stable inflation rate may also be necessary to make labour markets function efficiently. Even if average real wage rates are rising, there will be some labour markets in which real wages must fall in order to maintain a low rate of unemployment. When prices are completely stable (i.e. when the inflation rate is zero), to cut real wage rates, nominal wage rates have to fall. To save jobs, workers may be willing to accept falling real wages caused by nominal wage rates rising at a slower rate than inflation. However, workers are much less willing to accept cuts in nominal wage rates. Thus, with zero inflation, the changes required in relative real wage rates, which are needed to make labour markets function efficiently, fail to take place. Labour markets function best when inflation is low but stable. By contrast, absolute price stability produces wage stickiness, which results in unnecessarily high unemployment.

Some of the costs or disadvantages of inflation are:

- **Distributional effects.** Weaker social groups in society on fixed incomes lose, while those in strong bargaining positions gain. Also, with rapid inflation, real rates of interest may be negative. In this situation, lenders are really paying borrowers for the doubtful privilege of lending to them, and inflation acts as a hidden tax, redistributing income and wealth from lenders to borrowers.
- **Distortion of normal economic behaviour.** Inflation can distort consumer behaviour by causing households to bring forward purchases and hoard goods if they expect the rate of inflation to accelerate. Similarly, firms may divert funds out of productive investment in fixed investment projects into unproductive commodity hoarding and speculation. People are affected by **inflationary noise**. This occurs when changes in relative prices (i.e. a rise or fall in the price of *one* good) is confused with a change in the *general* price level or inflation.
- **Breakdown in the functions of money.** In a severe inflation, money becomes less useful and efficient as a medium of exchange and store of value. In the most extreme form of inflation, a hyperinflation in which the rate of inflation accelerates to a minimum of several hundred percent a year, less efficient barter replaces money and imposes extra costs on most transactions.
- **International uncompetitiveness.** When inflation is higher than in competitor countries, exports increase in price, putting pressure on a fixed exchange rate. With a floating exchange rate, the exchange rate falls to restore competitiveness, but rising import prices may fuel a further bout of inflation.
- **Shoe leather and menu costs.** Consumers incur shoe leather costs, spending time and effort shopping around and checking which prices have or have not risen. By contrast, menu costs are incurred by firms having to adjust price lists more often.

Should a government aim for complete price stability or for a low rate of inflation?

Achieving a completely stable price level and controlling inflation are not necessarily the same thing. A completely stable price level means the percentage rate of inflation must be zero. By contrast, controlling the rate of inflation usually means achieving a rate of 2% in the UK. The reason why the UK government aims to achieve a low, but not a zero, rate of inflation is the greasing-the-wheels of the economy argument I explained earlier. A low but stable rate of inflation may be necessary for markets to function properly. It is also possible that zero inflation may slip quickly into deflation, i.e. a falling price level. However, when prices are falling and people believe tomorrow to be a better day than today for spending, falling aggregate demand may lead to recession.

examiner's voice

Students often wrongly assume that controlling inflation and achieving complete price stability always mean the same thing.

Why it is important to diagnose correctly the causes of inflation

Just as a government must correctly diagnose the cause or causes of unemployment when implementing policies to reduce the level of unemployment, so it (and its central bank) must first determine whether inflation is caused by excess demand or by cost-push factors when deciding on the appropriate policies to reduce or control inflation.

The Bank of England has assumed in recent years (for a number of reasons) that UK inflation has been caused by excess aggregate demand. The low rate of increase in UK labour productivity has meant that incomes, and thus spending power, have grown at a faster rate than output. The growth of aggregate demand has also been fuelled by the rapid rise in house prices, which has boosted consumer spending. Rising house prices increase aggregate demand in two different ways. First, house owners become wealthier, and are thus more willing to spend on consumption. Second, rising house prices enable home owners to extend their personal debt by borrowing against the increased value of the assets they own. The resulting increase in personal debt has been a major contributor to the emergence of excess aggregate demand in the UK.

The increase in aggregate demand that occurred in the 1990s and early 2000s was accompanied by an absence of cost-push inflationary pressure. This was partly due to the success of the supply-side policies implemented in the 1980s and 1990s. These policies improved labour market flexibility, for example through attacking the power of trade unions. The economy also benefited from the benign effect of globalisation, which reduced the prices of imported manufactured goods.

As long as the assumption holds that inflation is caused primarily by excess aggregate demand, **raising or lowering interest rates** (i.e. **monetary policy**) remains the appropriate policy for controlling inflation. Indeed, the fact that interest rate policy kept the rate of inflation within the government's target range in virtually

every month between 1997 and 2007 gave further support to the view that UK inflation has been primarily of the demand-pull kind.

However, some economists now believe that cost-push inflationary pressures have become much more significant in recent years, particularly those stemming from the increased prices of imported energy and commodities such as copper. If this is the case, raising interest rates to reduce aggregate demand can be an ineffective policy for tackling cost-push inflation, unless it is argued that the economy should suffer a severe recession in order to reduce the demand for imported oil, gas and industrial raw materials. If this argument is correct, UK governments now have to face up to the fact that they lack policy instruments, apart from interest rates, for controlling the rate of inflation.

Extension material

Inflationary expectations and the psychology of inflation

Inflationary expectations

It is now widely accepted by economists that people's expectations of future inflation can affect the current rate of inflation. Along with the quantity theory of money, expectations of future inflation are an important part of the monetarist theory of inflation. The leading monetarist Milton Friedman was one of the first economists to draw attention to the role of expectations in the inflationary process.

Theories of expectation formation are complicated. However, the central idea is simple: if people expect that the rate of inflation next year is going to be high, they will behave in an inflationary way now, and their behaviour will deliver high inflation next year. Trades unions and workers will bargain for higher wages and their employers will raise prices now, in anticipation of tomorrow's higher expected inflation rate. Workers and firms try to get their retaliation in first, to avoid being left behind if the inflation rate they are expecting materialises.

Likewise, when people expect the inflation rate to fall, they behave in a way that enables low inflation to be achieved. Governments therefore try to talk down the rate of inflation by convincing people that government policies are credible and that the government (and its central bank) know how to reduce the rate of inflation. The UK government's decision to make the Bank of England operationally independent in 1997 was part of an attempt to convince people (and financial markets) of the credibility of government policies and of its determination to keep the rate of inflation low.

The psychology of inflation

Until the 1990s, one of the factors that made inflation difficult to control in the UK was the existence, built up over decades, of an 'inflation psychology'. Over the years, many groups in British society, including house owners and wage earners in strong bargaining positions, did extremely well out of inflation. For example, house owners with large mortgages had a vested interest in allowing inflation to continue in order to reduce the real value of their personal debt. (Indeed, house owners do even better when house price inflation exceeds the general rate of inflation. In this situation, the real value of houses increases while the real value of mortgages falls.) In the 1990s and until recently, UK governments successfully cut through much of this inflation psychology by convincing most people that inflation (with the exception of house

price inflation) would remain low and around the target inflation rate of 2%. Because of this benign effect on people's behaviour and their expectations, it became much easier to control inflation.

However, even in these years, some economists argued that circumstances could change quickly for the worse, and that inflationary dangers should be regarded as dormant rather than dead. By 2008, it appeared that the inflation beast was once again stirring and that expectations of future inflation were rising.

Summary

- Inflation is a continuing or persistent rise in the average price level.
- In the UK, the retail price index (RPI) and the consumer prices index (CPI) are used for measuring inflation.
- The RPI is used for the indexation of welfare benefits, while the CPI sets the inflation rate target.
- In the UK, the rate of inflation of services is generally higher than the rate of inflation of goods, which in recent years has sometimes been negative.
- The two main causes of inflation are demand-pull and cost-push.
- Demand-pull inflation results from the fact that when aggregate demand increases, firms are only prepared to produce and supply more output if prices increase.
- Cost-push inflation results from higher costs of production experienced by businesses.
- Demand-pull inflation and cost-push inflation can both be illustrated on *AD/AS* diagrams.
- Whether the benefits of inflation exceed the costs of inflation depends on the rate of inflation, its stability and on whether the rate of inflation can be anticipated correctly.
- It is important to diagnose correctly the cause(s) of inflation when selecting policies to reduce the rate of inflation.

Questions

1 Define inflation.
2 Explain the difference between deflation and disinflation.
3 Why may the UK government prefer the CPI to the RPI as a measure of inflation?
4 Distinguish between demand-pull and cost-push inflation.
5 Illustrate demand-pull and cost-push inflation on the *same AD/AS* diagram
6 What causes demand-pull inflation when the economy is on its production possibility frontier?
7 Why is cost-push inflation often associated with recession and stagflation?
8 List and briefly explain four costs of inflation.
9 Why does the UK government aim for a low and stable rate of inflation rather than for a completely stable price level?
10 What might happen if the government tries to control inflation by reducing aggregate demand when inflation is solely caused by rising oil and commodity prices?

Chapter 22

The balance of payments

Whenever international trade takes place between countries, payment must eventually be made in a currency, or other means of payment, acceptable to the country from which the goods and services have been purchased. The balance of payments is the part of the national accounts which attempts to measure all the currency flows into and out of the economy within a particular time period, such as a month, quarter or year. However, the balance of payments is only an estimate of the currency flows. Activities such as smuggling and money laundering mean that the balance of payments accounts are never completely accurate.

Learning outcomes

This chapter will:

- distinguish between the current account of the balance of payments and capital flows
- advise on what you need to know about the balance of payments
- explain the main items in the current account: exports and imports
- describe how investment income provides a link between capital flows and the current account
- apply *AD/AS* analysis to the current account of the balance of payments
- consider whether or not current account deficits and surpluses pose problems for countries

The current account of the balance of payments and capital flows

The balance of payments accounts are the official record published by the government of all the currency flows into and out of the country. Since they are published by the government, the presentation of the currency flows depends on how the government decides to group and classify all the different payment items flowing into and out of the country.

There are two main parts to the balance of payments: the **current account** and **capital flows**. The current account, which includes exports and imports, is so called

because it measures income generated in the current time period flowing into and out of the economy.

By contrast, capital flows occur when residents of one country acquire capital assets such as factories, shopping malls, and property such as office blocks located in other countries. For example, Tesco recently decided to expand into the US supermarket industry. The payments it made when purchasing US supermarkets were a capital outflow. By contrast, the payments made several years ago by Toyota when building car plants in Derbyshire were a capital inflow from Japan to the UK. Tesco's investment is an example of **outward investment** from the UK. Toyota's investment is an example of **foreign direct investment (FDI)** into the UK.

key term

The **current account** is the part of the balance of payments measuring income currency flows, especially payments for exports and imports.

examiner's voice

The specification states that candidates are not expected to have a detailed knowledge of the construction of national income accounts.

What you need to know about the balance of payments

The Unit 2 examination does not require a detailed knowledge of the structure of the UK balance of payments. Likewise, it does not require knowledge of capital flows, which are an A2 topic. Knowledge is, however, required of the different items in the current account of the balance of payments, and especially those that relate to trade flows, i.e. exports and imports.

Although knowledge of capital flows will not be tested in the Unit 2 examination, there are two specification topics for which some knowledge of capital flows is useful. The first is a non-trade item in the current account, labelled 'income'. This used to be called investment income, but the name has recently been shortened to 'income' in the UK balance of payments accounts. Nevertheless, investment income, which I explain later in the chapter, is its main component.

The second topic is monetary policy. Some knowledge of capital flows helps when developing an understanding of the link between interest rates (the main monetary policy instrument) and the exchange rate, which in the UK is the price at which the pound exchanges for other currencies such as the dollar and the euro.

examiner's voice

Examination questions will only be set on the current account of the balance of payments, but some knowledge of capital flows is useful.

Exports and imports and the current account

The main items in the current account that generate currency flows between countries are **exports** and **imports**. Exports occur when people living in the rest

key terms

An **export** is a domestically produced good or service sold to residents of other countries.

An **import** is a good or service produced in another country sold to residents of this country.

of the world buy goods and services produced in the UK. The goods and services have to be paid for, so currency flows into the UK in payment for the goods and services that are flowing out.

In the case of imports, both the trade and currency flows are reversed. UK residents sell pounds and buy foreign currencies in order to finance the purchase of goods and services that other countries produce. Goods and services flow into the UK, while currency flows out to pay for the imports.

Non-trade items in the current account

Exports and imports generate trade-related currency flows. There are also two significant non-trade items in the current account. These are **investment income** (which I have already mentioned) and **transfers**.

To explain investment income, I shall return to the earlier example of Tesco investing in US supermarkets. Since Tesco is a business and not a charity, its main aim is to make a profit. The outward flow of capital that occurred when Tesco expanded overseas generates profit, which flows back to Tesco each year. Tesco's shareholders benefit from the inward flow of profit, both from higher dividend income and from the increased value of Tesco shares. Provided the US supermarkets continue to be successful, profit flows each year from Tesco's subsidiary company in the USA to Tesco's UK headquarters. This profit contributes to UK investment income (a *current* account item), whereas the investment that created the ability to make the profit in the USA was a *capital* outflow in the years in which the investment took place.

> **examiner's voice**
>
> Knowledge of non-trade items in the current account (income and transfers) may be tested in objective test questions.

> **key terms**
>
> **Investment income** is profit and interest income flowing into a country that is generated from assets that residents of the country own abroad.
>
> **Transfers** are payments flowing between countries in forms such as foreign aid, grants, and gifts.

Interest payments flowing between countries are another form of investment income. For example, UK residents depositing money in offshore bank deposits in other countries (a capital *outflow*) receive interest payments (an investment income *inflow*) in subsequent years. At the same time, profit and interest payments flow in the opposite direction, out of the UK to the overseas owners of physical and financial assets located in the UK. The outward income flow includes profits paid to Japanese and US multinational companies operating in the UK and interest payments to overseas owners of deposits in UK banks. **Net investment income** is the difference between these inward and outward profit flows.

Transfers form the second non-trade item in the balance of payments on current account. Examples of *outward* transfers from the UK include British aid donated to developing countries, Britain's contribution to the European Union budget, and income sent overseas by immigrant workers to their families living in the countries of origin, such as Poland, Bangladesh and Jamaica. An *inward* transfer would be

money paid by rich American parents to support the lifestyle of their children studying at British universities.

The importance of the current account

The current account is usually regarded as the most important part of the balance of payments because it reflects the economy's international competitiveness and the extent to which the country is living within its means. If the currency outflows in the current account exceed the currency inflows, there is a **current account deficit**. If receipts exceed payments there is a **current account surplus**.

Many people think that a current account deficit is bad for the country, whereas a surplus is a source of national pride. While there is an element of truth in this view, there are circumstances in which a deficit can be good for the economy and a surplus bad. I shall explain the arguments for and against current account deficits and surpluses later in the chapter.

The balance of trade in goods

The UK's **balance of trade in goods** for 2006 is shown in Table 22.1, along with the other items in the UK's balance of payments on current account. A plus sign (+) indicates a credit item (currency flowing into the UK), and a minus sign (–) indicates a debit item (currency flowing out of the UK). The balance of trade in goods used to be called the balance of visible trade, and the balance of trade in services is part of what used to be called the balance of invisible trade.

key terms

The **balance of trade in goods** is the part of the current account measuring payments for exports and imports of goods. It is sometimes called the balance of visible trade.

A **current account deficit** occurs when currency outflows in the current account exceed currency inflows. It is often shortened to 'imports exceeding exports'.

A **current account surplus** occurs when currency inflows in the current account exceed currency outflows. It is often shortened to 'exports exceeding imports'.

examiner's voice

Exam candidates often confuse the balance of trade in goods with the whole of the current account, and the current account is confused with the balance of payments as a whole.

Table 22.1 The UK balance of payments on current account, 2007 (£ billions)

The current account *(mostly trade flows)*	
Balance of trade in goods	–87.649
Balance of trade in services	+38.450
Net income flows	+5.280
Net current transfers	–13.876
Balance of payments on the current account	**–57.795**

Source: ONS website, 9 April 2008

The balance of trade in goods shows the extent to which the value of exports of goods exceeds the value of imports, and vice versa. Table 22.1 does not indicate the absolute levels of exports and imports, which were respectively £220.857 billion

and £308.506 billion in 2007. The balance of trade in goods was therefore in deficit to the tune of £87.649 billion. This figure is shown in the top row of Table 22.1.

The balance of trade in goods can also be disaggregated (broken up) into different forms of trade in goods, such as the balances of trade in manufactured goods and non-manufactured goods. Some of the different ways of disaggregating the balance of trade in goods on this basis are shown in Table 22.2.

Table 22.2 Selected items from the UK balance of trade in goods, 2007 (£ billions)

Balance of trade in food, drinks and tobacco	−14.940
Balance of trade in raw materials	−3.491
Balance of trade in oil	−2.840
Balance of trade in manufactured goods	−65.120
Balance of trade in automobiles	−16.966
Balance of trade in all goods	−87.649

Source: Monthly Digest of Statistics, March 2008

e*xaminer's voice*

It is useful to have some knowledge of the balances of trade in items such as manufactured goods, oil and automobiles.

Table 22.2 shows that the UK is a net importer of primary products (food and raw materials), and had also become a net importer of oil by 2006. Up until 2005, Britain enjoyed a balance of trade surplus in oil, as a result of the development of the North Sea oil and gas fields in the 1970s and 1980s. However, depletion of these fields means that the UK is now a net importer of energy, and most of the coal used in the UK is also imported.

The balance of payments deficit in manufactured goods is significant. Apart from the periods during and immediately following the First and Second World Wars, Britain was a net exporter of manufactured goods from the beginning of the Industrial Revolution in the eighteenth century until the 1980s. In the middle part of the nineteenth century, Britain was said to be the 'workshop of the world'.

All this has now changed. In the early 1980s, the UK became a net importer of manufactured goods. The manufactured goods deficit is now huge, reflecting loss of competitiveness, the resulting deindustrialisation of the UK, and the fact that most manufactured goods are now produced in the newly-industrialised countries (NICs) of Asia, and particularly in China.

Box 22.1 Record number of cars built for export

The number of cars produced for export reached record levels last year, according to official figures published yesterday. However, a fall of 9.1% in the number built for the home market meant that car production in 2004 was a fraction lower than the 2003 total.

According to the Office for National Statistics, 1,179,753 cars were made for export last year (3.1% more than in 2003). Production for the home market reached 467,020, bringing full-year total production to 1,646,773 (0.7% less than in 2003).

Christopher Macgowan, chief executive of the Society of Motor Manufacturers and Traders warned against complacency: 'The UK hosts some of the most productive car plants in

Europe, but rising raw material and fuel costs, as well as unfavourable exchange rates, play their part in threatening future prosperity, particularly for companies in the supply chain'.

Production of commercial vehicles in 2004 was up 10.8% on 2003, at 209,293. As with car production, growth was strongest for the export market, rising 24.5% to 128,107. Production for the home market, however, was down 5.5% at 81,186.

The hopeful picture for UK vehicle production contrasts with the travails of specific British car-makers. Loss-making Jaguar Cars is ending production at its Coventry home and cutting 1,150 jobs (15%

of its workforce). MG Rover has so far failed to halt a slide in sales since BMW sold the company to the Phoenix Group of Midlands businessmen for a token £10 in 2001.

Jonathan Moules, Financial Times, 25 January 2005

Jaguar Cars is ending production in Coventry

Follow-up questions

1 What has happened to MG Rover car production in the UK since the extract was published in 2005?

2 Suggest reasons for the change in the fortunes of the MG Rover Group.

The balance of trade in automobiles, shown in Table 22.2, is a partial exception to the decline of manufactured exports and the growth of manufactured imports. Although the trade balance for automobiles was in deficit to the tune of £16.966 billion in 2007, a large number of cars continue to be manufactured in the UK, albeit in the Japanese-owned plants created by foreign direct investment in the late 1980s and the 1990s. Cars to the value of over £36 billion were imported in 2007, but exports of UK-made cars were over £19 billion. The UK plants owned by Nissan, Toyota and Honda are modern. They incorporate state-of-the-art technology, and labour productivity (output per worker) is high. Following the closure of MG Rover's plants in 2005, there is every prospect that car manufacturing will avoid any further deindustrialisation. However, ownership of Jaguar and Land Rover has moved to India, raising fears that production may eventually move there.

The balance of trade in services

Table 22.3 Selected items from the UK balance of trade in services, 2007 (£ billions)

Balance of trade in transport	−2.315
Balance of trade in travel	−16.970
Balance of trade in communications	−239
Balance of trade in insurance	+4.286
Balance of trade in financial services	+28.914
Balance of trade in computer and information services	+3.587
Balance of trade in all services	+38.450

Source: ONS website, 9 April 2008

Largely because of the decline of manufacturing and the growth of service industries, the UK now has a post-industrial and service sector economy, a fact that is reflected in the **balance of trade in services** shown in Table 22.3.

Box 22.2 Financial services see rapid growth this year

The future is bright for financial services in London after business in the Square Mile 'paused for breath' in the third quarter. Yesterday, International Financial Services London, an industry body, reported that international financial services transactions in the UK continued to grow rapidly in 2006.

The encouraging trends come as Deloitte, the accountants, publish forecasts for the financial services industry today. Advantages such as the use of English, the location of London, copious expertise, consistent regulation and relatively low personal taxes have helped the UK gain market share. Deloitte says that financial services could come close to eclipsing manufacturing in economic importance by 2011.

Roger Bootle, economic adviser at Deloitte, said: 'The onward march of globalisation opens up a realm of new international markets which the UK can take advantage of. There is a huge accumulation of savings in Asia, which will gradually become available to invest around the world.'

Chris Giles, *Financial Times*, 7 November 2006

Follow-up questions

1 What is a service industry?
2 How has the crisis in financial services, which started in 2007, affected the growth of the UK financial services industry?

Whereas most manufactured goods are internationally-tradable, the same is not generally true for services such as retailing, education and the provision of healthcare. Services such as these are produced and consumed in the non-internationally traded economy, or sheltered economy. However, many services which were previously produced within the UK are now being imported. This is an important part of the **globalisation** process.

UK companies, which used to produce services 'in-house', now outsource or buy-in the services from outside suppliers, often located in cheap-labour countries. UK-based companies are locating 'back-office' service activities overseas, including many financial and ICT related services. Many call centres providing customer services and direct marketing services have moved to India.

Nevertheless, as Table 22.3 shows, Britain is still a significant net exporter of financial, insurance and ICT services. These industries illustrate Britain's competitive advantage

in service sector industries, though the picture is not as rosy in industries such as travel and tourism, where Britons now spend much more in other countries than overseas residents spend in the UK.

Extension material

'Balance', equilibrium and disequilibrium in the balance of payments

It is important to avoid confusing balance of payments equilibrium with the balance of payments actually 'balancing'. Balance of payments equilibrium (or external equilibrium) occurs when the current account more or less balances over a period of years, and is perfectly compatible with occurrence of short-term current account deficits and surpluses. Fundamental disequilibrium exists when there is a persistent tendency for payments for imports to be significantly greater or less than payments for exports over a period of years.

The balance of payments is a balance sheet and, like all balance sheets, must balance in the sense that all items must sum to zero.

In practice, however, the estimates of the items in the balance of payments never sum to zero. This is simply because trade flows, and most of the other items in the balance of payments, are inaccurately measured and recorded. For example, a drug dealer flying a light aircraft into a remote landing strip in Essex is hardly likely to declare the value of the cocaine he is illegally importing. Hence, a balancing item to make the balance of payments sum to zero is necessary.

The balancing item is a 'mistakes item' which exactly equals the number required to make the balance of payments sum to zero. The statisticians who construct the UK balance of payments use a continuous revision method of measurement. When the estimates of the balance of payments for a particular year are first published soon after the end of the year in question, the balancing item is usually large.

In this situation, the estimated figures should not be trusted completely. However, in subsequent months and years, the balancing item usually decreases. In the light of new and previously unavailable information, the statisticians whittle away the balancing item, allocating it to one or more of the real trade, investment income, or capital flows in the balance of payments.

Applying *AD/AS* analysis to the current account of the balance of payments

In Chapter 18, I explained the meaning of aggregate demand in the economy, together with the aggregate demand equation or identity: $AD = C + I + G + (X - M)$. I then explained in Chapter 19 how, in an *AD/AS* graph, an increase in *any* of the components of aggregate demand (C, I, G or $(X - M)$) causes the aggregate demand (*AD*) curve to shift right, leading to a new macroeconomic equilibrium.

This chapter is about the balance of payments, so I shall now use *AD/AS* analysis to explain how a change in the last of the components of aggregate demand in the aggregate demand equation, net exports or $(X - M)$, affects the national economy.

As I have explained, the current account includes non-trade items (income and transfers) as well as exports and imports. However, for the rest of this section, I shall assume that exports and imports are the only two items in the current accounts of the balance of payments. Given this assumption, there is a current account surplus when net exports are positive, i.e. $X > M$, and a current account deficit when net exports are negative, i.e. $X < M$.

Exports are an injection of spending into the circular flow of income, whereas imports are a leakage or withdrawal of spending from the flow (refer to Figure 18.7 in Chapter 18, and to the accompanying explanation of the circular flow diagram.)

Suppose that initially $X = M$, which means there is neither a surplus nor a deficit in the current account. Note also that in this situation, given my assumption of no non-trade flows in the current account, foreign trade injections into the circular flow of income exactly equal foreign trade withdrawals from the flow. When $X = M$, the current account has a *neutral* effect on the state of aggregate demand and on the circular flow of income.

However, suppose that at the next stage, overseas demand for British exports increases, but UK demand for imports remains unchanged. This means there is a net injection of spending into the circular flow of income. The current account moves into surplus, with $X > M$.

In the AD/AS diagram in Figure 22.1, the increase in exports shifts the AD curve right. What happens next in the economy depends on the shape and slope of the $SRAS$ curve around the initial point of macro-economic equilibrium (point X in Figure 22.1).

However, point X shows the economy in deep recession, suffering from deficient aggregate demand. In this situation, *any* event that increases aggregate demand increases the level of real output in the economy and causes demand-deficient unemployment to fall. An increase in exports is just such an event. In Figure 22.1, increased exports shift the AD curve right from AD_1 to AD_2. This causes real output to rise from y_1 to y_2, though at the cost of some inflation, since the price level rises from P_1 to P_2.

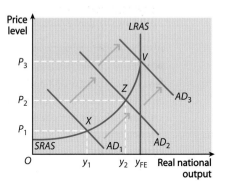

Figure 22.1 How an increase in exports can affect the national economy

Following the rightward shift of the aggregate demand curve to AD_2, macro-economic equilibrium is now shown at point Z. As the $SRAS$ curve becomes steeper, moving up the curve, the diagram tells us that the main effect of a further shift of the AD curve from AD_2 to AD_3 falls on the price level rather than on output and jobs. Output increases, from y_2 to y_{FE}, but the price level also increases to P_3. As full employment approaches, export demand has becomes *inflationary* rather than *reflationary*.

Nevertheless, in this situation, the growth in export demand eliminates the demand deficiency previously existent in the economy. The economy ends up on its long-run aggregate supply (*LRAS*) curve, with macroeconomic equilibrium at point *V*.

Once point *V* has been reached, what may happen next in the economy depends on assumptions made about the nature of short-run and long-run aggregate supply. According to Figure 22.1, when the economy produces on the vertical *LRAS* curve, any further increase in the demand for exports leads only to the price level rising above P_3, without any sustained increase in real output. However, there is another possibility. Foreign demand for a country's exports often creates favourable supply-side conditions in which the *LRAS* curve shifts right. This means the economy can produce and supply the goods needed to meet the increase in export demand without generating inflation. This is an example of **export-led growth**. The German and Japanese economies enjoyed export-led growth from the 1960s to the 1980s, and China is now enjoying similar benefits. However, the world-wide growth of demand for Chinese exports has begun to cause inflation in the Chinese economy.

examiner's voice

You must be able to use the *AD/AS* model and the circular flow of income to analyse how changes in exports and/or imports affect macro-economic performance , i.e. growth, employment, inflation and international competitiveness.

A fall in export demand and/or an increase in domestic demand for imports triggers an opposite effect to the one described above. There is a net leakage of demand from the circular flow of income, the *AD* curve shifts left, and both real output and the price level fall (or more realistically in the latter case, the rate of inflation slows down). Overall, the effect is *deflationary*.

Box 22.3 Export-led growth

Export-led growth is economic growth caused mainly by overseas demand for a country's exports, rather than by the growth of domestic consumption or investment. Export-led growth is usually short-term growth (or economic recovery from a recession). However, if sustained (as in China), export-led growth can be long-term growth that shifts the economy's *LRAS* curve to the right and its production possibility frontier outward.

When economists talk of export-led growth, they usually refer to growth in Asian economies such as China, Japan and South Korea. As the extract below indicates, it has been more difficult to achieve export-led growth in European economies such as the UK and those in the eurozone (which comprises European Union (EU) countries that use the euro as their currency).

The eurozone economy is getting weaker, and this downtrend is almost certain to continue in 2006. It is arithmetically impossible for Europe to have an economic recovery unless consumers spend more and save less. An export-led recovery is impossible for two reasons. First, exports, at 12% of GDP, are simply not large enough to drive the eurozone economy as a whole. Second, exports to the three main EU markets outside the eurozone — Britain, the USA and China — have been slowing since early 2005 and are likely to get even weaker.

There is, admittedly, another possible source of growth for Europe: consumer spending, fuelled by a British or American-style house-price and mortgage-lending boom. In several European countries, a combination of low interest rates and financial deregulation has already set off a self-reinforcing interaction of rising house prices, lending growth, booming consumption, improving employment opportunities and still higher house prices.

This kind of virtuous circle has been powering the Spanish economy since the start of the decade, and similar interactions have more recently become apparent in France,

Italy and Greece. In all these 'Club-Med' countries, house-price inflation has been considerably higher in the past 3 years than in the USA or the UK – and late last year was still running at 12-month rates of 10–15%. As a result, consumption and employment in the southern eurozone have been stronger than might be supposed by European central bankers and politicians who have been seeking the mirage of German-style export-led growth.

Anatole Kaletsky, *The Times*, 20 February 2006

Follow-up questions

1 According to the extract, what have been the main recent causes of economic growth in eurozone countries?

2 The opposite of the 'virtuous circle' is a 'vicious circle'. Explain how a collapse in demand for a country's exports could set in motion a 'vicious circle' of economic decline.

Does a current account deficit pose problems?

While a *short-run* deficit or surplus on current account does not pose a problem, a persistent or *long-run* imbalance indicates fundamental disequilibrium. However, the nature of any resulting problem depends on the *size* and *cause* of the deficit: the larger the deficit, the greater the problem is likely to be. The problem is also likely

Can a current account deficit be justified in a country such as Nigeria?

to be serious if the deficit is caused by the uncompetitiveness of the country's industries. Although in the short run a deficit allows a country's residents to enjoy living standards boosted by imports, and thus higher than would be possible from the consumption of the country's output alone, in the long run, the decline of the country's industries in the face of international competition lowers living standards.

In a poor country, a current account deficit can be justified because of the country's need to import capital goods on a large scale to modernise the country's infra-structure and to promote economic development. However, there is always a danger, as the experience of countries such as Nigeria has shown, that the deficit soon becomes the means for financing the 'champagne lifestyle' enjoyed by the country's ruling elite.

Does a current account surplus pose problems?

While many people agree that a persistent current account deficit can pose serious problems, few realise that a balance of payments surplus on current account can also lead to problems. Because a surplus is often seen as a sign of national economic virility and success, a popular view is that the bigger the surplus, the better must be the country's performance.

Insofar as the surplus measures the competitiveness of the country's exporting industries, this is obviously true. There are, nevertheless, reasons why a large payments surplus is undesirable, though a small surplus may be a justifiable objective of government policy.

Some arguments against a persistently large surplus

One country's surplus is another country's deficit

Because the balance of payments must balance for the world as a whole, it is impossible for all countries to run surpluses simultaneously. Unless countries with persistently large surpluses agree to take action to reduce their surpluses, deficit countries cannot reduce their deficits. Deficit countries may then be forced to impose import controls from which all countries, including surplus countries, eventually suffer. In an extreme scenario, a world recession could be triggered by the resulting collapse of world trade.

At various times since the 1970s, the current account surpluses of the oil-producing countries have led to this problem, as has the Japanese payments surplus, which at times has matched the US trade deficit. On several occasions, the US government has faced pressure from US manufacturing and labour interests to introduce import controls and other forms of protectionism. When introduced, US protectionism undoubtedly harms world trade.

Non-oil-exporting developing countries, almost without exception, also suffer chronic deficits, though these are very different from the US trade deficit. The imbalance of trade between more developed and less developed countries cannot

be reduced without the industrialised countries of the 'North' taking action to reduce surpluses which have been gained at the expense of the developing economies of the 'South'.

A balance of payments surplus can be inflationary

A balance of payments surplus can be an important cause of domestic inflation, because it is an injection of aggregate demand into the circular flow of income, which increases the equilibrium level of nominal or money national income. If there are substantial unemployed resources in the economy, this has the beneficial effect of reflating real output and jobs. However, if the economy is initially close to full capacity, demand-pull inflation results.

Summary

- The balance of payments measures the currency flows into and out of an economy.
- The two main parts of the balance of payments are the current account and capital flows.
- The main items in the current account are exports and imports.
- Balance of payments equilibrium occurs when exports more or less equal imports.
- A current account deficit usually occurs when imports are greater than exports. With a surplus, exports generally exceed imports.
- The balance of payments always 'balances', even when there is a deficit or surplus.
- Changes in exports or imports shift the *AD* curve right or left.
- An increase in exports or a fall in imports may be reflationary or inflationary, depending on circumstances.
- A decrease in exports or an increase in imports is deflationary.
- Current account deficits and surpluses both pose problems, though both may also have some advantages.

Questions

1 State and briefly explain the main items in the UK current account.
2 How have the balances of trade in goods and services changed in recent years?
3 Explain the link between capital flows and net income flows in the current account of the balance of payments.
4 What is the purpose of the 'balance' item in the balance of payments account?
5 What has happened to the UK balance of trade in oil in recent years?
6 What has happened to the UK balance of trade in manufactured goods in recent years?
7 Why is the production of financial services significant for the UK current account?
8 Explain the meaning of 'balance of payments disequilibrium'.
9 Does a current account deficit pose problems?
10 Why may a balance of payments surplus pose problems?

Chapter 23

Managing the economy: monetary policy

This is the first of three chapters that cover the three main elements of macroeconomic policy. This chapter explains monetary policy, while Chapters 24 and 25 examine fiscal policy and supply-side policies. Monetary policy is an example of demand-side policy, which means it is used mainly to manage aggregate demand. Along with fiscal and supply-side policies, it is also used to create a stable macroeconomic environment in the economy.

By contrast, fiscal policy is mostly used these days as a supply-side policy. Supply-side policies are aimed at improving the economy's supply-side performance, and they are not used to manage aggregate demand.

Learning outcomes

This chapter will:
- explain the meaning of monetary policy
- describe the Bank of England's role in implementing monetary policy
- distinguish between the objectives and instruments of monetary policy
- explain the meaning of the money supply
- discuss the extent to which UK monetary policy is 'monetarist' or 'Keynesian'
- use *AD/AS* analysis to distinguish between contractionary and expansionary monetary policy
- explain how changes in interest rates affect exports and imports via the exchange rate
- investigate how changes in the Bank of England's interest rate affect the economy

The meaning of monetary policy

Monetary policy is the part of economic policy that attempts to achieve the government's macroeconomic objectives using monetary instruments, such as

controls over bank lending and the **rate of interest**. Before 1997, monetary policy was implemented jointly by the Treasury (which is part of central government) and the Bank of England, which were known as the 'monetary authorities'. The Treasury abandoned its hands-on role in implementing monetary policy in 1997 when the government made the Bank of England operationally independent. Unless leaned on by the Treasury, there is now only one monetary authority, the Bank of England.

The Bank of England and monetary policy

Most banks, such as Barclays and HSBC, are **commercial banks**, whose main aim is to make a profit for their owners. The most significant exception is the **Bank of England**, which is the UK's **central bank**. For most of the period since its foundation in 1694, the Bank of England was a private enterprise company. Its principal function (besides printing bank notes) is to implement monetary policy on behalf of the government. Although profit is not its main objective, the Bank is highly profitable. However, as it is a nationalised industry, the profit goes to the state.

key terms

The **central bank** implements monetary policy on behalf of the government.

A **commercial bank**, such as Barclays, aims to make a profit from commercial banking business.

Monetary policy is the use of interest rates to achieve the government's policy objectives.

The objectives and instruments of monetary policy

To understand monetary policy, it is useful to distinguish between its objectives and instruments. A **monetary policy objective** is the target or goal that the Bank of England aims to hit. A **monetary policy instrument** is the tool or technique of control used to achieve the objective. Controlling inflation is the main monetary policy objective of the Bank of England, and the rate of interest is the main monetary policy instrument.

Box 23.1 What is money?

For most people, money is so desirable and so central to everyday life that what actually constitutes it hardly merits a second thought. For people living in England and Wales, money comprises coins and Bank of England notes, and any funds on deposit in banks such as HSBC and Barclays. Residents of Scotland and Northern Ireland would also include notes issued by local Scottish and Northern Irish banks. Building society deposits are now also regarded as money, though this was not the case until recently.

Where do we draw the line as to what is money? Is a credit card money? Is a foreign currency such as the US dollar or the Indian rupee, given the fact that we may not be able to spend or even exchange a foreign banknote or coin in the UK? Do we include financial assets such as National Saving Securities, which possess some, but not all, of the characteristics of money?

Consider also the social relationship that takes place whenever modern bank notes are spent on goods or services. Why, for example, are shopkeepers prepared to hand over new and valuable goods to strangers, in exchange for grubby and unhygienic pieces of paper with no apparent intrinsic value of their own? The answer lies in a single word: 'confidence'. In a modern economy, people are prepared to accept such tokens in settlement of a contract or debt, because they are confident that these notes and coins will also be accepted when they decide to spend them.

The functions of money

Economists cut through these issues by defining money in terms of the functions it performs in an economy:

■ **The medium of exchange function.** Whenever money is used to pay for goods or services, or for the purpose of settling transactions and the payment of debts, it functions as a medium of exchange or means of payment.

■ **The store of value (or store of wealth) function.** Instead of being spent, money may be stored as a wealth asset in preference to other forms of wealth, e.g. property or financial assets such as stocks and shares.

■ **The unit of account function.** Money is the unit in which the prices of goods are quoted. The unit of account function of money allows people to compare the relative values of goods even when they have no intention of spending money and buying goods, for example when we window-shop.

■ **A standard of deferred payment**. This function allows people to delay paying for goods or settling a debt. Goods may be provided immediately, but payment occurs at a later date, at a price (in money units) agreed today.

Is a credit card money?

Follow-up questions

1 To function as money, an asset should possess the characteristics of durability, portability, divisibility, scarcity, uniformity and acceptability. Explain why these characteristics are important.

2 Assess the case for and against keeping all of one's wealth in the form of money.

The main monetary policy objective: controlling inflation

For the last 30 years, control of inflation has been the main objective of UK monetary policy. However, at a deeper level, control of inflation should be viewed not as an *end* in itself, but as the *means* of creating the 'sound money' deemed necessary for competitive markets to deliver improved economic welfare.

> **k**ey term
> A **policy objective** is a target or goal that policy makers aim to hit.

Since the 1990s, central government has set the inflation target for the Bank of England. In recent years, the target set by the Treasury has been a 2.0% rate of inflation (measured by the rate of change of the consumer prices index (CPI)). From 1997 onward, the Bank of England's Monetary Policy Committee (MPC) has implemented monetary policy to try to achieve the inflation rate target set by the government.

Are there any other monetary policy objectives?

Prior to May 1997, monetary policy was concerned only with getting the inflation rate at or *below* the target set by the government. Critics argued that the policy had

a built-in deflationary bias (i.e. reducing inflation was favoured at the expense of achieving other possible macroeconomic objectives).

This is no longer the case. The MPC is also now required to reduce interest rates to stimulate output and employment if the Committee believes that, on unchanged policies, an inflation rate below 2.0% will be accompanied by an undesirable fall in output and employment. In the government's words: 'The primary objective of monetary policy is price stability. But subject to that, the Bank of England must also support the government's economic policy objectives, including those for growth and employment.'

UK monetary policy has thus become symmetrical, in the sense that the MPC is just as prepared to use monetary policy to increase aggregate demand as it is to deflate the economy. Indeed, if the inflation rate falls below 1%, the Bank of England has to explain to the government why the inflation rate target has not been met, in the same way that the Bank's governor must write a letter of explanation when the inflation rate rises above 3%.

> **examiner's voice**
> The Bank of England's name is often shortened to just 'the Bank'. In the past, the Bank has also been called the 'Old Lady of Threadneedle Street' and the 'East end branch of the Treasury'.

Extension material

Why UK monetary policy no longer imposes controls on banks to limit the amount of credit they can create

In the Keynesian era, from the 1950s to the 1970s, UK governments and the Bank of England imposed restrictions on how much banks could lend and on the type of customer they could lend to. Business customers requiring credit to finance investment or exports might be given a high priority, with consumer credit being relegated to a much lower position in the queue for advances or loans.

However, controls on bank lending have not been used as a monetary policy instrument in the UK since about 1979. Two main factors explain why. First, UK governments swung round to the view that free markets are far more effective than interventionist policies in achieving efficient and competitive resource allocation. Second, abolition of foreign exchange controls in 1979 meant that UK-based banks which were subject to restrictive controls could no longer compete profitably for banking business with their overseas competitors. Controls, which meant that British banks competed internationally on an un-level playing field, led to banking business moving 'offshore'. Removal of these controls meant that banking business became 'onshore' once again, thereby promoting the growth of the financial services industry in the City of London.

Monetary policy instruments

As I explained in Chapter 16, **policy instruments** are the tools used to achieve policy objectives. In this chapter, I have already briefly mentioned that the Bank of England's interest rate is the main monetary policy instrument.

> **key term**
> A **policy instrument** is a tool or set of tools used to try to achieve a policy objective.

Each month, the MPC either raises or lowers the **Bank's interest rate** (usually by a quarter of 1%), or, more often, leaves the interest rate unchanged to try to keep the inflation rate within a target range between 1% above and 1% below the 2.0% CPI target (i.e. between 3% and 1%). Various other names are sometimes used for the Bank of England's official rate of interest, including Bank rate, the Bank of England's base rate, and its lending rate.

It is important to realise that interest rate policy acts on the *demand* for credit and loans. When interest rates are raised, people generally decide to borrow less, because the cost of loans becomes too high. Conversely, falling interest rates encourage people to borrow more.

How changes in the Bank of England's rate of interest affect lending and credit in the economy

In order to understand how a change in the Bank of England's rate of interest affects credit or loans provided by commercial banks and other financial institutions, it is necessary to understand how a commercial bank makes a profit. A bank such as Barclays or Lloyds TSB is profitable because it 'borrows short and lends long'.

A bank 'borrows short', for example, by accepting deposits of money from people who have opened **current accounts** in the bank. The bank then lends this money to other people who wish to borrow from the bank. Most bank loans given to customers are long-term loans, for example 25-year **mortgage** loans, or 5- or 10-year term loans. This type of banking business is profitable because the rate of interest a bank pays when borrowing 'short' is less than the rate of interest it charges when lending 'long'.

key terms

The **Bank of England's interest rate** is the rate of interest at which the Bank of England lends cash to commercial banks to increase their liquidity.

A **current account** is a bank account that allows its owner to withdraw cash immediately by using a cheque or a plastic debit card.

Liquidity measures the ease with which assets can be turned into cash quickly and at a pre-known rate or price. Cash is the most liquid of all assets.

A **mortgage** is a long-term loan to a house owner that is secured by the property.

However, there is an element of risk in this. If customers who have lent 'short' to a bank suddenly decide to withdraw most or all of their funds, it might be difficult for the bank to repay them. If other customers then fear that the bank cannot honour its liabilities, they may also decide to withdraw their funds. In a worst case scenario, there is a run on the bank; the bank then crashes and goes out of business. This happened to the Northern Rock bank in 2007, before it was nationalised by the government.

To maintain confidence in the commercial banking system, the Bank of England promises to lend to major banks in the event of large unexpected cash withdrawals, in order to preserve the **liquidity** in the banking system and to prevent runs on banks. The guarantee is part of the Bank of England's **lender of last resort**

function. Even in 'normal' times, when there is no fear of a run on a bank, the Bank of England deliberately keeps the commercial banks slightly short of cash. It does this in order to engineer a situation in which, as a matter of routine, commercial banks have to borrow from the Bank of England. However, the rate of interest the Bank charges when lending to the commercial banks is penal, usually set higher than the rates of interest commercial banks charge when lending money to each other (the LIBOR rate).

At the next stage in the process, an increase in the Bank of England's interest rate generally causes the commercial banks to increase the interest rates they charge their customers, because it now costs more for the banks to borrow from the Bank of England the funds they wish to lend on to their customers. Thus, an increase in interest rates leads to bank loans becoming more expensive. Households and firms then reduce their demand for credit and repay existing loans wherever possible. This reduces the **money supply**, or stock of money in the economy.

> **key terms**
>
> The **lender of last resort function** is the Bank of England's willingness to lend cash to commercial banks to increase their liquidity and to maintain confidence in the banking system.
>
> The **money supply** is the stock of money in the economy, that mainly takes the form of cash and bank deposits.

Conversely, when the Bank of England cuts its interest rate, commercial banks also generally reduce the interest rates they charge their customers, because the cost of borrowing the funds they lend on to customers has fallen. If a commercial bank did not reduce its own interest rate, it would lose business and make less profit.

Box 23.2 The Bank of England's interest rate and the LIBOR

Commercial banks borrow money from people who open current accounts and saving accounts with them, as well as from each other. The rate of interest a bank pays when borrowing money from another bank is called the LIBOR rate (the London interbank offered rate). The extract below explains the relationship between the 3-month LIBOR rate and the Bank of England's interest rate.

In 'normal' times, the LIBOR rate hovers just above Bank Rate, but during the 'credit crunch' which followed the sub-prime mortgage crisis in the USA in the second half of 2007 the gap between the two rates widened. One of the factors affecting interest rates is the risk attached to a loan. The credit crunch made loans between banks much riskier, and banks worried that if they lent to other banks the debts would not be repaid. This caused the LIBOR rate to rise and drift away from Bank Rate. It also produced a situation in which the cut in the Bank Rate from 5.75% to 5.5% in December 2007 had little or no effect on mortgage interest rates, which are more determined by the LIBOR rate than by Bank Rate. Fears were expressed that, if the LIBOR rate continued to drift away from Bank Rate, the effectiveness of monetary policy would be undermined.

Unlike Bank Rate, which is set directly by the Bank of England, LIBOR rates are set by the demand and supply of money as banks lend to each other to balance their books on a daily basis.

LIBOR covers lending from overnight up to 1 year. The focus now is on the 3-month LIBOR rate. This normally trades at a small

premium of around 0.15% over where the market thinks the Bank Rate will be in 3 months' time. Recently, it had been hovering at just over 6%, since Bank Rate was widely expected to be raised from 5.75% to 6%.

But 2 weeks ago the rate shot up to 6.6% and has stayed around that level, hitting an eight-and-a-half year high of 6.7% yesterday. This reflected a reluctance by banks to lend to each other for fear that the counterparty may have problems related to the US sub-prime mortgage crisis and not be able to pay the money back.

Anatole Kaletsky, *The Times*, 20 February 2008

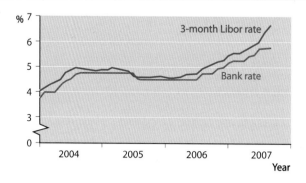

Figure 23.1 The LIBOR rate and Bank Rate, 2004–07

Source: Bank of England

Follow-up questions

1 Why do banks borrow from each other, as well as from the general public?
2 What was the US sub-prime mortgage crisis and why did it contribute to UK banks being reluctant to lend to each other?

Extension material

Pre-emptive monetary policy

In the UK, monetary policy is meant to be pre-emptive, i.e. based on foreseeing undesirable events likely to take place in the economy, and taking action *now* to prevent these events happening in the *future*.

The Bank of England's MPC estimates what the inflation rate is likely to be 18 months to 2 years ahead (the medium term) if policy (i.e. interest rates) remains unchanged. If the forecast rate of inflation is too far away from the target rate set by the government, the Bank may decide to change interest rates immediately to prevent the undesirable outcome becoming a reality.

The MPC is also prepared to raise or lower interest rates to head-off any likely adverse effects of the inflation rate or an outside shock affecting the economy. A good example occurred in 2007 when the 'credit crunch' caused by the US sub-prime mortgage crisis destroyed confidence in the UK banking system. After a period of dithering, the Bank of England cut its interest rate — even though the inflation rate was rising — to try to restore confidence in UK banks. Arguably, however, when monetary policy is determined in this way, it is *reactive* (responding to events that have already occurred in the economy), rather than *pre-emptive* (anticipating future events).

Monetarism and the money supply

When people react to higher interest rates by reducing the amount of money they borrow from banks, the stock of money in the economy shrinks. The stock of money in the economy is the money supply.

When macroeconomic policy in the UK was **monetarist** (from the late 1970s until about 1985), monetary policy attempted to control the rate of growth of the money supply. However, as I explained in greater detail in Chapter 15, monetarist monetary policies did not last long, largely because they never worked properly.

Nevertheless, although the money supply these days is neither a policy objective nor a policy instrument, it does function as a **policy indicator**. Despite the money supply having been dropped as a monetary policy target, when setting the Bank's interest rate, the MPC still take account of changes in the money supply.

First, changes in the money supply provide information about the 'tightness' or 'looseness' of monetary policy. Second, changes in the money supply indicate whether monetary policy is 'on course' to achieve the inflation rate target.

> **key terms**
>
> **Monetarism** is the belief that, as inflation is assumed to be caused by excessive growth of the money supply, monetary policy should be used to control this growth.
>
> A **policy indicator** provides information about what is happening in the economy.

Is UK monetary policy now Keynesian?

Since the dropping of monetarist monetary policy in the 1980s, some commentators have argued that monetary policy is once again being used in a Keynesian way to manage aggregate demand.

However, current policy differs in significant ways from the Keynesian demand management policies practised for many years before the advent of monetarism:

- Only monetary policy, and not fiscal policy, is used in a discretionary way to manage aggregate demand.
- Control of inflation, rather than full employment, remains the principal (but not the only) policy objective.
- Control of inflation is regarded as a pre-condition for the success of the government's supply-side policies.
- Monetary policy is implemented by an independent Bank of England, which is unlikely, unless 'leaned on' by the government, to succumb to the temptation to engineer an inflationary boom.

> **examiner's voice**
>
> Make sure you don't confuse monetarism with monetary policy.

Box 23.3 Hawks and doves at the MPC

The Bank of England's Monetary Policy Committee has nine members. Four are Bank of England officials, and four are 'independent' members appointed by the government. The governor of the Bank of England is the ninth member of the MPC, and has the casting vote.

It has become fashionable to divide the members of the MPC into 'hawks', who tend to resist interest rate cuts, and 'doves', who are much more prone to cutting interest rates and to resisting interest rate increases. The following extract divides the members of the MPC into those with hawkish and those with dovish tendencies. (Independent members lose their position on the MPC and are replaced every 3 years, so the doves and hawks may have changed by the time you read the extract.)

Mervyn King, Governor of the Bank of England
Instinctively hawkish, and increasingly prepared to cast dissenting votes.

Bank of England employees

Rachel Lomax, Deputy Governor, Monetary Policy
After hawkish beginnings, her recent form marks her as a dove, second only to David Blanchflower.

Sir John Gieve, Deputy Governor, Financial Stability
Relatively hawkish.

Charles Bean, Executive Director and Chief Economist
Marginally dovish.

Paul Tucker, Executive Director, Markets
Until January 2007, Paul Tucker was the most hawkish member of the MPC; he remains a hawk, but less decisively.

'Independent' members (government appointees)

Kate Barker, MPC member
The least likely to cast a dissenting vote. Her voting record suggests dovish tendencies but she is best described as neutral — a swing voter.

Professor Tim Besley, MPC member
One of the two leading hawks.

Professor David Blanchflower, MPC member
The arch dove.

Dr Andrew Sentance, MPC member
With Tim Besley, a leading hawk.

The Times, 2 August 2007

Follow-up questions

1 In the light of this information, how might the government be able to influence the decisions of the MPC, especially in the medium to long term?
2 Is the Bank of England really independent when it implements monetary policy in the UK?

Using *AD/AS* diagrams to show how monetary policy affects the price level and real output

Monetary policy, rather than fiscal policy, is now used to manage the level of aggregate demand in the economy. To understand how monetary policy is used in this way, it is worth restating the aggregate demand equation or identity:

$$AD = C + I + G + (X - M)$$

Whereas fiscal policy can affect aggregate demand by changing the level of government spending (G), monetary policy affects the other components of aggregate demand, C, I, and ($X - M$). An increase in interest rates causes the AD curve illustrated in Figure 23.2 to shift left, from AD_1 to AD_2.

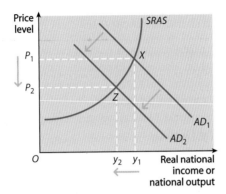

Figure 23.2 How an increase in interest rate causes the AD curve to shift to the left

There are three main ways in which an increase in interest rates decreases aggregate demand. Two of these are:

- **Higher interest rates reduce household consumption (*C*).** First, higher interest rates encourage people to save, and higher saving means that less income is therefore available for consumption. Second, the cost of household borrowing increases, which increases the cost of servicing a mortgage and credit card debt. Borrowers have less money to spend on consumption because more of their income is being used for interest payments. Third, higher interest rates may cause asset prices to fall, e.g. the prices of houses and shares. These falling prices reduce personal wealth, which reduces consumption. Fourth, falling house and share prices reduce consumer confidence, which further deflates consumption.
- **Higher interest rates reduce business investment (*I*).** Investment is the purchase of capital goods such as machines by firms. Businesses postpone or cancel investment projects because they believe that higher borrowing costs make the purchase of capital goods unprofitable. This is likely to be exacerbated by a collapse of business confidence and increased business pessimism.

How changes in interest rates affect exports and imports via the exchange rate

The third way in which an increase in interest rates leads to a decrease in aggregate demand works through the effect of higher interest rates on net export demand ($X - M$).

As I explained in Chapter 22, in the context of the balance of payments, higher interest increases the demand for pounds by attracting capital flows into the currency. The increased demand for sterling causes the pound's exchange rate to rise, which makes UK exports less price competitive in world markets and imports more competitive in UK markets. The UK's balance of payments on current account worsens, which shifts the *AD* curve left.

By contrast, a fall in interest rates triggers a capital outflow in the balance of payments. The exchange rate then also falls. Exports become more price competitive, and the current account of the balance of payments improves. Aggregate demand increases and the *AD* curve shifts right.

Contractionary monetary policy

Contractionary monetary policy involves raising interest rates in order to shift the *AD* curve left. However, the extent to which the price level then falls (or, more realistically, the rate of inflation falls), and/or real output falls, depends on the shape of the economy's *SRAS* curve. In Figure 23.2, the shift to the left of aggregate demand from AD_1 to AD_2 causes real output as well as the price level to fall. The price level falls from P_1 to P_2, and real output falls from y_1 to y_2. This illustrates the possibility that a contractionary monetary policy, which aims to control the rate of inflation in the economy, might also cause the economy to sink into a recession.

Expansionary monetary policy

An expansionary monetary policy operates in the opposite way to a contractionary one. When the Bank of England cuts interest rates, saving is discouraged, while consumption and investment in capital goods are encouraged. Net export demand also increases because lower interest rates lead to a fall in the exchange rate. This makes exports more price competitive than imports. For these three reasons, the *AD* curve shifts right, with the resulting effect on the price level and real output depending again on the shape and slope of the economy's *SRAS* curve.

Neutral monetary policy

The Bank of England now generally prefers a neutral monetary policy, rather than one that is overtly contractionary or expansionary. In a neutral monetary policy interest rates neither boost nor hold back aggregate demand. It is broadly consistent with the economy growing at its sustainable trend rate over the medium term, i.e. without positive or negative output gaps.

AQA AS Economics

chapter 23

Evaluating the success of recent UK monetary policy

In May 1997, Gordon Brown, the incoming Labour chancellor of the exchequer, transferred to the newly-independent Bank of England the task of using monetary policy to hit the government's inflation rate target. (Initially the target was 2.5% measured against the RPI, but it was later changed to the current 2.0% target measured against the CPI.)

Figure 23.3 shows that for most of the time between the late 1990s and the end of the second quarter in 2007, the UK inflation rate has been within its target range of 1% above and below the central target rate of 2.0%. Indeed, until 2005, the inflation rate was always below 2.0%.

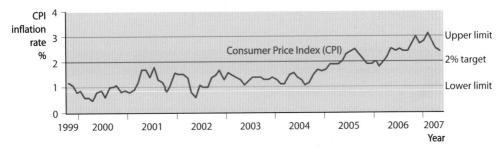

Figure 23.3 The UK consumer prices index (CPI), fourth quarter 1999 to second quarter 2007

So, has the success in controlling inflation been due to UK monetary policy, or have other factors been mainly responsible? Supporters of the government and of the Bank of England claim that 'the proof of the pudding is in the eating'. Monetary policy has aimed to control inflation — inflation has been low, ergo, monetary policy has been successful.

The Labour government's critics argue that, although monetary policy has been *partly* responsible for bringing down the rate of inflation, other factors have also contributed in significant ways. First, there has been the success of the supply-side reforms, introduced by Thatcher's Conservative governments in the 1980s. When introduced, under the dictum 'first the pain and then the gain', supply-side policies contributed to high unemployment and a widening of income differentials. This was the 'pain'. From the mid-1990s onward, the 'gain' arrived in the form of more competitive and efficient markets, which resulted in lower inflation rates.

Second, the policy makers were 'lucky' in the last decade of the twentieth century and in the first few years of the twenty-first century. These were benign times, in which commodity, raw material and energy prices were generally falling, and a period in which the ICT revolution increased productivity in manufacturing, communications and retailing.

More recently, times have been much less benign. Rising oil and commodity prices, agri-inflation (the rising prices of crops such as wheat and corn) and the

beginnings of inflation in Chinese manufacturing industries have triggered a severe bout of cost-push inflation, which UK monetary policy is not designed to control. Government policies other than manipulating interest rates may be needed if the rate of inflation is to remain low.

Monetary policy and inflationary expectations

UK monetary policy was successful in the 1990s and early 2000s partly because the Bank of England managed to control inflationary expectations. As long as monetary policy is credible, so the argument goes, people believe that the Bank of England can continue to control inflation. Policy credibility reduces expectations of future inflation and causes people to behave in ways consistent with the policy's future success. (Once credibility dissipates, however, the 'genie escapes from the bottle', threatening an accelerating rate of inflation.)

Extension material

'One club golf' and macroeconomic policy

In recent years, UK governments have been accused of relying on the 'one club golfer' approach to macroeconomic policy. The accusation is based on the following analogy.

Tiger Woods is arguably the greatest golfer in the world today. Imagine, however, Tiger playing in the Masters Golf Tournament in the USA with only one club in his golf bag. However great his talents as a golfer, Tiger can't hope to win a major tournament playing under these conditions. Different golf clubs are needed for different shots: a driver for teeing-off, a wedge iron for playing out of a bunker, and a putter for finishing off a hole on the putting green. So that Tiger can show off his skills as a top-rate golf player, at the start of an 18-hole round, Tiger's caddy places ten or more different clubs in the golf bag to be carried round the greens. Part of Tiger's skill then lies in selecting and using a particular club for a particular shot.

In the same way that Tiger Woods selects different golf clubs for different shots, so the government needs different types of economic policy and policy instruments for achieving different policy objectives. Good government policy shouldn't rely just on interest rate policy or monetary policy. However sensible it is to raise interest rates in order to tackle demand-pull inflation, interest rates do not provide a panacea for *all* the macroeconomic problems a government faces, particularly when policy conflicts and trade-offs are involved.

Tiger Woods could not win a tournament with only one club

Box 23.4 'Boring' monetary policy

I mentioned earlier in the chapter that, although controlling inflation is the main objective of monetary policy in the UK, there are others. Along with fiscal policy, monetary policy tries to create a stable macro-economic framework, in which businesses and households are less likely to be surprised by unexpected events.

The governor of the Bank of England believes that macroeconomic stability means monetary policy should be as boring as possible. The extract below is taken from a speech given by the governor, Mervyn King, at the Indian Council for Research on International Economic Relations (ICRIER) in New Delhi, India, on 20 February 2006.

National economic policies are – or should be – trying to create stable monetary and fiscal frameworks to condition expectations of future economic policy. Policy surprises should not add noise to the news about economic fundamentals. It is in each of our national interests to avoid sudden or large changes in capital flows induced by volatile or unpredictable changes in economic policy. We want the monetary and fiscal decisions not only at home, but also in other countries, to be boring.

Follow-up questions

1 Explain what is meant by a 'stable macroeconomic framework'.
2 What is a 'policy surprise'?
3 Using an example, explain how an adverse 'policy surprise' may affect the economy.

Summary

- Along with fiscal policy and supply-side policy, monetary policy provides a way of managing the national economy.
- In the UK, monetary policy is implemented by the country's central bank, the Bank of England.
- Control of inflation is the main monetary policy objective, but there are other objectives.
- Central government sets the inflation rate target of 2.0%, measured by the CPI.
- The Bank of England's Monetary Policy Committee (MPC) implements monetary policy to try to hit the 2% inflation rate target.
- The Bank of England's interest rate is the main monetary policy instrument.
- Monetary policy is used to manage the level of aggregate demand.
- Changes in interest rates affect consumption, investment and net export demand, and shift the position of the *AD* curve.
- Monetary policy can be effective in controlling demand-pull inflation, but it is much less effective at controlling cost-push inflation.
- Monetary policy was successful in controlling inflation in the UK in the 1990s and early 2000s, but other factors also contributed to this success.

Questions

1 Define monetary policy.
2 Distinguish between the objectives and the instruments of monetary policy.
3 What are the main features of current UK monetary policy?
4 Why are direct controls no longer imposed by the Bank of England on commercial banks?
5 How do changes in the Bank of England's official interest rate affect bank lending and the economy?
6 With the help of *AD/AS* diagrams, distinguish between contractionary and expansionary monetary policy.
7 What is meant by neutral monetary policy?
8 To what extent has monetary policy been responsible for controlling inflation?
9 Why is monetary policy less successful in controlling cost-push inflation than in controlling demand-pull inflation?

Chapter 24

Managing the economy: fiscal policy

This chapter follows on from the coverage of monetary policy in Chapter 23. Unlike monetary policy, which is now used to manage the level of aggregate demand in the economy, modern fiscal policy is much more a supply-side policy used for influencing personal incentives, particularly those to work, save, invest and to be entrepreneurial. Examination questions are set on demand-side and supply-side fiscal policy, so this chapter covers both forms of fiscal policy. However, the explanation of supply-side fiscal policy here is short, largely because the topic is dealt with in greater detail in Chapter 25.

Learning outcomes

This chapter will:

■ explain the meaning of fiscal policy
■ describe the Treasury's role in implementing fiscal policy
■ explain Keynesian or demand-side fiscal policy
■ use *AD/AS* analysis to explain how fiscal policy can be used to manage aggregate demand
■ discuss the significance of the government spending multiplier
■ examine the nature of supply-side fiscal policy and its effect on the *LRAS* curve
■ explain how government spending and taxation affect the pattern of economic activity

The meaning of fiscal policy

Fiscal policy is the part of a government's overall economic policy that aims to achieve the government's economic objectives through the use of the fiscal instruments of **taxation, public spending** and the **government's budgetary position**. As an economic term, fiscal policy is often associated with Keynesian economic theory and policy. Between the 1950s and 1970s, Keynesian governments used fiscal policy to manage the level of aggregate demand.

*e***xaminer's voice**
Students often assume wrongly that fiscal policy is always used to manage aggregate demand.

However, it is misleading to associate fiscal policy exclusively with Keynesianism. These days, the Keynesian fiscal policy implemented in the UK in the three decades before 1979 has been replaced by a very different supply-side orientated fiscal policy. Before I compare **demand-side** and **supply-side fiscal policy**, I shall examine the government's budgetary position.

The government's budgetary position

Using the symbols G for government spending and T for taxation and other sources of revenue, the three possible budgetary positions of the government (and of the whole public sector) are:

$G = T$: **balanced budget**

$G > T$: budget deficit

$G < T$: budget surplus

A **budget deficit** occurs when public sector expenditure exceeds revenue. It is important not to confuse *financing* a budget deficit with *eliminating* a budget deficit. A budget deficit can be eliminated by cutting public spending or by raising taxation, both of which can balance the budget or move it into surplus. Assuming a budget deficit persists, the extent to which spending exceeds revenue must be financed by public sector borrowing.

key term

Fiscal policy tries to achieve policy objectives through the use of government spending, taxation and the government's budgetary position.

examiner's voice

Make sure you don't confuse the budget deficit with the balance of payments deficit.

key terms

A **balanced budget** is achieved when government spending equals government revenue ($G = T$).

A **budget deficit** occurs when government spending exceeds government revenue ($G > T$).

A **budget surplus** occurs when government spending is less than government revenue ($G < T$).

The budget deficit and public sector borrowing

Various official terms are used by the Treasury for **public sector borrowing**, including the 'public sector's net cash requirement' and 'net public sector borrowing'. However, because the Treasury changes its terminology frequently, the most important thing to learn is that public sector borrowing is 'the other side of the coin' to the budget deficit. Whenever there is a budget deficit, there is a *positive* borrowing requirement. Conversely, a **budget surplus** means the government can use the tax revenues it isn't spending to repay previous borrowing. In this case, the borrowing requirement is *negative*.

Keynesian fiscal policy and the budget deficit

During the Keynesian era, fiscal policy was used primarily to manage the level of aggregate demand in the economy. Keynesian fiscal policy centred on the use of

deficit financing to inject demand into the economy. Deficit financing describes a situation in which the government runs a budget deficit, usually for several years, deliberately setting public sector spending at a higher level than tax revenues and other sources of government revenue. For each of the years in which the government runs a budget deficit, the shortfall of tax revenue has to be financed through a *positive* borrowing requirement.

> **key term**
>
> **Deficit financing** means deliberately running a budget deficit and borrowing to finance the deficit.

Before the Keynesian revolution in the 1930s, UK governments believed they had a moral duty to balance their budgets. This has been called sound finance or fiscal orthodoxy.

The orthodox view was that a budget surplus placed the government in the moral position of a thief, stealing from taxpayers. If the government ran a budget deficit, it would be in the moral position of a bankrupt, perceived as not being able to manage its finances. Since both these budgetary positions were regarded as wrong or undesirable, the government's fiscal *duty* was to aim for a balanced budget.

However, in the 1930s, John Maynard Keynes established a new orthodoxy that legitimised deficit financing and overturned the view that a government should always aim to balance its budget. The new Keynesian orthodoxy lasted until the late 1970s, when, during the period in which monetarism held sway, there was a return to a belief in balanced budgets.

As I explained in Chapter 15, in the 1930s, Keynes argued that mass unemployment in the Great Depression was caused by deficient aggregate demand. He believed that, in the economy as a whole, too little spending was taking place because households and firms in the private sector were saving too much and spending too little.

Keynes went on to argue that, in this situation, if the government deliberately runs a budget deficit, the deficit can be financed by the government, first borrowing, and then, in its public spending programme, spending the private sector's excess savings. This injects spending into the economy and (in Keynesian theory at least) gets rid of demand-deficient unemployment.

Using *AD/AS* diagrams to illustrate Keynesian or demand-side fiscal policy

Before applying *AD/AS* analysis to Keynesian fiscal policy and its effects on the economy, it is worth reminding ourselves of the aggregate demand equation or identity introduced in Chapter 18:

> **key term**
>
> **Demand-side fiscal policy** is used to increase or decrease the level of aggregate demand (and to shift the *AD* curve right or left).

$$AD = C + I + G + (X - M)$$

Box 24.1 Budget day

The government's financial year runs for the 12 months beginning 5 April. A few weeks before, in March, the chancellor of the exchequer presents his budget to the House of Commons. Part of the budget speech, which is published in the 'Red Book' (formally called the Financial Statement and Budget Report (FSBR), but commonly named after the traditional colour of its cover), contains the chancellor's analysis of the state of the UK economy. This is the part of the budget which most interests economists.

By contrast, the general public is most interested in the announcement of tax changes, some of which come into effect within hours of the budget speech. Modern chancellors often use the trick of announcing tax increases a few months earlier, in the previous year's November Pre-Budget Report. The politician hopes that taxpayers will not notice the announcement of stealth taxes (as the tax changes have come to be called), because the higher tax rates will not be paid until a few months later. The extract below describes some of the more trivial aspects of 'budget day'.

Briefcase encounters

Budget day used to be a high-fashion occasion. Until recently, many MPs wore top hats and formal morning dress, and a Labour MP, Tom Swain, once taunted them by wearing a miner's helmet. Women MPs used to appear in their finery, with hats only marginally less spectacular than those worn at Royal Ascot.

The word 'budget' comes from the French *'bougette'*, a little bag, which explains why the chancellor 'opens' his budget. The traditional scarlet briefcase was made for Gladstone in 1860 and was used by every chancellor thereafter until 1965.

George Ward Hunt arrived at the Commons in 1869 and opened the budget box — to find, to his consternation, that he had left his speech at home.

When Norman Lamont was chancellor, in the early 1990s, the bag that was waved at photographers contained a bottle of whisky, while the speech itself was carried in a plastic bag by his then aide, William Hague.

Hugh Dalton, just after the Second World War, leaked key parts of his 1947 budget to a reporter from a London evening paper. The chancellor underestimated the speed at which newspapers work, and news of a penny on a pint of beer and a tax on dog racing appeared in the paper before Dalton had reached that point in his speech. He resigned the following day, with the prime minister, Clement Attlee, calling him 'a perfect ass'.

Virtually the entire contents of Kenneth Clarke's budget in November 1996 was leaked to the *Daily Mirror* on the eve of presentation, but the paper resisted the temptation to publish any of the contents, instead returning the documents to the Treasury.

Adapted from the *Guardian*, 16 March 2005

The traditional scarlet briefcase was first used for the budget in 1860

TOPFOTO

Follow-up questions

1 What is the purpose of budget day?

2 What is a 'stealth tax'? Why are stealth taxes unpopular?

Government spending (G) is one of the components of aggregate demand. An increase in government spending and/or a cut in taxation increases the size of the budget deficit (or reduces the size of the budget surplus). Either way, an injection into the circular flow of income occurs and the effect on aggregate demand is expansionary.

Figure 24.1 illustrates the effect of such an **expansionary** or **reflationary fiscal policy**. Initially, with the aggregate demand curve in position AD_1, macroeconomic equilibrium occurs at point X. Real income or output is y_1, and the price level is P_1.

examiner's voice
Make sure you don't confuse demand-side and supply-side fiscal policy.

key term
Expansionary fiscal policy uses fiscal policy to increase aggregate demand and to shift the AD curve right.

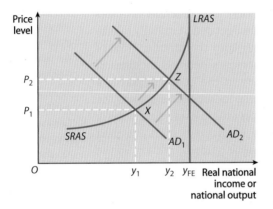

Figure 24.1 Keynesian or demand-side fiscal policy

To eliminate demand-deficient (cyclical or Keynesian) unemployment, the government increases the budget deficit by raising the level of government spending and/or by cutting taxes. The expansionary fiscal policy shifts the AD curve right from AD_1 to AD_2, and the economy moves to a new macroeconomic equilibrium at point Z.

However, the extent to which expansionary fiscal policy *reflates* real output (in this case from y_1 to y_2), or creates excess demand that leads to demand-pull inflation (in this case an increase in the price level from P_1 to P_2), depends on the shape of the AS curve, which depends on how close, initially, the economy was to full employment. The nearer the economy gets to full employment, the greater the inflationary effect of expansionary fiscal policy and the smaller the reflationary effect. Once the full-employment level of real income is reached on the long-run aggregate supply curve at y_{FE}, a further increase in government spending or a tax cut inflates the price level. In this situation, real output cannot grow (except possibly temporarily), because there is no spare capacity. The economy is producing on its production possibility frontier.

Figure 24.1 can be adapted to illustrate the effect of a **contractionary** or **deflationary fiscal policy**. In this case, a cut in government spending and/or an increase in taxation shifts the AD curve left. The extent to which the demand

deflation results in the price level or real income falling again depends on the shape and slope of the *SRAS* curve.

The national income multiplier

The **national income multiplier** measures the relation-ship between an initial change in a component of aggregate demand, such as government spending or private-sector investment, and the resulting larger change in the level of national income.

Suppose for example that government spending increases by £8 billion, but tax revenue remains unchanged. The resulting budget deficit initially injects £8 billion of new spending into the circular flow of income. This spending increases people's incomes. If we assume that everybody in the economy saves a small fraction of any income increase and spends the rest, the £8 billion generates multiple and successively smaller further increases in income, until the next stage is so small that it can be ignored. Adding up the successive stages of income generation, the total increase in income is a multiple of the initial spending increase of £8 billion – hence the name **multiplier theory**. If the size of the multiplier is 5, an increase in consumption spending of £8 billion causes national income to increase by £40 billion.

To capture the flavour of the multiplier process, think of ripples spreading over a pond after a stone is thrown into the water. Each of the ripples resembles a stage in the multiplier process. However the ripples in a pond last only a few seconds, whereas the ripples spreading through the economy following a change in aggregate demand can last for months and even years.

key terms

Contractionary fiscal policy uses fiscal policy to decrease aggregate demand and to shift the *AD* curve left.

The **government spending multiplier** is the relationship between a change in government spending and the resulting change in national income.

The **investment multiplier** is the relationship between a change in investment and the resulting change in national income.

The **national income multiplier** is the relationship between a change in aggregate demand and the resulting change in national income.

The **tax multiplier** is the relationship between a change in taxation and the resulting change in national income.

examiner's voice

You will not be expected to calculate the value of the multiplier in AQA AS exams.

There are in fact a number of different national income multipliers, each relating to the component of national income that initially changes. Besides the **government spending multiplier**, there is an **investment multiplier**, a **tax multiplier**, an **export multiplier** and an **import multiplier**. Taken together, the government spending and tax multipliers are known as **fiscal policy multipliers**. Likewise the export and import multipliers are **foreign trade multipliers**. An increase in consumption spending can also trigger a multiplier process.

In some circumstances, the multiplier process can reduce rather than increase national income. This happens when government spending, consumption, investment or exports fall. It also happens when taxation or imports *increase.* This is because taxation and imports are leakages from the circular flow of income, rather than injections. The tax and import multipliers are always negative.

The multiplier and Keynesian fiscal policy

During the Keynesian era from the 1950s to the 1970s, governments in many industrialised mixed economies, including the UK, based macroeconomic policy on the use of fiscal policy to manage the level of aggregate demand. This became known as **discretionary fiscal policy**. To achieve full employment, governments deliberately ran budget deficits (setting $G > T$). This expanded aggregate demand, but sometimes too much demand 'overheated' the economy. Excess demand pulled up the price level in a demand-pull inflation, or pulled imports into the country and caused a balance of payments crisis. In these circumstances, governments were forced to reverse the thrust of fiscal policy, cutting public spending or raising taxes to reduce the level of demand in the economy. The Keynesians used demand-side fiscal policy in a discrete way (supplemented at times by monetary policy), to 'fine-tune' the level of aggregate demand in the economy. Government spending and/or taxes were changed in order to stabilise fluctuations in the economic cycle, and to try to achieve the macroeconomic objectives of full employment and economic growth, without excessive inflation or an unsustainable deterioration in the balance of payments.

The larger the government spending multiplier, the smaller the increase in public spending needed to bring about a desired increase in national income. Similarly, the larger the tax multiplier, the smaller the required tax cut. It follows that if the government spending and tax multipliers are large (for example, equal to 5 as in my numerical example on page 306), and if the multipliers affect *real* output more than the *price level*, fiscal policy used as a demand management instrument can be an effective way of controlling the economy.

The multiplier in the UK economy

In reality, particularly in the case of the UK economy, neither assumption may hold. Free-market economists believe an increase in government spending stimulates *prices* rather than *real output*, and that government spending merely displaces or **crowds out** private sector investment.

k *ey terms*

Crowding out is a situation in which an increase in government or public sector spending displaces private sector spending, with little or no increase in aggregate demand.

Discretionary fiscal policy involves making discrete changes to G, T and the budget deficit to manage and 'fine-tune' the level of aggregate demand.

Even without accepting this free-market argument, the size of the multiplier is likely to be small. The UK economy is open to imports, with relatively high income tax rates when national insurance contributions are included in the tax rate. A significant fraction of the income received from an increase in government spending leaks into taxation and imports, as well as into saving. This means that the main effect of an expansionary fiscal policy may be to pull imports into the

economy — even when there is substantial unemployment — with relatively little increase in domestic output and employment.

Extension material

A closer look at the government spending multiplier

The multiplier process is essentially dynamic, taking place over time. To explain the government spending multiplier, I shall assume there is demand-deficient unemployment in the economy, and that the levels of taxation and imports do not change when aggregate demand increases. To reduce demand-deficient unemployment, the government decides to spend an extra £10 billion on road building.

In the first stage of the multiplier process, £10 billion is received as income by building workers who, like everybody in the economy, are assumed to spend 90p of every pound of income on consumption.

At the second stage of the multiplier process, £9 billion of the £10 billion income is spent on consumer goods and services, with the remaining £1 billion leaking into unspent savings. At the third stage, consumer good sector employees spend £8.1 billion, or 0.9 of the £9 billion received at the second stage of income generation. Further stages of income generation occur, with each successive stage being 0.9 of the previous stage. Each stage is smaller than the preceding stage, to the extent that part of income leaks into savings (there being no taxes or imports that vary with the level of national income in this economy).

Assuming that nothing else changes in the time taken for the process to work through the economy, the eventual increase in income ΔY resulting from the initial injection of government spending is the sum of all the stages of income generation. ΔY is larger than ΔG, which triggered the initial growth in national income.

The multiplier process I have just described is illustrated in Figure 24.2, which captures the ripple-like nature of the process. In this example the size of the multiplier is 10.

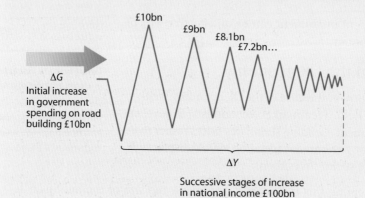

Figure 24.2
The government spending multiplier

£10bn
£9bn
£8.1bn
£7.2bn...

ΔG
Initial increase in government spending on road building £10bn

ΔY
Successive stages of increase in national income £100bn

Supply-side fiscal policy

Since 1979, no UK government, whether Conservative or Labour, has used fiscal policy to manage aggregate demand in the Keynesian or demand-side way I have described. Nevertheless, fiscal policy continues to be an important part of government economic policy, but is now used primarily as a supply-side policy. Successive UK governments have cut income tax rates in recent years, not for Keynesian reasons to stimulate aggregate demand (though this has been an unintended consequence of the tax cuts), but to create supply-side incentives in the economy.

key term

Supply-side fiscal policy is used to increase the economy's ability to produce and supply goods, through creating incentives to work, save, invest and to be entrepreneurial.

Along with other supply-side policies, supply-side fiscal policy is used to try and shift the economy's long-run aggregate supply curve (*LRAS*) curve to the right, thereby increasing the economy's potential level of output. The effect of successful supply-side fiscal policy on the *LRAS* curve is shown in Figure 24.3. (Note that an outward movement of the economy's production possibility frontier can also illustrate the intended effect of supply-side policies.)

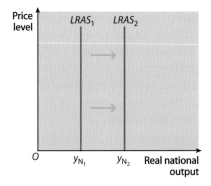

Figure 24.3 The intended effect of supply-side fiscal policy

To find out more about supply-side fiscal policy, read Chapter 25, on supply-side economics and policies.

Extension material

The code for fiscal stability

As Chapter 25 explains, supply-side fiscal policy tends to be microeconomic rather than macroeconomic. However, although it has not been used in a demand-side way, in recent years UK fiscal policy has nevertheless had an important macroeconomic objective: to achieve macroeconomic stability. Despite introducing stealth taxes, UK governments now believe that households and firms shouldn't be hit by unexpected tax increases that adversely affect consumer and business confidence and distort economic decision making.

To try to ensure the credibility of fiscal policy (i.e. to maintain the general public's belief in the government's ability to achieve macroeconomic stability), the Fiscal Policy Framework, introduced in 1998, includes a Code for Fiscal Stability.

Central to the Code are two fiscal rules:

- **The golden rule.** Over the economic cycle, the government should borrow only to invest in new social capital such as roads and schools, and not to fund current spending, for example

on welfare benefits. The golden rule means that the government commits itself over the cycle to a balanced budget or to a small budget surplus on *current spending*, but not on *capital spending*.

- **The sustainable investment rule.** Over the economic cycle, public sector debt (mostly central government debt, i.e. the national debt) is held at a 'stable and prudent' level of less than 40% of GDP.

The difference between current and capital spending explains the logic behind the golden rule. *Current* spending, for example on public sector wages and salaries, does not create assets available for future generations to use. If long-term debt is used to finance current spending, future generations have to pay taxes to repay past borrowing, without receiving any benefit in the form of useful goods and services. It is a case of 'live now, pay later', with people as yet unborn having to do the paying.

This is not the case with *capital* spending on assets such as roads, hospitals and schools. Providing social capital is maintained properly, future generations benefit from public sector investment undertaken now. Future generations should therefore pay part of the cost of capital spending. For these reasons, the Labour government in 1998 decided that, over a single economic cycle, the public sector's budget should balance with regard to current public spending, but run a deficit with regard to capital spending on assets to be used by future generations. The golden rule aims to protect necessary investment in social capital from public spending cuts, and allows fiscal policy to be used *in support* of monetary policy to manage aggregate demand, though not in a discretionary way.

Box 24.2 The US budget deficit

George W. Bush was president of the USA from 2000 until 2008. Although Bush was a pro-free-market politician, his Republican administration soon ran up a huge budget deficit (though as a proportion of US GDP it was not excessively large — approximately 4.2% at the time of writing of the extract below, in 2003).

The extract argues that the effect of Bush's deficit was Keynesian, though it is doubtful whether Bush intended this, or whether he had even heard of Keynes. Rather than being Keynesian in intent, the budget deficit resulted from two events close to Bush's heart: increased military expenditure to pay for the invasions of Afghanistan and Iraq, and supply-side tax cuts granted mostly to rich Americans.

George W. Bush

TOPFOTO

There is a case for the Bush administration running up huge deficits as it tries to stimulate a sluggish economy. After all, it is following the advice of the great economist John Maynard Keynes, who preached that governments should spend money and boost demand in times of recession. The Bush administration, taking that message to heart, has slashed taxes

unit **2**

and increased spending — especially on defence — to get the economy moving again after the 2001 recession.

As a result, the US budget deficit is expected to hit a record this year and next. In figures released yesterday, the politically neutral Congressional Budget Office (CBO) estimated that this year's budget shortfall will hit $401 billion (£254.7 billion) and $480 billion next year.

Yet, large as they seem, these budgets as a proportion of gross domestic product (GDP) are not alarmingly large. Next year's deficit — minus the cost of Iraq — will form just 4.2% of GDP, well short of the record 6% of GDP under the Reagan administration. Keynesians would have no problem with the current tide of red ink.

But there is a big difference between temporary budget deficits and fiscal irresponsibility.

Once budget discipline goes out of the window, it is hard to change tack. It is the prospect of huge entrenched deficits that has economists worried. ...

Douglas Hotz-Eakin, the director of the CBO, put his finger on the problem when he said that deficits were acceptable as long as the economy was operating below potential, in accordance with Keynesian prescription. The trouble would come if the US economy was saddled with high deficits once growth picked up.

...There are already signs of nervousness in the markets at the prospect of unsustainable deficits. Unless the White House and Congress show some awareness of the financial problems posed by large deficits, the markets will give them a rude awakening.

Mark Tran, the *Guardian*, 27 August 2003

Follow-up questions

1 Do you agree that there is a case for running up huge deficits to stimulate a sluggish economy? Justify your answer.
2 Are budget deficits acceptable as long as the economy is operating below potential?

How government spending and taxation affect the pattern of economic activity

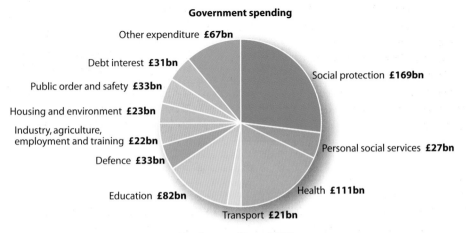

Government spending

Other expenditure **£67bn**

Debt interest **£31bn**

Public order and safety **£33bn**

Housing and environment **£23bn**

Industry, agriculture, employment and training **£22bn**

Defence **£33bn**

Education **£82bn**

Transport **£21bn**

Health **£111bn**

Personal social services **£27bn**

Social protection **£169bn**

Total expenditure: £619bn

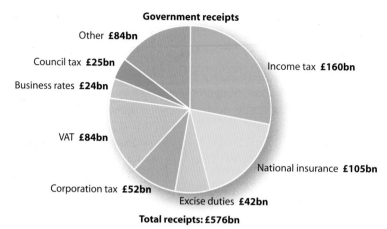

Government receipts

Other **£84bn**

Council tax **£25bn**

Business rates **£24bn**

VAT **£84bn**

Corporation tax **£52bn**

Income tax **£160bn**

National insurance **£105bn**

Excise duties **£42bn**

Total receipts: £576bn

Source: March 2008 Budget Report, HM Treasury

Figure 24.4 *Estimates of government spending and revenue, 2008–09*

As Figure 24.4 shows, at the time of the March 2008 Pre-Budget Report, total UK government expenditure and revenue (mostly tax receipts) were expected to be £618 billion and £575 billion respectively during the financial year 2008–09. This means that the budget deficit for 2008–09 was expected to be £43 billion.

Perhaps more significant than the absolute totals of public expenditure is the ratio of public expenditure to national income or GDP, which indicates the share of the nation's resources taken by the government. Apart from the periods 1914–18 and 1939–45, which saw rapid, but temporary, increases in government spending to pay for the First and Second World Wars, the twentieth century witnessed a steady but relatively slow increase in government expenditure from around 10% to over 40% of GDP, reaching 46.75% in 1982–83. The ratio continued to rise in the early 1980s, fell in the late 1980s, before rising and falling again in the 1990s. By 2006–07, as Figure 24.5 (a) shows, the ratio had increased again to over 42%.

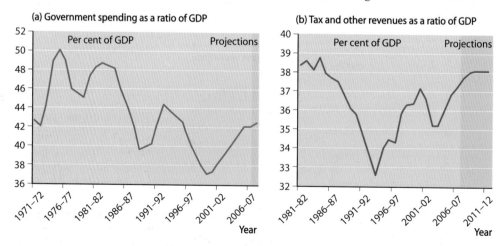

Source: March 2007 Budget Report, HM Treasury

Figure 24.5 *Government spending and revenue as proportions of GDP*

A main explanation for the changes in the ratios of government spending and taxation as ratios of GDP lies in changes taking place in employment and un-employment, which in turn relate to the economic cycle. As Figure 24.4 shows, spending on social security (under the heading social protection), which includes unemployment-related benefits, is by far the largest single category of public spending. When the economy booms, unemployment falls, so spending on social security also falls. The reverse is true in a recession.

Recent increases in the proportion of GDP going to the government in the form of tax revenue before being spent by the government mean that more economic activity is taking place in the public sector of the economy, with less economic activity occurring in the private sector.

Transfers and interest payments made by the government

A large part of government expenditure takes the form of **transfers**, for example the state pension and unemployment-related benefits. Transfers do not involve a claim by the government on national output, or a reduction in private sector economic activity. Instead, spending by the government on transfers merely redistributes income and spending power from one part of the private sector to another — from taxpayers to recipients of state benefits and pensions.

When transfers are excluded, government spending falls from around 42% of GDP to between only 20% and 30%. This figure is a more accurate measure of the share of national output directly commanded by the state (and thus unavailable for use in the private sector) to produce the hospitals, roads and other goods and services which government collec-tively provides and finances, for the most part, out of taxation.

Figure 24.4 also shows the interest paid by the government to people who have lent to the state (i.e. to holders of the **national debt**). In 2007–08, interest payments on the national debt were expected to be £31 billion, or over 5% of public spending. For an obvious reason, this item of public spending rises when interest rates rise. However, *total* interest payments are also affected by the government's budgetary position.

A budget deficit generally increases interest payments because it increases the total *stock* of government debt. Conversely, a budget surplus allows the government to reduce the national debt by paying back past borrowing.

> **key terms**
>
> The **national debt** is the stock of all past government borrowing that has not been paid back.
>
> **Transfers** are the part of government spending in which tax revenues are paid to people such as pensioners, without any output being produced in return.

> **examiner's voice**
>
> Don't confuse the national debt with the budget deficit. The national debt is a stock, but the budget deficit is a flow. Note that a budget deficit adds to the stock of the national debt, whereas a budget surplus allows the government to redeem part of the national debt.

Microeconomic ways in which government spending affects the pattern of economic activity

Taxes and subsidies are used to alter the relative prices of goods and services in order to change consumption patterns. Demerit goods such as alcohol and tobacco are taxed in order to discourage consumption, while merit goods such as healthcare and education are subsidised and sometimes publicly provided. Taxes are also used to finance the provision of public goods such as defence, police and roads. Under the 'polluter must pay' principle, taxes are also used to discourage and reduce the production and consumption of negative externalities such as pollution and congestion.

> **examiner's voice**
>
> At AS, knowledge of public goods, merit and demerit goods, and externalities is tested in the Unit 1 exam and not in the Unit 2 exam.

How taxation and government spending affect people's spending power

The price mechanism is 'value-neutral' with regard to the equity or social fairness of the distributions of income and wealth resulting from the action of market forces in the economy. If the government decides that the distributions of income and wealth produced by free-market forces are undesirable, taxation and transfers in its public spending programme can be used to modify these distributions and reduce this market failure resulting from 'inequity'.

Before 1979, British governments of all political complexions used **progressive taxation** and a policy of transfers of income to the less well-off, in a deliberate attempt — albeit with limited success — to reduce inequalities in the distribution of income. A tax is progressive when the proportion of income paid in tax *rises* as income increases. Progressive taxation, combined with transfers to lower-income groups, reduces the spending power of the rich, while increasing that of the poor. However, some taxes, particularly those designed to reduce consumption of the demerit goods alcohol and tobacco, are regressive and fall more heavily on the poor. A tax is regressive when the proportion of income paid in tax *falls* as income increases.

> **key term**
>
> A **progressive tax** is one where the proportion of income paid in tax rises as income increases.

Regional and EU considerations

Government spending and taxation also contribute to a redistribution of income between different regions and member countries of the UK. On average, people living in London and southeast England receive higher pre-tax incomes than those living in Northern Ireland, Scotland, Wales and in western and northern England. However, part of the tax revenue collected from households and businesses in the southeast is transferred and spent by the government in the poorer regions of the UK.

The UK is also a net contributor to the European Union's budget. Although the poorer parts of the UK benefit from EU spending on regional regeneration projects, taken as a whole, the UK pays more into the EU budget than it gets out. The UK's net contributions are expected to average almost £6.5 billion for the years 2011–13 — double the average of the decade 1997–2006, which averaged £3.25 billion.

The influence of supply-side theory on government spending, taxation and the pattern of economic activity

Between 1979 and 1997, and under the influence of supply-side theory, Conservative governments changed the structure of both taxation and public spending to *widen* rather than *reduce* inequalities in the distributions of income and wealth. The Conservatives believed that greater incentives for work and enterprise were necessary in order to increase the UK's growth rate. For the Conservatives, progressive taxation and transfers to the poor meant people had less incentive to work harder and to engage in entrepreneurial risk. The ease with which the poor could claim welfare benefits and the level at which they were available created a situation in which the poor rationally chose unemployment and state benefits in preference to wages and work. In this dependency culture, the unwaged were effectively married to the state. Many of the poor, obviously not enjoying this marriage, drifted into antisocial behaviour, attacking bus shelters and other public property, as well as privately-owned property.

Since 1997, successive Labour governments have tried to use fiscal policy, both to improve the economy's supply-side performance and to make the distribution of income once again more equal. The policy has only had limited success. Although the real incomes of most of the poor have increased, income inequalities have continued to grow, largely because high incomes have grown at a much faster rate than low incomes.

Summary

- Fiscal policy uses government spending, taxation, and the budgetary position to try to achieve the government's economic policy objectives.
- Keynesian fiscal policy (or demand-side fiscal policy) manages the level of aggregate demand.
- Changes in the government's budget deficit (or in its budget surplus) are important in Keynesian fiscal policy.
- The size of the government spending multiplier affects the power of Keynesian fiscal policy.
- Government spending is a component of aggregate demand.
- Changes in government spending and/or taxation shift the *AD* curve.
- The effect on real output and employment depends on the shape and slope of the *SRAS* curve.
- Supply-side fiscal policy affects the position of the *LRAS* curve.
- In supply-side fiscal policy, tax changes are used to try to change incentives in the economy.

- In the financial year 2007–08, the ratios to GDP of government spending, taxation, and the budget deficit were expected to be 42%, 38% and 4%.

- A significant proportion of government spending takes the forms of transfers and debt interest payments.

- Progressive taxation and transfers have redistributed income from higher-income groups to lower-income groups.

Questions

1 Distinguish between fiscal policy and monetary policy.
2 How does Keynesian fiscal policy differ from supply-side fiscal policy?
3 What is the difference between eliminating and financing a budget deficit?
4 Distinguish between a budget deficit and a budget surplus.
5 Relate the budget deficit to the government's borrowing requirement.
6 How have the budget deficit (or surplus) and the borrowing requirement changed in recent years?
7 Distinguish between the government spending multiplier and the tax multiplier.
8 Use *AD/AS* analysis to show the effects of income tax cuts in demand-side and supply-side fiscal policy.
9 What are the main forms of public spending?
10 Define progressive and regressive taxation.

Chapter 25

Managing the economy: supply-side economics and supply-side policies

This is the last of three chapters which explain the different forms of economic policy used to manage the national economy. Supply-side policy has already been mentioned in Chapters 23 and 24, and I introduced the meaning of supply-side economics in Chapter 15. In Chapter 23, I mentioned that monetary policy, which is now used to manage aggregate demand, has little to do with supply-side economics, except in the sense that supply-side economists deem 'sound money' and control of inflation as essential prerequisites for successful supply-side policy. As Chapter 24 explained, things are different with fiscal policy.

In this chapter, I explain how when supply-side economics first came into existence, it was based on a rejection of Keynesian fiscal policy and on the need to use taxation to create incentives rather than to manage aggregate demand. Most economists now agree that the economy's supply side is important, though many argue that the central premise of supply-side economics, that lower taxes pay for themselves through the extra tax revenue they generate, is not proven.

Learning outcomes

This chapter will:
- explain the meaning of supply-side economics
- relate supply-side economics to the free-market revival
- distinguish between the original meaning of supply-side policy and its later, broader meaning
- use *AD/AS* analysis to contrast supply-side and Keynesian views on the macroeconomy
- examine the role of fiscal policy in supply-side economics
- describe a number of supply-side policies that are used, or have been used, in the UK

The meaning of supply-side economics

Supply-side economics provides a framework of analysis which relies on personal and private incentives. When incentives change, people's behaviour changes in response. People are attracted towards positive incentives and repelled by the negative. The role of government in such a framework is carried out by the ability of government to alter incentives and thereby affect society's behaviour.

Professor Arthur Laffer, University of Southern California, 1983.

> **key term**
>
> **Supply-side economics** is a branch of free-market economics, arguing that government policy should be used to improve the competitiveness and efficiency of markets.

The term **supply-side economics** was first used in 1976 by Jude Wanniski, a journalist at the *Wall Street Journal*, and by Herbert Stein, a professor at the University of Virginia. A few years later, in 1980, supply-side economics became an important part of the economic policy programme promised by Ronald Reagan in his successful campaign for the US presidency. These policies became known as **Reaganomics**.

The ideology and policies of other free-market orientated governments were also strongly influenced by supply-side theories in the 1980s, in particular the Conservative administrations of Margaret Thatcher in the UK from 1979 to 1990. During the 1980s, Thatcherism became the UK equivalent of Reaganomics in the USA.

Margaret Thatcher in 1986

Box 25.1 Jude Wanniski: The man who 'invented' supply-side economics

The term 'supply-side economics' was coined in 1976 by Jude Wanniski, then an economics journalist for the *Wall Street Journal*. Wanniski got his ideas from two right-wing economists, Herbert Stein and Art Laffer, who themselves went on to become prominent supply-side economists. Wanniski's crude but popularist arguments in favour of tax cuts, especially from which the rich would benefit most, were adopted by US President Ronald Reagan in the 1980s (becoming perhaps the most important part of 'Reaganomics'). In recent years, Wanniski's arguments in favour of tax cuts have formed an important part of the neo-conservative (neo-con) political agenda in the USA, an agenda adopted by the Republican president George W. Bush.

The extract below has been taken from the obituary written by Dan Miller, published on 1 September 2005 in the *Chicago Sun-Times*, following Jude Wanniski's death at the age of 69.

To really appreciate his influence, one had to live through the 1970s immersed in business. Inflation was advancing at 15% a year, devouring the wealth and incomes of Americans with utter indifference to race or creed.

In such a hyperinflated economy, traditional economics predicted feverish growth and business activity. Instead, US unemployment grew, and business activity stagnated. The result was an unprecedented period of stagflation, all the more fearsome because its cure was beyond the knowledge of leading economists and politicians. As a nation, we were bereft of leadership and ideas.

Except for the pages of the Wall Street Journal, where Jude Wanniski explained the practical applications of the classical economic theory he described in 1976 as 'supply-side economics'. The USA of the 1970s was in thrall to Keynesian demand-side economics: if it increased demand through government spending on social programs and public works, the USA could spend its way out of stagflation.

Supply-side economics rejected this theory and predicted that increased personal income for individuals would result in increased investment, increased productivity and increased pace of business activity. Against ferocious opposition from traditional conservatives, Wanniski pressed the intellectual arguments for deficits of a different kind: through tax cuts.

Follow-up questions

1 What is meant by 'supply-side economics'?

2 Contrast the views of Keynesian and supply-side economists on the role of tax cuts in fiscal policy.

Supply-side economics and the free-market revival

As I explained in Chapter 15, supply-side economics grew in significance in the 1980s as a part of the free-market revival. The growing fashion for the term 'supply-side economics' was partly a response to the decline of monetarism, which for a number of years in the late 1970s and early 1980s had been the label most often associated with the free-market revival. Free-market economics, monetarism and supply-side economics all accompanied and contributed to the decline of Keynesianism.

> **examiner's voice**
> Refer back to Chapter 24 to find out more about demand-side fiscal policy.

> **examiner's voice**
> It is important to understand that supply-side economics is part of the free-market revival.

Although there is some disagreement over points of emphasis and detail, free-market economists believe in the virtues of capitalism and competitive markets, a belief which is matched by a distrust and dislike of big government and the role of state intervention in the economy.

The original meaning of supply-side economic policy

When supply-side economics first came to prominence around 1980, it focused narrowly on the effects of a fiscal policy on the economy. During the Keynesian era, most economists regarded fiscal policy — and especially taxation — as a demand management tool. In Keynesian economics, the government's budget deficit lay at the centre of fiscal policy. The Keynesians largely ignored the impact of public spending and tax changes on the supply-side of the economy, focusing instead on how changes in government spending and taxation affect aggregate demand.

By contrast, supply-side economics initially grew out of the concern expressed by free-market economists in the 1970s about the microeconomic effects of demand-side Keynesian fiscal policy. Indeed, in many respects, supply-side economics is a revival of the old classical public finance theory that largely disappeared from view during the Keynesian era. The central idea of supply-side economics is that a tax cut should be used, *not* to stimulate aggregate demand Keynesian-style, but to create incentives by altering relative prices, particularly those of labour and leisure, in favour of work, saving and investment and against the voluntary choice of unemployment.

The wider meaning of supply-side economic policy

Supply-side economic policy now encompasses more than just fiscal policy; it is the set of government policies which aim to change the underlying structure of the economy and improve the economic performance of markets and industries, and of individual firms and workers within markets. For the most part, supply-side policies are also *microeconomic* rather than simply *macroeconomic*, since, by acting on the motivation and efficiency of individual economic agents within the economy, the policies aim to improve general economic performance and the economy's underlying production potential.

> **key term**
> Interpreted narrowly, **supply-side policies** focus on the role of tax cuts in increasing personal incentives. Interpreted broadly, they aim to improve the economy's ability to produce and supply more output.

Supply-side economists, and free-market economists in general, believe that the economy is usually close to its equilibrium, or 'natural', levels of output and employment. However, due to distortions and inefficiencies resulting from Keynesian neglect of the supply side, towards the

> **examiner's voice**
> You should appreciate that supply-side policies tend to be microeconomic rather than macroeconomic.

end of the Keynesian era these equilibrium levels became unnecessarily low. To increase levels of output and employment (and to reduce unemployment), supply-side economists recommend the use of appropriate microeconomic policies to remove distortions, improve incentives and generally to make markets more competitive.

During the Keynesian era in the 1960s and 1970s, government microeconomic policy in the UK was generally interventionist, extending the roles of the state and of the planning mechanism. Interventionist policies, such as regional policy, competition policy, and industrial relations policy (which were known collectively as industrial policy), generally increased the role of the state and limited the role of markets.

By contrast, supply-side microeconomic policy is anti-interventionist, attempting to roll back government interference in the activities of markets and of private economic agents, and to change the economic function of government from provider to enabler. Along with tax cuts to create incentives to work, save and

invest, and cuts in welfare benefits to reduce the incentive to choose unemployment rather than a low-paid work alternative, supply-side economic policy includes policies of **privatisation**, **marketisation** (commercialisation) and **deregulation**.

In essence, the supply-siders, together with the other free-market economists, wish to create an enterprise economy. In this broad interpretation, supply-side policies aim to promote entrepreneurship and popular capitalism and to replace the dependency culture and statism that had been part of the Keynesian mixed economy.

key terms

Deregulation involves removing previously imposed regulations.

Marketisation involves shifting provision of goods or services from the non-market sector to the market sector.

Privatisation involves shifting ownership of state-owned assets to the private sector.

Extension material

The Laffer curve

Supply-side economists believe that high rates of income tax and the overall tax burden create disincentives, which, by reducing national income as taxation increases, also reduce the government's total tax revenue. This effect is illustrated by a Laffer curve, such as the one in Figure 25.1.

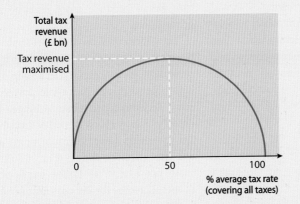

Figure 25.1
A Laffer curve

The Laffer curve, named after the leading supply-side economist Arthur Laffer quoted at the beginning of this chapter, shows how the government's total tax revenue changes as the average tax rate increases from 0% to 100%. Tax revenue must be zero when the average tax rate is 0%, but Figure 25.1 also shows that total tax revenue is also assumed to be zero when the tax rate is 100%. With the average tax rate set at 100%, all income must be paid as tax to the government. In this situation, there is no incentive to produce output other than for subsistence, so with no output produced, the government ends up collecting no tax revenue.

Between the limiting tax rates of 0% and 100%, the Laffer curve shows tax revenue first rising and then falling as the average rate of taxation increases. Tax revenue is maximised at the highest point on the Laffer curve, which in Figure 25.1 occurs at an average tax rate (for all taxes) of 50%. Beyond this point, any further increase in the average tax rate becomes counter-productive, causing total tax revenue to fall.

Supply-side economists argue that the increase in the tax burden in the Keynesian era, needed to finance the growing size of the government and public sectors, raised the average tax rate towards or beyond the critical point on the Laffer curve at which tax revenue is maximised. In this situation, any further tax increase has the perverse effect of reducing the government's total tax revenue. Indeed, according to supply-side theory, if the government wishes to increase total tax revenue, it must cut tax rates rather than increase them.

A reduction in tax rates creates the incentives needed to stimulate economic growth. Faster growth means that total tax revenue increases despite the fact that tax rates are lower. Arguably, the effect is reinforced by a decline in tax evasion and avoidance, as the incentive to engage in these activities reduces at lower marginal tax rates.

Box 25.2 How supply-side economics came into being

In the mid-1970s, a group of men in Washington DC invented a whole new approach to economics. In the past, it was thought that if you wanted to cut taxes, you had to ploddingly pay for it by either cutting spending or increasing borrowing. This was no more, as the new group preached 'supply-side economics', which claimed that you could cut taxes, increase public spending, and hold down borrowing and inflation, all at the same time. It's easy, they said: if you cut taxes, the economy will grow even faster — and make up the difference.

The supply-siders were the economic consultant Arthur Laffer, the journalist Jude Wanniski and the Republican president Gerald Ford's chief of staff — a man called Dick Cheney.

Laffer said he had uncovered the secret key to economic growth. To explain this idea, Laffer drew a parabola-shaped curve. The premise of the curve was simple. If the government sets a tax rate of zero, it will receive no revenue. If the government sets a tax rate of 100%, it will also receive zero tax revenue, since nobody will have any reason to earn any income. Between these two, Laffer drew an arc, which suggested that at higher levels of taxation, reducing the tax rate would produce more revenue for the government.

The Laffer curve became the supply-siders' 'Sermon on the Mount'. For Cheney, it was 'a revelation, for it presented in a simple, easily digestible form the messianic power of tax cuts'. Economic performance hinges almost entirely on how much incentive investors and entrepreneurs have to attain more wealth, and this incentive hinges almost entirely on their tax rate. The Laffer curve was an economic recipe for tax cuts for the rich.

Almost everyone else saw the idea as preposterous. However, a string of eccentrics began to preach the gospel — and they were swiftly employed by Ronald Reagan's burgeoning presidential campaign.

Johann Hari, the *New Statesman*,
15 November 2007

Follow-up question

Do income tax cuts necessarily increase the incentive to work? (See the Extension material on page 325.)

Using the *AD/AS* model to contrast supply-side and Keynesian macroeconomic theory

To explain the nature of supply-side macroeconomics, I shall use the aggregate demand/aggregate supply (*AD/AS*) macroeconomic model introduced in Chapter 19.

Two versions of the *AD/AS* model are illustrated in Figure 25.2. Panels (a) and (b) respectively show a Keynesian long-run aggregate supply (*LRAS*) curve and the vertical *LRAS* curve favoured by supply-side and other free-market economists.

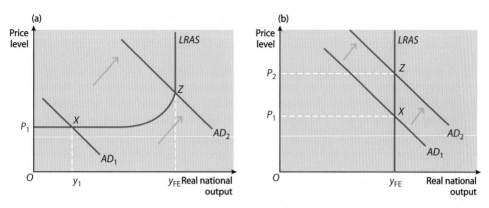

Figure 25.2 The Keynesian 'inverted-L'-shaped LRAS *curve and the supply-side vertical* LRAS *curve*

The 'inverted-L'-shaped *LRAS* curve in Figure 25.2 (a) illustrates the Keynesian view that an economy can settle into macroeconomic equilibrium at a position such as at point X, at which the level of real output (y_1) is significantly below the full-employment level of output (y_{FE}).

In this situation, and before the advent of supply-side economics, Keynesian economists recommended that fiscal policy should be used to increase aggregate demand. They believed that when used in this way, expansionary fiscal policy *reflates* real output to a greater extent than it *inflates* the price level. Following an increase in aggregate demand, which shifts the aggregate demand function from AD_1 to AD_2, real output increases from y_1 to y_{FE}. Macroeconomic equilibrium is now at point Z. Firms respond to increased demand by increasing output, and the price level rises more rapidly as full employment approaches. Once full employment is reached at the level of real output y_{FE}, any further increase in aggregate demand causes the price level rather than real output to increase.

By contrast, Figure 25.2 (b) shows the vertical *LRAS* curve that is central to supply-side macroeconomic theory. Along with other pro-free market economists, supply-side economists believe competitive markets ensure that in the *long run*, the economy produces at or close to the full-employment level of output.

Macroeconomic equilibrium (shown initially at point X in Figure 25.2 (b)) is at the full-employment level of real output y_{FE}. Because output and employment are at their long-run equilibrium levels, any expansion of aggregate demand, for example from AD_1 to AD_2, causes the price level to rise, in this case from P_1 to P_2, but with no effect on the levels of real output and employment, at least in the long run.

The role of fiscal policy in supply-side economics

The logic of the supply-side argument I have just outlined is that fiscal policy should *not* be used to manage aggregate demand. Supply-side economists, along with other free-market economists, believe that expansionary fiscal policy simply leads to inflation, with no long-run increase in real output.

To understand supply-side fiscal policy, it is important to distinguish between *extreme* and more *moderate* supply-side economists. The early popularisers of supply-side economics (for example, Arthur Laffer and Jude Wanniski) were 'extreme' in the sense that they believed, despite the fact there was little or no evidence to support their views, that tax cuts are self-financing. They argued that the incentive effect to work and to be entrepreneurial, which results from tax cuts, boosts the economy's growth rate to such an extent that *total* tax revenue rises, despite the lower tax *rates* that people pay. Extreme supply-siders also believed that, although the rich would benefit most from tax cuts, the poor (whom the rich employ, for example as servants and gardeners) would also benefit through a **trickle-down effect**. Many economists, especially Keynesians, question the strength and even the existence of trickle-down effects. J. K. Galbraith, for example, caustically quipped the less than elegant metaphor that if one feeds the horse enough oats, some will pass through to the road for the sparrows. Galbraith went on to argue that 'we can safely abandon the doctrine that the rich are not working because they have too little money and the poor because they have too much.'

> **Key term**
> The **trickle-down effect** is income paid by rich people to the poorer people they employ.

Extreme supply-side theory went out of fashion in the late 1980s when, far from reducing the US budget deficit, President Ronald Reagan's tax cuts led to a massive worsening of the US fiscal position. The term 'voodoo economics' was coined to describe extreme supply-side theory. However, promises of tax cuts are always popular with voters, despite the lack of economic evidence to justify them. For this reason, virtually every presidential candidate in the USA promises to cut taxes, using the supply-side argument to support the case. In recent years, neo-conservative politicians in President George W. Bush's administration used the supply-side argument to justify greatly increased government spending on arms, combined with large tax cuts, especially for high income earners. The neo-conservatives believe that higher tax revenues allegedly resulting from the tax cuts pay for military spending, without the government's budget deficit growing.

However, as was the case in the 1980s, the evidence does not support this extreme supply-side argument.

Nevertheless, few economists or politicians now call for continuous large budget deficits as the way to achieve growth and full employment, and there is general agreement that the tax structure should be used in a supply-side way to create incentives for work, entrepreneurship, saving and investment. Many Keynesian economists now accept *moderate* supply-side arguments, though they continue to reject extreme populist calls for swinging tax cuts and greater income inequality.

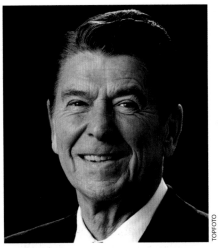

President Ronald Reagan, 1981

Extension material

Microeconomic theory and the effect of supply-side fiscal policy

The supply-side theory of the effects of taxation on labour market incentives, which lies at the heart of free-market supply-side economics, depends significantly on the shape of the supply curve of labour.

Supply-side economists usually assume a conventional upward-sloping supply curve of labour. Such a curve, which is illustrated in Figure 25.3 (a), shows that workers respond to higher wage rates by supplying more labour.

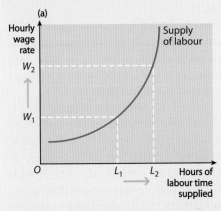
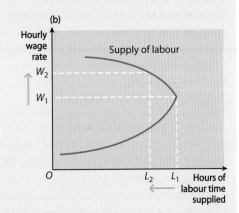

Figure 25.3 Labour supply curves

Since a cut in the rate at which income tax rates are levied is equivalent to an increase in the wage rate, the upward-sloping supply curve implies that workers respond to cuts in the marginal rate of income tax by working harder. (The marginal rate of income tax is the percentage of the last pound of income paid in tax.) If this is the case, a reduction in income tax rates creates the

incentive for workers to supply more labour (and for entrepreneurs to become more enterprising), while an increase in income tax rates has a disincentive effect on effort and the supply of labour.

However, as the extension material in Chapter 4 noted, the supply curve of labour need not necessarily slope upward throughout its length. The backward-bending labour supply curve drawn in Figure 25.3 (b) is another possibility. It shows that, above the hourly wage rate W_1, any further wage rate increase (or income tax decrease) causes workers to supply *less* rather than *more* labour. In this situation, workers prefer to enjoy extra leisure time than to work. Following an increase in the hourly wage rate from W_1 to W_2, the hours of labour time supplied fall from L_1 to L_2.

It is important to note that if supply curves of labour bend backward, the strength of the supply-side argument, that tax reductions increase national output and efficiency through their effect on labour market incentives, becomes much weaker.

Far from encouraging people to work harder, a wage rise or income tax cut might have the opposite effect, causing people to work fewer hours and to enjoy more leisure time instead.

Box 25.3 A criticism of supply-side economics

One of the most authoritative and articulate critics of supply-side economics is the famous US economist Paul Krugman, Professor of Economics and International Affairs at Princeton University. The following is an extract from one of his many books.

What is supply-side economics? It is not, as some of its apologists would have it, simply the recognition that the supply side of the economy matters; one would be hard-pressed to find a card-carrying economist who disagrees with that proposition. Nor is there anything distinctive about the recognition that high marginal tax rates can hurt economic growth — this, too, is an utterly conventional insight.

What defines supply-side economics, in other words, is not what it includes, but what it excludes. Supply-siders believe that only the supply side matters. They believe not only that taxes affect growth, but that virtually all bad things that happen to the economy are the result of tax increases, whereas all good things are the result of tax reductions. The implication of these views is that supply-siders think tax cuts are always a good idea — whatever the state of the economy or the government's budget.

Of course, supply-side economics will not vanish in a puff of smoke. ...Any ideology whose main policy prescription is lower taxes on the rich is likely to have extra staying power: those who preach it are not going to have trouble putting bread on the table. The supply-siders will be with us for a long time to come.

The supply-side idea — that tax cuts have such a positive effect on the economy one need not worry about paying for them with spending cuts, does not persist because of any actual evidence in its favour.

The kind of economics covered in the textbooks is a technical subject that many people find hard to follow. How reassuring, then, to be told that it is all irrelevant — all you really need to know are a few simple ideas! A significant number of supply-siders have created for themselves a wonderful alternative intellectual history in which John Maynard Keynes was a fraud, and the true line of deep economic thought runs from Adam Smith straight to them.

The Accidental Theorist: And Other Dispatches from the Dismal Science, Penguin 1999

Follow-up questions

1 Explain what is meant by a 'high marginal tax rate'.
2 Do you agree that 'only the supply side matters'? Justify your answer.

Examples of supply-side economic policies

I shall conclude the chapter with some examples of supply-side policies other than those that relate to the effect of fiscal policy on personal incentives.

All the policies listed below have been implemented in the UK over approximately the last 25 years. However, some policies, such as creating internal markets in the provision of state healthcare and education, have been partially implemented and then largely withdrawn.

Industrial policy measures

- **Privatisation**. The sale or transfer of assets such as nationalised industries from the public sector to the private sector.
- **Marketisation (or commercialisation)**. Shifting economic activity from non-market provision (financed by taxation) to commercial or market provision for which the customer pays.
- **Deregulation**. The removal of previously imposed regulations in order to promote competition. It removes barriers to market entry to make markets contestable, and gets rid of unnecessary 'red tape' or bureaucracy, which had increased firms' costs of production.
- **Internal markets**. In the National Health Service and education, where the state continues to be a major producer and provider of services, internal markets can be introduced to provide a form of commercial discipline and to improve efficiency. In an internal market, which is a substitute for privatisation, the taxpayer continues to finance hospitals and schools, but hospitals and schools 'earn' the money according to how many patients and pupils they attract.

Labour market measures

- **Lower rates of income tax.** Reducing marginal rates of income tax to create labour market incentives, and raising tax thresholds or personal tax allowances to remove the low-paid from the tax net.
- **Reducing state welfare benefits relative to average earnings**. Lower benefit levels create incentives to choose low-paid employment in preference to claiming unemployment-related benefits. In addition, welfare benefits can be made more difficult to claim, and available only to claimants genuinely looking for work. Making benefits less attractive may also reduce the unemployment trap.
- **Changing employment law to reduce the power of trade unions**. Removing trade unions' legal protection, restricting their rights, and extending the freedom for workers not to belong to unions, and for employers not to recognise and

negotiate with unions. Replacing collective bargaining with individual wage negotiation and by employer determination of pay. Restricting the right to strike and to undertake industrial action.

- **Introducing short-term contracts.** Replacing 'jobs for life' with short-term labour contracts, and introducing profit-related and performance-related pay. Critics of these policies believe they lead to even greater poverty and inequality for ordinary workers in an increasingly casualised and exploited part-time labour force.
- **Repealing legislation which limits employers' freedom to employ.** This makes it easier for employers to 'hire and fire' workers.
- **More flexible pension arrangements**. Encouraging workers to 'opt out' of state pensions and to arrange private pension plans so as to reduce the burden on taxpayers. Allowing workers to transfer private sector pensions between employers when changing jobs.
- **Improving the training of labour.** Establishing training agencies and City Technology Colleges and Academies to develop vocational technical education. However, UK governments have rejected the proposal to impose a 'training tax' on all employers to prevent free-riding by firms with no training schemes who poach trained workers from firms who do train their workers.

Financial and capital market measures

- **Deregulating financial markets.** Creating greater competition among banks and building societies, and opening up the UK financial markets to overseas banks and financial institutions. These reforms increase the supply of funds and reduce the cost of borrowing for UK firms. Financial deregulation and the removal of foreign exchange controls also encourage 'inward' investment by overseas firms such as Toyota and Nissan.
- **Encouraging saving.** Governments have created special tax privileges for saving. They have also encouraged saving by giving individual shareholders first preference in the market for shares issued when former nationalised industries such as British Gas were privatised. However, most individual shareholders quickly sold their shares to institutional shareholders. This negated one of the main reasons for privatisation.
- **Promoting entrepreneurship.** Governments have encouraged the growth of popular capitalism and an enterprise culture. Company taxation has been reduced and markets deregulated to encourage risk taking.
- **Reducing public spending and public sector borrowing.** This has been done to free resources for private sector use and avoid crowding out, though again the policy has been reversed in recent years.

Summary

- Supply-side economics argues that government policy should be used to improve incentives and the competitiveness and efficiency of markets.

- In its early years, supply-side economics focused on how, via increased incentives, tax cuts promote economic growth and are self-financing.

- The growth of supply-side economics was part of the free-market revival.

- Supply-side economists are anti-interventionist and wish to reduce the economic role of the state.

- Along with other free-market economists, supply-side economists believe that the *LRAS* curve is vertical.

- This means that in the long run, fiscal policy used to increase aggregate demand leads only to inflation.

- There is little or no evidence to support the 'extreme' supply-side argument that tax cuts are self-financing.

- Nevertheless, most economists now accept the moderate or mainstream supply-side argument that the supply side of the economy is just as important as the demand side.

- Many supply-side policies are microeconomic rather than macroeconomic.

Questions

1 What is supply-side economics?
2 Distinguish between the 'narrow' and the 'wider' meaning of supply-side economics.
3 Distinguish between a government's role as provider and enabler.
4 With the help of *AD/AS* diagrams, explain the difference between supply-side and Keynesian views on the effect of an increase in aggregate demand on the economy.
5 Explain the role of fiscal policy in supply-side theory.
6 Distinguish between an 'extreme' and a 'moderate' supply-side economist.
7 Outline one supply-side industrial policy measure.
8 Outline one supply-side labour market measure.
9 Outline one supply-side financial market measure.

Index

Red page numbers indicate definitions of key terms

AQA AS Economics